The Six Day Horror Movie

A No-Nonsense Guide to No-Budget Filmmaking

Michael P. DiPaolo

McFarland & Company, Inc., Publishers
Jefferson, North Carolina, and London

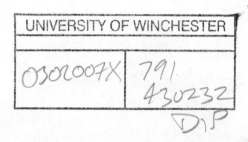
LIBRARY OF CONGRESS CATALOGUING-IN-PUBLICATION DATA

DiPaolo, Michael P., 1950–
The six day horror movie : a no-nonsense
guide to no-budget filmmaking / Michael P. DiPaolo.
p.   cm.
Includes bibliographical references and index.

ISBN 0-7864-1905-9 (softcover : 50# alkaline paper)

1. Motion pictures—Production and direction.
2. Low budget motion pictures.   I. Title.
PN1995.9.P7D52   2004   791.4302'32—dc22   2004018241

British Library cataloguing data are available

On the cover: Poster art for the 2003 independent horror film *Daddy*

Manufactured in the United States of America

*McFarland & Company, Inc., Publishers
Box 611, Jefferson, North Carolina 28640
www.mcfarlandpub.com*

The Six Day
Horror Movie

Table of Contents

Introduction

I've been in the room with more murderers than most cops ever will, video-taping over 2,000 confessions while working at the Brooklyn DA's Office. I have made five features that were loosely based on fictionalized variations of those confessions. Let me tell you, I've picked up plenty along the way, not just about making films and videos, but also about life and people.

And above all else, I've learned that you have to find out who to play with. I know that sounds simplistic, but let me explain. You will end up wasting more of your time, thus more of your life personally and professionally, by playing with the wrong people than anything else in your entire life. Think about it. All the weeks, months, maybe even years wasted on projects where the bottom falls out over "creative differences" or any close personal relationship that goes bad for whatever reason.

Now unfortunately, I can't help you solve any of your personal problems but I can help you avoid many of the pitfalls you'll come across dealing with the various inter-personal relationships that form *the* most crucial element of any low-budget production. This critical bond between the creative force behind any project (*you*) and the team you pick to make your dream a reality is usually given short shrift or left out of most film production books; it will be the main focus of this one.

In conjunction with this, I recently completed an intriguing "experiment in terror," which resulted in *Daddy*, my first digital feature after 16 years of struggling to create and distribute four other "underground" features. For the very first time, I was able to produce, edit and distribute my entire production exclusively through the use of just one computer and one camcorder. For me, however, the really challenging part of this experiment was that I shot the entire thing in only six days while paying the cast and crew, all for just over $5,000.

How'd I do that? Well, there's more than one way to skin the proverbial cat and it's in that particular vein that I'll provide you with a variety of tactics and strategies I've picked up over the years, which then helped me knock off my *Daddy* in only six days. These very same tactics and strategies will then give you a solid framework to make *your* film *your* way. Now why the hell is all this so important?

1

Well, to my mind, there are just too many damn people and books and workshops and whatever out there today telling beginning (and not so beginning) filmmakers how to do things the right way, i.e., their way. This can be very misleading, because hidden beneath this seemingly neutral "instruction" is the way your actual working style affects your finished film. There really is no right way to make a film or video, there is only the best way for you to make your film and hopefully this book will help you find your way.

So that's why I've included an early chapter with the somewhat strange title "Patron Saints of the Underground." All of these moviemaking mavericks, most of whom have worked on genre films outside the Hollywood system (including Edgar Ulmer, Val Lewton, Roger Corman, John Cassavetes, Ed Wood and Jean-Luc Godard), found that the only way they could continue making their films their way was to develop a unique working method suited to their own individual creative needs.

Another key concept that's especially relevant to anyone making genre films or videos, is cinematic Point-of-View. I believe Point-of-View to be of such fundamental importance, not only to genre filmmakers but anyone using a camera to tell a story, that I will devote an entire chapter to it. I dedicate it to Alfred Hitchcock, who more than any other filmmaker explored and exploited its possibilities both emotionally and artistically.

In a nutshell, your camera has a lens through which the image is fixed on the film or tape. Thus your lens becomes the spectator's eye and makes the statement "If you could only see things through my eyes" a reality for your audience. Your camera's point-of-view creates your cinematic style — not the story, not the characters, not the art direction, not the special effects, not the budget. And best of all, this is the one of the few elements of your entire production that does not cost you a dime.

I then break down the filmmaking process into what I believe are its six essential elements: The Story, The Plan, Your Team, The Ambush (Production), The Metamorphosis of the Ambush (Post Production) and Presenting the Ambush (Screenings). These six elements are all you need to make your film; everything else is open and negotiable.

In the end, all I'm trying to tell you is to listen to everyone, hell, listen to *any*-one, but ultimately do it your way; the only way you'll ever learn what your way *is*, is by knowing as much as you can about other filmmakers' working methods and then actually going out and shooting something, editing it and showing it to someone. Then starting all over again using what you've just learned.

In filmmaking you can only really know what you've actually lived through and that is the filter through which I will be recounting my experiences to you, but I hope you don't go out and attempt to replicate my experiences or anyone else's, but rather, critically assess them in relation to your personality, your experiences and your unique situation. Okay, enough about the book for now; how the hell did my experiment in terror actually begin?

PART I

Making a Horror Film in Six Days

1

Planning *Daddy*

It all started late one Friday at a local video store. I was browsing around when a couple of teen age girls came in and asked the clerk for something really scary. He recommended some recent studio stuff masquerading as horror like *I Know What You Did Last Autumn 3* or something lame like that when I suggested they check out Dario Argento's *Creepers* or William Lustig's *Maniac*.

Driving home, my mind wandered: What did I find really scary? And then it came to me, a *zombie rapist* (great title, just not for me, so go ahead and use it — titles are not copyrightable!) and the idea for *Daddy* — or, as it was originally called, *Rigor Mortis* — was born. Then all sorts of weird things began coming together the dark, deserted country road I was on and the crazed sheriff from Jim Thompson's *The Killer Inside Me*, except my sheriff would be a woman and her girlfriends would be the victims. Also a Greek tragedy called *The Furies*, some confessions from my 16 years videotaping them at the Brooklyn DA's office and, of course, Val Lewton's *I Walked with a Zombie*, Lucio Fulci's *Zombie* and George Romero's *Night of the Living Dead*, as well as Andrzej Zulawski's *Possession*.

Then I remembered that some friends had an old abandoned cemetery on their property that would be a perfect resting place for our zombie. Suddenly out of the blue I met Christopher Philippo, who expressed interest in helping me make an ultra–low-budget horror film in upstate New York around the Troy-Albany area. So I began writing, while searching for interesting locations that were both cheap and accessible.

The script mutated rather quickly into the story of Sylvia, the woman sheriff of a small resort community being plagued by a series of bizarre sexual crimes (by our zombie) and all the victims (surprise!) just happen to be her close personal friends. When the investigation intensifies, Sylvia begins to unravel, as long buried secrets (including our zombie) begin to implicate both her and her friends. Ultimately, as the powers-that-be conspire against her, Sylvia must confront them as well as her own inner (and outer) demons. A cliched story, to say the least, but I believed I could seriously twist it, while having some fun in the process.

Now let's hold up here for just a second or two before proceeding; There's no way in Hell I think anyone else in the world should make a film exactly in the way I will describe here ... unless there happens to be some other obsessive malcontent out there who might benefit, but I doubt it. What I want to get across to you is how I used the tactics and strategies covered in this book, which then enabled me to shoot an entire feature in only six days while paying, feeding, housing and transporting the cast and crew ... and all for the price of a relatively wrecked used car.

For the past few years, I've been pissed off with the misleading promises and ever-increasing greed of commercial film productions masquerading as independents who use deferred payment and various other ruses (we'll be sure to remember you when paying jobs come up ... sure!) to con cast and crew into working for nothing. Today, all too often, it's only a way to get something for nothing on films that are no more daring than some TV network's after-school special.

So the trick would be to treat my cast and crew fairly while still making a stylish horror film that had an interesting, but somewhat skewed take on well-worn genre. Unfortunately the reality was that I could only afford to shoot for six days with a very small crew — three people besides me, to be exact. It would consist of a production manager, a gaffer and a sound person. Of course I would have to pinch every penny until it screamed, using practically every shortcut I had ever picked up over the years and then some.

Underground/Guerrilla Filmmaking

The only way I knew to get it done, on time and on budget, was to use the Underground/Guerrilla mode of filmmaking, which meant that Che Guevara would somehow join philosophical forces with Roger Corman in the woods of Upstate New York to help make my DV feature a reality. Now I admit that a Communist, revolutionary, guerrilla fighter and an Off-Hollywood, capitalist, renegade movie maker seems like a very odd couple but for my purposes (and most low-no-budget productions), they are actually a match made in Heaven.

Che Guevara's basic premise of guerrilla warfare was that "Popular Forces" can win a war against "Conventional Forces" while Roger Corman felt (via one of the characters in his film *Atlas*) that, "A small band of efficient, dedicated, highly trained warriors [filmmakers?] could defeat any number of rabble."[1] Simply stated, those of limited means attempt to do battle on the same terms as those of unlimited means and transform their limitations into advantages. And as we all know, the main strategy all guerrillas employ is the ambush, which will serve as my main film production strategy as well.

What does this have to do with you making your film? By demonstrating how I directly benefited by adapting these methods to making my own on, *Daddy*, you will get a much clearer picture of what they can do for you. In addition, by covering Che and Corman in greater detail later, you will be able to see how their fundamentals can be successfully applied to just about any film or video production, anywhere and any time.

Budgeting

Now back to the harsh realities (aka … Money): Since we only had $5,000 to get this sucker in the can, many of the budgetary problems were instantly taken care of … we just didn't have money for most of the items found in a feature budget. However, there were a few non-negotiable givens, the first being that the smallest amount I could fairly pay the crew for six days work was $400, so that's $1,200 right off the bat. The lead actress, who would be working all six days, would get $500 while all the other cast members would get $200 for two or three days work, so that's another $1,700. Add $100 for casting expenses, and it now totals $3,000, leaving $2,000 for everything else. See how easy certain aspects of production can be when you don't have a lot of money!

Since I wasn't sure about all the locations we needed, I budgeted $700, which was way over what we actually spent but much of it eventually went towards covering those expenses I had underestimated. These included budget lines such as food and supplies that I had put at $200 each, while allocating only $100 apiece for set dressing and costumes. This all came to a total of $4550 plus a ten percent contingency fee of $455 which adds up to a grand total of $5005 — pretty damn close to what we had in our pockets.

The observant reader will have noticed that there is no budget line for transportation. The reason? We simply didn't have room in our budget for it, so I hoped to cover it (it came to $165) by the contingency allowance, which we ended up doing. All told, we eventually came in at $5,441 after a couple of unexpected expenses hit us fairly late in the game. So as you can see from all of this, the money did start us out, but it sure as Hell wasn't what actually made this movie work; it was my so-called dream team, those people who came together and made my dream (well, maybe more precisely my nightmare) a reality.

My Team

The first step in building my team was to put together a small but experienced crew that would include a production manager, a gaffer and a boom operator. I would act as the Art Director/DP/AD/Producer/Director with Christopher Philippo assisting on the upstate Producing chores. With a crew of only three, I had to be absolutely sure that I could depend on every single team member. Preferably, they should be people I had worked with before, be able to function independently and still fit in with the rest of the crew. Another important point, since this was a film about a zombie rapist: It would be extremely helpful if they were horror fans as well.

Justin Taylan, my production manager, had worked for me before in a variety of capacities. I knew him to be smart, reliable, hard-working and a lover of horror films. Originally he was set to be the boom operator, but when my gaffer screwed up his hand just before our start date, I had to juggle my crew choices around, so that Justin was "drafted" as the production manager. Remember, a guerrilla filmmaker must be able to adapt quickly to any problem at any time. Since Justin had never handled this particular chore before, it took him a while to get up to speed, but let me tell you, Justin was always there when you needed him as well as working the longest and hardest of anyone on the entire shoot.

Luckily for me, John Karyus (who would end up being the gaffer as well as acting in the role of the Sheriff's ex-husband) had caught my Internet postings for actresses and sent off an email asking if there were any male roles available. He added that he had worked on a variety of crew positions and didn't have a problem working long indie film hours without complaint. And for extra bonus points, he actually remembered some of my old *Film Threat* ads from years ago; he lived in the Niagara Falls area where I grew up; and he was more than willing to be the gaffer and act, all for the $400 crew rate, which sounded too good to be true. I asked John for several production-related references, which he quickly supplied. I checked them out and it seems everybody I talked to loved working with this guy. So did I; sometimes you just get lucky.

Last but not least was Brian O'Hara, my boom operator, whom I had known for years. He was honest, straightforward, reliable, and he had written and directed his own low-budget films including a great horror spoof called *Rock 'N Roll Frankenstein*. His being a few years older than John and Justin would add a little extra experience to what I found to be a perfect crew. All three were experienced, dependable, hard-working *and* horror fans…. The first part of my dream team was in place.

Casting

Next I had to find actresses who (most importantly for me) could act and (most importantly for them) be comfortable. Well, at least as comfortable as you possibly can get being naked while raped by a muddy, worm-ridden zombie. Finding those two co-existing attributes in the same actress isn't really that easy; however, the fact that I was paying something *really* helped.

Production manager Justin Taylan during a very rare lull in *Daddy* shooting (photograph by Christopher Philippo).

I went through my usual channels, people I had worked with before, and came up with some possibilities. But I still needed to see more actresses, so I put up some Internet postings. I was like a virgin to this approach and I did, in fact, get quite a few responses from all over the country. Unfortunately, many came in after I had finished casting.

Since my films deal with physical and emotional extremes, my usual interviewing method is to try and scare the prospective actors and actresses away. If they flinch ... they're history. If I can say anything now that puts them off, there's no way in Hell they'll be comfortable down the road, doing this kind of stuff in front of a small group of relative strangers on location. So usually within a minute or so during those first interviews, I knew if they were right. The minute they had a forced, twisted smile after the words "*zombie rapist*," I knew ... *next*!

After weeding out all the young ladies who didn't seem to fit the role, or scaring off the rest of them, I was left with three very talented actresses, Celia Hansen, Katherine Petty and Cynthia Polakovich. I knew I wanted all of them in the film, I just wasn't sure which actress I wanted in which part.

So I set up a series of auditions with my casting director Amy Wallin, who (being a great actress herself) helped out by reading and improvising with all finalists. Each

actress did the same short scene with Amy while I videotaped them, then we threw out the script and did a short improvisation from the script. My ulterior motive is to know that the auditioning actor or actress is playing with another talented player who has no ulterior motives. It just levels the playing field, while the improvisation lets me see who can think on their feet. Although Cynthia and Katherine did extremely well, only Celia seemed to be the angry woman sheriff I had written.

I always try to work with the same people and *Daddy* was no exception. David Shepherd (Dr. Vance) was the founder of America's first Improv theater, Compass, and I've worked with him over 27 years. Marc St. Camille (Deputy Daggot) has been trying to get used to my ways since 1993, playing the lead in my last two films Transgression and Death Desire, while my friend and fellow writer-director Murad Gumen (*Wonder Guy* and *Eve's Preyer*) would play the obnoxious State Police Lab guy.

Aaron Renning, my zombie,

Top: Daddy Gaffer John Karyus recounting horror film set war stories. *Bottom:* Soundman Brian O'Hara shares some experience with the rest of the crew on the set of *Daddy*. (Photographs by Christopher Philippo.)

Above: The ladies of *Daddy* (*left to right*): Bevin McGraw, Katherine Petty, Celia Hansen, and Cynthia Polakovich (photograph courtesy Celia Hansen). *Left:* Aaron Renning as the title character in *Daddy* (photograph by Jamie Renning).

was a friend from upstate who I knew to be a life long horror addict. I also knew that he was great with horror make up, having observed his Halloween get-ups over the years. Luckily for me, our shooting schedule also coincided with his summer vacation. Likewise, the rest of the cast was from upstate, including Bevin McGraw as one of the sheriff's girlfriends Walk of Fame video store owner Phil Sawyer, who would play a funny variation on himself, as well as friends Jamie Renning (the real-life wife of our zombie) playing the Nurse and Barbara Stubblebine as Sylvia's mother. Last but far from least, I should remember my crew, all of whom did double-duty as actors. Even I was understudying two different roles…. Everybody Does Everything! So, between the interviews, auditions and rehearsals with the key cast members in New York City, I was constantly bouncing back and forth between upstate and the city, searching for cheap (hopefully free) locations that were easily accessible.

Locations

According to the strategies of Che Guevara, as well as in the time-honored tradition of low-budget horror films like *Texas Chainsaw Massacre*, *Night of the Living Dead*, *I Spit on Your Grave* and countless others, I knew that isolated country locations, where all the action could be under our control, were the most desirable. And if they belonged to friends or friends' friends, I knew I wouldn't have to worry about insurance, permits, police, curfews or restrictions on what we could or could not shoot. Now that's entertainment!

And that's exactly the kind of locations I found. Our graveyard was isolated on a friend's piece of land way out in the country and also had some great backgrounds for pick-up shots of our zombie rambling around. Another friend's lakefront house was so large, with two totally different looks in the front and back, that we decided to use it for two separate victims' houses, thus saving all the time it would have taken to break down and travel from one to the other.

Finally, I traded with another friend for the use of her house that was conveniently located right across the lake from our base camp. In addition, our base would serve double or triple duty as two additional locations while coincidentally belonging to my wife and me. So when we ran out of money near the end of pre-production and either couldn't eat for two days or had to transform my bedroom into the sheriff's office, guess what happened?

Okay, all our locations belonged to friends or friends of friends and all were within a 20-minute drive from our base camp; now I had to make sure that every piece of our equipment would fit in with this lean and mean guerrilla approach to filmmaking.

Equipment

I wanted to carry the least amount of small, tough, highly mobile equipment I could find while still getting the quality I needed. So I picked the SONY PD-100 DVCam Camcorder, two Sennheiser Shotgun mics (one mounted on the camera and one mounted on a boom pole), a Lowell DP lighting kit with three adjustable (1,000, 750- and 500-watt bulbs) lighting fixtures (with a back-up kit that we seldom used) as well as four heavy duty 100-foot AC extension cords.

Since I didn't want to lug a lot of gear around, I had to be sure that what we did have would do the job. I had worked with the SONY PD-100 when it first came out and have always loved its small size, dependability and image quality. The Sennheiser shotguns (one on a carbon fiber boom and one on camera) and the Lowell DP lighting kit had been workhorses of mine over the years and have never let me down while providing the adaptability that we'd need during those rough six days ahead.

Knowing that we'd have to haul ass from set-up to set-up faster than a speeding bullet, I pre-visualized the entire movie by figuring out almost all the camera set-ups before we started shooting. I did this by hustling around to every location several weeks before our start date, then pre-lighting and videotaping practically every set-up. And let me tell you, having this easy access is another great reason why it really helps shooting at friends' places! This let us walk into every location during the shoot and know exactly where every light should go, how many A/C cables were needed and even which outlet to plug into. It saved us hours at every single location — time that I could then spend with my cast instead of looking for outlets or tweaking lights.

The Schedule

Now, this brings up one of the most crucial elements in the entire experiment — the schedule. When you attempt to shoot a feature in only six days, you sure as Hell better have every single move, no matter how small, scheduled and stick to it, come Hell or high water. (A copy of our timeline/schedule is included in the back of this book.)

First off, since I was paying the cast, I could only afford to have most of them on set for a couple of days. So I needed to bunch all of the scenes involving the largest number of cast members together, either at the very beginning or the very end. This then makes their arrival or departure logistically easier and also allows me to shoot their scenes together with some degree of continuity. Since the largest number of the cast came from New York City, it made sense/cents to have them come up with the main contingent at the very beginning of the shoot and complete all their scenes during the first two days.

The good news: By the end of the second day, I would be finished with most of the cast. The bad news: The first two days would be our worst logistical nightmare with more people, meals, moves and scenes. But if we did finish the first two days on schedule, it would be mostly downhill after that. So we scheduled our departure in two cars from New York City late Wednesday afternoon on July 31, arriving upstate together early that evening. This would give us plenty of time to settle in, for me to cook a large pasta dinner and, later, for everyone to get together and maybe even watch a video. I wanted a later bedtime to get everyone used to staying up late, as most of our shoots couldn't start until dark.

Day One

Our first day was scheduled to start at 3 P.M., giving us time to get our gear together. It would include the flashbacks involving all the lead actresses as well as the zombie's first attack. We would begin the day with the sheriff visiting the first victim, shot right inside our base camp. Then we'd break for an early supper since we were already at the base, before shooting all the "day for night" flashbacks at a location just across the lake. After the flashbacks were wrapped, we'd drive out after dark to the graveyard, then shoot all the graveyard flashbacks, while most of the crew would remain at base camp and set up for the first zombie attack and its aftermath. After nailing the graveyard flashbacks, we would rush back to the base and immediately begin shooting the first zombie attack that was already lit and ready to go, including our zombie's make up. We hoped to be finished by 4 A.M.

Scheduling Considerations

I also tried to take into consideration the emotional and logistical difficulties of each scene, so that the most difficult emotional scenes would be shot just past the middle of the schedule, giving Celia, our lead, time to build her part but before she might become too tired. I also tried to put off the scenes with the most complex staging until the second and third day, so we would have time to get used to each other's way of working. Finally, I tried to have the easiest scenes, both emotionally and staging-wise, set for the end of the schedule. Now, obviously, on such a short schedule, some of these principles were compromised, but I tried to stick to them as much as possible.

Day Two

For the second day we scheduled the second and third zombie attacks. By completing these scenes, we would be finished with most of the NYC–based cast and could send them home. All of the second day's action involved that one large house that was to be used double-duty, for two separate locations, which would hopefully save us quite a bit of time and energy.

We would "hit the beach" at 2 P.M. and begin shooting at 4 P.M. with a couple of twilight interior scenes, simultaneously setting up the lighting for the night exteriors. Then when darkness fell, we would grab all the night exteriors, which would be pre-lit, and then end the day with all the night interiors. And if we stayed on schedule, the NYC–based cast would catch an early morning bus or train, while the rest of us would head back to our base for a well-deserved rest.

Day Three

Since it was obvious that our second day would be the most grueling, I didn't schedule Day Three to begin until around 4 P.M., allowing everyone to sleep in a bit. The actual shooting wasn't set to go until 8–9 P.M., but since we were doing all the graveyard scenes at night in the middle of the woods, we would need a long stretch of daylight to run our extended cables, to help illuminate the graveyard. And since our cast had shrunk to only the Sheriff and Daddy, the amount of food and sleeping space required would drop dramatically.

This would be a long and difficult all-night-in-the-graveyard-in-the-woods shoot, but once the lighting was set up, only dressing the grave area and choreographing the fight scene would remain. If we could complete all these shots, we would be 60 percent completed by the third day and everything would much less frenzied.

Day Four

After three long days in a row, I knew everyone would be exhausted, so our fourth day was relatively laid back with a bunch of short pick-up shots requiring no dialogue. Once again the shots included the Sheriff and Daddy but luckily for the crew, I would only need one of them, since all the shots were available light … thank you, pre-production planning! The guys back at the base could take it easy and clean up our camp.

Day Five

Our fifth day would welcome two actors from New York City; they would rendezvous with us at the sheriff's house, right across the lake from our base, which was our sole location for the entire day. In addition, if there were any missed shots that had to be made up, they could be grabbed during a lull that day.

Day Six

By our last day I knew we would all be flagging, except for the two newly arrived actors, so everything would take place in a single location that was logistically simple since it just happened to be our base camp, in my bedroom-turned-sheriff's office. Since everything would take place in that one room, any of the crew not involved could put our base camp back in order, nice, neat and tidy. Hopefully we would finish early enough to have a wrap party, get enough sleep and take off the next morning back to NYC.

Now that I had a tight but realistic schedule, great-looking locations (which were mostly free), an experienced crew and a cast that was talented as well as attractive, I began rehearsals in New York City.

Rehearsals

Since I wanted all the actresses who were playing girlfriends to have a real sense of camaraderie and (I hoped) to form working relationships with each other,

Sheriff Sylvia Carlsen (Celia Hansen) dresses down Deputy Daggot (Marc St. Camille) in
Daddy.

I got them all together and did a series of videotaped improvisations. To the casual
observer, it probably looks like a bunch of silly dames messing around with nightgowns over their street clothes. But these improvisations allowed each actress to fill
in not only her own character but also her character's relationships with the
other characters—that is, her girlfriends. I also used the rehearsals to set up
shopping expeditions, to find costumes or for trying on outfits I brought from
upstate.

I also got Celia, who plays the Sheriff, together with Marc, who plays her Deputy,
to rehearse a scene that I had cut from an earlier version of the script. This brought
their weird, slightly sadistic relationship front and center, with them acting out each
character's desires that are, for the most part, repressed in the final film. But I guarantee you that everyone who watches *Daddy* gets a very strong indication of these
desires, even if they can't put their finger on them.

Because Celia had a strong theatrical background with little film experience, I
also did a series of camera rehearsals with her, so she could become more comfortable working with the camera. We did what is called "privileged moments," non-verbal moments when a character is alone with their thoughts or feelings, while only
the camera (and the audience) eavesdrops. It really helps the actress, see (via the
videotape) the difference between acting on stage and in front of a camera.

Using Video

You may have noticed that I videotape as much as possible during the pre-production process, whether I end up shooting on film or tape ... er, excuse me, Digital. I tape auditions, locations, rehearsals, lighting tests, costume tests, makeup tests, music, sound effects and any other sort of image or sound that will fit on tape. It really helps me to see images and sounds mediated through the lens of the camera and recorded for easy reference later on. Since I get most of my ideas through my eyes, videotaping is the best way for me to stimulate this. Okay, enough personal confessions.

Art Direction

By seeing on camera how everything looks, I know exactly which locations may need a little extra visual flourish. And although I try to find locations that need little or no set dressing, most places need some small changes to make them really belong to the character who lives there. For example, the house where our Sheriff lives was actually built by the architect who had lived there, so the Sheriff's father became a local builder in our story and the house's very stylized look played right into that. However, her bedroom had the wrong look; too "L.L. Beany," so I brought in blood red curtains (which were in my study) while also changing the bedding's color and thereby changing her character.

Also, since there would be quite a bit of mud, blood and worms, we would have to do a bit of "preventative" set dressing that would both match our movie's look while still protecting our friends' furnishings. So for every couch where the zombie attacked someone, we had to find a relatively thick but cheap cover that matched the room's decor. The local Salvation Army (Sally Ann's in our credits) was perfect for discovering the right color cover at the right (cheap) price.

However, for our one really bloody attack and killing, we could find no salvation at the Salvation Army, so we turned to a local hardware store. There we dug up leak-proof painter's drop cloths that came in a very pleasant shade of orange which would not only match the room, but also make a lovely contrast with our crimson Karo syrup blood.

Wardrobe

Just as we made sure that all of the interiors were color-coordinated, so too with our cast's wardrobe. Obviously, the Sheriff and her Deputy had to have realistic uniforms, so off I went to an Army Navy uniform shop opposite the Brooklyn Navy Yard for realistic uniforms. All of our police gear was supplied upstate by Walk of Fame video storeowner Phil Sawyer, who is *the* connection for almost any prop you're trying to locate. I also wanted all the girls' getups to be coordinated, which meant I had to rummage through all the local upstate Salvation Army stores, the New York City discount clothiers and various people's closets. You should have seen some of the looks I got while searching for the color-coordinated, period nightgowns for the flashbacks.

Last but far from least was our Daddy, who had to look like he had been gone underground five years earlier. The task of "distressing" his wardrobe also fell to me. First I found a discount clothing store in Manhattan where I bought two identical wool suits (polyester ones are difficult if not impossible to distress convincingly) for $60 — not apiece but for both of them! Then after researching how they had distressed all the uniforms in Sam Peckinpah's *The Wild Bunch*, I bought various grades of sandpaper, a torch and a few camouflage colored cans of spray paint. The sandpaper seemed to work the best, although it took the longest, while the spray paint (dull tan and brown) was extremely convincing as dust. It took time and effort, but all too often a low-budget film is betrayed by careless costuming or art direction — you know, a seventeenth century vampires with go-go boots!

Above: Daddy star Celia Hansen, as Sheriff Sylvia Carlsen, with Marc St. Camille as Deputy Richie Daggot, in convincing but cheap uniforms (photograph by Christopher Philippo). *Below:* Aaron Renning as *Daddy* shows off a well-distressed suit (photograph by Jamie Renning).

Make Up

The make up was applied by the cast themselves using a professional kit I own, for everyone except for Aaron, our zombie, who created his own look with his wife Jamie using special effects make-up I brought up from New York. I wanted a classic horror look which

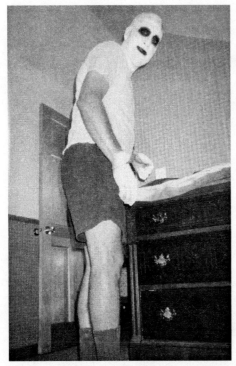

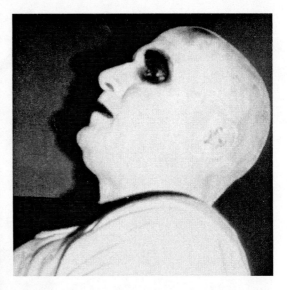

Left: Aaron Renning prepares to play *Daddy.* *Above:* Aaron Renning rests between scenes on the set of *Daddy,* showing his "classic" makeup. (Photographs by Jamie Renning.)

harked back to the 1920s and '30s and horror films like *The Unknown, Dracula, White Zombie* and others that I felt had a truly unsettling feel. I was after a surreal look rather than a more contemporary, explicitly scary one, which would have meant multiple layers of latex and hours each day tacked onto our schedule.

Food and Transportation

The last two pre-production arrangements were for food and transportation. And since good food or the lack of it has caused more mutinies on low-budget shoots than anything else, I wanted to be absolutely sure that we were covered in that area. First, I polled our cast and crew to make sure that there weren't any unduly esoteric diets, but to my surprise there were more than a few, most of whom I could accommodate. Some of the cast ended up supplying the own specialized diet, thus shaving a few precious dollars off of our already strained food budget. I then searched for someone upstate who'd buy the food and prepare it, all for a fixed rate. I thought I'd found someone until she found out that *Daddy* wasn't exactly a family film, but a zombie rapist film. So about two weeks before our shoot date, I still didn't have anyone to do the food.

With my back to the wall, I did some serious number crunching, adding up how many people, each day, we would have to feed and for how many meals. I knew exactly how many people would be eating at each meal on every day of the shoot. And if I could feed everyone breakfast as well as the first night myself, we could just about afford getting take-out food from a local pizza/Italian food joint for the rest of the shoot. That was mostly due to the fact that the number of mouths to feed would drop dramatically after the first two days.

Then two angels descended. The owner of The Crooked Lake Coffee and Tea Company graciously offered to donate our morning coffee and any leftover desserts for breakfast. And our friend, who was also donating her house as a location, would help get the coffee and munchies to our base camp the very first thing in the morning. We were saved and we actually came in under budget on the food, after we were told there was no way to do it. Of course, I had to go around to every Dollar Store in the area and pick up all their "On Sale" snacks, as well as stocking up on as much bottled Wal-Mart spring water as I could carry.

For the transportation, I just wanted to make sure we didn't have *too* many cars, as I had visited a local shoot one evening and found almost 20 cars for a scene involving three people talking in a barn. We never had more than four vehicles at any location for any scene. For moving our New York City cast and crew, we pooled our various crew members cars to get the NYC people upstate and Amtrak to get them home, if they were finished early.

Without the time-consuming, meticulous and often boring effort that went into the entire pre-production, we would never have been able to finish shooting *Daddy* on time and on budget. Take a close look at the schedule I've included; it's our original schedule and we stuck to it, only deviating when adverse conditions dictated that we become as flexible, adjustable, inventive and mobile as any guerrilla fighter.

2

Ambushing *Daddy*

On Wednesday July 31st, *Daddy*'s New York City contingent left late in the afternoon, packed inside two cars and arrived upstate at our base camp around 7 P.M. The whole gang then began settling in immediately, two people to a bed in the two bedrooms; our lead got her own small room with a single bed; and everyone else was camping out in the living and dining rooms. Around 8 P.M., I began whipping up a huge pot of pasta as everyone settled in. After a relatively late dinner, around 11 P.M. we watched a video of Andrzej Zulawski's *Possession*, to get us in the mood, then lights out around 1:30 A.M.

D-Day One

The next morning a few people were up early, but I lounged a little longer knowing that it would be my last full night of sleep for at least six days. After getting up, but while I was still gulping down my breakfast, we all started to get our gear in order. John, our gaffer, arranged all of our lighting equipment while Brian, our boom man, checked through all of his audio gear and Justin went driving off on one of his countless missions, this time to procure fresh worms. The cast readied their wardrobes and went over their lines together.

By 3 P.M. we were ready for our first shot, a long continuous take of the Sheriff visiting Alison, the zombie's first victim, the day after her attack. Although I had planned the lighting in advance, the way the sun was shining that afternoon made me change our lighting slightly by adding a warm spotlight coming in from a side window. I have this superstition about my first shot—it must be "perfect." So we did that shot about six times before getting it the exactly the way I wanted. We then had a quick dinner and "Next" became our constant refrain as we were off, never to look back.

We hauled ass directly across the lake to the Sheriff's house location, where all the flashbacks of the tragic slumber party were to occur. Since we would only be using one light and recording the wild sound by the camera mic, most of our crew remained at base camp. They began clearing up the inside where we would be shooting later that evening, as well as setting the lights and cables outside, while Daddy began putting on his face.

Back at the Sheriff's, I wanted the flashbacks to be in a contrasty black-and-white, so I set up a single weirdly angled key light blasting from the side. Most of the girls were already made-up from the previous scene and only had to quickly slip on their negligees. Since the sound wasn't critical, I was able to shout directions while shooting, making things move much quicker. We shot all the flashbacks in their chronological order, since I thought this would establish an emotional foundation for the rest of the girlfriends' scenes together.

Then we were off to the cemetery. You have to remember, we had only been at this remote location around 24 hours and these four actresses were now alone in car with me, driving down a dark and deserted country road into the middle of the woods to a cemetery they had never seen before. Realizing this, I thought by playing

Katherine Petty as Leslie Thornton prepares for shooting the *Daddy* flashback sequence (photo courtesy Celia Hansen).

Bernard Herrmann's score from *Cape Fear* (from the recent Scorsese version) as we drove up there, I wouldn't really have to direct them, only document their actual fear and uncertainty. It worked: We got to the cemetery and I just started shooting (using only the car lights for illumination) and, let me tell you, there wasn't much acting going on, which is just how I like it. Then we high-tailed it back to our base for the first zombie attack, which we started right in on, since the lights were all set and Daddy was made up.

Back at our base, even though we were doing extended, traveling takes (often over two minutes) things moved along quite smoothly until the zombie starts hitting Alison. I am very careful when doing stunts involving violence, as most inexperienced people think that you have to be violent to appear violent. *This is not so!* The action must only appear violent and it's by judicious camera placement that this

In *Daddy*, Sheriff Sylvia Carlsen (Celia Hansen) comforts her friend Alison Headly (Bevin McGraw), the first victim (photograph by Christopher Philippo).

is accomplished, not by putting your cast in jeopardy. I set up a dynamic angle to cover this action that looked real but was safe enough that the zombie's fist could be 12 inches from Alison's face and still appear to be hitting her. The only snag was that the actors weren't experienced in this kind of film fakery, so it took over a dozen takes until we coordinated everyone's movements just right.

Our second problem was *the worms*. We had purchased two varieties of real worms (earth and mealworms) to supplement our fake rubber ones. It seems mealworms are similar in appearance to maggots and if they're good enough for Dario Argento, Hell, they're good enough for me. The only problem was getting the suckers to move when you wanted them to move. This sticking point of the worm's motivation was further complicated by the fact that our zombie actor was now lying on top of our negligee-clad actress, who was then having cold mud and worms smeared all over her naked thigh. I just have to thank our production manager–worm wrangler Justin Taylan, who had the patience to coax these slimy little performers into squirming on cue.

Now, however helpful Justin was with the worms, there was one teeny, tiny thing that I had overlooked. He was also Bevin's boyfriend. So that when it was time for her to be sexually molested by our zombie, it wasn't too smart of me to have Justin sitting around. So Bevin called me over and mentioned what should have been obvious and I had Justin go off and begin setting up our next scene.

The Worms!

Daddy (Aaron Renning) surprises Alison (Bevin McGraw).

After that, things went smoothly and we finished the first day's shoot by 5 A.M., a little late, but we got all our shots and Bevin (who was playing Alison) was all finished and on her way home. Tomorrow would be our longest and most grueling day; the weather forecast warned there *might* be rain. But one thing in our favor was that we would be doing two very different locations all at the same house.

D-Day Two

We headed out around 2 P.M., after a fairly decent night's sleep. Upon our arrival we began setting up an interior scene between the Sheriff and her friend Jamie as the predicted thunderstorm seemed to be rolling in. I decided to go ahead and shoot since the scene we were doing would come late in the finished film, thus needing no continuity regarding the weather. I then placed the actresses in front of a window that looked out on the dark incoming clouds. As the thunder began rumbling louder, I quickly decided to try shooting immediately, which was

Daddy director Michael DiPaolo after a very long, very tiring day (photograph by Jamie Renning).

possible only because I was shooting long extended takes. If you take a look at the finished movie, you'll see that my gamble paid off as the thunder crashes loudly at precisely the right climactic moment and, let me guarantee you, it was not dubbed in!

While we were grabbing that scene, the rest of the crew was setting our lights (not actually plugging them in) outside under plastic covers, in case the threatening skies decided to let loose. They never did, they just misted and rumbled in the background. But because we weren't sure about the storm, we decided to change our schedule and do two more interiors with the Sheriff and her girlfriend Leslie before attempting to venture outside for exteriors. This abrupt shift in our plans, in response to the uncertain weather, would never have been possible if both of our locations were not in this same house.

So the next set-up, an extended dialogue between the Sheriff and her friend, was shot "day for night," since most of the windows were supposed to be shuttered and it was already twilight. Things moved right along until we got to the end of that scene, where the two friends sit down for a drink. Unfortunately, we had left our prop booze bottle back at our base camp, so we thought we'd save time and just use a bottle from the house. We left $10 figuring that should cover it, but little did we know that we'd picked a specially imported bottle that ended up costing us $40. Oh well … I guess it pays to know your wines.

Luckily, the storm mostly passed us by and we were able to get all the night exteriors with Daddy relatively quickly, as well as knocking off a short scene with the Sheriff and her Deputy. This left zombie attacks two and three, so that as the midnight hour quickly approached there was still quite a bit to cover. *Next!*

Coming up was Daddy attacking Jamie in her kitchen and parlor, which went fairly well, *until the worms.* This time when the zombie attacked Jamie, he was supposed to upchuck a mouthful of mud and worms all over her exposed breasts. Now let me tell you, it's one thing to figure out using coffee grounds for mud and fake fishing grubs (which had to be thoroughly cleansed of their sickening fish-attracting scent) for maggots, but it's whole other thing to get them all in an actor's mouth and

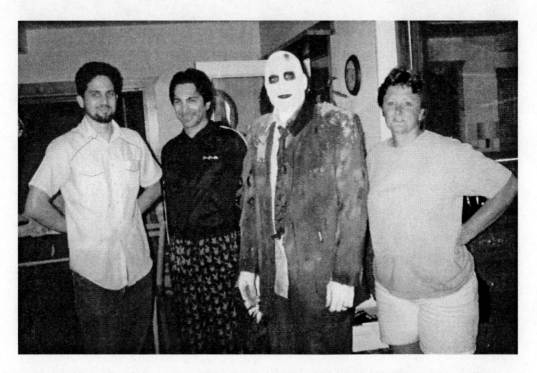

Justin Taylan (production manager) and actors Marc St. Camille, Aaron Renning and Jamie Renning take a break during the second day on the set of *Daddy* (photograph courtesy Celia Hansen).

Daddy (Aaron Renning) attacks Jamie (Cynthia Polakovich).

spewed up on cue while falling precisely into the thin streak of light falling on the actress' exposed breasts. I really have to thank Cynthia Polakovich, whose professionalism and good humor really helped us get through all of this without too much angst, as well as Aaron Renning, who had to actually put that strange concoction into his mouth ... thanks all!

Next we had to kill the Sheriff's closest girlfriend, Leslie, after she had been raped by our zombie. This is where my discovery of the orange drop cloth really paid off. We were able to smear her and splatter the couch, rug and drapes with our Karo syrup blood without worrying too much about ruining the room. It was getting so late that it was beginning to grow lighter outside and our next scene was supposed to be in the middle of the night as the Sheriff drives up to Jamie's after her attack. This forced me to shut down our lens a couple of stops to make things look appropriately dark. Luckily, we were helped by the fact that the dawning day was overcast and drizzly. By stopping down, we were able to make the outside appear a very beautiful deep blue with our exterior spotlights back-lighting the morning mist over the lake.

We quickly knocked off the Sheriff running inside, her short talk with Jamie, then finally an argument with her Deputy, which we switched to the outside, just because it looked so damn beautiful and only needed one light. It was around 5:30

A.M. and we were done with the New York–based cast, so Justin drove them to their various bus or train stations, while the rest of us packed up and dragged ourselves back to base camp. Mission accomplished: We had finished just under half the movie in our first two days and we were on budget and on schedule.

A Note on Teamwork

Before going on, I should mention something that was becoming more apparent after our second day and that was a decided difference in the cultural preferences of our cast and crew. As I mentioned, when I put the crew together, I wanted to have all horror film aficionados, which I did, with a vengeance. Unfortunately, not all of my cast shared these preferences and herein lay the seeds of discontent.

So you could always find the entire crew plus my co-producer Chris Philippo talking and/or arguing films (mostly horror) from the moment they woke in the morning (I know because I could hear them) right up until the moment they drifted off to sleep. Even during meals, you would often find them hunched around Chris' laptop watching some rare cult horror DVD.

A tired *Daddy* director (the author, left) with his cast Aaron Renning, Celia Hansen, Marc St. Camille, Cynthia Polakovich (photograph courtesy Celia Hansen).

Since most of my cast did not share this particular enthusiasm, they set up their own sort of social club with somewhat more refined conversations concerning Edina and Patsy from *Absolutely Fabulous*, for instance. And me, I was stuck somewhere in the middle, maybe a little bit like the movie I was making. But don't get me wrong, there wasn't really any nastiness or one-upmanship, just two very distinct camps who, luckily for me, came together when it was time for the work to begin.

Not that our set was some tranquil Garden of Eden — we did have some very real kinks that had to be ironed out. As I mentioned, Celia came from a classical theater background while the only cast member who had any experience in anything resembling horror films was Cynthia. The crew, on the other hand, had been mostly involved on a variety of low-budget genre film sets. However, I don't think they were exactly used to working with actresses who took their craft so seriously.

One of your main problems and/or responsibilities will be to make sure that all of these divergent backgrounds come together to work as one team. So that's what I did, making sure the actresses knew they could come to me with any problem and that, once alerted to an actress' problem, the crew would do whatever they could to make the set more "actress friendly." Usually this would only entail taking down the decibel level of their film-related conversation or discreetly moving into another room while the cast prepared. It wasn't a lot, but it helped and made a big difference. Then when most of the cast returned to NYC, our lead Celia was left alone with "the guys." I could sense her feeling of isolation, so I tried to spend a little bit more time with her and a little bit less with the crew; it seemed to help.

D-Day Three

Our third day was both simpler and more complex for now we only had to deal with two characters, Sylvia and Daddy, in just one location, the graveyard. But we would have our work cut out for us, as we had to run cables through a long stretch of woods (since a generator going all night would have bugged the hell out of the locals) and we would have to do considerable set dressing at the grave site itself. We would also be stuck in the middle of the woods for most of the night dealing with mosquitoes and other assorted bugs with only our flashlights to guide the way. Anticipating this, I had equipped everyone with mosquito repellent, mosquito-netting headgear, flashlights and plenty of batteries.

I should add that most of the grave "construction" was done weeks before shooting began, so the woods would help make it blend right in. Our grave "building" was necessitated because, although we had total access to the graveyard, we were asked not to dig *down* in creating Daddy's unmarked grave, so we built *up* a new grave on a sloped area of the graveyard using bags of mulch, wood chips, dirt and leaves.

We headed out around 3 P.M. after a decent night's sleep and began setting up our temporary base camp outside while running cable and dressing the grave. So while everyone else prepared the location or their makeup or costume, Justin drove off to pick up our take-out supper, which we wolfed down just before dusk.

We used the twilight to get some really great shots of Daddy silhouetted against the sky, then as soon as we lost the light we went straight to the cemetery and started shooting there. Once again the entire cemetery shoot was based on guerrilla filmmaking principles.

Earlier, I had a choice of a generator, which would have given us a brighter, more adjustable look, but with a considerably reduced period of time to shoot, due to the inevitable noise it would have created. Or I could run a single 1K spotlight off of four daisy chained 100-foot extensions from our friend's house, supplemented by propane lantern or car lights, thus enabling us to shoot quietly and uninterrupted for the entire night. For a guerrilla filmmaker, it was a no-brainer, we went with the one light and I know it was the right decision.

Quite remarkably, there were no real difficulties doing any of the cemetery scenes until we got to the final confrontation between Sylvia and her Daddy at the gravesite. It was just another relatively relaxing evening at the deserted cemetery in the middle of the woods. Perhaps a little too relaxing, as when it came time to do the fight scene, we were running behind schedule. Part of this was because I had added a couple of new shots involving some relatively bizarre objects I had discovered while shooting Daddy's twilight ramblings.

One of these was a weird, discarded doll that we eventually hung upside down from a tree on the cemetery road. The doll's hair reminded me of Elsa Lanchester's in *Bride of Frankenstein* and together with a nearby feathered boa, which I thought might look like a dead bird if it was wrapped around the doll, I hung this all from a low tree branch. This slightly surrealistic scene worked really well, but we were certainly behind schedule when it came to our final confrontation at the grave.

As I said before, staging fake fights with people who haven't done that sort of thing can be kind of tricky and our final fight was no different. It was further complicated by the addition of a saw, shovel and rock which were to be used in the course of the confrontation. Since our fight involved a real saw and shovel (our rock was fake), I had to make doubly sure that every shot was safe but looked real, very, very real. To accomplish this, I broke the entire fight down into small short shots that would individually be safe but when cut together they would appear to be extremely violent.

I always rehearse the action for every stunt shot, several times in slow motion, then several more at half-speed, so that the actors know and are comfortable with their movements. The only sticking point was that it was very late, the actor and actress were very tired, they had never done this kind of stunt before and it was getting fairly close to dawn. So on the very first take, Aaron didn't hear me say "Cut!" and continued with the action beyond what we had rehearsed. In the process, Celia almost twisted her ankle, something that we definitely did not need.

Since it was nearing the end of a very long, very stressful day, everyone was close to their limits, including me. I knew that I had to take it one precise step at a time or risk hurting someone, which would have helped no one. This despite the fact that it was now clear that dawn was approaching and it would ruin our entire scene if we didn't get all these shots soon, very soon. So from then on I made sure that my "Action!" and "Cut!" were loud and precise.

Things moved forward, slowly but they did move, until we got to the final shot, where Daddy, after faking unconsciousness, rises up, grabs Sylvia and pulls her into the grave with him. He immediately smashes her with a (prop) rock and begins his final attack. The camera was then supposed to slowly wander up to the car, all in one long continuous take. We obviously weren't going to be able to do this kind of complex shot before the dawn arrived, so I decided to leave the camera on a shot of the grave as Daddy attacked Sylvia; then maybe we could dissolve into the grave at dawn.

We did this four or five times, finally getting a couple of good takes just as the dawn broke. It was very, very close but we made it and I guess as a consolation, it looked like the sun might end up shining directly on our grave if we waited a bit longer. We did wait and the sun shined precisely on our grave for our final, but totally unplanned shot. A guerrilla always adapts and takes advantage of changing conditions and sometimes you just get lucky.

D-Day Four

It would be mostly downhill after that, so we all slept late the next day, which I had planned as our lightest, a day of relative rest. But just in case we had not been able to get everything, we would make it up on this, our fourth day. The

At the end of another long hard day of shooting *Daddy*, Phil Sawyer (left) rehearses with Celia Hansen as the director listens in (photograph by Christopher Philippo).

only shots we didn't grab at the cemetery were a couple of our zombie strolling through the woods, so we added them as well as a shot of the Sheriff leaving Alison's house.

Most of our shots were relatively simple, involving nothing more than driving to a location, jumping out, grabbing our shot with available light, jumping back in and driving off to the next one. Since our first shot didn't have to be set up until about 8 P.M., we had a leisurely dinner, then I set off with a skeleton crew, accompanied by Celia and Aaron, without his makeup, as all of his shots would only be in silhouette.

Our first shots were picturesque vistas where we silhouetted our zombie walking towards camera, then it was a short drive to Walk of Fame Video, where we grabbed another quick but complicated shot of the Sheriff picking up her date, Phil Sawyer, the video store owner. Next we were off to a deserted road in the countryside where the Sheriff rides along with her red light flashing.

Finally, we ended the night near the cemetery location where the Sheriff looks around a dark wooded area and is scared by a passing car, as well as a couple more shots of Daddy wandering around the woods. But since we didn't have any of our movie lights, we ended up using the car headlights instead. They worked fine and we were done for the night. And while we were roaming around the countryside, the rest of the crew stayed at the base camp and cleaned up what had become a semi-chaotic crash pad. It was an early night, so we had time to watch another video, *I Walked with a Zombie*, of course.

D-Day Five

Our fifth day found us rested and ready to go; we awaited the arrival of two New York–based actors. Our sole location for the entire day was to be the Sheriff's house, which was just across the lake from our base. We had a leisurely set-up in the afternoon since all of our day interiors would use only the available light coming through the windows. This left the crew plenty of time to get ready for our night exteriors, while we knocked off all the interior shots with the Sheriff.

Then it was time to do the scene where the Deputy goes looking for the Sheriff at her house and she pulls her gun on him. This was the scene that we rehearsed in New York City, using the cut scene from the script. Because I knew that we would be using available light, I hadn't planned the blocking of this scene as precisely as most of the others.

So we felt the scene out first, I knew I wanted a circling, tango-like effect, but until I was there with the cast, it really didn't click. Then all the preparation we had done in the rehearsals kicked in and we got what I consider to be one of the best-acted scenes in the film. I loved the relationship between the Sheriff and her Deputy; I found it very real and very touching in an almost sad way.

We wrapped that scene and headed to the lake for a couple of pick-up shots of Sylvia canoeing to Jamie's house. Then I realized the shot we had previously done of Sylvia walking up to Jamie's didn't include her carrying the crucial bag containing

A *Daddy* flashback shot of a young Sylvia (Celia Hansen) watching her father (Aaron Renning) attack her mother (Barbara Stubblebine) (photograph by Christopher Philippo).

the shovel and saw, so while everyone else ate dinner, Celia and I rushed back to the Jamie's house location and grabbed that shot. Then back to the Sheriff's house for her bedroom scene with the video store guy, which because of Celia's skill as an actress and Phil's natural gift for acting was completed flawlessly in only two takes.

Next up was a drunken woman sheriff alone in bed with her .38, a sort of weird shotgun marriage of Ingmar Bergman and sleaze cinema. Since I knew this would be one of Celia's most difficult scenes, I emptied the set of everyone except the two of us. We talked over a couple of things and then decided to give it a try to see if we could find our way by just doing it. There was no rehearsal and we did it on the first take. Sometimes you know when you're getting it and I knew. After a few more shots we were done and back at camp, exactly on schedule after five very tiring days.

D-Day Six

The sixth and last day dawned with the arrival of David Shepherd, who had driven all the way from Massachusetts to appear in the role of Dr. Vance. David and I go back to 1976, when I produced, shot and edited his improvised video movie *Sopha*. Since I was still sleeping, my friend and fellow director Murad Gumen made David

During the making of *Daddy*, David Shepherd (left) rehearses with Murad Gumen (photograph by Christopher Philippo).

feel at right at home by finding him some breakfast and then going over his lines with him. When I found out that David was already on location, I immediately got up and welcomed him. This allowed the crew to move in and begin stripping my bedroom, then transforming it into the Sheriff's office.

Needless to say, it didn't take too long before we were all set up and ready to go. David and Murad were fresh and ready to go, while Celia, not to mention all of the crew, myself included, were beginning to feel the effects of five continuous days and nights. All the scenes for the entire day were to be shot in that one room, and once we got our general lighting scheme, there wasn't much for John and Justin to do. So they began getting everything ready for our departure.

One unavoidably harmful effect of a six-day schedule is the damage it inflicts on your cast members' performances, since you often have to move to the next set-up knowing full well that they could have done much better with just a few more takes. And since the last day's scenes were more like ensemble pieces involving actors

In *Daddy* Sylvia (Celia Hansen) confronts Dr. Vance (David Shepherd).

with three totally different styles, they really needed that extra bit of time to merge into a single piece. I really felt that the last day's performances, more than any others in the film, could have benefited from just a little more time. Now this may all sound like sour grapes and I guess it sort of is, but I just want to add that we shot a little over 18 pages of dialogue in just one day that began shooting at noon and was totally completed by 7 P.M.!

We were fully wrapped by 9 P.M., then it was time for farewells from everyone leaving that night and party time for those who stayed. It wasn't too wild as everyone was exhausted, and also a bit surprised that the shoot had gone so smoothly, with no major problems. So after a good night's sleep, the remaining cast and crew headed back to New York City and a couple days of sleep.

While I enjoyed the peace and quiet after everyone had gone, I shot some wonderful shots of the moon on a cloudy night; later, some people thought they were created in After Effects, but were only me and my camera. I also realized that it would be a good time to grab some audio of night ambiences that might come in very handy during post-production. And one morning after I was awakened by a noisy flock of crows down the road, I sprang up, grabbed my camera and recorded the sounds, all of which were used in my final edit.

3

Finishing *Daddy*

Because there's nothing too different about my post-production process, I won't go into too much detail here, although I will cover the entire process more fully in the "Metamorphosis of the Ambush Chapter" later on.

Editing Quirk #1

I've developed a couple of quirks over the years that I will write about. The first is that I don't make selected takes (the "best" take or two of each shot) to edit from, I have to have all the footage in front of me. This comes from editing all my previous rough-cuts on a videotape-based S-VHS edit system that I've owned for years. I just make time-coded dubs on 60–minute S-VHS tapes and zip back and forth to my heart's content. In fact, I did my entire rough-cut for *Daddy* on this S-VHS system, even though I had access to Non-Linear systems. I find that being forced to look at all the scenes rush past me at 32 times normal speed while going between different takes forces me to constantly re-examine and re-think my footage.

And I can't begin to tell you how many times I found great bits and pieces that ended up in places other than where they were originally planned. It also forces me to constantly re-examine my preferred takes, which occasionally has made me change my mind about whole scenes as well as many of the shots in them.

A great example of this comes late in the film, where Sylvia lashes back at the Doctor and the State Police guy who are pressing her. My original choice was technically better, but by continually passing by this other scene, which had way better energy but two "mistakes," I realized I could disguise the mistakes and end up with a much better scene. I did make the switch and ended up with not only a better scene but also a better movie.

All too often the process of making selects, especially on a digital system, unnecessarily reduces your options, thus your creative flexibility, which is so vital during the entire editing process. So that in many cases, the only thing non-linear about non-linear editing is the machines, not the people or their working methods.

Editing Quirk #2

My other editing idiosyncrasy is that I never look at the script once I begin editing. I'm telling a story with the images and sounds that I captured, not conforming what I shot to what I wrote before I shot it. To me that's bass-ackwards. Since I wrote the damn thing, I better know what the hell the story is, so I just let my shots lead me. All too often, especially on low-budget, independent films, people are editing the script and not the footage they have in front of them — in other words, what they are supposed to have as opposed to what they actually do have.

The entire opening of *Daddy* was changed by this editing process, if I had followed my script, it would have been dead in the water early on. You have to stay open and let your actual footage lead you. In conjunction with this, I just have to mention Walter Murch's book on editing, *In the Blink of an Eye*; it's by far the best editing, hell, one of the best film books, ever written. It's short, concise and brilliant. It changed my editing life; get it, read it, it'll change yours.

Another great advantage to using this method is that I was able to more closely modulate the shifts in the Sheriff's character over the course of her story. When I wrote the script, I did some really dumb things; for instance, the morning after one of her best friends is raped, Sylvia begins laughing and joking with her ex-husband who drops in for a visit at her office. The scene was pretty good at introducing the ex-husband and the actors did a great job ... but what kind of insensitive shit would be laughing and joking the morning after an attack on her close friend? Reading the script, this didn't jump out at you, but the minute I tried editing those scenes together, it was apparent. Very apparent.

I tried editing that scene in eight million different variations and nothing worked, so it ended up on the cutting room floor. In the script this scene played a very important part, letting the audience in on Sylvia's past, as well as letting them know who the hell the peeping Tom outside her house was. Without this scene, the audience wouldn't know who her ex-husband was, even though he would keep popping up throughout the film. There was one other scene where the audience can easily infer that he's her ex-husband, but if I put that scene up front to replace the one I cut out, her ex-husband would make an early appearance, then sort of slowly disappear as the story progresses. Since I hate this kind of thing when I watch movies, I knew I'd better come up with something better than that.

Although it wasn't the greatest, what I came up with did work while adding an extra element of suspense. Since I had shot more than a few shots of Ed (her ex-husband) peeping in on Sylvia at her office and in the woods, I made him into this mysterious peeper for the first half of the story. In this way, the audience would be wondering who the hell this weirdo was, instead of wondering where he had disappeared to. Then I could place the scene where you finally find out who he is, and what he's doing, just past the halfway point of the story. Now the audience would have their questions answered, the Sheriff didn't seem like a heartless bitch and I had an extra element of suspense where there originally wasn't any. I killed three birds with one stone.

I also had a very powerful scene (the Sheriff contemplates suicide) which, in the script, took place very early. Watching the edited footage, it became readily apparent that it would be even more powerful if I placed it much later, directly after her best friend is murdered by the zombie as Sylvia lies unconscious nearby. Thus by making this switch from the beginning of the film until two-thirds in, the downward spiral of her character is much more pronounced and it's a hell of a lot more believable coming after the death of her best friend rather than after an argument with some one-night-stand.

Editing on the Computer

By the time I changed the edit over to my new Apple G4 computer with Final Cut Pro, the overall final shape of *Daddy* was there. Most of the fine-tuning was done on the computer, but the ease with which this is possible is a very, very large trap. You can infinitely tweak anything you want as long as you want and therein lies the danger. Perfection is death, as far as I'm concerned, and all too many movies today have been "perfected" via a cut every two seconds with a screaming over-designed, over-modulated soundtrack that's deadening after the first seven or eight deafening whirlwind minutes. Like people, films have to breathe — listen to their rhythms and let them breathe.

Sound Design

I don't want you to get the wrong idea: The digital sound design on *Daddy* took a long time and much effort. But I tried very hard to resist the "digital temptation" to overdo it. Since I don't have a lot of dialogue, music plays an extremely important part in my sound design and that's why I was so overjoyed when I found Lev Zhurbin, a young but very talented composer and violist to create my soundtrack. I wanted something different, a very modern but totally dissonant score that would create the impression that at any moment the ground could give way beneath you.

And I wanted real strings and voice, not synthesized ones. A very tall order on our minuscule budget, but Lev was totally up to the chore. After hearing just the first few seconds of his demo CD, I knew he was the man for the job. Nicole Renaud, who had previously worked with Lev, contributed the haunting vocals.

After I had locked my picture (completed the final editing of all the visuals) I then went through the entire edit and made a list of all the sound effects I wanted. Since I had been recording wild sounds throughout the production on the PD-100 camcorder and later on a DAT (digital audio tape) recorder, I checked what I had against what I wanted. I had managed to record some great night ambiences that included crickets and frogs as well as some early morning flocks of crows, songbirds and various takes of wind through the trees.

But I was missing some of the very specific sounds that I wanted, such as a variety of mysterious sexual and muddy worm-like rumbling sounds, as well as our zombie's footsteps. And since our budget was all gone, I also became the Foley department by creating many of the more esoteric effects, most of which had to be synched with the picture. This was done by playing my edit on an S-VHS deck while I watched from a quiet hallway, armed with my DAT recorder, Sennheiser shotgun mic and whatever gunk I was making my noises with. I made sure everything was recorded digitally, all digital in and all digital out, the secret to an efficient low-cost high-quality sound mix. The only problem is that I detest digital sound but then that's a whole other book.

For the sounds of the up-close and personal sexual intercourse, I used my finger in a jar of Vaseline petroleum jelly. To duplicate the zombie moving around underground, attacking his victims and walking around, I used a glass jar filled with a wet, gritty mud that I moved in various directions with the handle of a hair brush to create a variety of smooshing sounds.

I then gave every location a different sound effect that would act as its identifying ambience throughout the movie. For example, the Sheriff's house during the day always had the flock of crows in the background but at night it was crickets, while Alison's had a refrigerator, Jamie's had the frogs outside and Leslie's had an artificial silence. The graveyard had crickets and distant dogs and the Sheriff's office had the police band radio. The presence of the worms was accompanied by a very low frequency rumble.

In conclusion, my overall editing strategy is to try and inject a certain ambiguity in every single scene, so that the audience never really knows where the scene is going or how it will end. Of course, much of this can come from the script, but a good deal of this can be carried through right into the editing. I want to create a very clear "how" things occur combined with a relatively murky "why" things are done. In other words, show, not tell.

Now that you probably know more than you ever will want to about how I made *Daddy* in only six days while paying my cast and crew, it's time to move on to how you can use many of the methods I've just described to help you make your film your way. There's no better way to begin that by introducing you to those moviemaking mavericks who spent most of their lives making their films their way.

PART II

An Introduction to Guerrilla Filmmaking

4

Patron Saints
of the Underground

What in the hell is a "Patron Saint of the Underground?" It's a filmmaker who has a lifetime of consistent creative work, done under a variety of unfavorable situations, but has still managed, for the most part, to retain his integrity. Or as director Edgar Ulmer so succinctly put it, "I really am looking for absolution for all the things I had to do for money's sake."[2]

These "Saints" will serve as a historical precedent for many of the alternative methods of filmmaking I will cover in later chapters. Their perseverance in the face of adversity as well as their personal working methods can teach any filmmaker, beginning or experienced, some very valuable lessons. I must confess, I've borrowed quite a few of their methods myself, so if you've never heard of them or never seen their films, I urge you to check them out *now*!

Edgar G. Ulmer (1904–1972): Master of High Seriousness on a Low Budget

One man who gave Hollywood and subsequent generations of moviegoers "more bang for the buck" was Edgar G. Ulmer. He began as a designer with Max Reinhardt, F.W. Murnau and Fritz Lang in Berlin during the late teens and early 1920s. In 1925, now in Hollywood, Ulmer directed a slew of ultra low-budget Westerns for Universal and once again worked for Murnau as the production designer of *Sunrise*, *Four Devils* and *City Girl*, as well as art directing for Erich von Stroheim on *Merry Go Round* and Ernst Lubitsch on *Lady Windemere's Fan*.

In 1934, Ulmer got a break when he was assigned to direct and design *The Black Cat*, starring Boris Karloff and Bela Lugosi (their first picture together) and based on a haunting incident from the First World War (rather than Poe's short story). Ulmer turned this film into a strikingly stylized meditation on responsibility and revenge, modeled on the Medieval Morality play. The film was a success, but due to personal complications Ulmer was not able to make a another film in Hollywood until 1942.

In exile from Hollywood, Ulmer learned to pinch every penny until it screamed, turning out stylish exercises in Yiddish, Ukrainian and Black films on budgets that approached the invisible. Finally able to return to Hollywood in 1942, Ulmer chose the lowly Poverty Row studio PRC rather than MGM or 20th Century-Fox. His rationale was that he could bring his ideas directly to top management, who would then act quickly, unlike most other studios. He was also able to pick his own crew, which he then took with him from picture to picture.

One of the principal reasons Ulmer formed a dedicated crew (his wife was his script supervisor) was that an integral part of his style was the use of long choreographed takes, learned while working with Murnau. Now most "experts" say you shouldn't or can't do this on a limited budget. But with experience and a good crew, it can ultimately save you time and money. Ulmer was able to avoid "covering" the scene from multiple angles by using these long master takes while choreographing into them his medium shots and close-ups. This tactic kept his shooting ratio down, often as low as 2:1!

It was in this atmosphere that Ulmer directed a number of PRC pictures, most of which were shot in only six days! Averaging 80 set-ups a day! Their quality continues to amaze filmmakers and filmgoers to this day. He was even able to take a one-page outline called *Club Havana* and create a low-budget version of *Grand Hotel*, shot on one set in an amazing four days! So when you start complaining about how many set-ups you have to shoot in so little time, look to Edgar Ulmer and learn.

Now I'm not saying to go run out and do this without any experience, but it can be done and it can be done on a tight budget with a short schedule, but only if it's executed by a dedicated, experienced crew and by a director who knows when and how to apply it. Watch Ulmer's films *Detour*, *The Naked Dawn*, *Ruthless*, *Bluebeard*, etc., and you'll see how; then if you feel the need for that kind of camerawork to fulfill your vision, go out and find your own way to get it done. In fact, I've used my own variation of this tactic more than once.

Another of Ulmer's unique methods that allowed him to finish a feature in six days was the way he shot close ups. Because the close up was not an integral part of his style, which depended heavily on choreographed camera movement, he would save the shooting of his close ups until the last day of production. In addition, he always made sure that at least one part of every set had a bare gray wall. He would then put his actor against that wall and have them run through their speech for each close up, then (instead of cutting and re-slating) he would place his hand in front of the camera, quickly take it away and the actor would deliver their next speech from their next closeup. Thus saving considerable film, time and ultimately money.

One final lesson from Ulmer was his contention that "We've been looking, to my knowledge, for over 40 years to identify ourselves with our audiences."[3] And, in conjunction with that, you "have to have a viewpoint when you tell the story.... Don't do it from five viewpoints."[4] This insistence on the primacy of Point-of-View is repeated by other "Underground Saints" and will be the subject of this book's fifth chapter.

Val Lewton (1904–1951): Master of the Implied

Vladimir (Val) Lewton was one of the few Hollywood producers who was able to create his own distinctive style. He did so while producing horror films at RKO studios, working with unbelievably low budgets during the 1940s. The budgets were limited to $150,000, the films were not to last longer than 75 minutes and were given pre-tested and marketable titles such as *Cat People, I Walked with a Zombie, The Leopard Man, The Curse of the Cat People, Isle of the Dead, The Body Snatchers and Bedlam.*

Lewton's first order of business at RKO was creating a team, a hand-picked production unit made up of the very best people his limited budgets could afford. This was an important lesson he had learned while working for David O. Selznick at MGM in the '30s. Lewton listened to every member of his team, including his secretary, thereby making everyone feel special, a contributing member of his picture-making process.

This first group would include writers DeWitt Bodeen, Curt Siodmak, Ardel Wray, director Jacques Tourneur (*Out of the Past, Experiment Perilous, Curse of the Demon*) and editor Robert Wise (who would later move up to director for Lewton and then go on to direct *The Haunting, The Day the Earth Stood Still, West Side Story* and *The Sound of Music*). Later team members included editor Mark Robson, who would also move up to directing (later helming such pictures as *The Bridges at Toko-Ri, Peyton Place, Von Ryan's Express* and *Valley of the Dolls*). Lewton inspired his team to view their restricted budgets as a creative challenge, so that everyone pulled together, making for a very close-knit group.

Lewton, who had started out as a writer, would personally fine-tune every script before production began, using a variety of artful ellipses to impart important story elements (such as the use of an authentic folk song sung underneath a period lamp post to suggest a sense of place rather than going out and building an entire street set). He would study period paintings and engravings, picking up essential elements that could be added for next to nothing, only the cost of proper research.

Lewton really knew the value of withholding information from the audience. During the script-writing stage, the scenes that he and his writers chose to show as well as those they chose to omit contributed to a concise, almost abstract, audience-involving style of telling a story. His movies, in a sense, needed the audience's participation to fill in and complete them, a valuable lesson for any filmmaker.

Another of Lewton's methods for saving money while enhancing the overall look of the entire picture was to select one location where much of the action was to take place. He would then lavish special care on that one set, making it really stand out, thus giving the entire film a much more expensive look.

On his very first picture, *Cat People*, he used an ornate stairway from *The Magnificent Ambersons*, greatly enhancing the look of the entire picture but not increasing its budget. He later renovated the church from *The Bells of St. Mary's* for his production of *Bedlam*, recreating that infamous Mental Hospital of eighteenth century London. He turned the sets from *The Hunchback of Notre Dame* into the backgrounds for his *Mademoiselle Fifi*, one of the least expensive costume dramas ever filmed. So go out there and take the extra time to find that one striking location that not only looks great but also belongs to someone's relative or friend who'll let you use it for little or nothing.

In *Cat People*, Lewton began using suggestive shadows rather than showing the large cat directly, feeling that the dark patches on the screen would be filled in by the audience's own fears and anxieties. It was an artistic strategy he would employ for all of his films at RKO.

For the guerrilla filmmaker, this is one of the most important tactics at your disposal: *Shadows* are your best and cheapest special effect. Study painters like Rembrandt, Caravaggio and Vermeer or directors of photography like John Alton or Vittorio Storaro and see how they use shadows to increase the drama in a scene, then apply those lessons to your own work.

So many films are totally and unnecessarily over-lit. You do not need to see everything! The audience should only be seeing those elements which are necessary to the telling of your story. What you don't see, or don't show, can be just as important or even as revealing as what you actually choose to show.

Upon completing *I Walked with a Zombie* (one of my personal favorites) and *The Leopard Man* in 1943, both directed by Jacques Tourneur, Lewton was given the opportunity to become a producer of "A" films at RKO. But when he insisted that one of his team members direct his first "A" production, he was sent back to the Bs, now realizing he had more creative freedom in those low-budget features than with the more prestigious (and higher budgeted) "A" pictures. After Tourneur eventually left to direct "A" pictures, Lewton continued to produce exquisite little "B" picture gems such as *The Seventh Victim* and *The Curse of the Cat People* (one of the best children's films ever made, despite the title). Then in 1944, Boris Karloff came to RKO and worked with Lewton and his team to create a trio of atmospheric and haunting films: *Isle of the Dead*, *The Body Snatcher* and *Bedlam*.

In 1946, after problems at RKO, Lewton left for the seemingly greener pastures of Paramount (unfortunately not able to bring his valued team with him). In the years that followed, Lewton was never able to negotiate the treacherous Hollywood waters of bigger budgets, greater studio interference, personal betrayal and the new world of independent productions.

The few films he did turn out lacked his usual flair that had combined the literate and the visual into a small but glistening package. However, to this day, his RKO productions remain a glowing testimony to Val Lewton's grace, intelligence and taste in circumstances that constantly seemed to work against those very qualities.

Roger Corman (1926–): The Master of Artful Exploitation

"A small band of efficient, dedicated, highly trained warriors [filmmakers?] could defeat any number of rabble."[5]

—from Corman's film *Atlas*

To me, the most influential American filmmaker of the last 30–40 years isn't Orson Welles, but rather Roger Corman, King of the Bs. And below are just some of the valuable filmmaking tips that he's shared with young directors such as Francis Ford Coppola, Martin Scorsese, Jonathan Demme, James Cameron, Joe Dante, Dennis Hopper and countless others:

Thorough preparation.

Rigid scheduling.

Quirky plots.

Unconventional but well sketched characters.

A villain as interesting as the hero.

A good first reel (so the audience knows what's going on) and a good last reel (so the audience knows how things turn out).

Reuse standing locations.

Never say die, never say can't, never say quit.

A quick disciplined pace on the set.

At least twenty set-ups a day.

Act decisively when unforeseen circumstances arise.

Each scene should be shown through one character's POV (not necessarily a hand-held shot panning around).

Create a visual style expressed through the moving camera but always with a motivation for doing so.

Frame shots with an interesting depth of field.

Lead people into scenes with a moving camera.

Heighten tension with POV shots.

Use as many interesting angles as you can.

Don't repeat compositions in Close Up.

Solid performances.

Take advantage of accidents to "steal shots."

Reuse footage, either stock footage or from previous films.

And finally, Be tough with yourself in the editing.[6]

Some of the above-mentioned directors are now working with much larger budgets, but they are still utilizing many, if not all the lessons they learned at "The Roger Corman School of Filmmaking."

In his own films of the '50s, Corman evolved a style that combined comedy with horror and would lead to such films as *A Bucket of Blood* and *The Little Shop of Horrors*, the first shot in a remarkable six days, the second in an almost unbelievable two-day period! It was this combination of two seemingly disparate genres that would lead to his most famous series, the Edgar Allan Poe films from 1960 to 1964. Using such veteran actors as Vincent Price, Peter Lorre, Boris Karloff, Ray Milland and Basil Rathbone, as well as one of F.W. Murnau's cameramen from *Tabu*, Floyd Crosby, he created *The Fall of the House of Usher, Pit and the Pendulum, The Premature Burial, Tales of Terror, The Raven, The Masque of the Red Death* and *The Tomb of Ligeia*.

Corman's skillful and involving use of the moving camera and creative (and cost-efficient) casting, combined with an imaginative use of standing sets and a Freudian-influenced perspective on these classic tales, created a sophisticated '60s variation on Val Lewton's low-budget horror classics of the '40s. Once again those very same filmmaking elements are evident: putting together a small motivated team of creative individuals, cost-effectively reusing standing sets with only minor alterations, the intelligent placement of the camera to involve the audience rather than relying on expensive special effects, a script written with an awareness of the production's limitations and a stock company of experienced character actors playing sympathetic villains. The results both critically and financially were also relatively similar, even though over 20 years had passed and the mood of the country had changed considerably.

In the late '60s, Corman was to create two of the most archetypal films of that decade, *The Wild Angels* and *The Trip*, featuring actors Peter Fonda, Bruce Dern, Jack Nicholson and Dennis Hopper. As almost everyone knows, *Easy Rider* was in some way the bastard child of Roger Corman. Unfortunately, due to American International's restrictions concerning Dennis Hopper as the director, Hopper and Fonda took the picture to Columbia, via a connection from Jack Nicholson.

After his disappointment with *Easy Rider*, Corman made *Bloody Mama* for American International, starring Shelley Winters, featuring Robert DeNiro in the supporting cast and shot by John Alonso. This film, one of Corman's favorites, would be the model for more than a few sequels over the years, including *Big Bad Mama*, *Big Bad Mama II*, *Crazy Mama* and *Boxcar Bertha* (directed by Martin Scorsese).

Due to continued editorial interference from American International in the early '70s, Corman formed his own production and distribution company, New World Pictures, which had the somewhat schizophrenic personality of distributing Ingmar Bergman, Akira Kurosawa and Federico Fellini while simultaneously making and distributing *The Student Nurses, Private Duty Nurses, Angels Die Hard, Angels Hard as They Come, The Big Doll House, Women in Cages* and *Rock and Roll High School*. He made money on both, having the unique distinction of putting Ingmar Bergman into American drive-ins!

In 1983, to get out of the distribution end of the business and take advantage of a very lucrative offer, Corman sold New World Pictures and turned right around and formed Millennium solely for the purpose of production. Unfortunately, things did not go the way Corman had planned and he found himself in 1985 once again producing and distributing via his new company Concorde Films. With the rise of cable TV, Corman's "quality on a budget" has found new and expanded markets, and he continues to offer opportunities to up and coming filmmakers.

John Cassavetes (1929–1989): Master of Character

"The emotion was improvisation, the lines were written."[7]

— John Cassavetes

During the 1950s, John Cassavetes acted on live TV in New York City before appearing in several films as a juvenile delinquent. He turned an appearance on a New York radio talk show into his first film directing opportunity by suggesting that the audience should send him money to create an alternative to Hollywood-style films. To his amazement, around $20,000 was sent in, allowing him to begin production on what was to become *Shadows*.

Produced over a two-year period, this improvisational feature was shot with a hand-held 16mm camera and featured a score by the great jazz composer, Charles Mingus. The film was originally improvised and shot in 1957 and presented in 1958, but a second version which was written using the 1957 improvisations was shot and presented in 1959. The 1959 version is the one which is now seen but, in appreciation to the actors, Cassavetes left the "totally improvised" end credit.

After successful screenings in Europe, *Shadows* found only limited distribution in the U.S., but it did lead to directing assignments in Hollywood, including *Too Late the Blues* and *A Child Is Waiting*. As fate would have it, Cassavetes left after a bitter dispute, effectively banishing him as a "difficult director."

After acting in a few more Hollywood films, Cassavetes used his earnings and converted a stageplay into what would become his second independently produced feature, *Faces*. This film would act as the model for the remainder of his directing career. He gathered a group of friends (Seymour Cassel, Al Rubin), relatives (his wife Gena Rowlands) and experienced (John Marley) and aspiring actors (Lynn Carlin) into the cast.

His friend Al Rubin, who would end up working for the next 20 years in a variety of production capacities from cameraman to producer, was sent to New York City with $8,000 to buy as much equipment as he could. It included a 16mm Arriflex, assorted tripods, a lens, an audio recorder, microphones and lights. Cassavetes also acquired a 16mm Eclair which would became his camera of choice because of its adaptability for hand-held work.

The actors worked for deferred (sound familiar?) payment, which they had to do on *all* of Cassavetes' independent productions, and he shot with short ends of film. The main locations were Cassavetes' house and his mother-in-law's, while the film was cut and mixed in his garage. If there is any founding father of "American independent film" as we know it today, John Cassavetes is it, pure and simple. Anyone else is an also-ran.

Faces ended up costing $200,000 and took six months to shoot, using nights and weekends since everyone involved had a "day" job. Principal photography began on New Year's Day 1965 and finished in June of that year. It was shot mostly in continuity, something practically unheard of in studio filmmaking.

Cassavetes' reasoning for this approach was that studio filmmaking methods worked against the actors, who he believed should be of prime importance. He also believed, rightly, that shooting schedules were set up more with the crew's requirements than the actors, thus making it almost impossible for an actor to give an emotionally nuanced performance.

Cassavetes thought that the manner in which individual scenes were shot (a master shot, then the over-the-shoulders or medium shots, then the closeups or reaction shots), also worked against the actor, making it difficult to build or sustain an emotion. This, as well as constantly having to hit marks, Cassavetes believed, benefited the cameraman more than the actor. In the method of shooting he was to develop, this was all changed.

It must be mentioned that not all Hollywood directors shoot in this coverage style and that many of those directors who are most recognized for their individual styles found alternative strategies for realizing their visions. And so should you *if* you are uncomfortable with the typical method of covering a scene.

Cutting down the coverage from multiple angles saves on the amount of film that you use, but of course Cassavetes used this saving of film in his own unique way by shooting many more takes of each shot to get exactly the performance he was after, routinely shooting a million feet of film per picture, averaging 10 to 12 takes. His process was inseparable from what he wanted to say; in a sense, it was what he wanted to say.

In the same vein, Cassavetes wouldn't tell an actor what he wanted or how to play a character but would let them find it themselves. He didn't correct them, but would have them reassess it and do it again and again, leading to multiple takes. This process was his means of getting at an emotional reality in the only manner he considered truthful, sometimes doing as many as 50 takes— not unlike Stanley Kubrick, but in an entirely different context.

Cassavetes never wanted to let actors know when the camera was running, seeking to avoid that self-consciousness actors seem to put on when they know film's rolling. He did this to experienced as well as inexperienced actors, sometimes talking an actor through a scene while actually shooting it and then later erasing his voice from the soundtrack.

Cassavetes said that his films didn't matter, but the process of making them *did*. Because, to him, each film was an exploration, an open-ended proposition, and the ending was only possible after going through the entire process of making that particular film.

The actual shooting could and would shift emphasis if something happened along the way that intrigued him or changed his mind (and because he shot mostly in continuity, this was not the major problem it would otherwise be). The final edit was also continually shifting and changing, existing as totally different retellings, sometimes using scenes deleted from other versions. Thus, with no deadlines other than his own, he created this luxury for himself.

Premiering in 1968, *Faces* was a critical and financial success. In the '70s and '80s, Cassavetes went back and forth between his totally independent productions, including *A Woman Under the Influence*, *The Killing of a Chinese Bookie* and *Opening Night*, and studio productions over which he had control, including *Husbands*, *Minnie and Moskowitz*, *Gloria* and *Love Streams*.

Unfortunately his last film was named *Big Trouble*, a studio production which was exactly that. Cassavetes took over the directing reins in midstream to help out his friend and frequent collaborator Peter Falk. Falk, together with Cassavetes' wife Gena Rowlands, his friend Seymour Cassel and Ben Gazzara made up the nucleus of Cassavetes' acting company throughout his entire independent directing career, creating a galaxy of unforgettable characters in unique collection of totally original films.

"As an artist, I feel that we must try many things—but above all, we must dare to fail. You must have the courage to be bad—to be willing to risk everything to really express it all."[8]

Cassavetes—Post Script, vol. II, #2

Edward D. Wood, Jr. (1924–1978): Master of Persistence

Many years ago, I saw a film on TV and it was the weirdest damn thing I ever saw, more surreal than anything Luis Buñuel or Salvador Dalí had ever attempted. It was only much later that I learned that it was *Glen or Glenda?* and its star, writer and director was Edward D. Wood, Jr., dubbed "The World's Worst Director." In addition, I learned that it was autobiographical in the extreme, beyond almost any other feature film that I knew of.

If Wood was so bad, why did this imagery (not just the visuals but their crazy juxtapositions as well) linger for so long? What qualities made him "the worst"? He was honest, he dared to go where others feared to tread (by putting his own ass on the line, on- and off-camera), he did the best work he was capable of, he devoted his life to his work, he had developed a team (actors and crew) that stayed with him over the years, the films were unique in ways few others were, the acting was mostly terrible, the stories practically unbelievable and the sets were from hunger.

But how many films have I seen that had great acting, totally believable stories in gorgeous settings, that were dishonest, conformist and could only have come about with the calculated indifference of all involved? The unfortunate answer is most and it seems to apply now more than ever. I'm still not sure whether I think Ed Wood is a good or bad director or if it even matters, but I am sure that he has much to teach the underground filmmaker.

After a few years of working on the fringes of the Hollywood film industry, Wood was given his chance. In 1953 he wrote, directed and starred in *Glen or Glenda?*, a very, very thinly veiled autobiography masquerading as a scientific examination of the then-popular Christine Jorgensen sex change controversy. The script took only a few days to write, but was obviously brewing in his mind for a long time, so when the opportunity arose, he took full advantage of it. It paralleled his relationship with his live-in girlfriend Dolores Fuller and put Wood, his angora fetish and his transvestitism right out in front of the camera for all to see.

Wood would only have five days to shoot the entire film, putting his earlier experiences to good use. As many of his co-workers have attested over the years, nothing would stop Ed Wood. From endless hours poring over stock footage, which was available for little or nothing, Wood would fashion his convoluted narratives, adding an extra visual dimension otherwise unavailable on his meager budget.

From his directing of commercials and a failed stint as an actor-writer-director of Westerns, Wood was able to organize the production with a limited number of locations, a small cast and crew, indefatigable energy and improvisational skills in the face of any emergency, all the while bringing the film in on time (five days) and on budget ($26,000).

When Wood was making a film, it was a 24–hour-a-day commitment, living with it, sleeping with it and driving cast and crew to the limits of their endurance — which mercifully lasted only 4 or 5 days. But his infectious spirit was to rub off on almost everyone, so that even with the rock bottom budgets, crazy schedules, everyone doing a little bit of everything, as well as constant funding problems, Wood was able to attract and hold a loyal team of actors and crew. They would include William Thompson on camera, Harry Thomas doing makeup, Dale Knight recording sound and actors Bela Lugosi, Tor Johnson, Criswell, Dolores Fuller, Lyle Talbot, Tim Farrell, Kenne Duncan, Conrad Brooks and Paul Marco.

Even today, cast and crew alike still remember the way Wood would pitch in anywhere he was needed — strapped to the top of a car with a watering can to create a rain effect or scraping together the cardboard and paint necessary to make an improvised coffin, helping to steal a rubber octopus from a studio prop shop or even taking over the role of someone's mother when the actress failed to show up!

This crazy camaraderie Wood created would carry him through many difficult scrapes. Thus the example *you* set, from the very first minute of the very first day of production, is one of the most valuable commodities you'll have as low-budget filmmaker. And how you go about using and/or abusing that responsibility will have a major influence on the smooth sailing of your production, especially if things go wrong. And they will, I guarantee it!

Unfortunately, monetary problems would plague Ed Wood for most of his career. He would often begin production without the total budget being in place, and was forced to raise the remainder in bits and pieces while filming progressed. If he couldn't, shooting was sometimes suspended. He often lost most or all of his financial interest in his films this way.

And herein is another valuable lesson for the guerrilla filmmaker: It is definitely not the best strategy to go into production without all of your funding in place, because once anyone (investor, producer, distributor) knows that you need *their* money to finish (whatever stage you're at), you are at a disadvantage. And any deal you make, will almost always work against you, decreasing how much of your own film you end up owning. So think through all your options first, don't rush into anything. It's always better (although not necessarily feasible) to have the entire budget in place before beginning.

Wood continued writing, producing and directing films such as *Bride of the Monster, Night of the Ghouls* and the film he considered to be his masterpiece, *Plan 9 from Outer Space*, introducing the iconic images of Tor Johnson rising from the grave and Vampira stalking through the mist into our collective consciousness. This child of the American Pulp Pantheon has finally found his place among them.

Jean-Luc Godard (1930–): Master of the Intellectual/Improv

"The lords of imperialism have transformed technology and sexuality into instruments of repression."[9]

—from Godard's Le Gai Savoir

From his very first feature *Breathless* through *My Life to Live, Contempt, Alphaville, Masculin/Feminine, Pierrot, Weekend, Tout Va Bien, First Name Carmen, Hail Mary, Forever Mozart* and *In Praise of Love* to his most recent film and TV work, Jean-Luc Godard has, more than any other filmmaker working today, questioned every aspect of filmmaking with a rigorous intelligence. Godard believes that the "New Hollywood" is an arrogant usurper of contemporary cinema, forgetting its own creative past and unthinkingly imposing rigid rules and regulations, instead of constantly reinventing itself.

He has said that he feels more at ease with the methods of the silent era's "King of Comedy," Mack Sennett, than with current filmmaking practices. The main reason for this preference is Godard's perception that the early cinema was inventing itself as it went along, so that those working in film were never bored and that their creative energy was transferred directly onto the films they produced. It's a quality he finds sadly lacking in most contemporary cinema.

A prime example of his inventive quest is Godard's continued use of improvisation, especially during principal photography. He prefers to call this improvisation "last-minute focusing" because of his extensive preparation which includes detailed notes and an overall plan. His overall plan consists of the film's seven or eight key moments or scenes, which then provide the plot. Thus, during filming, when a new idea arises, Godard only has to decide which moment or scene that new idea fits into. This method offers him maximum flexibility while maintaining a clear path to the film's completion. A "well-written script" is only necessary if you find it to be necessary. If you don't like using or writing scripts, there are other methods.

Godard's goal is to create a working method that uniquely suits him, not anyone else. He is only against any rule that says there is only one way to do something. Thus, because his need to take extra time to think during production is a prime necessity, his process reflects this. Whereas most directors spend quite a bit of time setting up every shot and very little time on the set, actually thinking about what's being filmed, Godard would rather have the shot set up quickly (hence his extensive use of natural lighting), giving him more time to think.

He also incorporates into his schedules an extra amount of production time, figuring in long waiting periods for the cast and crew, while ensuring they're well paid for all of their time. This is one of the prime reasons Godard has constantly worked with low budgets over his entire career. Low budgets allow him the luxury of time, a contradiction according to Hollywood, but not Godard, who feels that once a budget reaches a certain height, the film becomes the producer's, not the director's.

This is not to say that Godard doesn't appreciate the work that a producer contributes, because as he's said, they're one of the very few people who will tell you without hesitation, what they think of your film (see *Forever Mozart*). And in some strange way, he feels that when you're speaking about money with the producer, it can sometimes be a way of speaking about art (see *Contempt*). For Godard the money always figures twice, once when you're raising the funds and then again when it is made apparent in your film's images.

The problem arises when you as the director are making a different film from what your producer envisions. This has led Godard to be just as careful in his selection of producers as in that of his crew, actors or actresses. An important lesson for any filmmaker negotiating that ever-shifting line between producer and director.

Another reason Godard prefers small casts and crews is because he asks for a personal involvement from every member, feeling that he can only achieve this type of intimacy with a small group. He can ask them questions, not only about the film, but about their lives and how they personally relate to what they're now working on. Whereas with large crews, communication is often limited to "Hi" and "Bye."

In 1972, Godard moved his production company to Switzerland, first to Grenoble, then Rolle, where he sometimes would take on the additional role of producer, while continuing to keep his budgets low and his crews small. Ultimately for Godard, making a movie is making life and in big films there is an unavoidable division between labor and love, when in his mind they should be united, so that in the making of his small (in budget and crew size only) films Godard finds that unity, in life and cinema.

Now as you've seen, each one of these "Saints of the Underground" has demonstrated over the course of their career a singular vision, a unique Point-of-View, which coincidentally happens to be the subject of our very next chapter.

5

Point-of-View

(Or, what Alfred Hitchcock, Master of Metaphysical Manipulation, taught us)

In a cheap motel bathroom, a nude, young woman steps into the bright white shower and closes the curtain. She turns the water on, scrubbing vigorously, attempting to wash her guilt away. Suddenly the bathroom door opens and a dark silhouette approaches.

The shower curtain is ripped back and violins shriek as an old lady–like silhouette violently slashes the young woman in the shower. She is totally defenseless and it's only a matter of time before the young woman's lifeless and bloodied body slides slowly down. The audience as well as the victim are left drained, all victims of Alfred Hitchcock's mastery.

But why such utter devastation? Is it because *Psycho*'s star has been killed off less than a third of the way through the picture? Possibly … but on careful analysis it's more, much more than that. The entire movie, right after the very beginning when the camera moved into an anonymous hotel room, has been told exclusively from that one particular woman's Point-of-View, everything has been visualized *Through Her Eyes*. We, the audience are privileged to no other Point-of-View in the movie, until Norman Bates looks through the peephole as Marion Crane undresses.

So that when Marion is murdered, we the audience have no other choice than to follow Norman Bates, the only other Point-of-View made available to us. We have no other character to identify with, to sympathize with, except Norman Bates, the transvestite. And this truly audacious cinematic reversal of audience identification has been pulled off by Hitchcock's selective and rigorous use of Point-of-View. Therefore, I dedicate this chapter to Alfred Hitchcock, who more than any other filmmaker, has successfully explored and exploited Point-of-View's emotional and artistic possibilities.

POV (Point-of-View) is *the* defining element of narrative film and indispensable to any understanding of feature filmmaking. Simply put, the camera has a lens through which the image is fixed on the film or videotape. This Point-of-View through the camera's lens is the only perspective made available to your audience. Your lens becomes, in effect, the audience's eyes and makes the statement "if you could only see things through my eyes" a controlling reality for your audience.

The choice and positioning of your camera's lens is your prime responsibility as a filmmaker; everything else follows from that decision, including how consistently you apply it and when you decide to change it. This creates your *cinematic style*, not the story (literature), not the characters (drama), not the art direction (painting), not the special effects (technology), not the budget (business). Even though those other elements combine and contribute to your film's overall effect, *every single one of them can be subverted or enhanced, altered or aided by your camera's POV*. And best of all for the filmmaker on a tight budget, this is one of the few elements in your entire production that does not cost you a dime! The price tag is only your consistent and informed use of this unique and powerful tool.

Alfred Hitchcock, more than any other director, fully utilized the expressive power of POV, but he was by no means the first or only director to benefit from the use of this fundamental tool. In the bustling, creative atmosphere of 1920s Berlin there were three young filmmakers who would make extensive use of POV during their long careers. Fritz Lang, then the most famous of the three, was making his *Dr. Mabuse* and *Niebelungen* films; Edgar Ulmer was art directing Lang's *Niebelungen* films as well as Murnau's *The Last Laugh*; while Alfred Hitchcock, over from England, was writing and art directing a film called *The Blackguard*.

As Edgar Ulmer mentioned in the last chapter, "We've been looking, to my knowledge, for over forty years to identify ourselves with our audiences."[10] and that as a filmmaker you "have to have a viewpoint when you tell the story.... Don't do it from five viewpoints."[11] This sentiment is echoed by Fritz Lang who has said, "First of all, I use my camera in such a way as to show things, wherever possible, from the viewpoint of the protagonist: in that way my audience identifies itself with the character on the screen and thinks with him."[12]

Alfred Hitchcock has said that he thought his film *The Wrong Man* would be interesting if all the events were told from the POV of the innocent man and, apropos of Marion Crane in *Psycho*, "I always want the audience thinking what she's thinking."[13] Hitchcock's absolute insistence on the strict observance of POV is echoed by Marshal Schlom, his script supervisor on *Psycho*: "He wanted the camera, being the eyes of the audience all the time, to let them [view the action] as if they were seeing it with their own eyes."[14] This led Hitchcock to insist that most of *Psycho* be shot with a 50mm lens, which he felt most closely approximated normal human perspective.

This valuable lesson has not been lost on such talented filmmakers as Roman Polanski and Brian DePalma. Regarding his film *Rosemary's Baby*, Polanski has said, "Much of the film is seen through Rosemary's eyes. In trying to convey this subjective immediacy, I often staged long, complicated scenes using short focal lenses that called for extreme precision in the placing of both camera and actors."[15] He too shot most of *Rosemary's Baby* and *Chinatown* with primarily one lens, 25mm for *Rosemary's Baby* and a 40mm Anamorophic for *Chinatown*.

DePalma, talking of his film *Body Double*, has said, "You the audience have seen exactly what I have seen. It's the point of view shot, and it's unique to cinema. You have communicated to the audience information in its most basic form, without any transitional thing to go through..."[16]

Now that I've finished with this barrage of heavyweights talking about their use of POV, let me mention that most of these filmmakers utilize a style that stresses the subjective approach, attempting to put you, the audience, inside the character by seeing what they see. Almost all filmmakers attempt this in one way or another at one time or another, but the consistent and rigorous application of this approach is practiced by very few filmmakers. However, you can see by the directors who use this approach, and the films they have made, how successful this approach can be.

Most other filmmakers prefer to remain more "objective" with only the occasional subjective angle. Prime examples of this more objective style can be seen in the work of Howard Hawks, who favored a loose medium two-shot, almost always at eye level, or John Ford, who preferred tableau-like long shots from a lower angle, creating more dynamic compositions of light and shadow.

Later, Orson Welles created a baroque variation on John Ford's style by shooting almost exclusively with a wide angle lens set very low, while his actors were choreographed through the deep focus he preferred, or were followed with stately camera moves. This continued and consistent stylization by Welles created his own unique POV (a very subjective objectivity) which resembled sitting in the orchestra of a theater watching a play, while the movement of his camera resembled, at times, the stage rotating before us. One could go on and on mentioning acclaimed directors and their distinctive camera placement and lens choice, i.e., their cinematic POV, but I think I've made my point.

Obviously, I'm not saying that everyone should go out and use this subjective approach in their film or that a more "objective" style isn't the best way to approach your story. It's not a matter of one style being right or wrong, it's a matter of you finding out what works the best for you, whether it comes about instinctively or through a conscious search on your part. However, let me leave this chapter with a quote from Brian DePalma, "The Point-of-View shot is a basic building block of cinema. You build movies around people seeing things," not saying things.[17]

6

Two Fundamental Theories

I'll begin this chapter with one of the fundamental theories of filmmaking — the Eastwood Theory of Limits, which as most of you have guessed by now, if you're at all familiar with Clint Eastwood's films, is, "A man's got to know his limitations."[18] Now of course we all know this applies to men as well as women and the women probably knew it way before the men did. But I digress. Most films are made with a team of people, making it impossible for any one person to do everything. Hell, even Stanley Kubrick had to delegate, although he could probably have done most of the jobs on a film set himself.

The very nature of film production necessitates that you learn to delegate certain tasks to other people. But what exactly has to be delegated and what can you handle yourself? An entire industry has been built up in this country telling you exactly what and who you need to complete your film. But these people have never met you, they don't know your strengths or your limitations. The only person that does know that is you.

And this leads me to my second fundamental theory — the Lucca Theory of Negotiation. A few years ago, film director Michael Mann, then a TV producer, hot off the success of his hit TV show *Miami Vice*, began producing a second TV series entitled *Crime Story*, about detectives in 1950s Chicago. I loved that show, even more than *Miami Vice*. (Yes, I liked that too!) It again showcased visually stylized, pop music–driven shows featuring feature film directors like Abel Ferrara who ensured that the proceedings sped along at a very high energy level.

One of the characters in this series was named Lucca, Italian for wolf. As played by Anthony Denis, he was of course a gangster, an up-and-coming bad ass in the mob. He quickly fought his way up to a certain level of authority by an accomplished and almost exclusive use of violence.

Lucca had now reached a level of authority where the use of violence became less and less desirable, more the last resort than the first. You know, it's bad for business, etc. Anyway, he went to a meeting with another mid-level mobster to negotiate a turf war between them, but the older, more experienced thug "negotiated" rings around Lucca.

Outsmarted and angry, Lucca went to an old friend, his mentor in mobdom. After recounting the humiliating details of the meeting, Lucca confessed to his mentor that he just wasn't any good at negotiating. After a carefully orchestrated pregnant pause, his mentor looked Lucca square in the eye and told him that *If You Can't Negotiate ... Don't Negotiate*!

Lucca instantly grasped this profound piece of wisdom and quickly set up the next meeting to "finalize" the negotiations, and eliminated the competition in one, swift, bloody blow. Lucca had learned one of life's hardest lessons: All of us cannot hope to be good at everything, so we must fully utilize those qualities that we do possess.

And this, budding film/video maker, is my number one piece of advice to you. Jean-Luc Godard could not have made the films he made if he had tried to make them just like Roger Corman, no more than Roger Corman could have made the films he made if he had tried to make them like Jean-Luc Godard. That's why any film book or course or teacher or seminar cannot teach you the one best way to make your film or video. There is no one best way to make a film, it all depends on your own various strengths and limitations. As a filmmaker, you must closely examine yourself before you can examine the world around you.

What are you good at? What can't you do? What can you learn to do? And what will you never be able to learn to do well? Before you start out on anything, you have to ask yourself those hard questions and give yourself the sometimes deflating answers. But you will be way ahead of the game if you do.

Let me give you a few examples from my own experiences. When I was first starting out as a video producer-director for a department store chain, I hired a guy whose technical skills were okay, but he was very good at relating to the fashion models we used.

I felt comfortable handling the technical side, but I really wasn't too comfortable working with women. I had been a football player and frat boy in college, so my "feminine nurturing side" wasn't too well developed at that point. So this guy was a great help getting the models ready and patching things up if I inadvertently pissed them off, which at first was quite often.

As we did more productions, I learned that this guy was much better with the more emotional women, but tended to get on the nerves of the more intellectual ones (yes, there are intellectual models): So I hired a second guy who was more comfortable around the more intellectual ones. His technical abilities also weren't as good as mine, but I was able to maintain the level of program quality I was after. However, I was still stuck running camera, even though I was supposed to be a producer-director.

Sometimes, you eventually gain some of the skills you lack. For example, I now get along just as well or better with the women in my cast and crew as I do with the men. Ultimately, there are no easy, tried-and-true methods, it's a constant process of self-evaluation and the more honest you are with yourself, the better you will get at doing it, becoming in the process a better filmmaker.

7

Strategy and Tactics

"Know yourself as well as your adversary and you will be able to fight 100 battles without defeat."[19] This old Chinese proverb provides the key to successfully winning any guerrilla war — at least, according to Latin American guerrilla leader Che Guevara in his book *Guerrilla Warfare*. And since the key to Underground Guerrilla Filmmaking is in converting your disadvantages into advantages, what better way to get a solid grasp of this dynamic process than to briefly study Che's strategy and tactics, which he drew from his personal experiences in the Cuban Revolution.

Basics

The basic premise of guerrilla warfare is that "Popular Forces" can win a war against "Conventional Forces" — or, as Roger Corman had one of the characters in his film *Atlas* say, "A small band of efficient, dedicated, highly trained warriors [filmmakers?] could defeat any number of rabble."[20] This is accomplished by using the conventional army's own resources against them, taking maximum advantage of the country's indigenous population as well as capitalizing on that country's specific geographical characteristics.

Yeah, yeah, I know you're not fighting any stinkin' war, you just wanna make your film, but as many distinguished directors from Stanley Kubrick to Samuel Fuller to Jean-Luc Godard have observed, the making of a film has many of the same characteristics as fighting a war, requiring many of the same skills.

As we go through this next section, I will be relating many of the tactics and strategies that guerrilla fighters and low-budget filmmakers have in common. But the specifics of how to fully utilize them in the filmmaking process will be covered later and in greater detail by those chapters that specifically deal with those individual aspects of film and video production.

Starting Out

One of Che Guevara's original premises was that it's not necessary for all the conditions for making the revolution to exist; the insurrection itself can create them. Over the 20–plus years I've been in the business, I've seen scores of friends, enemies and those in between, waiting for the perfect conditions to make their film. Whether it was the budget, a certain investor, the perfect script or story, the right actor, the correct political climate or maybe even the proper astrological sign, almost all of them are still waiting.

For most of us, the perfect conditions will never exist and sometimes it becomes necessary to take the initiative and start the ball rolling, hoping that along the way others will catch your dream. Sometimes it doesn't take much, but what it does take is your unswerving commitment and vision, plus a small but dedicated group of "co-conspirators" armed with a realistic strategy.

Strategy

Location, Location, Location

Now we're getting into the nitty-gritty, ladies and gentlemen. What kind of planning does it really take to get it done? For the guerrilla fighter, the most important elements are picking the right spot to begin operations and the cooperation of the people living in that area. And after you have your story, scenario, script, storyboard or whatever, that's exactly where you should start. If you're from a Hollywood studio or even a middling production company, you begin with a location that you turn into a set with a great deal of equipment and manpower. But most of us don't belong in either one of those boats, so what can we do?

Well, according to Che, there are two kinds of locations, favorable and unfavorable. For the guerrilla as well as the filmmaker, favorable areas are those where you can do more types of activity for longer periods with a larger group while enjoying relatively easy access and good communications. Ideally it is immediately accessible to your cast and crew while no one, governmental or otherwise, is likely to interfere.

And as guerrilla fighters and filmmakers alike have found out, this usually means an isolated part of the countryside, hopefully belonging to one of your cast, crew, friends or family. Think of all the first films or low-budget wonders (*Texas Chainsaw Massacre, Night of the Living Dead, Evil Dead*) set in an isolated countryside location. The reason for this is that the closer you move into populated areas and the denser the population of the areas you move into, the greater your need for a smaller group, less equipment, more secrecy, greater mobility, better communications or *More Money*.

And the more unfavorable the areas you move into, the more you will have to worry about and deal with curious locals concerned about their property being

Setting up a lakeside shot for *Daddy*: Michael DiPaolo, Celia Hansen, Brian O'Hara and John Karyus (photograph by Christopher Philippo).

messed up or their neighborhood being misrepresented in your film or their sleep and/or parking being disrupted. It is also more likely that the authorities (police, fire, sanitation, etc.) will come around to make sure you're doing only what your permit allows (if you can even afford the insurance to get a permit!), creating a much greater need on your part for a higher degree of mobility and secrecy.

It's now easy to see why the area you pick is so connected to the absolute necessity of getting the people in that area on your side, working with you, not against you. And of course that's why it's always better to be in an area where you or your cast or crew is both known and liked. Boiled down, this just means it's easier to shoot on your Uncle Harry's farm than it is in Grand Central Station and the closer you move to Grand Central from your Uncle Harry's farm, the more difficulties you'll encounter. Not that there aren't ways to shoot in Grand Central (if you have little or no budget) but your mobility, need for secrecy, scaling-down of equipment and amount of pre-planning all increase dramatically.

That's why many books on low-budget filmmaking will tell you to limit the number of your locations, but I never thought that films should be made just because of their locations; rather, they should be made because you have a story that has to be told. And if it needs to be shot in a difficult location or 25 different ones, it's up to you to devise a plan to accomplish that within the confines of how much time and money you have available.

But the general rule for all the locations on a low-budget shoot, as well as in guerrilla warfare, is an absolute and detailed knowledge of each and every location you use. You should know each location like your very own neighborhood. And when I cover Locations later on, I'll go through some of the alternative ways to find and secure the locations you need without going broke or crazy.

Win Every Battle You Fight

Another important strategy of the guerrilla fighter is that no battle should be fought unless it can be won and that by winning all of those many small battles you will eventually win the war. But how many times have I seen a small production sabotage itself by biting off more than it can chew? Too many, unfortunately.

I once consulted with this small group who wanted to shoot a digital feature in various locations around a small college town. So far so good, but they wanted to do "Hollywood" lighting in a local diner using a Lowell lighting kit with only three lights! I tried to explain that what they wanted to do wasn't really possible, but if they used whatever fixtures and/or natural light was already available in the dinner, supplemented with their Lowell kit, they could get a very natural and pleasing look. Well, they still wanted the "Hollywood" look and they were going to find a way to do it with their small kit. Two weeks later, production had ground to a disappointing halt.

Make sure you can accomplish what you set out to do, because nothing kills the morale of a cast and crew, especially on deferred pay, more than seeing their producer and/or director biting off more than they can chew, thereby substantially decreasing the possibility that the film or video will ever be completed. No one wants to waste their time and energy, especially when they're not being paid in cash.

Take Advantage of the Enemy's Weak Points

Take advantage of the enemy's weak points; or, what do you have that Hollywood doesn't? *Time!* Time to research, reconsider, rewrite, reconnoiter, recast, re-use, revise, re-shoot, re-think, re-edit, reflect or re-finance. With thousands of dollars riding on every minute and thousands of cost accountants keeping track of every minute and every dollar, most of Hollywood has lost the luxury of time.

Listen to the oldtimers from the 1920s and '30s talk about waiting for the light, that is, waiting for the natural light to break into a beautiful effect before beginning to film. Do you think any Hollywood filmmaker has the ability to wait for the right light today? Before you answer, remember, Stanley Kubrick is gone. Also remember that by staying small, Jean-Luc Godard can actually incorporate the extra time to rethink and reflect into his budgets, his own personal luxury. A luxury that Hollywood can no longer afford.

Take your time, rewrite your script, get other's opinions and, if necessary, rewrite it once again until you get it where you want it. Take the time to look for that special actor or actress who really brings your character to life. If you and your actors are into rehearsal, take all the time you need. If you need to shoot in an unfavorable area, meet the locals, take the time to learn the lay of the land, when to shoot and when to lie low. If a scene's not working, stop and re-think it with the help of your actors or crew. You have time, sometimes before shooting, sometimes during shooting, sometimes after shooting. Find it and use it, to your advantage.

Use Light Weapons

A guerrilla fighter uses light weapons almost exclusively, while using his ammunition sparingly, mainly because he doesn't have any to spare. And so should the underground filmmaker take advantage of the newer lighter equipment, which fortunately also means less gear to lug around. With today's fast film stocks, the necessity for large lighting packages has decreased enormously, while sound gear from the audio tape recorders to the microphones has continued to diminish in size while increasing in sensitivity. The cameras have also gotten smaller and lighter, while new, lighter and more mobile systems have been developed to ensure smooth camera movement.

And as the digital revolution progresses, the equipment for an entire production could conceivably fit into a large suitcase. With this reduction of equipment comes a reduction of non-essential crew, a reduction of vehicles needed, and an increased mobility resulting in substantial savings while allowing greater flexibility, all to your advantage.

Use Less Ammunition

Che Guevara remarked on how you can always tell a guerrilla fighter from conventional forces by the way they fire their weapons. The conventional forces shoot in long bursts utilizing a great deal of ammunition, while the guerrilla fires one shot at a time, making each shot count.

What better parable for the low-budget filmmaker's use of film stock? Your shooting ratio (the amount of film stock exposed during principle photography compared to the amount utilized in the final edit) should be much lower than any Hollywood production. Some filmmakers have been able to get away with a 2:1 ratio, but I find that most low-budget shooting ratios range from a low end of 3:1 to a high end of 10:1, with most falling in the middle.

Hollywood can afford to shoot as high a ratio as 100:1, because, as Penny Marshall once explained and/or rationalized (as she does have an extraordinarily high shooting ratio), on a typical Hollywood production, film stock is one of the cheapest expenses compared to many of the other elements in a Hollywood film's budget. But for the underground filmmaker, film stock is one of the most expensive budget items as well as being crucial in determining your film's final appearance.

The director of *Daddy* (the author) sets up a crucial scene with his light weapon of choice.

Obviously with the advent of today's inexpensive Digital videotape, the direct costs are not of great concern. However, there are hidden costs that should be taken into consideration. These can include the cost of extra tape dubbing, extra digitizing costs in post, longer logging time and editing time and wearing your cast out by repeated takes. All too often, inexperienced filmmakers attempt to use multiple takes to mask their lack of preparation. However, if you're really using this Digital advantage as an integral part of your working method and not being lazy, go for it!

Keep Moving

Like a shark in the water, the guerrilla must keep moving, making continuous blows against the enemy — or, as Roger Corman advises, maintaining a quick disciplined pace on the set with at least 20 set-ups a day. This gives you, as well as your cast and crew, a certain momentum, an energizing push toward your ultimate goal of finishing on time and on budget. It also keeps to a minimum the amount of time your cast and crew have to become disgruntled with their less than plush circumstances, while encouraging everyone to remain involved and interested.

How many times have I've read about a Hollywood actor or actress complaining how difficult it is, when the crew is setting up the next shot, to keep their energy and concentration at a certain level during those long periods? And how they would prefer things to move along at a quicker pace, which as you may remember was an

Stealing a shot, guerrilla-style: Daddy (Aaron Renning) comes home.

important element that John Cassavetes always incorporated into his productions, realizing how beneficial it is for an actor's or actress' performance.

Secrecy

If a guerrilla fighter is found out, he is captured or killed. Luckily the penalty for filmmakers isn't as severe, but at times and in many different ways it can be extremely disadvantageous to the underground filmmaker who is shooting with a low to non-existent budget. Unless you are working in a movie studio or have paid off everyone in sight, it is to your advantage to keep as low a profile as is possible on every location you use, whether it's a favorable or unfavorable location.

The reasons for this are practical as well as logistical. A movie set, by its very nature, is a chaotic environment, and unwanted intrusions on your set will only add to its inherent chaos. People walking through shots and looking into the camera or making any sort of unwanted noise or distraction will cost you time and therefore money. And the more interruptions, the more time and money … is this what you need? I don't think so.

But by keeping a low profile, you can actually turn this disadvantage to your advantage, by using the natural elements (people, vehicles, buildings, etc.) of your location as extras and props which can only heighten the production values of your movie and not cost you a dime.

I used this technique in my feature *Requiem for a Whore*, while shooting scenes with my actresses who were playing streetwalkers. By choosing an area near where real prostitutes actually worked the streets, in this case New York City's meat packing district, and utilizing only the street lights for illumination as well as an unobtrusive hand-held camera, I was able to shoot the actual johns cruising for prostitutes as unpaid extras, unpaid extras who also graciously and unknowingly donated the use of their cars, saving me money on both extras and rental vehicles, all the while adding a very real ambiance to our scenes.

Group Homogeneity

Almost all of the "Patron Saints of the Underground" as well as Che Guevara stress the prime importance of a homogeneous group, a small but committed band who fully understand and agree with both the goals and methods of their band. You as the producer-director must be just as careful with the selection of your crew as you are in the casting of your actors and actresses. It does your film no good if you hire an ace cinematographer who does mostly commercial work, if he can't alter his method of working to fit in with your shortened schedule and reduced budget.

Now, of course, almost anyone trying to get a job, be it actor or actress, cinematographer or production assistant, will tell you they totally understand what you you're trying to do and are absolutely familiar with and totally into your way of working. Beware ... beware ... beware! Most of them are lying through their teeth just to get the job (yeah, even if it doesn't pay), so you have to separate the wheat from the chaff, dig hard and find out who really understands and agrees with what

Daddy producer Christopher Philippo, soundman Brian O'Hara and gaffer John Karyus take a break by watching a DVD — horror, of course! (photograph by the author).

you're doing as opposed to those just looking to move up to the next step up on the career ladder. If they're not working on your side, then they're working against you and on a smaller production this can have disastrous consequences.

Strong Base of Operations

Last but not least of the strategic considerations is the necessity of having a strong base of operations. Now of course, for most of you, renting a production office is out of the question, but as guerrilla fighters over the centuries have shown almost anywhere can function as a base of operations, as long as it contains the essential elements required by your production. These elements include accessibility, sufficient space, adequate communications and, ideally, 24–hour access.

Your apartment, a friend's loft, an empty room in someone's office, an old warehouse, whatever you can get your hands on for little or no money is or can become ideal. It should be geographically central to all of your locations, easily accessible by cast and crew, have enough space to store equipment, supplies, props and wardrobe and act as home for all your office and communications equipment. It could even serve as a kitchen for your culinary needs or anything else you deem essential to your operation. And as I mentioned earlier, it's ideal to have 24–hour access without bothering too many other people, as guerrilla filmmakers tend to go rather late into the night or have to be up extraordinarily early.

Once the production actually begins principal photography, the base becomes less important in direct relationship to the size of the crew, the smaller the cast and crew, the less important the base becomes. In effect, your daily location becomes your base when principle photography begins and you should try to retain as many essential office operations as is physically feasible, although in reality, probably no more than a laptop computer, cell phone or beeper is possible or practical.

Tactics

Now that we've covered the fundamentals of strategy in guerrilla warfare, how do you go about applying them in the real world? What skills are needed? And how can use them to make your film your way?

Flexibility

The guerrilla fighter and the underground filmmaker are first and foremost flexible, aware of and adjusting to the prevailing conditions, converting all "accidents" to their advantage. Now these same tactics could apply to any film or video production regardless of their size or budget, but to the low-budget production they become essential.

The only consistent element of a guerrilla production is that the unexpected is

Daddy director DiPaolo (left) confers with production manager Justin Taylan before setting up the graveyard location (photograph by Christopher Philippo).

sure to occur. Your cameraman will get a paying job while instantly and totally forgetting they had promised to stay on for your entire production schedule; there may be a technical problem with your developed film; the guy who promised you the use of his apartment for two days can now only give you one unless, of course, you cough up some more money; the actress with black hair you shot last week has, without warning, dyed her hair blonde; the actor you cast with shoulder length hair now has a buzz cut; your lead actress breaks her ankle two weeks before principal photography which absolutely, positively must begin in two weeks or you lose the rest of your cast and crew; on the first night of shooting, one of your principal actresses, who you've worked with before, walks off, saying she can't handle the conditions; your artificially bloodied ropes and sheets from that torture scene you "stole" in that hotel room (paid for with your credit card) were left behind for the maid to find; and, last but not least, the local pimp is flashing his gun to your cast, even though you've already paid him off. Believe it or not, all of the above, in one way or another, has actually happened on my productions.

Adjustability

You must constantly adjust and improvise or you, as well as your film or video, are dead meat. But as I found out early in my career, one of the best ways to deal with the unexpected is to plan on alternatives of practically every aspect before you begin shooting. Look through all your plans, search for possible weak links, people you think may be unreliable and anything you think or even have the faintest feeling may go wrong and plan alternatives, have backups—hell, have backups for the backups. You think I'm going too far? Well I've used my backed-up backups more than I care to admit, but I'm sure as hell glad I had them.

Remain open, open to your actors and actresses, open to your crew, open to what the location is offering you that you hadn't seen before, open to changing anything that isn't working, either in front of or behind the camera, open to what's going on across town, to the weather, the light, the sounds and most of all to the whispering that always seems to be going on right behind you.

And once you've detected a weakness or discovered a strength use it to your advantage or change it. You're now caught on a huge wave of circumstances, some of them disastrous, some of them wonderful and you can't get off until the wave's over, so take advantage of the wonderful ones and try to turn the disastrous ones into new wonderful ones. But stay alert, stay mobile, adjust and keep moving like those damn sharks.

Inventiveness

Che Guevara encourages the guerrilla fighter to invent every minute, an echo of what we heard Jean-Luc Godard say earlier, about being more at ease with the methods of the silent era's "King of Comedy" Mack Sennett than with current filmmaking practices because the early cinema was inventing itself as it went along. This has the added benefit of ensuring that those working on your film become more involved, less bored and their creative energies are being transferred directly onto your film or video.

Mobility

Sylvia (Celia Hansen) is lost in thought during a *Daddy* flashback. The evocative lighting, a car's dashboard light, was an on-the-spot invention.

What tactics can you use that will ensure your ability to react and take advantage of every situation whether positive or negative? In a word, *Mobility*, the ability to move quickly and efficiently by using small bands of people. Obviously, if you have less people in your cast and crew, then you will have less bodies to move around, less mouths to feed, less people mulling around between takes and, if you're on location, there will be less people to house, less interpersonal problems, less transportation needs and *Less Money*! Now all

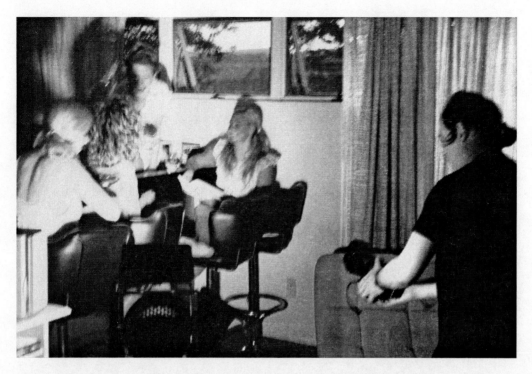

The author shoots a *Daddy* flashback scene with (from left) Bevin McGraw, Katherine Petty, Celia Hansen and Cynthia Polakovich (photograph by Christopher Philippo).

of these "lesses" add up to greater mobility, making it easier for you to alter your plans and adapt to constantly changing conditions.

We've talked about the benefits of using lighter and less equipment earlier, but along with this reduction in equipment comes a reduction in the size and number of vehicles that you'll need. Remember, always use the smallest, most mobile form of transportation, and whatever Hollywood uses is probably not good for you. If the subway's faster, use it (just make sure whatever you're carrying is camouflaged; remember secrecy in unfavorable terrain). If your equipment can fit in a station wagon or sedan instead of a van, rent them instead; if you can improvise a portable makeup and changing room in the back of van instead of a trailer, do it; if taking taxis costs less than the renting, parking and gassing up of cars, start flaggin' those suckers down. Hell, if a bicycle gets the job done, hop right on.

However, if something or someone is holding up shooting at your location, obviously the speediest remedy is called for; therefore, sometimes you have to sacrifice money for speed. If your assistant bought DAT audiotapes instead of recordable mini-discs and your're shooting that scene next, then now is the time to send someone out, grabbing the nearest taxi and speeding back, no matter the cost. And when that moment comes along (and it will!), don't cut your nose off to spite your face, just dig into your pocket and pay the extra bucks.

Jamie (Cynthia Polakovich) breaks down in a *Daddy* flashback.

The Ambush

Now we come to the culmination of all the aforementioned strategies and tactics, *the* model for all guerrilla filmmakers; *The Ambush*. The ambush synthesizes all of the above information into one flexible package that can be altered to fit anyone's personal idiosyncrasies, in any situation and in any terrain.

The ambush, as Che Guevara explains it, follows the *Minuet* (yeah, that's right, the minuet!) *Maneuver*, utilizing a surprise attack with the minimum number of personnel and maximum engagement concentrated at a key strategic point selected in advance. This is followed by a swift but totally passive withdrawal which in turn is again followed by another attack of maximum engagement at another key strategic point. This is repeated until the maximum damage has been inflicted while sustaining little or no damage to the guerrilla force, which then quickly retreats to their staging area. This tactic avoids full frontal attacks of any kind.

Now, translating this minuet maneuver to moviemaking terms, we see that by virtue of superior planning, that "small band" of [filmmakers] we referred to earlier could "defeat any number of rabble."[21] This is that strange twilight zone where Che Guevara, the Cuban Revolutionary meets the America's Maverick Capitalist, Roger Corman, and the really intriguing thing is that both of these disparate individuals were able to take on the system and win, using the very same strategy and tactics.

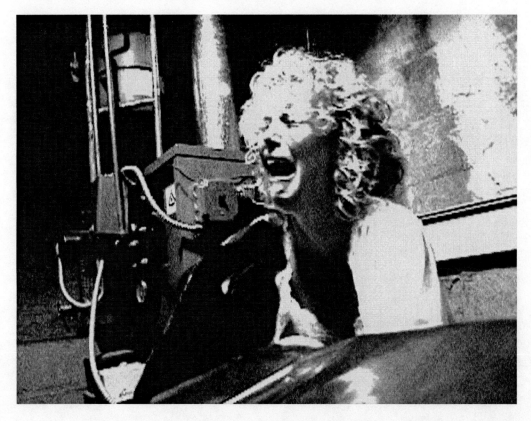

Leslie (Katherine Petty) reacts hysterically during a *Daddy* flashback.

How does this *Ambush* maneuver apply to you and your film or video? Well, reducing it to a Yankee-Imperialist-show biz cliché, you get more bang for your buck with the added advantage that its guidelines are elastic enough so that anyone can successfully adapt these basic principles to their own individual personality and working habits. Go back over the chapter on the "Patron Saints of the Underground" and see how many of them used the strategies and tactics described in this chapter … all of them!

In conclusion, by superior planning, first-hand knowledge of the terrain, the cooperation of locals, using small amounts of lightweight equipment and using only essential supplies, keeping a low profile and staying mobile, a small but dedicated group of filmmakers can continuously grab their shots while creating an effective and low-cost alternative to the Hollywood machine. Now on to the actual step-by-step process of "The Art of the Ambush."

PART III

How to Be a
Guerrilla Filmmaker

8

The Story

Since the focus of this book is feature films, specifically narrative feature films, I will begin at the beginning—that is, the story. Picking your story will, more than any other element, determine where your filmmaking odyssey will take you. It will dictate who you'll need to assist you as well as where and how far you'll have to go to realize your vision.

What is a story and how do you pick yours? To me, a story is a series of events that must continually answer the audience's question "What Happens Next?" I think you can start anywhere and end anywhere you want, just as long as you keep the audience constantly engaged in asking that question. I really believe it's just that simple; successfully realizing it is the difficult part. However, if you listen to Aristotle or Syd Field, your story must have a beginning, a middle and an end, but if you listen to Jean-Luc Godard, not necessarily in that order.

I have to be personally moved by the story I pick. Then, hopefully, I will be able to communicate that initial response of mine to the audience as well. This is one of the most difficult aspects of the entire filmmaking process—the ability to constantly inject every scene with your initial personal, intellectual and emotional response. If you can keep that initial stimulus as your point of reference throughout the arduous process of making your film, you'll be way ahead of the game.

The story can be your own personal story or a fictionalized variation, a tactic many beginning filmmakers successfully use for their first film, since it adds a much-needed dose of authenticity to what can be an extremely artificial process. But it's important to realize that for a continuing career in film and video, you must learn to develop a theme or a style, preferably both.

Ultimately, you must become a servant to your story and every element, whether it's the lights, camera, action, acting, sets or the music. They must all serve your story, not distract from it. That's why it's so important to pick the right story ... right for you ... right for moving pictures ... and, you hope, right for your audience.

That's one of the reasons it takes some directors, like Stanley Kubrick for instance, so long to find the just the right kind of story to make into a movie. Generally novels must be compressed, short stories expanded, plays opened up and true events padded with fictional elements. And in the process, novels lose their unique, rich complexity, the short story's original premises are altered, plays lose their focus and the anarchy of actual events becomes over-rationalized. For my money (or lack of it, right now), the best films come from original screenplays first and foremost, followed by short stories, which have been expanded with an eye to the requirements of the screen.

Aristotle and Syd Field ... Separated at Birth?

This Is the Hollywood/"Indie" Way ... If That's What You Want, Learn It! ... Live It! ... Love It! If Not, Read On At Your Own Risk!

Even though my films are based on actual events with people I find sympathetic, I'm always being told my characters are passive and unsympathetic, while my stories are unbelievable,. And I'm always reacting against it, resisting any preconceived perceptions, while attempting to remain faithful to the people, relationships and events I've witnessed first-hand. Which admittedly, after videotaping confessions for the District Attorney's office for over 16 years, gives me a slightly "skewed" perspective

To me, this is like saying I haven't seen what I've seen and haven't heard what I've heard. I believe by limiting your lead characters to easily sympathetic ones, you severely restrict which realities you can present and if you happen to be attracted to idiosyncratic stories that reveal hidden, less attractive aspects of human behavior, a great many people probably won't believe you, even if your stories, although improbable, are actually true.

They would rather believe what a friend of mine has called "the lies we live by." They want to believe the TV cop shows which are always told from the POV of the police or the lawyers and are nowhere near the reality of what I've witnessed first-hand while working at the District Attorney's office. I've always wondered where this zombie-like mantra (sympathetic characters, no passive lead characters, beginning, middle and end, etc.) comes from. Well, I've discovered the culprit: none other than that pesky, old Greek philosopher, Aristotle.

The question then becomes, why has Aristotle's Poetics via Syd Field and numerous others taken such a hold on Hollywood? The answer, at least to my mind, is because it's a handy formula for success with a classy pedigree that also mirrors the lives of those powerful white males who make most of the decisions in Hollywood.

The result is thousands and thousands of movies where a "Flawed Male" who underneath is really sympathetic (you know, every male action star who makes over $20 million a picture and is only a substitute for some sonofabitch studio exec, who would like to believe he's really nice, but isn't), takes action, enabling him to overcome various reversals in a plot-heavy narrative. This tired formula is even beginning to wear thin on those stars who have made millions and millions from it, i.e. Stallone and Schwarzenegger, to name only two of many. But where does all this bat guano come from?

Well, according to Aristotle, tragedy and comedy both came from sacred, improvisational dance performances. Those very elements which Aristotle, with the precision of a surgeon, handily removes from what he thinks constitutes a perfect tragedy, which he defines as a serious, complete action which has magnitude and embellished speech. Voila: the imposition of literary values on a previously, non-literary medium is born. According to Aristotle, "the potential of tragedy does not depend upon public performance and actors."[22] Now, I have to admit, that's one way to save money I never thought of; however, what does all this mean to you making your film or video today? It's relatively simple: *Follow the Rules or Suffer the Consequences*. But what are the rules?

Aristotle thinks the most important element of tragedy is the plot, where each action must probably or necessarily lead to the next one and the play must represent a single complete action with a beginning, middle and end (in that order) wherein everything is tied up in a nice neat bundle by the end ... just like your life, huh? Starting to sound familiar? Read on...

And of course, you have to stress universals over particulars, but not events that have happened, but rather those events that may probably happen and if this becomes too boring (which it quickly does), add a twist, i.e., a plot twist or a plot point as Syd Field calls it, or (as Aristotle referred to it) a reversal. It's all the same thing. But it can't be any kind of reversal, oh no, you shouldn't show good men going from good fortune to misfortune, nor bad men going from misfortune to good fortune, because that's not *the* lesson we're teaching here and all these rules are about perpetuating *the* lesson, whether it's actually true or not. And *the* lesson is that rationality rules and rewards those "few good men" who practice its precepts and "take action."

To Aristotle, since the plot is the single most important element, the actual characters are relegated to secondary importance. But what kind of characters is he talking about? Not everyone is an appropriate character to Aristotle; he says they should be good, appropriate, lifelike and consistent.[23] But what happens to characters that are bad, inappropriate, lifelike and inconsistent? Tough luck; if they don't fit into Aristotle's view of the world, they are conveniently excluded or made into the villains, who are usually much more interesting by virtue of the fact that they are allowed to be portrayed more realistically. How many films have you seen where the "bad guy" is more interesting, more multi-dimensional than the good guy? Probably most of them.

Now I'd like you to listen to what Aristotle thinks about women characters: "It is not appropriate for a woman to be so manly or clever."[24] And you wonder why so many talented actresses seem to disappear from the screen after reaching age 40 (when they can no longer maintain the illusion of a young, fertile, unmanly, not-too-clever support for the male star who takes "action") or why there are so few rounded woman characters of any age today, except for those quasi-males toting heavy weapons, or else those 20–something, interchangeable models of the month. If you think I'm overstating my case, go back to the pre–Code films of the '30s and earlier, while watching the work of Clara Bow, Louise Brooks, Lillian Gish, Greta Garbo, Marlene Dietrich, Joan Crawford or Bette Davis.

Now, I don't know what most women think of this particular tidbit, but to my mind, this reductive view of character not only tends to exclude anyone but a combative male from leading roles, but it also encourages a very simplistic "either-or" syndrome — that is, either a character is good or they are evil. And although this rationalistic "either-or" matches the reality of a computer's zeroes and ones, it doesn't correspond to the real world, only a biased rationalistic reduction of it. And you thought the good guy in white and the bad guy in black was just a Hollywood invention.

But what happens when your good guy, who's based on an actual person, has a bad habit or two? Aristotle's answer for that is to make sure you add a few redeeming characteristics to offset those pesky bad ones. He mentions how the poet Homer made Achilles good as well as being a stubborn jerk, to illustrate the correct way to offset undesirable traits in your lead character.

This has always been one of my pet peeves and, of course, it too comes from Aristotle. I've always hated how plays and films attach particular character traits to make the lead character more sympathetic (remember Arnold Schwarzenegger discretely blowing away thousands of knee caps instead of killing anyone in the kinder, gentler *Terminator 2*, yeah right) or making the villain less sympathetic shortly before you kill them off (think of Glenn Close making rabbit stew in *Fatal Attraction*). I call this "the handle," which makes it easier for the audience to pick up on or discard a particular character, even though "the handle" seldom has any basis in that or any other character's reality.

Okay, Okay, this is all Greek to you, get to the point! Here it comes: The ultimate contradiction of this entire theory, which Aristotle writes not once but twice, is that "events which are impossible but probable should be preferred to those which are possible but improbable."[25] Academics often call this "Aristotle's paradox," but to me it reveals the foundation of total bullshit beneath this entire thesis and how it distorts truth to further Aristotle's rationalistic agenda at whatever cost to representing reality in anything approaching a truthful manner. Or as Christian Metz says in his book *Film Language*, "the Plausable is a reduction of the possible; it is an arbitrary and cultural restriction of real possibles; it is, in fact, censorship...."[26]

Aristotle always prefers the probable. An example he gives is the statue of a man who has been killed falls on and kills the man who killed him. He thinks that this makes for a finer composition; I think it's phony moralistic crap, plain and simple. Let's *stop* this 2000 years of probable lies generated by powerful white males who control the processes of discourse, destroying or marginalizing all those who would disagree with them.

The goal of Aristotle's Poetics is the instruction and fostering of a society based on reason, while anything that does not contribute to the advancement of this agenda is to be excluded or its value diminished. Thus truth becomes a victim to be sacrificed on the altar of rationality. Aristotle's priority is always a rationalistic construction favoring plot over character, probability over actuality, action over contemplation (or mediation), the mainstream over the marginal, white over black (i.e. good or evil with no in between), men over women, the rulers over the ruled, consistency over inconsistency, universals over particulars, tragic over comic and, above all else, rational over irrational.

So, if you want to go Hollywood, learn, live and love Aristotle and Syd Field *et al.*, but if you're female, black, Latino, Asian, American Indian, victimized or abused, marginalized in any way, start looking for the dramatic forms that will foster your POV, just as Aristotle's has fostered that of the powerful, rationalistic, warring white males of the last 2000 years.

To Script or Not to Script?

As far as I'm concerned, there are only two writing instruments used in the creation of a film or video: the camera and the microphone. As you may have guessed, I'm not a big fan of scripts and the main reason is that I believe when movies were born, a new way of telling stories, first with images then later with sounds, was born. And this new method of storytelling had an almost universal appeal, beyond any single language, directly affecting the audience's emotions, much in the same way as music does.

It was a revolutionary advance which, once its vast power to move, persuade and influence vast numbers of people was recognized, began to be taken over and co-opted by those in power. And when films became both influential and profitable, these powers moved in, first by creating the role of the producer to control and standardize the entire creative process, where before there was only the director and his individual approach. Next, those in control of the industry began utilizing the script as their primary means of control, first financially, then later creatively.

The "accepted wisdom" is that a well-written script is the necessary backbone of an efficient film production and good films cannot be made without them. However, D.W. Griffith did not have a script when he shot *Intolerance*, one of the most complex narrative films ever made. A very loose scenario was the usual written communication at that time, if anything was written down at all.

Recent discoveries of Charlie Chaplin's outtakes reveal that he would create his films on camera as he went along, constantly retaking, rethinking and reshaping a scene until it worked. Of course, by then he owned his own studio, but all of his films made in this manner were successful, then and for as long as film survives.

In his book *The Parade's Gone By*, Kevin Brownlow wrote, "None of the great comedians, Chaplin, Lloyd or Keaton, ever worked from a script until talkies came in. But then few silent comedies were shot from a conventional scenario; that was their secret."[27] He also shows a one-page outline that was written by Douglas Fairbanks, Sr., as the basis for his feature film *Robin Hood*.

Edgar G. Ulmer, who also started in the silent days, had the ability to efficiently create an entire feature without a script. In the 1940s, as I mentioned before, he took a one-page outline called *Club Havana* and created a low-budget version of *Grand Hotel*, shot on only one set in an amazing four days! And as you may remember, Jean-Luc Godard's creative process emulated the early silent filmmakers' engaged attitude towards filmmaking by forcing himself as well as his cast and crew to constantly invent on the spot, rather than relying on a detailed written script.

I can tell you from first-hand personal experience that you don't need a script to shoot a full-length feature film with quality and efficiency. I have shot two features with only a three- or four-page outline and one other with a 20–some page outline. And all of them were shot in two weeks or less (one in only six days with a one-page outline). It only became necessary to start writing scripts when I started raising outside money for my productions.

Most people you approach in order to raise money for a low-budget production will want to see a script, even though most wouldn't know a good script if it came up and bit them on the ass. But it's become the norm, so if you need to raise outside money, start writing … if you've already got your money or are flying so low on the budget radar you don't have to worry, a script is only an option, not a necessity.

However, if you decide to use a script, do you write it yourself or have someone else write it for you or do you start looking for something already written? I think many of the filmmakers that I most respect, do not write their own scripts, and that most directors who start out as writers are lousy directors. There are some exceptions to the rule, like John Cassavetes, Sam Fuller, Sam Peckinpah and Jean-Luc Godard, but the most fruitful avenue seems to be the filmmaker collaborating with the writer, seldom taking actual screen credit for the script or actually splitting the writing-directing credit between the writer and the director like Michael Powell and Emeric Pressburger. Think of the great films by F.W. Murnau written by Carl Mayer, or those by Josef von Sternberg written by Jules Furthman, John Ford's work with Dudley Nichols, Alfred Hitchcock's work with Michael Hayes, Nicolas Roeg's films with Paul Mayersberg or Allan Scott, Martin Scorsese's ongoing relationship with Paul Schrader and Mardik Martin, etc., etc.

Unfortunately for many low-budget filmmakers, it is often difficult to connect with someone who is sufficiently sympathetic to your vision to form a creative partnership. Or if by chance you *do* actually find someone simpatico, having enough money to fairly compensate them for their services can be a problem. That seems to be the reason so many low-budget films are written and directed by the same person, not necessarily because it's better.

My only collaboration was with Y York, a woman playwright and writer whose prose mirrored the damaged qualities I wanted the lead in one of my early videos to possess. And she hit the nail right on the head, mixing despair with optimism, so much so that when an experienced actress up for the lead wanted to change some of her lines to make the character more sympathetic, I told her that the writer's words would stay … so she went.

If you do choose to write your own script or to work with someone else, there are a thousand and one books out there to help you. Almost all of them are in the Hollywood/Indie (there's no difference between the two any more) vein. The most widely read (I refuse to say the "best") are *Story* by Robert McKee, *Screenplay* by Syd Field, *The Screenwriter's Bible* by David Trottier, *How to Write a Selling Screenplay* by Christopher Keane and Julius Epstein and *Adventures in the Screen Trade* by William Goldman. There are literally hundreds of others and if this is the avenue that you chose to pursue, knock yourself out.

My own particular method that I followed when I had to write a screenplay for prospective investors was to read a few screenplays from writers I admired, "borrowing" from them, while attempting to remain faithful to my own vision. Contemporary screenwriters I find particularly worth studying (and "borrowing" from) are Paul Schrader (*Raging Bull, Taxi Driver, The Last Temptation of Christ*, etc.) and Paul Meyersberg (*The Man Who Fell to Earth, Merry Christmas Mr. Lawrence, Eureka, Captive, The Croupier*). I also love Jules Furthman (*Rio Bravo, The Big Sleep, To Have and Have Not, Only Angels Have Wings, Blonde Venus, Shanghai Express, Morocco* and *The Docks of New York*) who wrote many classic scripts for Josef von Sternberg as well as Howard Hawks. And I can't forget Philip Yordan (*The Fall of the Roman Empire, 55 Days at Peking, El Cid, King of Kings, The Big Combo, Johnny Guitar* and *Reign Of Terror*), who wrote for Anthony Mann and Nicholas Ray. These two talented screenwriters from Hollywood's glamorous past are especially informative for any aspiring screenwriter.

If you're going to use a script but choose not to follow the Aristotle–Syd Field–David McKee route, I would still advise that you follow the general page layout (see *Daddy* Script Excerpt in the back of the book) only because it's the industry norm and if you're using a script, it's easier to give your cast and crew a format they're familiar with. This said, if you feel the need to mess around with that form … be my guest. But when I have to resort to using a script, I go with the flow, as there are many other more important battles to fight.

One of the largest discrepancies I find when using the standard script form is the "preferred" length of the finished script, that is, no less than 110 pages and no more than 120 pages. Most of my scripts run only 70–80 pages, but when actually made or when "timed out," they all run at least 90 minutes. The adage, one page of script equals one minute of screen time, is only accurate for dialogue-heavy dinosaurs. I believe the script for *Terminator 2* only ran 70 pages, the reason being if you have an action scene which lasts only one paragraph in your script, you really have no accurate estimation of how long it will last on the screen unless you have storyboarded it all out.

Using a script doesn't necessarily mean that your structure or story or characters have to follow any particular form. Some of the most original plays in our Western cultural tradition, those of Elizabethan England just before, during and after Shakespeare, most certainly did not take Aristotle's theories as their model. To mention but a few of those many talented playwrights, beside Shakespeare, there's Christopher Marlowe (*Dr. Faustus, The Jew of Malta, Edward II*), Thomas Middleton (*The Changeling, Women Beware Women*), John Ford, not the film director (*'Tis Pity She's a Whore, The Broken Heart*), John Webster (*The White Devil, The Duchess of Malfi*) and Cyril Tourneur (*The Revenger's Tragedy*).

Just one word of caution. I've known a few people who gave up writing screenplays entirely after reading through many of the available books out there, having become more discouraged than encouraged. Remember, none of them are the "Bible" and you should be ready to use or discard any or all of what they have to say, depending on how they correspond to your own personal vision.

There are a great many other cultural traditions which can offer the scriptwriter looking for alternative forms a fertile field for research. Try looking into the Japanese

Here you may have to be a bit of a detective, because most people looking to work on a project will almost always tell you they have complete sympathy with any and all ways of working (short of indentured slavery) while totally understanding where you're coming from. And of course much of this is complete b.s. and it's your job to separate the wheat from the chaff, so to speak.

Getting back to the scenario, it usually gives a brief description of each location, the characters involved and what they do and say. This can include actual dialogue, but usually not, or if it does, then usually not too much. It should be clear enough so that your crew knows how to dress and light the location and your cast understands who their characters are and what they have to achieve in each scene. Some scenarios are more detailed in this area of character development, others less so, depending on the director and his or her relationship with the actors and actresses.

Speaking of character, I would like to talk about a vital aspect of using a scenario or outline, instead of a script. Because of their very nature, scenarios and outlines cannot give your actors and actresses as much in-depth information about their characters as a script can. But it's your job as a filmmaker to know all your characters in such great detail that you can help your actors and actresses create convincing, well-rounded characters. This is where you can tell if a director is just being lazy about the script and only using the scenario as a means of avoiding work.

I find that before principal photography begins on a production using a scenario or outline, it is absolutely necessary to rehearse your actors and actresses together so that they can understand not only their own character, but also their character's relationships with the other characters. In conclusion, excellent examples of scenarios can be found in *Godard on Godard* and *Hitchcock's Notebooks*.

The Outline ... What's Necessary? ... What's Not?

The method I use most often (when I don't need a script to raise money) is the outline. To me, it is the most creative *and* efficient means of making a film or video. But bear in mind, this is only my own personal preference. Most scripts actually begin life as an outline and many script-writing books suggest working out an outline as a road map of your entire script before actually beginning to write.

An outline is the skeleton of your movie (see *Daddy* Outline Excerpt in the back of the book), listing the scenes in the order they will appear on the screen. Although your original, preliminary outline should only list your scenes, a production version that will be given to your cast and crew should also give the locations, the characters involved and what happens in each scene. Like the scenario, how much or how little information you include is up to you.

This doesn't mean that you haven't done as much work as the scriptwriter, it only means that you haven't formally written it all down. Jean-Luc Godard probably does more research before beginning a film than most writers and directors combined, but he works mainly from detailed notes, preferring to invent on the spot.

Before setting anything in stone, i.e., print, it may help when you're beginning your outline to put each scene on a 3x5 card. Lay them all out on a table or pin them up on a wall, which allows you to see the structure of the entire film or video all at one glance. You can also shift scenes around and try out different orders and/or structures. This has the added advantage of letting you see if you have bunched together too many similar types of scene (dialogue, exposition, action, etc.) and allowing you to break up that monotony.

For example, if you find that you have three or four rather static dialogue scenes in a row, it would probably be to your advantage to break them up with some kind of non-verbal action scene in between, unless of course all your scenes are static dialogue scenes ... and if they are, you shouldn't be reading this book anyway.

This will also allow you to more easily see where you could place any scenes that you want to double or echo previous scenes. For example, at the beginning of the film there's a confrontation between the good bad guy and the bad good guy that sets up a confrontation later in the film, you might want to have a variation of this scene somewhere later in your film or video. Having all the scenes laid out before you allows for an easier placement of the second scene.

While the outline is particularly good for keeping the overall structure of your film or video in constant sight, you have to be careful that it doesn't distract you from fully shaping each individual scene. Make sure before you start shooting that you have a general shape or idea of how each and every scene should progress or unfold.

Are you trying to create suspense? Are you trying to reveal something hidden in one of the characters? Are you setting up a scene that comes later? It may be the simplistic (personally I hate this reductive approach, but many people find it useful) "What does each character want in this scene?" Or it might be achieved by setting up an interesting dramatic situation and seeing what your actors or actresses (by now totally in touch with their characters) can bring to it.

A good scene always contains a certain ambiguity about its eventual outcome, one that creates an aura of suspense in the audience, keeping them both involved and guessing about the scene's eventual outcome. The trick is too keep them guessing but in a manner you've charted out for them. Using clichés is a guaranteed way to lose any audience. The instant the audience knows or can anticipate what's going to happen next, you've lost them, unless of course you're setting them up for later suspense or an unexpected twist. The key is to look at these situations with a fresh eye, a new perspective and twist it in unexpected directions.

Another advantage of using an outline is that you can discover themes and visual motifs during production that you might never have thought of while writing the script. They only become evident during the actual shooting of the film and thus can become in a certain sense, more relevant and potent. Let me give you an example. A few years ago we were making a short film in a local park and although we had planned the shoot around a small stream, I started placing quite a few of the scenes near some type of water we found in the park, including a lake, a pond and the original stream. Thus water become a strong visual motif not only mirroring the emotional state of my lead character, but also adding another interesting visual element. This was something I probably would never have scripted, but the possibilities made themselves evident on location during the actual production.

An outline allows for more flexibility during shooting, whether it's changing a scene in midstream or taking advantage of a spontaneous event. An example: I was shooting a scene from my feature *Bought & Sold*, a young girl had just been mugged, losing all her belongings, and was sitting on an empty street when a group of young women (not connected with the production) coming from a local restaurant passed by. They saw us shooting and began to make faces, but on camera it looked like they were making fun of the young girl in her distress, adding an element of big city callousness to the scene. I had to change how the scene ended to include this spontaneous moment but the scene was immeasurably enriched by it.

I have shot a feature film in six days with a one-page outline while I have shot another in two weeks with a 20–some page outline; the only difference between the two was the size of the crew. This meant that I had to delegate more responsibilities to more people, necessitating a more detailed outline that would provide the information the extra crew needed to do their job.

The outline should provide you, your cast and crew with the locations, the characters, the action, possibly the wardrobe and/or props as well as your estimated timings of each scene. You must provide the rest. It should only tell you where you've been and where you're going, not how you're getting there. Think of the outline as journey where you continuously create your own itinerary as opposed to the script's guided tour where you always know exactly where you're going next.

In conclusion, an outline is the most general, least specific road map you can have for your filmmaking journey, but it allows for the most exploration, the most interaction, the most invention, the most excitement and the most risk. Hopefully, we all haven't become the slaves of the marketing department or actuarial tables ... yet.

Storyboards or Story Boreds?

Before I go any further, let me inform the uninitiated among you what storyboards are. They are a series of small drawings (usually 4–12 per page) which can run the gamut from simple black-and-white stick figures to highly detailed color computer simulations, representing and breaking down the individual shots that constitute a complex film sequence, usually depicting some kind of action.

For someone like Alfred Hitchcock, it did much more, but in general this is the major function of storyboards. It helps you pre-visualize your movie on paper before having the difficult task of getting it all down on film or video. There is no clock running when you're alone in a room doing storyboards, you can try things out, discard them, re-edit them, do whatever you want, all for the cost of electricity to run your computer or the price of the pencil and paper.

Speaking of the price of paper, for the low-budget filmmaker storyboard paper is expensive and I've always found that 3 x 5 cards cut to the correct aspect ratio are much cheaper and more flexible. You can switch them around, shot by shot, without having to do the whole board over. Additionally, it's relatively simple to mount them on a piece of 8½" x 11" paper or board, making it easy and cheap to reproduce them. And if you are not too good at drawing, a stick figure can work fine;

A sample storyboard from *Daddy*.

or there are several computer software storyboard systems that can quickly remedy that.

Directors of genius like Alfred Hitchcock can make extensive use of storyboards and achieve astonishing results—*Psycho* anyone? But at times even in Hitchcock's films, I can see the storyboards peeping through and lessening the moving picture experience. Think of Tippi Hedren at the diner in *The Birds*, just before the gas pump explodes … looks like a storyboard to me … always has.

And here in a nutshell are the plusses and minuses of using storyboards. The Plusses: 1) pre-visualizing your scene, 2) breaking complex actions into single shots, 3) ensuring the shots will cut together, 4) allowing you to shoot more efficiently without extra angles or excessive coverage or extra cash.

The minuses: 1) sequences resembling a series of static drawings, 2) forcing your locations to become recreations of your drawings while ignoring more powerful elements right in front of your eyes, 3) making your actors into substitutes for the simplistic figures in your drawings while under-utilizing their unique expressive capabilities, 4) inadequately being able to represent the movement *between* shots that creates a three-dimensional element unique to film and video.

Now obviously, for a complex action sequence like a battle scene or a bank robbery or a fire burning down a building, it helps immeasurably to have a very specific number of shots, sketched out before hand, allowing you to focus you and your crew's attention on those small pieces that will enable you to create an entire convincing action on screen. It should also be obvious that this is a much more cost efficient method than constantly repeating a battle or robbery or fire for your cameras until you think and/or hope you have enough coverage.

But today, it seems that more and more people are storyboarding their entire movie. Of course, this will help you save money, no doubt about it, but is it necessary and what are the hidden costs to your film's or video's eventual quality? The problem with most of what are called "independent" films is that they almost always are too static, the compositions of each shot too studied, too perfect. There seems to be little or no connection *between* shots—that is, they resemble *Story Boreds*.

The problem with storyboarding everything is that subconsciously you begin to try and replicate your storyboards on the set. You're trying to recreate instead of create. Instead of utilizing all those wonderful and variable elements that you have there in front of you, you're forcing them into a preconceived idea. And that's what so many of today's films look like, play like, sound like—preconceived ideas, not experiences that live and breathe.

As Shakespeare said, "Action is eloquence." And in action sequences, the filmmaker has a great opportunity to create the most truly moving cinematic moments possible. And for these scenes, story boards *are* a great tool for cost-effectively breaking down and structuring complex actions into their individual shots. And especially for the low-budget filmmaker, a well-storyboarded sequence can save you considerable time, money and effort.

Say, for example, that you're doing a low-budget (or next-to-no-budget) film that involves multiple killings and you don't have the time, money or connections to do the special effects that have become a standard in this genre. What can you do to ensure that you deliver the thrills that an audience demands without putting you into the poor house or way behind schedule? One has only to think back to instances when masters of the genre have done so much with so little.

One of the most memorable was a scene in Val Lewton's production of Jacques Tourneur's *The Leopard Man*, where a young girl is returning from the store at night in a small town where a leopard is loose. The individual shots, their relationship to each other as well as their growing orchestration of the young girl's (and the audience's) terror is truly masterful, building to an understated but truly chilling climax. It is obvious that this scene could not have been made up on the set, but was carefully storyboarded in advance, especially if you are at all familiar with the budgetary restraints Lewton and Tourneur worked under. Now I'm not going to tell you how the scene ends, you'll have to rent the video to experience that thrill first-hand, but it's a prime example of using a well-thought-out visual sequence to create the maximum of suspense with the minimum of expense.

The very important lesson this carries for the low-budget filmmaker is that the effectiveness of action scenes can be dramatically increased without spending extra time or money, but by intelligently using your storyboards to create a visual abstraction of your action. Huh? Watch some old Westerns on TV — which fight scenes look fake and which look real? Invariably, the most effective are the ones where the action is broken up and the violence is simultaneously communicated and covered up by the cuts. Long shots of bar brawls, where people probably really got hurt, are almost always less convincing that expertly staged and edited fights.

And usually they are safer too. All too often beginning filmmakers make the mistake of thinking just because they show an action scene all in one shot, it is somehow more authentic or more exciting to an audience. It is not necessarily what you show but *how* you show it that will ultimately involve and move your audience. Thus, the storyboard is a cost-effective weapon in the low-budget filmmakers arsenal for increasing audience involvement without increasing your budget.

9

The Plan

Now that you have your story and some sort of written version, whether it be script, scenario, outline or storyboards, you are ready to begin your journey toward making it a reality.

The Schedule

How long will it take to shoot this sucker? A critical question that needs to be answered as realistically as possible. It is here and now that "A man (or woman) has got to know his (or her) limitations." Your schedule will not be arrived at by figuring how much money you have, divided by how many people you'll need, but by a very honest appraisal of your resources and your personal abilities.

The first thing is to sit down with your written version of the story, whether script, scenario, outline or storyboards, and make a list of every scene, no matter how small, including the location involved. Then group every scene that happens at the same location together. This is where using the same location for as many different scenes as possible comes into play, saving you time and money. This will also give you a fairly good idea of how many "moves" of equipment and people you will have to make. Obviously, with a low budget, the less moves the better—for your budget that is. But then again, maybe not for your story.

The next step is to figure out how long it will take to shoot all the scenes at each location. This is where being realistic with yourself is of prime importance. With over 20 years of experience, I now know pretty much how long it will take to shoot a particular scene or bunch of scenes, but if you're starting out how do you figure this out?

When I'm working as a line producer on other people's films, the first thing I do when I get to this point to call a meeting with the director, the director of photography and occasionally the art director. We then sit down around a table and go through the script scene by scene, talking about what each one needs to successfully accomplish each scene. This way I can get a better idea of what a realistic schedule will be.

My reason for doing this is to figure out how many individual camera-lighting set-ups a day are necessary as well as practical to complete each scene. My main considerations are:

1. Does the director shoot using multiple-angle coverage with long shot, medium shot, closeup and reversals? Or do they only shoot what they need with a minimum of coverage?

2. Is the director organized and well-prepared in advance or do they seem to prefer flying by the seat of their pants?

3. Does the director improvise or like to use camera movement?

4. Does the director rehearse before or during shooting?

5. How quickly does the d.p. light a typical scene?

6. How many lights does the d.p. use to light a typical scene?

7. What size crew does the d.p. have?

8. How many actors or actresses are involved with each scene?

9. Is any special set decoration needed before and during shooting?

10. Does the scene have any special needs— special effects, extra lighting, crowd control, special weather conditions, etc.?

This then will give you a pretty fair idea of how many days it will take to shoot your film. Remember, if you begin fudging things here, it will only be to your disadvantage later. I only mention that because this is the stage where a great many people begin deluding themselves about their project's feasibility. It is better to cut a scene here in pre-production, where you can choose what to cut, taking into consideration the scene's relationship to the entire picture, rather than later, when you will have to cut a scene just because it happens to come at the end of your schedule.

Does the amount of days you estimate match up with the days you can actually afford to shoot? If so, you're ready to continue scheduling, then budgeting, then shooting. If not, you either have to begin to find ways to shorten the way you plan to shoot your scenes, or shorten the scenes themselves, or cut the scenes altogether, or begin raising more money. If you know beforehand that these figures do not match up and you begin production anyway, you're only asking for trouble.

One way to economize is the manner in which you arrange the schedule of your shooting days. In other words, are you shooting 12 days straight, or are you shooting only weekends or nights? Sometimes it's cheaper to shoot all at once, especially if your cast and crew only have limited availability or you're getting a price break on your equipment rental. However, sometimes it's cheaper (especially if everyone has other jobs and can't afford to take off any amount of straight days in a row) to shoot only on weekends or nights as some equipment houses will give you an extra day or two if you rent over the weekend. The worst situation that sometimes occurs is when you may only be able to shoot when you get the extra money which you need to continue, little by little. And while I don't recommend this particular way, it is an alternative that has worked for some people.

I have worked on straight schedules and weekend-only schedules and I find that the straight schedule is by far the best method for the overall quality of your finished picture. It allows your cast and crew to get up to speed and become a more efficient unit much quicker, while also maintaining a momentum and unity that just is not feasible working only weekends or nights. Of course, this is not always economically feasible.

Now that you have decided whether to shoot straight days in a row or weekends, you must begin placing your individual scenes and locations in that calendar. I have always found it best to schedule some relatively simple scenes for the first few days, as this is the time when the cast and crew are learning to work together, often requiring adjustments along the way. I also try to schedule simple scenes for the last couple of days, because by that time your cast and crew will be tired and not at their very best. In addition, if you leave an extra afternoon or evening free near the end of the schedule, you can use that time to make up for any scene or shot that you may have had to skip because of time constraints earlier on.

I then try and schedule the most important, most difficult logistical scenes around the end of the first third of the schedule and the most important, most difficult emotional acting scenes some time after the halfway mark. The difficult logistical scenes need teamwork especially among your crew, which can only built after working with one another for a few days.

The most difficult emotional acting scenes are the ones that have to be right, have to work for your movie to work. They can't be rushed and every single member of your cast and crew has to be working at maximum efficiency. I believe that there are usually three or four key emotional scenes in every film that must work for the film to work. They are the keys to your film and they must contain magic. In all the other scenes you should be trying to hold your audience, making sure their interest is piqued, but in those three or four key scenes they must be *moved*. So in all my schedules I leave extra time for those particular scenes.

Before moving on, I just want to mention the scheduling or extended scheduling that some low-budget productions utilize in shooting a project over an extended period of time, such as six months to over a year or two. It has been done and done successfully, but the main concentration of this book is on a production that will be shot in one go, either in a continuous block of days and/or weeks or a continuous string of weekends. But many of the same principles apply, only they apply for each small amount of time that you are actually shooting and are much more forgiving if you do not complete a scene in its allotted time period. However, most productions are completed during some continuous period and that will be our concentration.

To conclude this section, every director has his or her own priorities and they should be evident in their schedule, whether they include extra time to set up special effects or allow for improvisation or cut down the number of scenes to be covered to accommodate complex camera moves or letting you just sit down and rethink in the middle of a scene. This is the time and place where your ideals, your priorities can be made practical. Once you have settled on your schedule it is time to move on to your budget.

The Budget

All of your hopes, thoughts and dreams must be translated from your written version into things, the things that go into making a film or video. I believe that it was director Douglas Sirk who said something to the effect that films are made with things, that is with mirrors, flowers, furniture, etc. You get the drift: Now you must begin breaking down your written story into the things that you will need to make your vision a reality.

Before breaking down my script, outline, whatever, I always go over, sometimes on paper and sometimes only in my mind, what my top priorities in making this particular film are to be. Especially on a low-budget production, you can't always get what you want, but sometimes you just can get what you need! But what do you need?

This is a very important question, as it may mean the difference between your idea laying dormant on a shelf as an unproduced script or actually being made. And before you begin, you should know the difference between what you want for your film and what you need. Obviously, you should go after what you want but always bearing in mind what you need.

Over the years I have seen many friends and colleagues talk about what they were waiting for before they would begin making *their* film. Well, I hate to tell you, almost all of them are still waiting. You will never have enough time, enough money, enough people, enough of anything. Listen to those guys making $100 million dollar movies, they're still complaining about being rushed, not enough money, problems with cast or crew. It is never going to be perfect.

Compromise is always an integral part of making a film; the trick is knowing the difference between what you want and what you need and this applies not only to physical matters like budget, cast, crew, schedule, props, special effects, but also to creative matters such as how you are going to shoot a scene or working with a particularly troublesome actor or crew member or editing decisions before your final cut, up to and including any questions regarding distribution or sales.

Now this doesn't mean that you must compromise your vision so much that it loses all resemblance to your original concept. What it does mean is that you are the only one who will know when that line is crossed. Everyone has a different line and, believe me, when those moments of compromise appear, you will intuitively feel where your particular line is. I hope that when those moments do arise (and they always will!), you won't cross your own line. And by working on a low-budget production, you will have much more input, more ability to effect those compromises than on a larger budget production. This is one of the main lessons learned for the "Patron Saints of the Underground."

Okay, enough of this philosophical b.s., let's start making this sucker! What do you need? $$$! How much? Well, first you have to break down your script, scenario or whatever. *You only need ten things* (besides the money) to make your film and they are:

1. Actors
2. Crew
3. Equipment
4. Locations/Sets
5. Film/Video Stock
6. Supplies
7. Wardrobe
8. Props
9. Food
10. Transportation

There are two optional categories depending upon on how dangerous you choose to live. They are:

11. Insurance?
12. Lawyers?

So let's go through each of the ten necessary, plus the two optional, budget lines to get your project *in the can*. I have also included my budget breakdown for *Daddy* (see *Daddy* Budget in the back of the book), which will give you a realistic picture of a low-budget budget. Then due to its complexity, I will have a separate section dedicated to your post-production budget.

Budgeting Actors

Go through your script and make a list of all the characters mentioned. Then go back over this list and rearrange it by how many scenes those characters appear in the script, with the character who appears in the most scenes at the top of the list and go on down your entire list. This will give you a pretty fair idea of how many days you will need each actor or actress. The most important thing to the actor or actress (after whether they think it's a good or interesting part or not) is how much time they will have to devote to their role in your project. Since in all probability you will not be paying top dollar, let alone scale, this becomes a very, very important consideration.

The decision whether or not to pay your cast is an important one that will always have a direct influence on your finished film. If you do have money in your budget for paying the cast, I believe that it's one of the best investments you can make, as it acknowledges their importance to your project and creates good will that will count for plenty when you run into hard times such as long nights, little sleep, uncomfortable working situations — you know, all the conditions of a low-budget shoot. They are also much more likely to show up, hopefully on time.

If you are not bound by union rules, and probably most of you shooting low budget are not, I find the best way of calculating what to pay the actors and actresses is figuring out what you can afford for the entire cast, then arriving at a day rate that fits within that dollar amount. I would also advise that you have a different day rate for your lead actors and bit actors. So that if you are planning on a ten-day shoot with your three leads (@$100/day) each working nine out of ten days and ten bit parts (@ $50/day) at one day apiece, your total acting budget would come to $3,200.

In recent years, because of the marked increase in low-budget independent productions, the actors' unions have come up with a variety of plans for lower-budgeted productions. However, what they define as low-budget may not exactly fit what you define as low-budget. This can put the underground filmmaker in a very tricky situation, as most of us would love to be able to pay everyone on our productions the going rate. But if you are unable to do that, I also believe that should not prevent you from trying to attain your vision, as long as you treat your cast and crew fairly and with common decency.

If you do choose to use union actors and actresses, you should contact your local Screen Actors Guild (SAG) (movies) or American Federation of Television and Radio Artists (AFTRA) (television) and ask about their limited release or low-budget contracts. These may allow you to pay less than scale along with certain relaxed working conditions. Some may include restrictions on where you can screen your finished work. These concessions will usually mean a reduced day rate while still contributing to the union's pension fund (fringes), which may be a motivating factor for an actor looking to work enough days to qualify for their union's health plan. But if you're sure you want to use union actors and have any questions, do call your local union office for details, as they are becoming more flexible towards low-budget productions.

However, if you are not able to pay your cast, it is usually advisable, whenever possible, to at least provide some kind of per diem ($) that will cover any transportation to and from work, any special dry cleaning or hair cutting or any other incidental expense that may arise, as well as providing their meals when they are working for you. It shows a concern on your part that you are aware of the sacrifice that they are making for your project and you don't want them to have to spend any their own money while involved with your project.

Budgeting the Crew

Determining the size, selecting the members and budgeting for your crew will have more influence on how smoothly your production runs as well as how much it will eventually cost you than any other decision you make in pre-production. You will be spending more time with your crew during the production of your film or video than anyone else, including the actors, actresses and even your own family, girlfriend, boyfriend or whatever. So it is of utmost importance, especially for the underground filmmaker, to "cast" his crew as carefully as you cast your actors and actresses.

The first question to ask is how many people do you really need to shoot a feature film or video? A film can be shot with as few as six people and a video with as few as four. The positions needed for a film shoot are the director of photography, assistant camera, sound recordist, boom operator, line producer/production manager and a production assistant. Everything else is negotiable and/or extra. For a video shoot you need a director of photography, boom operator, line producer/production manager and a production assistant; everything else is negotiable and/or extra.

I have known directors, including myself, who have doubled as the director of photography and I would advise against this, as it always has a negative impact on the performances. You just do not have enough time to spend with your actors and actresses if you are also physically involved with setting up lights and tripods and cameras. It also makes it that much more difficult to gauge performances during the actual shooting by losing the critical distance you need to be able to adjust your cast's performances midstream. Use a DP or a camera operator, it's worth it, I *guarantee* it.

Now that I've convinced you (or not) to have an extra person on your crew by not shooting your picture yourself, I will try and convince you from this point on to use as few people as necessary for the remainder of your crew. The reason for this is that on a low-budget production, for every single budget line you increase, you will automatically add at least two or three other budget lines. How can this be?

On larger Hollywood-type productions, adding an extra person usually means very little to the final budget; however, the addition of even a single day can have tremendous repercussions. Some large productions are probably spending in the area of $200–500,000 a day. This is because the various departments on large films function relatively independently of each other. But on an underground film, the opposite is true. Every single budget line is dependent on practically ever other budget line and because the overall scale is so reduced, any small increase, especially in personnel, can have major repercussions in more than one area.

This means that if your DP says that he needs a truck for his lighting needs, you will not only add the cost of the truck and driver to your costs, but you will probably need at least one gaffer and probably more, along with their additional expenses. This also may mean additional expenses for parking or permits. It also means you will not be able to move as fast and your lighting set-ups will involve more lights which means more time which means a longer schedule. See what I mean?

On a great many guerrilla productions, one last consideration is that you can only afford to pay some of your crew. Who do you pay and how do you decide? And do you let other crew members know who's getting paid and who's not? For my money (and it often has been) the prioritized list of who should get paid goes like this: the director of photography, the sound team, the line producer or unit production manager, the hair/makeup person(s), the art director, the camera crew, the director's crew and finally the production assistants.

Part of the rationale for this list is that the people at the top of the list will quite often be bringing in their own equipment, camera, lights, microphones, make up, whatever, thus making it easier to rationalize why they're getting paid to the other crew members who aren't. Whether you actually inform everyone who is and is not being paid up front is a decision that each individual filmmaker must make depending on their own personality.

If you do have money in your budget for paying the crew, I believe that it's one of the best investments you can make, for the very same reasons as paying your cast: creating goodwill during those inevitable hard times, as well as increasing the likelihood of them showing up on time.

If you decide that your cast or crew's pay will be deferred, make sure you let them know this is a relatively unlikely event, as most of them will be aware of this already and appreciate your honesty. However, if you are not able to pay your crew, it is usually advisable, whenever possible, to at least provide some kind of per diem

($) that will cover any transportation to and from work or any other incidental expense that may arise, as well as providing their meals when they are working for you. It shows a concern on your part that you are aware of the sacrifice that they are making for your project and you don't want them to have to spend any of their own money while involved with your project.

For the underground filmmaker, every decision you make will have repercussions along your entire budget line. That is why it is absolutely necessary to scrutinize every crew position you have. Do not add someone just because "that's the way it's done." If you don't need them, don't have them. With that in mind, I'll now go through most of the crew positions with my thoughts on what is and is not necessary.

BUDGETING THE DIRECTOR'S CREW

By this I mean any assistant directors, script supervisors, continuity persons, assistants and production assistants (PAs). Most budgets will include this category, but for a low-budget production, I don't find it particularly useful. I personally have never had anyone of the above positions, except for a few PAs, working on any of my feature productions. And I believe with the more experience you have as a director, the fewer of the above positions you'll need — unless of course you are involved with a relatively large-scale production.

The first AD, or assistant director, is the one who keeps things running smoothly on the set, making sure that the production stays on schedule and under budget. They are usually the "bad cops" who yell at people to get to work while making the director appear to be the "good cop." The second ADs help with the extras, attend to the necessary paperwork like releases, etc. and help set up each days schedule with the first AD.

I find that ADs are only necessary if you have large groups of people involved with a scene, whether it's a group of extras or a complicated scene with multiple logistical elements that need to be coordinated at precisely the right moment. However, the moment you begin thinking that you need an assistant director, first or second, on a low-budget production is the moment you should start worrying that your budget may be starting to get out of hand. A true underground director is usually their own best first AD.

In my experience, I've found that most PAs can handle these situations when they arise, if you've taken the time to pick a mature, responsible person for that job. However, when you find yourself in a position of needing large amounts of people, cast and crew, in a relatively large number of your scenes, then you may need an assistant director and possibly another investor.

The script supervisor and/or the script person and/or the continuity person is usually the same individual on a low-budget production. But the only time they are necessary, once again in my experience, is when you are shooting material that needs to have strict continuity — that is, either coverage with master, medium, closeup and reversals or where scenes are shot partially on one day at one location, then finished on another day at another location. In these specific instances, they can be invaluable, assuring continuity for editing, if they are observant. But when you are shooting on anything other than film, they are not particularly necessary; just rewind your tape and play back. Polaroid or videos taken on location can also be helpful for continuity problems and help you eliminate one more budget line and mouth to feed and body to transport.

Last, but far from least in my mind, is the production assistant. On a guerrilla production the PA is an important and necessary element for the underground director's successful shoot. Quite often, you will find productions bringing on as many PAs as possible, with little or no experience for little or no pay and not treating them particularly well, making them seem expendable. That's one of the stupidest things you could possibly do.

Personally, I have always found that you should search out the best qualified, most experienced people for production assistants and then give them as many responsibilities in as many capacities as they can handle. In return you should give them whatever title and/or crew credit they want, as long as someone else hasn't worked in that position. I think this is a more than fair trade and it doesn't cost you a cent. Hell, I've credited PAs as Assistant Producers and was glad to do so, because of the great job they had done.

Let them learn and gain experience in as many production areas as is feasible, but only have as many on your crew as you can keep *constantly* busy. They should never be sitting around, but rather they should become your swing crew, so that if they are not helping with the lights they can be helping with the set decoration or getting props or preparing wardrobe or maybe even start getting the next location prepped. They also should be the youngest people on your crew, participating fully, turning it into a learning experience instead of being relegated to a menial "gofer" status. In this way you'll find that you can considerably cut down on your crew size without cutting down on your efficiency.

BUDGETING THE CAMERA CREW

The director of photography (who should also double as the camera operator–gaffer) and his assistant (who should also double as the focus puller–gaffer) are the only absolutely necessary camera crew you will need on a film shoot, while for video you can get away with only a DP. This is obviously much more work for the DP and his assistant, also necessitating that you and anyone else not actively engaged must assist them in hauling equipment or setting up the lights and camera, when needed. This is where a somewhat experienced and willing production assistant really becomes invaluable.

But depending on the DP that you choose, there may be various other positions they deem necessary, before they agree to work on your project. This will be one of your most important negotiations having a very direct influence on your bottom line as well as the your final product. Most DPs will tell you what they consider to be the minimum amount of people and equipment that they need to do what they consider a professional job. If you want them because of the skills they've demonstrated in past projects and they seem compatible with your vision, method of working and budget, then you probably should listen to their advice.

The more experience you have, the more able you will be to successfully negotiate their conditions, because I've found that most DPs have a way of working that
they're comfortable with and prefer to stay with that. Unfortunately for many low-
budget productions that may not be the best approach. Many of the DPs that you'll
meet haven't done a feature, but are willing to work on less than advantageous terms
(your low-budget wonder) to get a feature credit.

For the DP, a low-budget feature will be different from just about any other production that he/she has been involved with. He/she will never have the time to get
things just the way they want, there will always be pressure to move faster with the
worst case scenario being that because of the DP's meticulousness and/or slowness
scenes must be cut or severely shortened.

Additionally, some DPs may not be used to working with relatively inexperienced talent or temperamental actors or actresses on a low-budget feature and forget that ultimately it's what the actors or actresses do in front of the camera that
counts. So make sure that your DP is sensitive to the needs of the actors and actresses
as well as his or her photographic needs. And if they aren't, let them know immediately, and if they can't change their way of working, make sure you minimize their
interaction with the cast.

And no one will have more influence on the speed or lack of, as well as the quality or lack thereof, than your DP. Many people walking onto sets often think the DP
is the director because of the control they exert on a film set. There's nothing more
destructive on a film or video set than a DP and director at odds over either the style
or the mode and/or pace of the production. So spend a lot of time making sure that
your d.p. shares not only your cinematic vision, but your budgetary vision as well.

Productions with a lot of camera gear and/or elaborate camera set-ups and/or a
lot of locations in a short amount of time may need a second assistant camera, but not
usually on a guerrilla-style production. If you are using more than a couple of lighting kits for your lighting needs or will be tapping into electrical outlets on location or
are using a lighting truck, you may need a gaffer or two, depending upon the amount
of lighting instruments used. But if you and/or your DP decide you need gaffers, see
if you can set your schedule up so that those particular scenes with special lighting
requirements can be bunched up together over several consecutive days rather than
spread out over the entire production. Just another way to cut costs, not quality.

If you will be moving your camera on a dolly, then you will need experienced
grips to lay the track and/or move the dolly, allowing you to hit your marks. My
advice on grips is that if you are going to use dolly shots, then you should have the
most experienced grips and best dolly equipment you can afford or beg or scrounge
for. In the long run, the time lost with inexperienced dolly crews is usually just not
worth the few dollars you will save.

This said, there are many time-honored guerrilla methods of camera movement.
The first and foremost is hand-held with a wide angle lens allowing for greater depth
of field (and no focus puller) or sitting your DP on a wheelchair or stand them on a
skateboard or have them wear roller skates. Sometimes a slow-moving car can make
a perfectly acceptable dolly shot and if the surface is a little rough, just let a little air
out of the tires.

Noh and Kabuki theaters, Antonin Artaud's Theater of Cruelty, the Balinese Theater with its percussive Gamilian instrumentation and expressive dancers, the Folk and/or Fairy Tales of almost any region, the oral traditions of the American Indian, the African Griot, the street corner storytellers of India, the rituals of almost any religion or any other storytelling tradition that you may feel a kinship to.

And whether you're searching for new forms, a more collaborative method of working or attempting to utilize new technologies in a more interactive manner, you may find that the written script is no longer a satisfactory way of working. So for those of you who happen to be looking for alternative methods of structure, read on.

Scenarios

What exactly is a scenario? Basically, it's your story or storyline or plot, usually written in prose, running somewhere between 20 to 70 pages. A scenario summarizes the action of your story from beginning to end. The amount of detail included (see *Daddy* Scenario Excerpt in the back of the book) will vary according to your own individual needs and preferences. These details should include where the action is taking place, who is present and what they are doing.

But it may get into much greater detail both in terms of location and character. I have seen some scenarios written as poetic evocations of each scene while others were as dry and factual as a police report. Whatever amount of information you need to get your creative juices flowing is the right amount of detail.

In other words, are you the type of person who will stay awake all night worrying about every aspect of the next day's scene? Then I would suggest being as specific and detailed in as many areas as possible. Are you the type of person who becomes bored having everything planed out in advance? For you, limiting the amount of information, forcing you to invent on the spot, might be the trick.

Another important element of both the scenario and the outline is gauging the approximate screen time of each scene. I believe it's important to have a clear idea in your head, before you begin, just how long each scene should last. When you're not using a script, the one area that can lead you the most astray is allowing scenes to run much longer than they should. And if you use improvisation, this is an added risk.

Setting a timing for each scene forces you to weigh the value of each individual scene in relationship to the whole movie. It lets you see and gauge, beforehand, what scenes are important and need time to develop while limiting the duration of the scenes which are not as vital to your overall story. It also allows you to better judge how long it will take you to shoot each scene and how much time to set aside for their shooting on your schedule.

Of course this now brings up another aspect of using a scenario. To many cast and crew members, a script is like a security blanket and without it they may feel lost at sea. Most the productions they have worked on use one and they will have become used to it. This is something that should be brought up well before you bring anyone, cast or crew on board.

And although the Steadi-Cam may be great for higher-budgeted films, the Steadi-Cam Junior works just fine for most small Digital camcorders (although most of them feature steadying features which work pretty well) and there always is the Sam Raimi-Cohen Brothers' early method of securing your camera to a large piece of wood that is held by one person on each end, allowing you to get exciting, swooping, low-angle shots.

BUDGETING THE SOUND CREW

On a guerrilla production, the sound crew consists of a sound recordist and a boom operator, nevermore, quoth the Raven, nevermore. And if you're shooting on video, you can usually get away with only a boom operator. However, if you can find a talented and experienced sound person, recording on DAT (Digital Audio Tape) as opposed to a Nagra Reel-to-Reel, who can boom and record and monitor simultaneously (I know it can be done because I had someone do it on one of my features and very successfully), go for it.

Make sure they are extra-vigilant about distortion (more about this later) which can be alleviated by having two inputs from your boom with one on an optimum setting and the other at 20 dbs below the optimum. One note of caution about sound on a guerrilla production: The easiest way to tell a low-budget production is by bad sound. This seems to be the area where most people will skimp and cut corners. Don't do it. The only two crew areas you should absolutely not skimp on are the camera and sound crews. And if no one else gets paid on your crew, they should be, and as fairly as possible.

BUDGETING THE LINE PRODUCER, UNIT PRODUCTION MANAGER AND LOCATION MANAGER

These are the people or person (depending on your budget or ability to hustle) who are the organizational backbone of your production. They are the one(s) whose job it is to ensure that your locations are secured and that everyone and everything gets to where they're supposed to be at the time they're supposed to be there. Sounds simple, but it's one of the most complicated and necessary functions in a low-budget production.

The line producer or unit production manager is the one who makes sure everything and everyone gets where they need to be. They arrange locations, make living arrangements, set up transportation, help in the hiring and with the payroll, if there is one. When a shoot has a large number of different locations, there may be a location manager whose only job is set up and oversee each and every location.

But on an underground production, almost all of these chores will fall in the lap of one person, who is in charge of all the practical, logistical arrangements, which will probably include: setting up the schedule (in collaboration with the producer, who may also be the line producer and/or UPM and/or location manager); obtain and secure the locations; arrange transportation for cast and crew and equipment; arrange for meals (craft services are only for larger productions where you can afford to pay someone to do this); and make sure that all the necessary equipment, props, wardrobe, sets and anything else that is needed for shooting will be at the location when needed.

They will also act as damage control and/or juggle schedule changes necessitated by unforeseen events, such as finding an alternative locations if you are forced to move from your scheduled location, whether by weather, angry neighbors, power failure, the police or any other "Act of God." They also will search out and find that last-minute, "forgotten" prop, piece of equipment or actor who hasn't shown up. And of course, on a ultra-low-budget production, you the director will be probably be acting as the line producer/u.p.m./location manager, while the DP probably will deal with the camera package and the sound person with the audio package.

BUDGETING THE ART DEPARTMENT

The only time I had what is considered a "proper" art department, everyone in it, except for one person, was more bother than they were worth. Of course, part of it had to do with the fact that they weren't getting paid and were not the most qualified people around and part of it was because I had started out as a artist (a painter) and was and still am extremely selective (fussy) about every single visual element in all of my films.

If you have the time and the eye, I would suggest you spend or make that extra time and act as your own art director, while delegating to a production assistant with some visual flair the actual tracking down and purchasing of items you have either found or okayed. However, if you can't match your shirt to your pants, I would suggest trying to entice a beginning art director, whose work you have seen and admired, with an opportunity for creative freedom, within your practically non-existent budget. Or try and finding an art director working in another field (i.e., advertising, print, industrial, short films) and offer them the opportunity to design an entire feature. You'd be surprised how many very creative people are looking for just that opportunity.

And if all that fails, try searching out a painter or sculptor who has never worked in film before and give them a shot, as well as a chance to acquire a portfolio piece for any future film work. This particular method has worked well for me in the past. Of course, nothing helps so much as having friends with fabulous taste in apartments, who will allow you to shoot in their places that need little or no alteration.

BUDGETING HAIR AND MAKEUP

Hair and makeup (especially makeup) is the other area that betrays low-budget deficiencies almost as much as poor sound quality. There are only four options available to you: hire someone experienced for as little money as possible, find someone with talent who is just starting out and needs the experience, use professional performers who know how to do their own makeup or pay an experienced hair/makeup artist to show each lead actor or actress how to apply the makeup that is best for them. And if your lead actors and actresses are forgetful, videotape the session for each of them to help refresh their memory should they need it.

The makeup person is the last stop for your actor or actress before actually shooting and it seems as if the makeup person is *always* delaying the shoot. While this may seem so at the time, it usually isn't and I must confess that I have been as guilty of this as any other director. So take this into consideration before getting on the back of your makeup person: They have a job to do and it is important, let them do it.

At any rate, you should pay for all makeup (make sure it's made for film, so it won't melt under the lights!) and don't cheap out on this! As you may have noticed, I do not believe in cheaping out on anything that will eventually show up on the screen, because it *will* show up on the screen and reflect badly on you and your production.

When you have finalized your crew requirements, list all the positions and what they are to be paid. For underground productions, it's usually wiser to pay a flat rate for the entire shoot. Although it may be based on some basic day rate, the flat rate gives you a little more flexibility, especially if you fall behind and/or you need an extra day somewhere. Just remember not to abuse this by tacking an extra week or two onto your schedule, as any good will you've won by actually paying people will be quickly lost.

If you must pay a day rate, make sure it is for at least a 10–hour day and preferably a 12–hour day, as that is a relatively average day for standard underground, low-budget production. And if at all possible you should negotiate for a weekly or bi-weekly or monthly discount on the day rate.

Once again, as with the actors and actresses, the respective craft unions have been recognizing the growth in the independent film production and are offering reduced fee schedules, if your production qualifies. And what I said before about the cast and unions goes for the crew and unions as well: If you can afford that range of pay, you should definitely talk to the unions about their low-budget agreements, which offer a reduced day rate and the relaxation of some hourly requirements, as well as helping their members to qualify for health and pension benefits. But again, as I mentioned before, what they consider low-budget and what you consider low-budget may not be exactly the same thing.

Budgeting the Equipment

Remember back in the chapter on guerrilla warfare about carrying the absolute minimum necessary to do the job? Now is the time when you begin practicing what you preach. What do you need to accomplish your objectives? A camera, a microphone and a device to record audio; everything else is extra. Sound far-fetched? With today's high speed films and low-light digital video cameras, this is now a reality. There are many considerations to be made concerning the type of equipment you will use for your production. Some are aesthetic and will be covered later, but most are related to financial considerations and will be covered in this section.

BUDGETING THE CAMERA EQUIPMENT

What kind of camera are you going to use, film or video— oh, pardon me, I mean *digital*? Is it going to be all hand-held or do you need a tripod? Do you need a truck full of lights or a Louma Crane or just a doorway dolly? Should you record your sound digitally or on the faithful Nagra?

Before making these important decisions, you have to ask yourself why or for what end purpose are you doing all this work? Obviously, if you just want to make a film, no matter what, or there's no way in the world you can afford film, these decisions have already been made, but if you're at some point in the middle, these are some considerations you should take into account, at least, as of today.

If you want theatrical distribution, it's still best to shoot on film, first choice 35mm, second choice Super 16mm, third choice 16mm, fourth choice digital video transferred to 35mm film. If you want to go to film festivals, it's still best to shoot on film, no matter what is being said about digital video. And 35mm is still preferred, if you can afford it, then Super 16, then 16mm and finally digital video (being the new hip, "in" thing) but still not preferable to film, unless of course you are an already established film director.

For television and video distribution, film is still the preferred medium, but instead of 35mm, you can probably get away with 16mm transferred to Digital Beta for editing and mastering. This is followed by Digital Beta, then DV, mini or DV Cam transferred to BetaSP or Digital Beta for your edit and master. Although I must add that digital video, whatever format has the industry buzz, and even though the quality is not as good as film, it is a very cost-effective alternative. I haven't mentioned high definition, because it's usually way beyond the pockets of most underground, guerrilla budgets. So you must decide what you want to do with your production, where you want to go with it and whether you want to increase or decrease your odds of being accepted, bought and anything else in between.

Now you can go out looking for the camera you need, film or otherwise. But how can you get the best deals without putting yourself into more risk than you've already assumed by deciding to make a feature? Without a doubt, the best deals are to be found by using a camera package that belongs to your director of photography. In this way you can a negotiate a price that includes the DP and his equipment, often throwing his lighting equipment into the package as well.

The only problem with this approach is *if* you find you have a problem with your DP once production begins, you will not only have to get rid of him, but you will now have to find and negotiate a deal for a new camera package and/or lights as well. I have seen where this can lead to a DP practically blackmailing their helpless producer and/or director into making the production a calling card for the DP with little concern over the producer/director's dramatic and/or financial concerns. Obviously, this is the worst case scenario, but I have seen it happen and you should always be aware of these possible implications before deciding to use a DP and his own personal camera package.

Of course, not all DPs own their own equipment, but they often can recommend people they know or rental houses where they might have connections to get you a favorable deal. I believe this is preferable to renting just a camera package from an individual owner, although it may cost less money to rent from an individual. The rationale for this is that if an individual's equipment malfunctions, you're stuck and will have to go looking for another equipment deal; but if you're renting from a rental house, they'll have replacements for any of their malfunctioning equipment. But once again, if your DP has used a particular package from an individual successfully in the past, you have some assurance about its upkeep.

Some rental houses will give you a one-day rate if you rent one of their cameras over the weekend, in effect giving you a three-for-one deal, which is one of the reasons so many micro-budgeted features are shot over weekends. I have also found if you plan shooting your project during slow periods, holidays, etc., you can often negotiate a better deal for camera packages.

Everything beyond the basic camera package should be carefully chosen by you and your DP after close scrutiny of your script, scenario, etc., and its requirements. The key to hiring your DP is summed up by one word and that is *trust*. And although this is not easily arrived at, the more you know, the more people you talk to, the more research you do beforehand will help you make that crucial decision. Look at their reel, ask questions about particular shots, how they were set up. And ask for references, making sure that you talk to at least two or three people they've worked with in the past.

Ultimately your camera package is more an issue of trust with your DP than any technical data you can find, unless you know more than your DP and that doesn't happen too often now that Stanley Kubrick's gone.

BUDGETING THE LIGHTING EQUIPMENT

On a low-budget production, one of the key logistical decisions will be about the size of the lighting package needed. With today's faster film speeds, faster lens and increasingly sensitive video cameras, the amount of light needed to illuminate a scene satisfactorily has been greatly reduced but, contrary to popular belief, not done away with.

Two things give away an amateur production faster than anything else, bad lighting and bad audio. And there is one simple way of remedying this ... experience — either yours or the person you have chosen to handle this responsibility. The more you know, the less lighting fixtures you'll need to light well. The prime example of this is John Alton, who photographed a great many Hollywood classics in the late 40s and early 50s. He used so few lights and thereby fewer people that he was given a hard time, especially at large studios like MGM, where directors Vincent Minnelli and Richard Brooks insisted on using him over the objections of that studio's camera department. Study his films, especially his superior, low-budget film noirs (*T-Men, Raw Deal, The Black Book*) with Anthony Mann directing and you'll discover maximum beauty with minimal resources.

Remember the sun is the original key light and can give you more beautiful light than any combination of artificial light and it's free. Use this to your advantage, by scouting locations in advance and checking out what times of the day the natural light is most advantageous for your film.

The only problem with this approach is that you sometimes have to wait for the light, if it's an overcast day or the weather turns against you. The earlier filmmakers would often wait for just the right cloud or lighting effect, but in today's budget-conscious world only the low-budget filmmaker can afford this luxury. This is one way you can create stunning visuals that are on a par with any Hollywood super production and the only cost is your time.

When Hollywood moves into a location, they usually change that location into a set, but you should do the opposite. Use the lighting that already exists at the location and only supplement it with your own. One of the prime prerequisites for picking a location should be the quality of available light at that location, whether it is natural or the fixtures already there.

I believe that a low-budget film/video with a small cast that doesn't have to light huge night exteriors should be able to do with no more than five lights! However, these five lights (preferably capable of using either 1,000 watt, 750 watt or 500 watt bulbs) should be versatile, rugged and equipped with stands, clamps, barn doors, scrims, diffusion, colored gels, a way to bounce light, a way to sculpt the light and enough heavy duty A/C extension cords.

The light stands should be sturdy and secured with sandbags (or large bags of kitty litter) if there's any chance they might fall or pedestrians might trip over them. The clamps should be specifically made for film lights (and use a safety chain), the barn doors should allow you flexibility in shaping the light, the scrims will allow you to cut down the amount of light without reducing color temperature, diffusion (spun glass or the translucent sheets) will allow you to soften the light, colored gels will allow you to add color or balance different light sources, a reflective umbrella or just white foam core or show card will allow you to bounce the light for a softer affect and C stands with flags and/or patterns or black wrap (black aluminum foil) will help sculpt the light. And don't forget a bag of the wooden pinching variety of clothes pegs.

However, if you have to light daytime exteriors (of which there are many ways to avoid using lights), you will probably have to rent HMIs with ballasts. If you have to film night exteriors, you will also need a generator, unless you can "borrow" power from a nearby building or convenient street lamp.

The bottom line is that if you have the experience, you can greatly cut down on the amount and type of lighting fixtures that you need, but if you don't have the experience, discuss things with your DP. Show them films or videos that you like the look of and also explain your budget and schedule limitations. But remember, most DPs habitually bring more lights than they'll ever need because they don't want to be left short. If you have the time, go to each location with your DP and discuss your ideas; it will be time well spent. If they don't have the time, videotape them or take Polaroids, especially at those times of day that you will be shooting.

BUDGETING THE SOUND EQUIPMENT

Luckily the sound equipment isn't anywhere near as complex a situation as the camera, but it is just as critical. For DV and most other video situations, you will probably be recording the audio with your camcorder, although you might want to have it go through a mixer first. However, for a double system recording set-up, where the audio recording is taking place on a machine other than the camera and which includes almost all film-based systems or possibly as a back-up for some video ones, there is either the Nagra reel-to-reel or the DAT (Digital Audio Tape) cassette recorder.

The Nagra is preferable (to me) because it's more forgiving in terms of loud (over-modulated) sounds, but it is more expensive (to rent or buy) and a little more cumbersome. The DAT is usually cheaper and lighter to carry, but is unforgiving if your sound is over-modulated. That means anything above the Zero setting on a DAT recorder will distort and be unusable, whereas with a Nagra there is a wider range where the sound can still be usable, even if not perfect. Also make sure, if at all possible (that is to say affordable), to get one that records time-code, otherwise you will have to pay later to have all the audio tapes time-coded to be able to use them most efficiently during post-production.

Some people also say the Nagra sound is "warmer" and the DAT sound is "colder," but I will leave that subjective opinion up to you. Some people even say the DAT sound is too good, but I've never understood what they mean by that. Your sound recordist may have a preference and if you trust them, you should trust their choice.

For film you will need a clapboard to sync the sound. An electronic one that connects to your audio recorder while laying down timecode is the best and preferable method, but the old-fashioned slate still works just fine. And although recording sound along with your video doesn't require a clapboard because the sound is automatically in sync with the picture, some people still prefer to use this method, believing that it makes identifying their clips easier. However, I think that it wastes precious minutes on the set and is more efficiently accomplished when you're logging your takes later without the clock ticking. But whatever the DP and sound person are comfortable with is fine by me.

For double system audio recording, most professionals prefer using a mixer that modulates the audio signal before it's recorded. However, on an low/no budget production, it's not a necessity, as you can adjust the levels right on the Nagra or DAT. But if you're recording your audio on your camcorder, it's a good idea to have it go through a mixer first. This way your sound person can monitor and adjust levels on the mixer before it's recorded on the camcorder. This is important, as it's next to impossible to simultaneously monitor and adjust audio levels on the camcorder while you're recording. And as I mentioned before, relying on the automatic gain of the camcorder is the sure sign of an amateur.

Although not recommended, there is a way around this if you are using only one source of audio and have the ability to set levels and record on two separate audio tracks. If you split your single audio feed from your mic into two separate channels, while setting one channel's level to the optimum recording level, established before the take, and then set the other channel 20dbs below the optimum level. That way if any part of the channel that is recording your sound at the optimum level over-modulates, you are backed up by the other channel set at the lower level. This works

99 percent of the time, but nothing beats having a mixer that allows you to monitor and adjust simultaneously.

Next we come to the microphone, an item often neglected with the resulting poor audio a testament to the filmmaker's lack of experience. For most of your production needs on low-budget features, a good shotgun microphone on a boom, handled by an experienced operator, will cover 95 percent of the situations you run into. This is another area you should not skimp on. Rent or buy the very best shotgun microphone that you can afford. A shotgun microphone has an extremely tight, narrow pick-up pattern; that is, it only records the sound from the precise area that it's pointed at.

And this is where the necessity of having an experienced boom operator becomes so important. All too often the microphone is handed off to a trustworthy PA with little or no experience booming and the results usually reveal this lack of experience very quickly. It is very easy to record audio using a shotgun mic and a boom pole, practically anyone can do it, but very few people can do it well. Take the time to find someone to do it well or you will be spending quite a bit of your time (and money) in post-production fixing the inadequacies of your poorly recorded sound.

And make sure that your sound person is not hesitant about informing you of any audio problem before you move on. A shy sound person can also cause many problems that only become evident in post, costing you a lot more than you might wish or can afford.

For recording large crowds or long shots without dialogue, an omni-directional microphone may be fine, but under no conditions should one be used to record dialogue. Just as your camera selectively frames the visual material you want to include or exclude, your microphone should be doing exactly the same with the sound and nothing does this better than the shotgun mic on a boom pole.

Boom poles come in variety of materials and lengths. The lighter the pole, the more expensive, with the Carbon fiber ones being the lightest and most expensive, but a lightweight aluminum one being an acceptable substitute. For most low/no budget productions, a 12–15 foot Carbon Fiber boom pole should cover almost any situation you run into. The lighter pole also will save your sound person's energy for later in a typically long day, when you just might need it.

You will also need a shock mount that isolates the microphone from the pole, eliminating any sounds arising from bumps or shaking. But once again, you should consult with your sound person, as they may prefer something different from the above or even have their own equipment. And as always, I would defer to their judgment.

In addition, if you're going to be doing any shooting outside, a windscreen is absolutely necessary and probably a good idea inside also, just in case you have to swing the boom around quickly. You may also want to use some type of clip or tie to hold your cable to the boom pole to keep it from rattling. Some people use those small ponytail holders, but whatever works for you is fine.

If you are shooting DV/video and recording your sound on the camera, you will have to connect your sound person's mic to the camera. There are basically two ways of doing this: You can either connect them via a cable or have a wireless transmitter going from the sound recordist to a wireless receiver on the camera/camera-man.

For connecting via a cable, I advise that you have an XLR output from your mic and go into an XLR input on the camcorder. But if you have one of the smaller DV camcorders that only have a mini audio input, I recommend the use of those little audio adapters that fit on the bottom of the camera and have two XLR inputs that go into the single stereo mini input of those camcorders.

And if you want the control of changing levels during the take, it's best to have a small portable mixer allowing your sound person to mix the sound and ride levels during the take, so that your camera operator doesn't have to worry about sound levels. They have enough problems without adding that. And because you will be connected via this cable, it's best to make a large loop, giving you plenty of slack, then tucking the looped cable into the camera operator's belt, so that if either of you move quickly, you won't be pulling or tugging the other around.

The other alternative is to have a wireless transmitter from your sound person's boom or mixer feeding the audio to a small receiver on your camera operator, who then has a short cable running into their camera or the small adapter on the bottom. The sound person may also mix a wireless mic on one of your performers with their own boom before sending the mixed signal to you.

With rapid advances in the technology of radio mics, they are now affordable for the low-budget auteur as well. But the cheaper units are prone to interference, especially in cities and the better ones with diversity switching (they will automatically switch to an alternative channel if they pick up interference) are still relatively expensive to rent. But nothing can beat them for picking up conversations, when your camera is placed at a distance from your talent, either by intent or by the practical necessity of (for instance) stealing a location.

All wireless mics have a transmitter sending the signal off to the receiver, which is then connected to the audio recorder. Before the advent of wireless mics, a long, cumbersome cable was needed to accomplish this and hiding it was a major chore. But with the advent of wireless mics, this bothersome umbilical cord has been cut.

The lavaliere version, which is that small, peanut-sized microphone (the one you see on almost all TV commentators), is connected by a wire to the transmitter. Make sure this is hidden by the actor's clothing, watching that it isn't actually rubbing against any of the material. This set-up has been the standard wireless outfit used in features, but there is an increasing use of a wireless shotgun mic that frees the sound person from being physically connected to the recorder, allowing them much greater mobility and cutting down on the amount of "boom shadow" problems.

Also, if you're using two radio mics, your sound person has to be careful to avoid crosstalk — that is, the one mic is picking up the audio from the other person as well as the person that it's on.

However, for the guerrilla production, I not convinced of their viability, unless of course you're getting them and the operator for free or you're stealing most of your shots. If you're stealing most of your shots, wireless mics are great, especially recording dialogue in crowded places without calling attention to yourself or your actors.

But for most guerrilla shoots, a good shotgun and boom with an experienced operator is the key.

One guerrilla method of covering a long distance conversation is to have a DAT or small analog audio recorder or Mini Disc recorder and lavaliere mic hidden on your talent and record the sound that way, syncing it up later in post-production. It really works and, because the talent is further from the camera, exact sync with their lips moving becomes much less noticeable.

I just want to add a personal note. For one of my 16mm features, we did all the sound with a DAT, with the boom operator also recording the sound. It was a small SONY DAT with a mini stereo plug, it did not record time code and we ended up using an old-fashioned clapboard. We added the time code afterwards while cloning the master tapes and it synced up perfectly, even on some two- or three-minute, extended takes. The only problem was two overmodulated takes we missed on location, but luckily were able to fix in post.

This method saved considerable time and money, but was only possible after I discussed everything with the recordist–boom operator who was experienced in doing both jobs and convinced me he could do as well on our production. The only thing I would change if I did this again would be having a small portable mixer to allow two separate inputs from your boom, with the level for one input set to the optimum setting and the other at minus 20 dbs below optimum setting, to prevent over-modulating.

Equipment Considerations. This first question you have to answer regarding equipment is whether your should you rent, borrow or buy the equipment you will be using on your production. And of course, there's no one answer for everyone.

I'll start off with renting the equipment, since that's probably the option used most often by low-budget filmmakers. But before I proceed, I must mention that with the advent of low-cost digital cameras and editing systems, more and more guerrilla film and video makers are buying their equipment and this option will be more fully explored later in this section.

When you rent your equipment, most often you are getting it from a rental facility that specializes in film and video, whether it be cameras, sound equipment or lighting. They will usually have more than one piece of each type of equipment and they are, for the most part, well maintained. And if something goes wrong during production, it's relatively easy to go back to them and either have them fix it quickly or exchange the malfunctioning piece of equipment for one that works. However, when you rent from an individual, this is usually not an option, since they only own the one piece of equipment. Which means you'll have to go out find someone else with similar equipment and make another deal ... quickly!

The trade-off in this situation is usually cost. You can almost always get a better deal with an individual and, they may not require equipment insurance on your part. A rental house will almost always require an equipment insurance policy that covers the replacement cost of their equipment and often (especially if you've never done business with them before and are a relatively low-budget production) a security deposit.

What do these extras buy you? *Security* ... knowing that you will have properly functioning equipment for the entire period that you have all your people there. Wasted time on a guerrilla production is the number one morale killer for both cast and crew, since they are most often giving you their time for little or no financial consideration.

I am always willing to spend a little extra in those key areas where I can ensure that no one's time will be wasted for the entire duration I have them on location. Whether it be renting the best possible equipment, or liability insurance that allows you to get permits and not be interrupted by the police, or spending extra time scouting a location to ensure that you have all your set-ups covered. Remember: *Good people and good equipment are essentials; everything else is negotiable.* This having been said, most of the times I have rented from individuals (mostly due to cost factors), their equipment has functioned satisfactorily.

However, if you are going to an individual renter blind, ask for references from previous jobs, then make sure you follow them up, especially asking for any additional renters they may know of, since the individual renting the equipment will only give you their most satisfied renters for reference. Ask around, ask other rental centers what they think of them (then take it with a pinch of salt), compare, shop around and don't jump into anything, no matter how tempting it may first appear.

Before we leave this section, I'd like to give you a few cost-cutting tips for rentals. The cheapest rental places are community-run (and subsidized) access centers, where equipment is available (once you become a member) for rental fees far below the going rate. Unfortunately this gear often shows the wear and tear of its many and varied renters, so beware. Some local universities also rent their equipment out at lower than market rates; ask around.

At the larger rental houses, the longer you continuously rent the equipment, usually the bigger the discount. Often, paying cash up front can get you a discount. Belonging to trade organizations such as the Independent Feature Project, Association of Independent Video and Filmmakers, etc., will also get you discounts. Often, if you rent during a slow period such as a holiday or weekends, you can get a discount. On weekends, many places will let you rent their equipment for the entire weekend while only paying for one day. These are all considerations you should take into account when putting together your budget and schedule.

A subdivision, so to speak, of renting equipment is renting equipment from the person who will be doing the actual job, such as renting your DP's camera or your sound person's DAT or Nagra. This is usually the way you'll get the best rental prices and the most favorable terms, but of course it comes with a big catch. If your DP or Sound person decides to walk, you're in deep trouble. This complication, which anyone renting their equipment and services is well aware of, can lead to subtle or not-too-subtle forms of blackmail on your set.

The lesson I learned from this was that I had to audition my crew, especially if I was going to be using their equipment, as carefully as my actors. I have done exactly that since then and have had no more problems like that. It's a matter of trust and experience, so if you are going to rent your DP's camera, lights, etc., make sure they're on your wavelength and they can be trusted.

The next option is to buy the equipment. Some people, especially control freaks, like to own the "means of production," which on a film or video production means (to most people) the cameras, lights and sound equipment. The catch to this is that, to me, the means of production are the *people*, not the equipment. Many people think that just because they own the equipment, they can take all the time they want to shoot their project. But I've found, even when I owned all the production equipment, it's the requirements of your cast and crew that will determine the length and duration of your schedule, not you owning the equipment. However, it does come in very handy if you have to go back after principal photography to get material you missed or for B roll material.

In addition, with today's ever-evolving technology, the equipment you buy today may be obsolete tomorrow, so you had better be sure there are other ways to get a return on your investment, beyond the production of this one project. Now of course, this doesn't take into account the "techie" or "gear-head" who lives for owning the next shiny new piece of state-of-the-art whatever.

If you are a techie, you probably have this aspect of the production puzzle solved, but make sure that the technology doesn't blind you to the people necessary to complete your vision. Films and videos are always *by* people and *for* people and if you become too enmeshed in the technical side, you can tend to block out those pesky people, who aren't as easy to manipulate as pixels on your computer screen.

I can best exemplify this problem by a young college grad, who had consulted with me regarding the lighting on his first no-budget feature. He wanted to light large locations, using only a small Lowell lighting kit, *and* to make it look like a Hollywood film. I told him he couldn't make it look like Hollywood, but that a perfectly good lighting effect could be achieved — if he only scaled his plans down. He ultimately decided not to take my advice and immediately ran into problems during production, which caused him to leave the project, letting his partners finish it without him.

A year or so later, he came to me again while planning his next production. He had come up with an incredibly complex plan using a confusing maze of technology involving wireless mics and mini disc recorders on all the actors — mainly, it seemed, to avoid interaction with a crew. Since the only rational for using this complex (and probably self-defeating) method was to avoid his unpleasant experience with the crew on his last production, I advised that it probably wouldn't work anyway and he'd be better off learning to work with a crew. The medium of film and video is not film, not video, not even money as Jean-Luc Godard likes to say, but *people*.

If you're buying equipment, obviously used equipment will be cheaper, but remember that all of its past problems will also come along with it when you purchase it. And if you're going to use it on your shoot, make sure you or someone else on your crew is well-versed in not only running it, but maintaining and fixing it as well. But even before you buy it, make sure you have an experienced technician look it over.

And run tests. If it's a film camera, run a few different rolls of film through it, develop them and scrutinize the projected results carefully. If it's a video camera, roll tape and check out the results, with a wave form monitor and vectorscope if at all possible. And make sure it's not stolen, if you can't get the original bill of sale; any reputable repair facility can probably do that for you for a small fee. Hell, maybe there's even a way that's free on the Internet ... if there is, I wish someone would let me know!

Obviously, buying new equipment poses fewer problems (other than the money) but probably requires more research to make sure it fits your needs. And remember, stay away from the fancy models with automatic everything, as nothing makes a film or video look or sound more amateurish than some automatic feature adjusting in the middle of a shot. That's always the mark of an amateur, especially if you're interested in trying to sell it later on. Every aspect of the camera, lighting and sound equipment should have the ability to be controlled manually.

As soon as you get the new equipment, check it out thoroughly by testing it under similar conditions to your shoot. Also, make sure you fill out and send in your warranty, but stay away from those extended service contracts many of the retailers try and sell you; they're generally a waste of money, since much of it is already covered by your original warranty. And it's almost always better to stick with the reliable brand names in the field. These equipment purchases are investments and you should take as much time researching and making them as you would any other large financial investment.

The main reasons for buying equipment are using it after your production to make money to pay back all the debts you'll accumulate on your own shoot or to satisfy your own personal need for technological involvement in the production process, allowing you to more fully achieve your dream or goal. Either is valid; just make sure you don't end up with an unused piece of equipment gathering dust in your closet. I wish I had a dollar for every unused digital camcorder.

Speaking of digital cameras, etc., now that the digital (it's still video!) revolution has been blessed by both the Sundance Film Festival and Hollywood, as well as almost everywhere else, I like to add a word about buying DV equipment. It's relatively cheap, it gives you more bang for the buck, 8.5 million people own one (okay, so I exaggerate a bit), people are hiring DPs according to what kind of DV camera they own, PBS is financing projects with the main criterion being that they be shot on DV and, like I said, most of this stuff sits in somebody's closet most of the time. If you will be using your DV camera quite a bit, go out and get one; if it's going to sit in your closet, go out and make a deal with someone, because there are an awful lot lying around. This includes edit systems as well. Just be aware that most of these people couldn't light their way out of a closet or cut a piece of paper, but some can and if you can find them, you might find a great deal.

Which leads us to our final category ... borrowing. Borrowing is by far the most financially viable option for the underground filmmaker, unless of course you break the stuff; then you're on your own because you probably won't have any insurance. But where do you borrow equipment? Friends, family, school, work, friend's family, friend's school, friend's work ... you get the picture. Anywhere you can talk someone into giving it to you or giving it to someone working for you.

Some people have enrolled in film school just to get access to the equipment (watch out for the waivers some of them have you sign regarding who owns the finished production). Some filmmakers have volunteered at Cable Access facilities or Community Film or Video Centers, some have interned at production facilities. Wherever there's unused equipment and a will, there's a way. Find it! Just make sure you take care of it like it's your own, because if you don't it may become yours, at a price you probably can't afford. To conclude this section, I just want to repeat: Check it out, check it out, check it out!

Equipment Insurance. Insurance and I have a love/hate relationship because it's becoming more and more necessary to have insurance while it's becoming more and more restrictive to get unless you're running a large production. But the good part is that once you have it, it allows you access to areas usually reserved for the *big boys*, i.e., Hollywood: free permits, free police, access to better equipment (if only to rent) and a certain legitimacy in the eyes of the powers-that-be. "Run and Gun" shooting with small digital video cameras makes it easier to "steal" locations, but nothing beats having a permit.

Regarding equipment insurance, it is necessary when renting from almost all (if not all) rental facilities. The amount will vary from place to place, so if you can find out in advance what the rental facility you choose requires, you may be able to save a few bucks here. But don't skimp on the coverage and don't lie on the forms; insurance companies love to turn down claims based on false information.

Guerrilla Insurance for Equipment. Guerrilla Insurance is alternatives and nowhere is this more vital than with equipment. Some piece of equipment invariably will go wrong during your shoot, usually at the most inopportune moment. Hopefully it's just a cable or light bulb, but make sure you have back-ups for every piece of equipment. Now I'm not saying to have a fully loaded truck full of lighting and grip equipment and a second camera sitting around, but what I am saying is to make sure that for every major piece of equipment, camera, tripod, lights, mics, audio recorder, you have arranged and/or anticipated an emergency situation so that you can replace any piece of equipment within a few hours.

In addition, because you may be getting your equipment along with the person who owns it and you probably are paying little or no money, it's very conceivable, no matter how much they may swear to the contrary, that they may leave you, taking their equipment with them, if a higher paying job comes along. Have back-ups, both for cast and crew as well as equipment, in mind; it never hurts.

And for the more heavily used but less critical equipment like cables, stands, scrims, etc., make sure that you have back-ups or someone in your crew who is competent to immediately fix whatever problem may pop up. There's nothing worse than 15 to 20 people standing around while someone has to rush out to buy an audio adapter for a back-up cable that doesn't have the correct connection. Having back-ups and easy alternatives to every piece of equipment is the best equipment insurance.

Budgeting Locations

The key to saving money on locations is finding as many as you can that cost little or nothing, then filming as many scenes as possible at those locations. They then can be supplemented with those locations you may have to pay a fee for. And remember, the old Val Lewton trick of having one really outstanding location where you try and stage as many scenes as possible. Now of course many independent films (*Night of the Living Dead, El Mariachi, Faces* and on and on) based their entire production on one particularly striking location or a variety of readily available ones, all owned by family or friends and costing nothing. But as I mentioned earlier, I've never believed that an available location should dictate your story, but rather your story should dictate your locations. It's up to you to find and secure them.

Liability insurance is one expense you may have to include, in order to reassure those people whose property you will be using that if anything does get damaged, it will be repaired or replaced. I personally recommend it, although I know of a great many filmmakers who have gone ahead without it. My rationale for having it is that it allows longer, uninterrupted access to more varied locations while putting the location owner more at ease. It will also allow you to shoot on public property such as parks, city streets, government buildings, etc., where liability insurance is a necessity. In places such as New York City, the local film commission will provide free police (if needed) for the cost of a liability policy, making the entire city your location.

The alternative is "stealing locations" which is a time-honored underground filmmaker technique. Just like a guerrilla fighter, you, your cast and crew swoop down into a location, set up quickly, get the shot(s) and are out of there before anyone can notice or complain. This requires a detailed reconnoitering before hand, to find out the lay of the land with any potential problems or special features, allowing you to anticipate any problems before they can occur.

The only snag with this approach is if you're found out and your shooting is stopped. Nothing can demoralize your cast and crew quicker than wasting their time by being chased from a location, especially if they are being underpaid or not paid. Of course, if your cast and crew are *into* this guerrilla filming approach (and I admit that it does cause the adrenaline to pump), then use this method as part of your filmmaking technique of getting your cast and crew up for their great adventure.

Once you've secured any and all of the locations you can get for little or money, go back over all those locations and see if, by minor adjustments, any of them can be made into a location you don't already have. As you may remember from the Patron Saint's Chapter, a great way to save money is by redressing an already existing set for little or no additional money. This will also save transportation costs of moving everyone to another location for something you may be able to pick up by moving to another room in the same building or apartment.

An example from my film *Death Desire*: For a scene that depicted a film being shot in a large loft space, we reused that same very same loft space dressed for a party scene, then redressed it as a smoky barroom, then redressed it again as the actress' bedroom, all without moving cast, crew or equipment. Doing this saved at least one day on our schedule, which on a 14-day schedule is nothing to sneeze at.

Once you have run down and reused all your free or low-fee locations, you have to begin negotiating for your other locations. This is where the liability insurance becomes vital, as most businesses or strangers will want to see this before allowing you into their spaces. However, if you are gifted with a silver tongue and not enough money for liability insurance, remember the allure that being involved in a film production has for most people.

After you begin negotiating for locations, it's usually best to emphasize how really low-budget your production is, but of course reminding them what a huge "up side" potential your project has, helping to promote their business, if and when your film or video is successful. Almost everyone wants to be part of the Movie's Magic and it's your duty to help people attain that (while keeping your own costs considerably lower). Make businesses see the promotional possibilities by appearing in your film or by donating products or services to your film. And if that doesn't work, try bartering your services to produce a promotional video and/or commercial for them.

Also remember to include as many locations into one setting when you're negotiating location fees. For example, say you need a hotel setting in a town where you'll have to house your cast and crew. See if you can negotiate a deal for a location which doubles for housing. I did that on my film *Transgression*, where we used our main location (the killer's house in the country) as our primary housing and meal-serving location. That was also a great way to save time and money going to and from the location.

In conclusion, remember there are two kinds of locations, favorable or unfavorable. Make sure that your production is based near the favorable ones, thereby saving yourself time, money and aggravation.

BUDGETING SETS

On a low-budget production today, unless you are getting a standing set for free or next to nothing, it will probably be too expensive. However, if it's a location that's impossible to find or get permission to use in your area, then it may be possible to build a low-budget variation for a fraction of the cost of securing the real thing.

Let me give you an example from one of my films. I needed a jail set and we found a convenient and available cell in a small town in New Jersey, as well as a more elaborate and expensive one via the New York City Mayor's Office for Film and TV. But we only needed the set for a half day. Needing to do a variety of lighting set-ups ruled out the New Jersey one, while the New York City one was way beyond our limited budget.

Our solution was to rent (for $100) a set of painted wooden jail bars and door from a local New York City outfit that did scenery for operas. We then hauled it upstate and put it in the corner of our set for the killer's hideaway. We then exposed the cinderblock wall and left the other side open, using the frame of the camera as our other wall. By keeping the light off the wooden bars, it was impossible to tell they were wood; when the door was closed, we dubbed in a loud metallic *clang*. This allowed us much more flexibility, saved time on our schedule and cost considerably less. It's not what you see, but what the camera sees.

You should build only when you cannot find or afford the actual location, and then build only what you absolutely need to see in that particular shot, keeping your material costs as low as possible. It only matters what it looks like on the screen, so never buy plywood when foam-core will do; never build a wall if you don't have to see it (either use your framing as the other unseen wall or fake it with drapery); never paint if you can drape colored fabric or gel your lights or camera lens. Finally, what you can't afford to build, leave in the shadows and "build and/or hide" it with your lighting. Hell, I "built" an entire prison and execution chamber with just light, shadow and one panel of Plexiglas.

Watch any of Edgar Ulmer's later films (especially *Detour* or *Bluebeard*) and you will learn more about making something out of nothing than you can find in any book on set design. If you use your imagination, so will your audience, so use yours and you may be surprised at the results.

Location and/or Set Considerations. Whether it's a phone booth on that lonely but photogenic corner or a cemetery in Brooklyn with a panoramic view of Manhattan, I'm always looking for and storing interesting locations in the back of my mind. The minute I walk into a friend's apartment, I size it up as a possible location and over the years this has served me well. To me, the *where*, the location, is of prime importance to the story I'm telling; whether it's a gritty realistic crime drama or a fairy tale for children, your locations go a long way in setting the unique visual tone of your story.

This also happens to be the most cost-effective way of finding locations: doing it yourself, long before production begins, before the script or story is even written. In this way you mold your future production to spaces that you've already been to, spaces where you may have already figured out the best angles, the best times of day, determined the accessibility to electricity and proximity to mass transit. And since they belong to a friend, you also have a pretty good idea that you can get permission for little or nothing.

Now of course, you probably aren't going to be able to find all the locations yourself. If this isn't something you're good at, how do you find the people to find the rest of the locations? Ask the people around you, those who you've already chosen for your production. Ask them to go through the story or script and see if they have any suggestions. Most of the time you won't even *have* to ask. Then make arrangements to go to the location and see it with them, if at all possible.

I think that it's vital that you actually go to the location before shooting to get an idea of it. Because although a film ends up as a two-dimensional illusion of a three-dimensional world, the actual making of the film is a very three-dimensional business between the camera, the sound recording, the lighting and the actors and actresses. The actual production is really a very sculptural experience and nothing prepares you for this better than physically being in the location.

Another source of people to assist in finding locations are those who have worked on your previous productions—another reason that it pays to build long-term relationships. Between these two groups of people, I have never had a bad or mundane location. But if you aren't good at or unable to find the right location, make sure you can find someone who can.

A great way of finding locations in a town where you don't have any contacts: visit a local real estate office. Often they will have fully furnished homes waiting to be sold, and they are more than happy to rent them out for a couple of days or weeks for what can be a lot of money for them and not too much for you. You can kill two birds with one stone by housing your cast and crew there as well.

Another way of finding locations is the want ads in your local paper. This can be especially effective for summer sublets outside of a city area that you might not know about. The excitement of being a movie location can be contagious; it's your job to spread it.

Last but not least is your area film commission. Whether it be local or state, they can be very helpful. Although they obviously can give more help to larger-scale productions, it's always worth it to check with them, because even if they don't give you the right place at the right price, they may put you in contact with someone who may. And this is where the question of liability insurance begins to come up. To take full advantage of the commissions, you will probably have to have a certificate of insurance on file with them, but I would bet you could make some use of them for awhile, without having any.

And if it's the first time someone's been approached about having their place used as a location, they will probably be more willing than if you've used their place before. Because even the most organized production will throw most households/ business locations into chaos for the duration of their usually brief stay and people who have never been "invaded" will not know this.

This brings up an important reminder for the guerrilla filmmaker: If you plan on making more than one film guerrilla-style, you must always treat each and every single location like your own home (for some of you, even better than your own home!) because you will probably, somewhere down the line, have to ask to use that particular place again. If you've treated them and their property with special care, you may be able to get back in again. If not, forget about it!

This matter of courtesy, respect and care must be instilled in each and every member of your crew as the number one rule while on location. The larger the crew, the harder this becomes, but it's your job to make sure it happens. Any "accidents" may have to be paid out of your pocket, even if you have insurance, as most policies will most likely have a deductible, which seems to grow larger year after year.

Personally, whether I have insurance or not, I prefer to keep a low profile, believing that it affords me more creative opportunities and/or options, *if* I can be quick enough to respond to them. But then that's my personal thing and how you choose to go about conducting yourself on location is your choice. Just be aware that how you go about it will in a large degree determine how well your production moves along or not.

Obviously the location must first of all *look* right or have the *ability* to look right with little or no alteration. Especially on a guerrilla production, the less set dressing a location needs, the better it is. This isn't a matter of accepting whatever's available and cheap, but a matter of spending the amount of time necessary to find just the right place.

When Hollywood goes out on location, they spend an inordinate amount of time making the area look like a set. The underground filmmaker's strategy should be the opposite, using what's there while intelligently highlighting all the visual elements which fulfill the needs of your story. Study the best times of the day (or night) for the light or the ambient sounds, study the furniture, the walls, then use the elements that enhance your film and hide those which don't, either by your lighting or shadows or artfully placed drapes, rugs or sheets.

If you have a production designer or art director, work as closely with them as time will permit. Show them, either by photos or films or videos, the kind of things you're looking for as well as the kind of budget you're working with. I prefer to do everything on video, because I like to see things mediated by the lens of a video camera. But if you prefer Polaroids or 35mm stills or drawings or whatever, be my guest. Let your designer know how much or little you want them to change your locations, how much or how little assistance they will have in doing this and, as much as possible, try and keep things visual when communicating with them.

The second important criterion of a location is how "filming friendly" it is, i.e., whether there's room to position the camera for the kind of shots you want with the lens you have, whether there is enough room for all your lights or your camera dolly, enough power for your lights, windows with good natural light or if they can easily be gelled or curtained. Are the floors quiet or squeaky, are the neighbors loud, how will they react to the filming, are there annoying ambient sounds, is there construction going on in the vicinity, is there adequate room for your cast and crew to stay out of camera range when shooting, is there more than one bathroom, can this location be used as a fall-back option if you're rained out of some exterior location, are the owners fussy or neat (watch out!), will you have to pay for the occupants to stay somewhere else while you film, how much work will the place need to make it look right for your scene, will you have trouble getting the equipment in and out, can you store it there overnight and a hundred other things depending on how fussy you are.

The third important consideration for the location is how accessible it is for your cast and crew. Basically, on an underground production you want to eliminate any expense you possibly can and what better way than to pick locations that are easily accessible to most of your cast and crew, eliminating the rental of extra cars or vans or having to pay to transport a large group to some distant location.

Especially in a large city, when you can set up most of the locations accessible to mass transit, you can't help but save money. But even in the countryside, by picking locations that are easily accessible for everyone, the amount of travel time is cut down and the amount of time available to sleep can be increased. This is especially important, because I have never been on a low-budget feature where everyone got enough sleep. And let me tell you, by the last few days, it really shows.

Another consideration regarding location is how accessible it is from the previous location and its proximity to the next location. This is especially crucial if you have multiple locations that you have to cover in a short period of time. If you have to do more than one move in a day, you had better make sure you don't have to cross a busy part of town at rush hour, unless you have a back door route set-up. Try to have all your locations in the same part of town or city, lumped together on your schedule; you'll save time, money and energy.

Another major consideration regarding your location choice should be the kind of neighborhood it's located in. Is it an area where you can slip in and out unobtrusively? Or is it an area where the neighbors will complain about the noise or too many parked cars or people walking on their lawn? If it's an exterior, will you have trouble controlling the heavy flow of people or is it anonymous enough that you can camouflage your production in the crowd? This was also covered earlier, in more detail, in the chapter on guerrilla warfare.

Once you have found the right location, you should immediately go about securing it for your production. If you know the people, it obviously going to be a lot simpler, but the same procedure should be used. First off, you should make sure that the location is available for the specific times you will need it, alerting them to the inevitable delays that may occur.

Then make sure that you agree on the financial terms, obviously for as little as possible. But you will be amazed how much the lure of being a movie location has for small business owners, who may only ask that you feature their sign in the film and/or put a little mention of their establishment in the credits. Work this angle for all its worth, it'll get you into some great locations and it's cheap.

You should assure the location owner that you and your cast and crew will treat their property with all the respect that you would your own home. By the way, you should also mean that! If you have insurance that should be mentioned right after this, as trying to secure a location from people you don't know is especially difficult without insurance.

Last but not least, you should try and sign a location agreement with the owner of the property; although it's not 100 percent necessary, it can be helpful. And make sure it's signed by the *owner* of the property — not the tenant or super. Only the owner or his legal representative can do this. This form can usually be found in a variety of production resource books or on the Internet. It gives the specific dates and times the location is to be used, the amount of money to be paid and any issues of liability as well as promising to leave the place as you found it. It also may entail a security deposit, which can sometimes be hard to get back, especially if the owner turns out to be an asshole.

Dressing the Right Location. Once you have secured the right location, your production designer, art director, etc., should begin to accentuate the positive and camouflage the negative. The first thing to remember about locations is that nothing matters except what appears on your finished film or tape. I'll always remember my first visit to a local TV station as part of a TV production class at Rochester Institute of Technology. We walked over to the News Room set and the lower part of the news desk including the station's logo was absolutely filthy with dust. I looked at that and wondered what the hell was going on. Well, they blasted the lights on (in those days they had to blast them on) and when I looked at the picture on the studio monitor, everything looked perfect.

It doesn't matter what you see; it only matters what the camera sees. To the camera, polyester can look as lovely as silk — sometimes better because it doesn't wrinkle. I've used cheap polyester jacket lining to make many of my sets look rich for only a few dollars. In fact on *Death Desire*, I was able to color coordinate all four bedrooms of four different couples with what looked like silk sheets, but was in fact only cheap polyester.

In *Daddy*, Sheriff Sylvia Carlsen (Celia Hansen) attempts to question her friend Alison Headly (Bevin McGraw), in Alison's home (our basecamp) (photograph courtesy Celia Hansen).

Often, just by eliminating certain elements at a location, you can achieve your desired effect with little or no cost. We were in a relatively nice studio apartment in New York City that was decorated with quite a few beautiful paintings, color photos and sculptures, but the place was supposed to belong to a poor slob of a writer. By taking down about a third of the paintings and most of the photos, then covering a lovely upright piano with an old blanket and replacing the custom drapes with an old dirty sheet, we were able to transform the entire apartment in a couple of hours.

It's very difficult and time-consuming to build a set from scratch; for the guerrilla filmmaker, low-budget dressing and redressing is the favored remedy. Think of your character who lives there and then take out everything that doesn't belong to them. If you can't remove it, hide it or camouflage it. If you can't do that leave it in the shadows or out of your camera's frame.

Re-dressing the Same Location. Re-dressing or reusing the same location is the best way to shave days off your schedule, saving time, money and your people's energy. It is a time-honored underground filmmaker strategy that is specifically singled out by Edgar Ulmer, Val Lewton and Roger Corman, while being used by practically all the "Patron Saints of the Underground."

Ulmer would shoot all of his closeups on the last day of shooting and against a neutral wall. Lewton would redress standing sets, turning a church into an insane asylum or the staircase for Orson Welles' *The Magnificent Ambersons* into the staircase for the young girl's apartment in *Cat People*. And one of Corman's key suggestions to new directors is to reuse standing locations.

I have used the same loft as a film set, a smoke-filled night club, a gangster's apartment, a party set and a porn queen's bedroom, all in my film *Death Desire*, and no one could tell. I also used my apartment, for same film, as a mob boss' apartment as well as the apartment of one of his underlings, just by moving the camera a few feet. Just by these two instances, I saved at almost two days on my 14–day schedule and if you don't think that made a huge difference, you might as well wait until Hollywood knocks on your door.

Look around you, you don't have to show every part of every location you use. But you should be thinking about trying to reuse every location you have as another location, either by using another room or another angle or re-dressing what's already there. Hell, you could probably use the same room for two different locations, if it's

For *Daddy*, the author's bedroom was transformed into the Sheriff's Office after a couple hours' work (photograph by Christopher Philippo).

large enough, just by turning the camera around and never showing the reverse angle (or cover the reverse angle in shadow or with a sheet or drape or whatever). Always think about multiplying your possibilities and you will save time, money and energy.

Finally, if you must travel to a distant location, make sure that any place that serves as a major location can do double duty as a place to house your cast and crew. Just make sure to try and keep the place where your crew is living separate from where you will be doing the actual shooting. Nothing can cause inadvertent continuity problems more than having coffee cups and such suddenly appearing in your shots, left behind by a forgetful crew member.

And if you have to use a hotel or motel, make sure that you somehow have incorporated some part of that location into your story. Hotel/motel rooms are great standing sets waiting to be used. And I guarantee you that I've used that routine more than once.

Guerrilla Insurance for Locations. Options! Options! Options! As I can't repeat too often, having creative alternatives for every aspect of your production is the best low-/no-cost insurance you can have. You should have a back-up location for every single location on your schedule. They probably won't be as good, visually or logistically, but they may save your ass if that time ever arises.

Exteriors are always vulnerable due to changing weather conditions, so have a sheltered exterior alternative or have a back-up interior location available at short notice. One that you saved for just that contingency or one that can be put off until the last day of principal photography.

Now you say that you have insurance, city permits, signed location agreements, assured cooperation, the whole nine yards ... why would you need to have back-ups? Let's say you have found the perfect apartment for one of your key scenes and, because it is so critical to your story, you've placed it near the end of your schedule. The day arrives, you're all set to start shooting and they suddenly start construction and/or demolition on the building next door. Do you go Italian Style and shoot without sound and dub later or shoot yourself right there?

Or as the day progresses, you keep inadvertently blowing out power, pissing off the upstairs neighbor who begins banging on their floor whenever you try a take. Or you've scheduled the last three days for exteriors and an unexpected storm decides to sit over your area for the next four days. Or you only got a certain actor or actress for one day on an exterior location and it begins to snow, not matching anything else you've already shot. Don't laugh, variations of all these things have happened. By having back-ups, I was able to avoid disaster. So can you, so should you.

Budgeting Film/Video Stock

Question: How much film or video stock will you need?
Answer: As little as possible.
But what is "as little as possible?" Well, that will depend how you plan on shooting your film or video. With video, this is not as crucial with film — but remember, every budget item has its hidden counterpart somewhere else. So that even though

videotape is quite a bit less expensive than film, the more you shoot, the more window dubs you may need for your rough cut, the more you may have to load or lose in your non-linear edit, the more you may have to sit through picking your takes and the longer (and costlier) your edit.

Most independent features have approximately a 10:1 shooting ration, that is, for every foot of film used in the final edit, ten feet have been shot to reach that point. This is a very general rule, as I know some films that have shot as low as 2:1, while others have gone as high as 20:1, with some as high as 100:1! My own films run about 5:1, even though I improvise and use a moving camera.

The amount of film you budget for should be a result of your (and your DP's) analysis of your script and your shooting methods. Obviously a two-hour film will use more film stock than a 75–minute film and a filmmaker who "covers" every scene from multiple angles will use more than a filmmaker who shoots only those angles they need for their edit. And of course, how much money you have in your budget may go a long way in determining what your shooting ratio may be. But whatever it is, only by consulting with your DP can you be sure that what you have (financially) matches up with what you want to do and how you want to accomplish it.

Coverage, that is shooting long shots, medium shots and closeups of every scene, uses up more film, and long, complicated shots use up more film —*unless* you are very organized with an experienced crew. *Then* they can actually use less film. Improvisation uses more film —*unless* you are very organized with an experienced cast and crew. Not knowing what you want, while only finding out on the set when shooting, takes up a lot more film. Being a perfectionist takes up more film than anything else.

What kind of film stock do you buy? Because I am visually biased, I always buy the best film stock I can possibly afford, which to me means Kodak. But this is an area where priorities come into play. If you feel you will need quite a bit of stock to shoot the way you want and can only achieve this by buying less expensive stock, then you should. If you believe you have to pay your actors or actresses more money to get the kind of actors or actresses that you need, but are not as particular about the look of your film, then pay your actors or actresses more.

One way to save money on film stock is to buy recanned film or short ends. Recanned film is a full roll or can of film that was bought but never used by someone else's production. There are brokers for this kind of film stock, especially in Los Angeles and New York, and they can save you considerable money. Make sure you consult with your d.p. first and have your lab do a test before you use any recanned stock.

Short ends are those leftover bits of film that were unused by filmmakers when they were shooting a scene and felt there wasn't enough left on the roll to finish their next take. (Or they changed the type of film stock for some reason.) These can come in practically any length and are the cheapest way of buying film.

The drawbacks are that your scenes may not visually match — even shots in the same scene may not match! Also, nothing is more annoying to an actor or actress than doing their *big* scene and having the camera run out of film in the middle. But this is the world of guerrilla cinema and they may have to get used to it.

One final note: With today's increasingly fast (ASA–wise) film stocks, there is a real savings to be had by using less lighting and camera equipment and still achieve striking professional results. Some of the newer stocks cost a little bit more, but what they save in reduced lighting, transportation and crew costs may more than compensate for their extra expense. And don't forget extra take-up reels, film cans and changing bags!

For videotape, things are slightly different. Processing the tape is not necessary; only the actual cost of tape stock is to be considered. Although even here there are options. Once again, as with the film stock, I have my prejudices. I prefer Maxell, TDK or Fuji tape stock to all others, this being my own personal preference over years using practically all the brands out there.

The main thing you should be looking for in videotape is that it has as few dropouts as possible and that the adhesive used to stick the metal (usually) particles to the tape have a durability to adhere for as long as possible. This also means that you should always buy the professional stock; although it costs more, it will more than pay for itself over the long run. I've been able to play and actually re-edit some of my videotapes from over 15 years ago because I bought the top-of-the-line stock, which has lasted. If you're in this for the long haul, you should see quality tape stock as an investment, not an expense.

There are various studies out there and some of the technical video magazines will periodically do tests. Your DP probably has a preference and if he does, sound him out as to *why* he prefers what he does. If it sounds reasonable to you, I would probably go along with his decision, but if you have any reservations, you should conduct your own research.

Because tape stock is relatively inexpensive compared to film stock, there is a tendency to shoot way more than you need and sort it out in the editing. Unfortunately, most films that do that usually look just like that. But there are additional expenses that will come around if you use a lot of videotape, such as having to have them time-coded for your rough cut as well as having to have your editor sit through it all. Shooting a lot of videotape also takes up time and your actors' and actresses' energy. Know what you want or what you're after and use as much as you need, but don't run tape because of your indecision.

Also, a word on the smaller videotape stocks like Hi-8 and DV. Once you shoot with these tapes, ideally, you should never play them back until the final edit, only making window dubs for your rough cut. The reason of this is that the small gauge of the tape stock makes them especially susceptible to tape dropout — and dropout on such small tapes can look like golf balls. *Avoid playback.* I know there's no way to avoid it entirely, just try and keep it to the bare minimum.

BUDGETING AUDIOTAPE STOCK

Obviously, the amount of film or videotape stock for which you budget will determine the amount of audiotape that you need to budget for. Once again, as with the videotape, I prefer Maxell, TDK and Fuji for my audio stock; do your own research or ask your sound person.

A personal quirk of my own is that I like to have my sound person do "wild takes" of any ambient sound they think may contribute to the project's final sound mix. It can be anything from a noisy refrigerator, to hot water pipes banging and sizzling, to a bird singing outside the window. I want my sound person to feel free to explore the soundscape of the shoot in the same way a camera operator shooting a B roll camera would. And for this, I usually budget an extra roll or two of audio tape. I also add two or three rolls for the post-production period, as I often will go out to find supplementary sounds for the audio mix, as well as occasionally doing my own Foley work.

Film/Video/Audio Stock Considerations. Where do you buy your film or tape stock? For film stock, it is in your best interests that the film all come from the same batch to assure a certain uniformity of manufacture. (In film much more than videotape, this is a consideration that can show up on the screen.) So buy all your stock at the same time and from the same source. I usually get all my stock directly from the manufacturer, but reputable dealers in your area will probably have enough quality stock for your needs. If you plan on using a stock that is not commonly used, I would suggest checking with them in advance as to its availability in the amounts that you'll need.

Once again, organizations such as the Independent Feature Project and the AIVF have discount programs for the purchase of raw stock, both film and video. But some people swear they get better discounts on their own and those organizations' discounts also can sometimes be limited to specific types and/or amounts of stock. It may be more worth your while to buy a particular non-discounted stock that is better suited to your production's needs. On one of my recent films, my DP and I had decided upon a new, faster stock of 16mm film that wasn't available at the member discount, but because the new film was more light-sensitive than the discounted stocks, we figured it would more than pay for the difference in the discount by our having to use less lighting. We were right and the effects we achieved were well worth it.

If you're buying recanned film in any kind of quantity, you should do a test before filming, to ensure its quality. And always try to buy from a reputable reseller, not from someone you've never met who is offering a great deal over the Internet. And if you're using short ends, good luck.

I usually have my DP store the film and bring whatever he deems necessary on each day of the shoot, although it's something I discuss with them beforehand. You don't want to be stuck on location and run out of film. Once you've brought the stock home it should be kept in a refrigerator, but must be restored to room temperature a full eight hours before filming.

Once you've exposed your film, get it to the lab as soon as possible, making sure that it's on a camera spool or on a core and put in a black paper bag. Then in the film can, with the can being taped around the edge. Most labs will provide a film bag where you can put all your exposed stock.

You will probably have to set up an account with the lab beforehand and make sure that when your film is dropped off, it's labeled with the title of the production, a description of the film materials, the amount of footage, the services you desire and whether you will pick it up (usually) or have it sent somewhere. And if you only want selected takes printed or dailies made, you will have to provide a copy of the camera report with the selects clearly marked. Once it's been processed, have your processed stock and the film or video dailies picked up as soon as possible. You want to be able to look at your first results as soon as you can to check for any camera or film stock or processing problems.

When you buy your videotape for your shoot, you should also buy all of the tape at the same time from the same supplier, although this is not as crucial as it is with film stock. Stick with the brand that you've decided upon with your DP and always try and get the top-of-the-line product, as it's much more likely to withstand the test of time.

Like film stock, videotape should be kept in a dry, cool, dust-free space away from any strong electromagnetic fields. Unlike the film stock, I store it and bring along with me. And once we shoot the video, I take back it with me, to make window dubs and store at my place. I try never to screen my master tapes (except to make the window dubs from which I will run any other copies) until the final edit, as running a videotape always entails the risk of adding dropout and even occasionally getting stuck in a player. At this stage, that's not a risk I want to run, but that's up to you. However, if you must check something shot on videotape while on location, never scan the tape; fast-forward and rewind, but try to avoid running the tape over the heads, and only play back the take you need to see.

Budgeting Supplies

Go through your script, outline, whatever you're using, and make a list of *anything* that will be used up during production (that you can't beg, borrow or steal from family, friends, cast and crew), with its approximate price. Then go through your written plan again; anything else you will need to achieve or build or that will aid in your production gets added, along with its price, such as: photocopies, still photography film, stationary, batteries, paint, brushes, fuses, makeup, shoe dye, towels, blankets, nails, screws, hammers, light fixtures, fog machine rental, coffee maker, paper cups, AC extensions, paper, ink markers, fluorescent light fixtures and everything else that you (or anyone else) can think of.

Budgeting Wardrobe

Most wardrobe on low-budget films is provided by the actors and actresses themselves, in consultation with the filmmaker, the art director and possibly the DP. When you are figuring out your wardrobe budget, you should be looking through your written plans for any piece of wardrobe that is out of the ordinary. It could be a uniform, a special pair of shoes, a bizarre piece of lingerie, anything that may be ruined in shooting or that you may need multiple copies of due to special effects (for instance, what if you're going to shoot a stabbing from four or five different camera set-ups?).

Then either go out and price those items or, if you have someone on board like an art director or a particularly fashion-conscious production assistant, have them go out and price them. Obviously, second-hand stores or flea markets can be of great assistance, as well as buying things from clothing stores and then returning them — that is, if they haven't been too abused during shooting.

WARDROBE CONSIDERATIONS

Every piece of clothing that your cast wears is important. If it isn't important to you ... find someone to whom it is. I personally dress every member of my cast. No, I don't go with them into the bathroom and help them on with their socks and shoes, but I either pick out or approve everything that everybody wears in my films.

Sometimes this causes problems because the actor or actress doesn't personally like what I have them wearing, but I don't care, because I know what their character would be wearing and that's what's important. I also know that it will fit into my color scheme for the entire film, something they don't have to be concerned with.

If you're not this fussy about what your actors or actresses are wearing, then you should find someone who is. It can be your production designer/art director or a student from a nearby fashion school or a local artist. They should have a good eye for color and fabric, know what does and does not look good on camera and know where to go for bargains that look great. If they can't be there on set all the time taking care of the clothes, they should at least be available to go out alone or with you and the cast to help select their wardrobe.

You really have to see how the clothes look on someone, how they move on the actor or actress, before buying them for your film. On my first couple of films, I had too many unpleasant surprises by not going along when the clothes were picked out or made. In addition, before you actually buy the clothing, make sure you ask your actor or actress their opinion about the garment. How it feels, is it comfortable, does it fit, etc.? They may have a valid complaint that you should listen too or they may not, but you want to know how they feel before you get on set in front of the rest of the cast and crew.

And remember, any clothing involved in an action sequence where it might get dirty or soiled has to be bought in multiples of the exact same piece for as many takes as you anticipate or can afford. In addition, to save the expense of a wardrobe person, I assign the responsibility of their wardrobe's upkeep to the individual actor or actress. I'm more than willing to pay the occasional dry cleaning bill if I can cut down on an extra crew member.

On a low-budget production, your actors and actresses can be your best way to save money on wardrobe by using their own clothing, as long as it fits into your visual scheme. But you must be willing to reimburse them for anything ruined or any cleaning bills due to the shoot. It's generally not a good idea to have them risk their own clothes in any kind of action or stunt, due to the ill will it can create. Buy your own low-cost multiples for these scenes.

This is another area where the additional expenditure of a few dollars may make the difference between your movie looking like amateur hour and a professional production. That's why it's so important not to compromise with what's going to appear on the screen. If someone offers to make you something and it looks like amateur night, thank them, then go right out and spend the money to make it look right.

Borrowing from People. For the underground filmmaker, the key to saving money is never pay for what you can borrow. And as I mentioned before, using your cast's own clothing should be your first stop when gathering wardrobe. I usually will go over to each actor or actresses apartment and look over what they have for their own character's wardrobe, while making mental notes of anything that might be appropriate for other cast members. And just as I used the cast and crew as a resource for finding a location, I also use them as a resource for finding wardrobe and props. They are motivated; use that motivation.

Also, I usually work with people who have their own small theater or dance company and over the years I've donated many of my leftover costumes or fabrics to their collections. (Of course, with the proviso that should I ever need to borrow them again or anything else they have, I may.) This has consistently worked out to all of our benefits. The value of a team approach over the years cannot be underestimated. Needless to say, this team approach to wardrobe can also be extended to your family and friends who are usually more than happy to help out, if they can.

"Borrowing" from Stores. After you've exhausted borrowing clothes from everyone you know, the next step is to borrow them from large stores. No, I don't mean stealing them, I mean buying, then returning them after production, an old trick I learned when working for a department store. They did it all the time with the stuff the models wore. Just make sure it looks like it did when you bought it. This is where a wardrobe person can come in handy; if you're "borrowing" enough clothing from stores, it may be worth it to add this extra member to your crew.

Any shoes should have their soles carefully taped over with gaffer's tape, making sure that it doesn't show on camera. It keeps them from getting scuffed and peels off without leaving any sticky residue. Labels should be taped or pinned back. Hems have to be pinned and folded but not pressed. And you constantly have to be on guard for the smearing of the actor's or actress' makeup on the shirt or jacket collars. If there are any stains, you should try and immediately remove them with a cold, damp cloth, then repressing or steaming them before you try to return them.

Last but not least, don't return everything at the same time. The returning should be handled by the person with the most experience or the most nerve. If it's not you, find out who is experienced in this department; there's usually at least one on every set.

Buying. And when everything else fails, you just have to break down and buy the right wardrobe. But never at full cost, unless it's absolutely, positively necessary. This means that the first place you begin looking is at flea markets and used clothing stores, including the Salvation Army. Now of course, by being a city boy, I've totally forgotten the yard or garage sale. In practically every small town and city in America, there are yard and garage sales going on all the time during spring, summer and fall (and winter in the warmer states); find them, as many as you can in your neck of the woods. As soon as you know you're going into production, begin scouring them for your wardrobe and prop needs. You should have a breakdown of every outfit you need and this is when you begin looking.

Your next stop is the smaller, off-chain, discount clothing stores that are all over, especially in the larger cities. Some of these places can give you better prices on new (although some are flawed) clothing than some thrift stores do for second-hand goods. In New York City, there are places where I can get great-looking new suits that are cheaper than the second-hand stores. It's in these places that you can also pick up any current fashion knock-offs for a fraction of the cost. Up-close and in person it's obvious the stuff is a cheap variation, but your camera probably won't be able to tell the difference. This is where you can get any T-shirts, underwear, socks, stockings, slippers, pajamas, etc., as well as many cheap props. After you've covered the off-chain discount stores, only then do you hit the larger national chains.

And your stop of last resort is the regular retail store or small specialty store where you know you can get what you need, but usually not for a price that you want to pay. Some of the more specialized stores in large cities will let you rent some of their more expensive items for a film or video shoot at a fraction of their cost plus a security deposit. Don't forget to try this option, adding that you will give them a nice large credit at the end of your film. Also remember to check out sales sections in all the stores, which are usually hidden somewhere in the back. Take one of your "shop-aholic" friends with you, I'm sure they'll know where to look. When you're in these places, look for damaged items and see if they'll knock the price down for you. Again, if it won't show on camera, it doesn't matter.

Guerrilla Insurance for Wardrobe. As with everything else on your list, make sure you have backups on any piece of wardrobe that you're not sure will look right on camera. When your actors and actresses come to the location, ask them to bring a couple of each item, if at all possible. You never know when something which looked perfectly fine in the store will look perfectly awful in your location. The more options you have, the better able you will be able to adjust.

One final note: I usually let the cast keep any piece of clothing that I buy for their character and can't be returned. Not only is it the least you can do, considering that you're probably not paying the going rate, but if they know that, they take better care of their wardrobe. And if you should ever need it on some future production, you'll know where to find that particular piece of wardrobe ... hey, ya never know.

Budgeting Props

I have included props as separate from supplies principally because I believe props to be of prime importance to any film or video. They are, in effect, your silent, immobile characters, capable of conveying great emotional story values, if chosen and presented with care. This doesn't mean that you have to spend a great amount of money, but you must have exactly the right object that the scene calls for.

It must *look* right to your camera's eye which will become the eye of the audience.

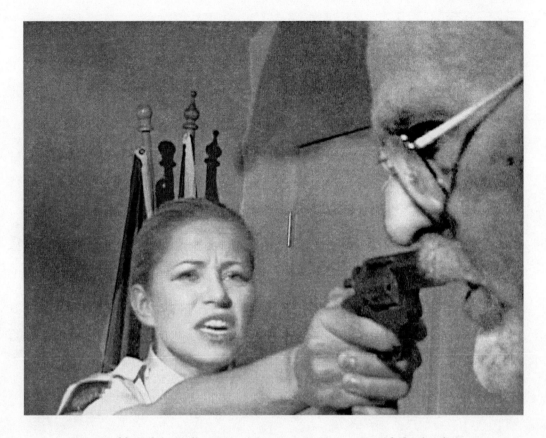

In *Daddy*, Sylvia (Celia Hansen) turns on Dr. Vance (David Shepherd).

For example, nice shiny satin polyester actually looks better on film than real silk (no wrinkles), so you can have a wonderful polyester bedspread that appears to be and *is* silk for the audience. Or in a long shot or at night, a fake plastic gun may appear to be as real as the actual weapon.

However, there are times when only the real thing will do and, if you want to convey this reality to your audience, you'd better go out and get the genuine article. For example in *Daddy*, the Sheriff contemplates suicide with her .38 caliber revolver, in closeup. There's no way to fake that, so we got a non-firing model that worked just fine. Too many low-budget productions reveal their limitations by cheap props masquerading as the real thing. If you need something real, find a way. It may take a lot of looking, but it will be worth it.

Prop Considerations

As I mentioned earlier, the director Douglas Sirk used to say that a film is made up of *things*. So by the proper selection of your things, that is your props, you can tell the audience more about a character than pages and pages of dialogue, thus enriching your film immeasurably without breaking the bank.

Think about the opening of Hitchcock's *Rear Window*: The camera moves slowly around James Stewart's character's apartment, highlighting his photos, his camera, his life, and by the time we see him with his leg in a cast (which was set up by an auto crash photo and broken camera), we know quite a bit about his character before he even opens his mouth.

This is another reason why you should know your characters so intimately before you begin shooting. The more you know them, the more precise you can be in selecting those visual elements that will help round them out as characters. It will also help your actors and actresses get a better fix on the character they're playing.

The first thing is to go through your script/ outline/scenario looking for any prop that is mentioned, whether water glass, comb or a gun. These are the props that you need and they should be listed by each scene. But remember that each prop isn't just a water glass or a comb or a gun, but rather a water glass, comb or gun belonging to a particular character, and the choices you make should tell the audience something about the character that they didn't know before.

On an underground production your choices are limited by your budget, but let me tell you that there an infinite number of low-cost choices available *if* you spend the time thinking about them, then searching them out. Don't settle for a generic-looking prop unless your character is a generic kind of person; find the slightly different piece that will illuminate their personality. Give them something totally offbeat and expand their personality instantly. I always remember the beginning of that Alan Ladd film *This Gun for Hire*. He played a hired killer with a kitten, which he petted on his way out. It was fantastic ... hmmm ... I wonder if Francis Ford Coppola or Marlon Brando remembered this for his first scene in *The Godfather*? But you see what I mean?

And since props also seem to be the one element most often forgotten on low-budget shoots, it's imperative that you put someone in charge, someone who is organized and responsible. This is where having a trusted production assistant comes in handy. Obviously, it would be better to have a dedicated prop person, but that usually isn't the case on guerrilla productions. So either your production designer/art director handles all the visual elements (including sets, wardrobe and props) or you assign a trustworthy PA the assignment.

Whoever takes over the job, make sure they have the schedule with the scene breakdowns that include the necessary props for each and every scene. Also try involving them in helping you to create the visual aspects of each character's personality, by asking for their suggestions. You should always try and take everyone's suggestions seriously *before* production begins, reserving the right to make the final decision. If you've chosen the right people you can reap the benefits.

A very similar process to the gathering of the wardrobe can be followed while gathering your props together, in fact, they often can be done at the same time and at many of the same places, killing two birds with one stone.

Borrowing from People. So first of all, you should show your prop list to the cast and crew, seeing how much you can find through this method. Usually it's quite a bit. Then I go back to former collaborators looking for stray pieces that I gave away and may be able to use again. Last but far from least is your friends and family once again.

"Borrowing" from Stores. It's not as easy to buy your props from the larger stores, then return them after your shoot, but it is possible. The trick is to find the stores in your area with the best return policy. Ask your "shop 'til you drop" friends or relatives, they will probably know. Then try and buy only one or two large props from each individual store in each chain, making sure to retain your receipt. Then treat the items carefully on your shoot and if you're lucky and nervy, you might get away with it.

Yard Sales. After you've covered all your family, friends, cast and crew, your best bet by far is yard sales. Especially with the props, yard sales are by far your best bet; hope that they will be in season just before you shoot. The yard or garage sale assures you of the most and the cheapest stuff in the best condition. These are followed by flea markets and second-hand or thrift stores. And with the second-hand and thrift stores, don't be shy about asking if you can only rent them or sell them back after you're done — hey, you never know.

You usually can't afford to buy any of the larger props that you may need but if you're in a metropolitan area there may well be a prop house or (in other areas) a regional theater or college theater group where you may be able to find just what you're looking for. Ask around, you may be able to find those jail bars you need at the college theater down the road, but you'll never know unless you seek them out and ask. Make a deal to videotape one of their productions and you may not have to pay at all.

Buying. Last but not least, you can pay full price for whatever you need — but try and wait for sales or look for damaged goods.

A final tip on props: You don't necessarily have to buy things that work, as long as they *look* like they work. There's a great place in New York City's Chinatown that sells a variety of computer and electronic items that are in need of repair. Mostly people go there looking for spare parts or for things to fix and sell, but they have the cheapest prices anywhere on some really unique stuff. You might also start taking trips around town the day before garbage collection day. It works — really.

Guerrilla Insurance for Props. As with almost every other budget item, having options is your best insurance. I once had a prop guy who, to put it plainly, wasn't too good. For one of our scenes we needed to have the lead character take communion before her execution (don't ask!) and we had secured about 20 unblessed communion wafers. Unfortunately our prop guy left them in a paper bag which happened to end up in a puddle of water. Well, 19 wafers were ruined, but one was salvageable and managed to survive until our one successful shot.

But if we didn't have back-ups, we could have been scrambling around trying to flatten some stale white bread! Especially if it's anything that's going to be used up, have more than you'll need, because you never know what may happen and it usually does, just when you don't want it to. This is not negative thinking, but experience. Take it or leave it ... at your risk.

Budgeting Food

The number one cause of cast-crew mutiny on low-budget shoots is food. Whether it's bad food or the same kind of food over and over again, food is the biggest cause of friction on a guerrilla shoot. And it doesn't have to be, because there are so many inexpensive ways to keep your cast and crew happy.

This is such a high priority on my shoots that I usually have my line producer or unit production manager handle it with the help of a PA. But whoever you put in charge should know that you consider it a top priority. Of course on a larger production they just hire a caterer to handle everything, but that's usually far beyond any guerrilla filmmaker budget, unless your mother or girlfriend happens to be a great cook and is willing to do it. Don't dismiss this, it's a great solution.

But usually having someone cook for you entails too much mess and effort to make it cost-effective for a cast and crew of about 15 or less. However, if you have well over 20 people or if you're away on an overnight location and have rented a house where your cast and crew are staying, then having a dedicated kitchen where one skilled person prepares large, tasty and healthy meals near a designated eating area is a definite possibility.

The principal method, though, is usually buying some kind of take-out food which is brought to your set. I personally poll each member of the cast and crew about their likes and dislikes, letting whoever is in charge of the meals know what kind of food they should be looking for.

This means you should also be scouting for food locations at the very same time you're doing your location scout, looking for quality take-out restaurants in the area and even going so far as collecting take-out menus for future reference. These are given to the person in charge of meals, who will also check with each location's owner for any other reasonable alternatives. You most definitely do not want to be stuck going to an expensive place when you're on location just because you haven't done your homework and the last cheap place closed a half-hour ago.

In the mornings I provide juice, coffee or tea and some sort of rolls, pastry or snack. I also have some kind of snack food, soda pop or seltzer available during the entire day. About an hour or two before I want to break for lunch, I have the designated person go around with the take-out menu, whatever that may be, and have them take orders. That way, they should be back with the food just when I want to break. I never have set times for any meal.

Also make sure that you vary your menu; almost no one wants pizza five days in row. If you're in a city, try pizza, chicken, Chinese, pasta, burgers, deli, etc., but if you're in a smaller place it might have to be Fast Food Chain #1, Fast Food Chain #2, Fast Food Chain #3, etc. But even there I'll bet there are smaller restaurants in the area. Hell, if you throw 'em enough business they may give you a package price that beats the fast food chains. Ask — you never know until you do. And remember, everything's negotiable.

If you're buying food, try and buy it fresh early every morning from some place that sells in bulk or at discount. Then make sure it gets to the set on time. There's nothing worse than a crew without their morning coffee. The same routine applies for dinner, especially if you're going late (and you probably will). Just don't go to the same place twice in the same day. And keep lots of water, juice, coffee, tea, soda pop or whatever else your cast and crew asks for around the set; it helps to keep them as well lubricated as your movie camera. And if your third ear begins hearing some griping about the quality or quantity of food, make sure you pay attention.

The hardest time to get your cast and crew moving is after meal breaks, so you should set a definite time to finish. Eat your meal quickly, then begin chatting about your film as soon as possible. After about 15 minutes before you want them to begin again, you should wander back to the set by yourself or with anyone else who will follow and start doing little things on the set: tinker with the lights, adjust the props, in other words, begin guilting them out early. By the time the break is over, you will be fully justified in making sure they return to work—of course, this is because you've feed them so well.

Budgeting Transportation

How are you going to get your stuff around? A relative's, friend's or team member's van is the best production vehicle available for a guerrilla production. Not only can it haul your gear and/or people from place to place, but it also can double as a low-budget dressing room or cast trailer when on location. It can provide warmth, shelter and privacy for cast and crew alike.

Second best is family, friend or team member cars, but remember that when you're borrowing someone's car for your production, you should always pay for their gas, parking and tolls. And the bigger the car, the better. Small compacts are usually not worth the expense.

Remember that public transportation in some cities (New York for example) is faster and more efficient than anything else; just make sure you camouflage anything of value. But when all else fails, look to rental companies for your truck, van or car needs, but try and avoid the major chains. Most cities have a local company that can give you much better rates, especially for vans. But when you need nice shiny new cars which will double as picture cars (those actually appearing on camera), it's better to go to one of the national outlets that will let you pick your models (and perhaps the color too) and be in much better shape. You don't want an advertisement on the side of your van that's going to appear on camera.

This part of your budget should also contain any travel per diems that you are giving to your cast and crew, any parking fees or special parking such as overnight secured storing of your equipment and/or van, gas allowances, tolls, taxis and anything else that has to do with anyone else in your cast or crew getting to some location you need them to be.

Transportation Considerations

Time is money (usually yours) when you're shooting. Therefore getting around quickly is more important than anything else during principal photography. People and things have to be where you need them, when you need them. So any of your decisions about what form of transportation to utilize should be based on that set of priorities.

You should only schedule vehicles for exactly when you need them. They should never be left unused for long periods of time. So make your schedule in a manner that lumps together, as much as possible, the days when you will need those vehicles. And if you don't need one for the full day, try to get it for a half-day. Often it may be cheaper to rent one of those "man and a van" set-ups, but only for those times when you are making large equipment moves, than renting a van for the entire production. But only by figuring all your moves out in advance can you accurately gauge this.

If you have to rent an extra van or car, make sure it's only for a few days and that in those few days you will be bunching together all those scenes that make that extra vehicle necessary. Always make sure that your rental cars do double duty both as transportation as well as appearing on camera. And when renting cars, always try and look for the small local company that can give better rates than the large chains.

But if you rent from some large chain, try their airport rental facility as they usually have much lower rates than that same company's branches in a nearby city. And again check your local organizations such as the Association of Independent Video and Filmmakers for applicable discounts. The big companies get discounts, why not you?

If you're out at night shooting in the city, you'll need a van to transport people and equipment as well as acting as a dressing room and makeup area. The cheapest way to set this up is to get a small cargo van (remember, no ads on the side so that you can use it in your shots if necessary) and set up a simple (100–watt) clip-on light in the back that runs off a small transformer that you can connect to the cigarette lighter. They cost about $30–40 and are well worth the money. A small mirror and a few plastic milk crates or stools with cushions and you have your own mobile production facility. It also will keep people warm on those cold and windy nights. The only problem is that you will probably have to have your driver or at least someone hang around the van to make sure you don't get ripped off.

To recap the transportation question, your priority should always be the fastest *and* cheapest. Your considerations must always include: What must be transported? What is the fastest means at that particular time of day? How long will it take? Will parking be a problem? How many people will be utilized? Below are some of actual examples of the priorities that should always be considered in your choice of transportation. One particular way is *never* always better; it will *always* depend on a combination of all the above factors.

Examples: Sending someone cross-town during rush hour whether by car or taxi *is not worth it*; have them take the subway. Someone who is willing to work for free and bring their car at a position that requires a lot of running around *is not worth it* if they don't know the area, unless of course you can separate them from their car, but even then the hassle of doing so probably *isn't worth it. It's not worth it* to send one person with a car to get something in Manhattan or any large city, because the parking is either too expensive in a lot or it will take too long to find a spot on the street. *It's not worth it* to send two people, just to have one sit in the car making sure it doesn't get a ticket. If one person can carry it, the subway's the way. A car that keeps breaking down, even if it's free, *is not worth it.*

Underground Budget Options

BUDGETING INSURANCE

As with other sections in the budget, I believe that if you can afford insurance (at the very least general liability and Workman's Comp), you should get it, but if that is the budget line that's stopping you from making your vision a reality, then you must do what you have to do to achieve your goal. If you decide on insurance, make sure that you go to a broker who specializes in entertainment insurance, not your father's car insurance salesman, unless of course he's the only one who will insure your production.

For film or video production, there are a variety of policies available, covering various aspects of production. They are: General Liability, which covers any damage or injury while on location; Automobile Liability, which covers any damage to or injury by or to anyone resulting from someone working for you on your production; Negative, which covers any damage or faults in your film stock, developed negative as well as the cost of re-shooting any "lost" scenes; Faulty Equipment, which covers any malfunctioning equipment and pays the cost of any re-shooting due to that equipment, 3rd Party Property, which covers damage to any third party's property; Miscellaneous Equipment covers rented or leased equipment; Prop/Set/Wardrobe covers just what it says; and Workman's Compensation covers any injury to your employees during production. Workman's comp cannot be purchased through your insurance agent, but must be purchased separately from your state's office of Workman's Compensation Insurance.

As with all insurance companies these days, there is usually a deductible (or how the insurance companies can increasingly fuck you) that will ensure that on a low-budget guerrilla production, the insurance company will probably never have to pay you a dime.

Very often trade organizations such as the Independent Feature Project or Association of Independent Video and Filmmakers have discounted rates for members; they should be your first stop. But even that doesn't necessarily mean they are the cheapest. Call around.

If you're having a hard time getting insurance from an entertainment-related company, and you know the exact types of insurance you want and/or need, you might want to call a couple of non-entertainment related companies. You might be surprised and it's only the price of a phone call. Even though it may not be preferable, some insurance is better than none, at least in my eyes. So shop around, as all companies will give you different prices for the very same policies. Usually it will be to your advantage to try and negotiate a package deal, which includes as many of the elements from that list as you think you'll need or can afford.

Most states will require that you have Workman's Compensation Insurance to cover injury to your employees. This is separate from your other insurance and can be obtained from your local state division. The premium is usually based on some percentage of your budget. Once again, only you know what you can afford, but to me this has become one of those necessities that I feel I need to be fair to all those willing to work with me.

There is also the problem that if your budget is too low, insurance companies may not even choose to ensure your production at all. However, if you do not tell the truth on your insurance request and/or claim and the insurance company finds out, you will not be paid for your claims. Since there is the possibility that you may not be able to get any insurance policy unless you "stretch" the truth, what do you do? In all honesty, I can't tell you. So, if you unfortunately get to that point, you'll have to make up your own mind.

There are couple ways of not having to pay for production insurance yourself. The most prevalent method is by bringing someone on board, usually a production company or producer, as some kind of partner and then using their policy. There may be a couple of variations on this which you will have to figure out for yourself, if you have a mind to.

Last but not least is the time-honored "Vigilant Guerrilla Mode of Non-Insured Filmmaking," which has been going on since film began and probably go on until media-making takes place entirely inside the computer. You will have to "steal" all your locations, hope that all your equipment works properly, that your film or tape is flawless, that no one gets hurt and that no one objects to you filming. And if any or all of this happens, you're stuck and probably liable.

This is the ultimate guerrilla mode of filmmaking and you need to follow most the previous advice to the letter; i.e., keeping a low profile, being extremely mobile, having as many options available as possible while taking advantage of absolutely anything that can help you accomplish your goals. The less you carry with you, the less attention you arouse, the faster you'll be able to move to take advantage of changing conditions. If you need to operate in this manner, make sure every single person working with you is on your wavelength and good luck! I remember when I was young and foolish too ... last week to be exact.

Budgeting Lawyers

Do you need a lawyer for your guerrilla production?
No.
Will you get screwed if you don't have one?
Yes.
Will you get screwed if you have one?
Yes.
Then why have a lawyer?
Hopefully you will get screwed less and at least you'll be prepared for who's doing it and possibly be able to take action against them ... if you can afford to.

Please remember, any advice I give in this book is not intended as legal advice or the practice of law, especially since I hate most lawyers and the way they think. But as with any legal document, you should consult a lawyer for exact interpretations of the law; if you can afford it is another story. If you have to set up any type of company or corporation or a partnership, limited or otherwise, as well as a stock offering of any kind, you will *need* an attorney.

However, if you use a lawyer on a low-budget underground production, they will probably end up being your highest budget line, when you can afford them at all. What will you be getting in return? As I said, a lawyer can draw up any type of business formation that you may be using such as a limited partnership, partnership or incorporation, but also your cast releases, location releases, crew agreements, deferred pay agreements, musician-composer agreements, collaboration agreements with your writer or anyone else who may need one.

Can you find all of the above for free? Yes, you can, on the Internet and in a variety of filmmaking resource books, but they will not be specifically tailored for your production and the particular way you work, thus leaving room for future problems. Can you live with that doubt? Most of the time, I have, but then, once again, it's your move.

When you are figuring out how much a lawyer should add to your bill, you should have no problem with them giving you a price for a certain amount of work. The only tricky part comes in if you ask for more then you originally agreed on. In that case, hold onto your wallet or at the least try and negotiate an up-front flat fee for all their work.

Budgeting Post-Production

This is without a doubt the most difficult part of any budget to estimate, especially because most of the problems you will run into during post-production are ones that will arise during your actual shooting and are impossible to anticipate. A general rule which seems to hold true for me is that post-production will be the same amount as it takes to get your film into the can or your tape into the box, unless of course you happen to own your own computer-based non-linear system as I now do now. I don't know if this is a low-budget thing or what, it just seemed to hold true.

For a film shoot and film edit you will have to include:

Film processing

Film or videotape dailies

A work print for editing

The actual editing or rental of a film editing machine, whether flat-bed or Moviola

A negative cut

An internegative print

An answer print

Re-recording your sync sound

A sound mix

Locking picture with sound

A safety print

A dubbing print.

A 35mm blow-up, if you shot on 16mm and want to go to 35mm

These prices are always changing, so that you should go to your local lab and find out what their rates are and if you can get a discount or deferral agreement.

For a film shoot with a non-linear tape edit and film finishing, you will have to include:

Film processing

Film-to-tape transfers (you can use your dailies, just make sure they're time-coded)

A non-linear edit

A negative cut from your non-linear edit list

An internegative print

An answer print

Transferring your sound to mag

A sound mix (you may have this or at least part of this from your non-linear edit)

Locking picture with sound

A safety print and

A dubbing print

A 35mm blow-up, if you shot 16mm and want to go to 35mm

The same goes for this process regarding prices, so hunt around and find the best deals or find an editor who (though they may cost you more) can help you through this maze with much less hassle.

For a tape shoot, edit and finishing you have to include:

Time code dubs of your master tapes,

A non-linear edit (unless you can get a cheap or free linear system to do your rough cut; then make an EDL [Edit Decision List] which will greatly reduce your non-linear edit time and budget)

Sound mix

An on-line edit (which can be skipped if you use a non-linear system that will give your broadcast quality video)

A Betacam SP or Digi Beta master from your on-line edit or broadcast quality non-linear edit.

These prices will vary even more, especially with the advent of the low-cost, high-quality Final Cut Pro system from Apple and the Avid DV Express. The full-blown Avid systems seem to be the high-end systems of choice.

If you want to transfer your video or digital video to film, there is an ever-increasing list of available options. The costs can range from the lowest for a simple kinescope (which won't look very good) to a high-end digital-to-film transfer that will cost thousands of dollars per minute.

Deliverables, another highly difficult area to budget, are often left out of the low- no-budget film's budget, but they should at least be considered when making out your budget whether you decide to include them or not. The amount of "deliverables," that is, what materials the distributor requires from you before you see any money from them, can cost as little as a few hundred dollars or more than $100,000, depending on the distributor. I will give you two deliverable budgets from actual situations and let you make up your mind how much or little you want to set aside for these purposes.

On the high end of the spectrum, you will have to provide:
A full list of credits
A copy of script
The director's bio
A blow-up to 35mm for theatrical release
An M & E (music and effects) track
A stereo mix
Film prints
A low–contrast print for video
Music clearances
NTSC Digi Beta master
PAL Digi Beta master (cost covered by foreign distributor)
A trailer (create one during your edit)
Color production stills
A poster
A dialogue list
E & O (errors and omissions) insurance (not always necessary)
An internegative/interpositive print (only for theatrical distribution)
All for a total of between $52–117,000.

But a smaller distributor who handles only video or TV may want only:
A Beta SP master (NTSC)
SVHS master (NTSC)
5–10 color photos
Full film credits
A synopsis
Any press, reviews, etc.
All for a total of around $500. And if a foreign deal is made, the foreign distributor should/would pay for the dubbing and PAL mastering.

Before finishing your budget, you should always add at least a ten percent contingency fee of the overall budget. This allows for anything that you overlooked or anything else that arises unexpectedly. And don't worry, something always will. If you're the type of person who has the tendency to underestimate your resources or over-estimate your efficiency, you may want to make your contingency percentage slightly higher, anywhere from 15–20 percent.

Please Note: The following diatribe is off the top of my head and I ask not to be held to any figure, but I'm willing to bet this is a lot more "on the money" than most people are willing to admit, at least publicly or in print. So to conclude this section on budgets, there are four or five levels of production for the underground filmmaker, with very definite limits, and little (if nothing) in between. The very first level on feature films (16mm) is approximately $25,000 to get it in the can and no one gets paid, except for maybe the DP and sound recordist (if they use their equipment). The lighting is restricted to one or two lighting kits of three to four lights in each kit, which can run off of house current, the locations are free, the insurance is minimal, the schedule is approximately two weeks and no lawyers are involved.

This automatically jumps to $40,000 if more lighting or dollies are used and anyone but the DP and sound recordist are paid, including lawyers and insurance agents. Post-production on a film print will be the same amount as you spend on production. Double this again if you shoot on 35mm. If everyone is paid, it will cost you just under $100,000 for a two- to three-week shoot, including post-production on film. Double this figure for 35mm. If you are shooting union, actors and crew double these numbers. If you have a "star," add their salary plus an additional 20–30 percent for the value they add as well as trouble they will cause.

Shooting on digital, Mini DV or DV Cam (which is still just a fancy way of saying "on video") can possibly save you 30–40 percent on the above costs, unless of course you drastically reduce your crew size to about three, lighting requirements (one kit with three lights), shoot it all in two weeks and do all of your post-production on a computer. Then it's conceivable that you could bring in a feature for under $8,000 if you don't pay everyone, $20,000 if you pay everyone and around $1,000 if you do everything yourself and call in all your favors. However, it'll jump to $40,000 if you use a better digital camera or digital Beta which means more equipment, more lighting, more people and a longer schedule. Adding extra locations that you have to pay for and/or building sets will add another $5,000–10,000. Paying everyone will jump the whole thing up to around $100,000.

With the constant advances in computers and computer software, there are many budgeting programs available that will do just this. More and more people are using these programs, but for the low-budget filmmaker, I believe they can be misleading.

My reasoning is that these programs are all modeled after Hollywood-style productions, and (as I mentioned in the chapter on guerrilla strategy and tactics) for the underground filmmaker the Hollywood way is the enemy. What these budgeting software programs do is entice you to believe that you need things that you don't really need, to include (thereby creating) job classifications and equipment categories that can only and almost always add extra and unnecessary costs to your budget. They also generate more, *much* more paperwork and forms than you actually need and in some cases can add an extra person to your crew, just to handle all the paperwork generated

I just recently went over a budget submitted by group who used a computer budgeting format for their first project. They had certain lines (i.e., expenses) doubled, they had certain costs included which they could easily have done without, they based their calculations on a totally unrealistic shooting schedule, their contingency percentage was half of what it should have been, etc. In other words, they had a ten-page budget, full of errors, when a handwritten, realistic one-page form would have served their purposes just as well or better.

If you're a line producer on a half million dollar or higher budget, then I think these programs can be of assistance, but even then I have my doubts for the same reasons listed above. On a true guerrilla production, you don't need computerized forms to show you how many budget lines you can't afford or budget lines you should have *if* you were a Hollywood production. You only have to sit down and figure out exactly what you will need and when; everything else is extra, a waste of time, energy and effort.

Raising Money

If you're reading this book, you're probably not someone who can go to your friends and family and immediately raise $100,000–500,000 for your production. If you can raise that kind of money, skip this chapter and immediately proceed to the next. However, if you're like a majority of underground filmmakers, you'll probably be getting by on a bit less … *quite* a bit less.

Obviously, the first place to look is to yourself. If you're not willing to put money into your production, to fulfill your vision, why should anyone else? Most beginning filmmakers have to use their own money because they are unproven and people are looking to see if you have that kind of financial confidence in yourself. In addition, there's an old adage that money attracts money, so start saving those nickels and dimes. And along with the confidence that your savings will project to people, you must also begin to demonstrate to everyone around you the confidence you have in your vision.

Your vision should consume you and drive you to find a way to make it a reality. It's something the people around you will sense and not have to be told; it will energize your every waking moment until you finally finish your film or it finishes you. And if you have that kind of "fire in the belly," your investors, your cast and your crew, hell, anyone who comes into contact with you will feel it and hopefully have some of it rub off.

But remember, for the underground, guerrilla filmmaker, all those team members who have "caught your dream," as the Martin Landau character in Coppola's *Tucker* said, will be your number one financial resource, since what they can bring to you, in terms of free or low-cost production necessities, will probably far outweigh whatever money you can raise. It's these non-financial elements which will ultimately decide whether you fulfill your vision or not. If it's only about money or fame, which seems to be more and more prevalent today, count me out and give this book to someone who can really use it.

Okay, so you've managed to stash away a couple of thousand dollars or more; now what do you do? Family and friends are obviously the first place to turn. These people will be investing in *your* dream; therefore you have to make them susceptible to "catching your dream." This particular job will remain with you continuously until you begin working on your next film after this one is finished. Everywhere you go, you will want the people you're meeting to somehow, in some way, "catch your dream," whether it's friends, family, prospective investors, prospective cast or crew members, festival directors, distributors, reviewers and ultimately the audience. How susceptible all these people are to "catching your dream" is determined by how well you can articulate your dream to them.

Before proceeding, in regard to your personal financial repercussions (which may differ by state), you should consult your accountant (if you can afford one is another story). And remember, anything I say is not intended as legal advice or the practice of law, especially since you may recall the issues I have with most lawyers and the way they think. But again, as with any legal document, you should consult a lawyer for exact interpretations of the law.

Outright gifts are the preferable form of small investments from family or friends because you will not have to create any formal business or investing entity. An informal personal loan is another possibility, but if the loan's formalized, you can be liable for the entire amount plus any penalties for defaulting. Especially if it's a secured loan, you can be liable to lose any security that you had to put up.

If you must form an investment group, the most frequent is the limited partnership, which makes you the general partner responsible for all the business and creative decisions as well as any liabilities, while the limited partners (your investors) have no say in the running of the business or production, while their only liability is their financial investment.

This must be drawn up by an lawyer and the financial terms may vary. Usually it's a 50-50 split, with the limited partner receiving the first funds received until their investment is paid off. Sometimes there are additional small percentages taken by the limited partner before the 50-50 kicks in and sometimes the percentages may be skewed in favor of the investor. But these are things that should be covered in more detail and can be found in a great many film financing books and articles or on the Internet.

Once you moved outside the circle of your family and friends, there are a variety of ways that you can proceed. One of the most used is the fundraiser. Whether it's a party or dinner or screening, it can help raise a *limited* amount of funds—unless, of course, you're really good at it, but most of us aren't. The most critical element is compiling the guest list, which you should gather from your family, friends, cast and crew. Anyone who might be in for as little as S50–100 should be included. Because if you can get together as few as 60 people paying $100 a pop, you should be able to go out and finish a feature shot on Digital Video.

Make sure that as much of the refreshments, entertainment and venue are donated as possible. And if one of your fundraisers works particularly well, you might think about trying a second or third. However, if you lose money, you either should find someone else to take over for you or consider another means of raising money.

You can also use the fundraiser as an opportunity to look for additional investments, leaving cards around for people to contact you later for additional information. If you can't raise money from someone, at least try and get the name of another potential backer or two. You never know who your next potential backer may be or where they can come from.

Another source of funding may be a local production company which may make some kind of deal where they lend you the use of their equipment and/or facilities (and maybe themselves as well) for a percentage or partnership in your production. They may also give you a deferral until the money starts coming in from your film. As with most financial arrangements, everything is negotiable. If it's formal financial relationship, a lawyer should be involved.

Now, of course, there are pre-sales from video distributors or feature film distributors, but at the budget range we've been discussing, forgetaboutit. There are also professional fundraisers who will attempt to raise money for a fee. Most often, on this level, they will only take your money and run.

Before I leave this section, I want to end with a dose of financial reality for all you aspiring millionaires and Hollywood wannabes. More and more what is called "independent" films are being made each year and if you include those made on digital video the number is even more astronomical. What that means for you, the individual putting up your own money, whether it be your savings, your credit card or your home (and if it's the last two you're really in trouble!), is that the odds of getting your money back or even making a small profit are in the same range of probability as winning the lottery.

Never put in more money than you can afford to lose. If you make a 16mm or 35mm film without *name* stars for more than $50,000, you will probably never make a dime. If you make a digital feature without *name* stars for more than $10,000, you will probably never make a dime. Even if you have two or three *name* stars and your budget is between $200,000–$1,000,000, the odds are such that you or your investors will never make back your investment, let alone make a profit.

Most first time filmmakers *never* make money; even *if* their film is successful, they only make it on their second film. And in my opinion, all this hype about people putting up their home or maxing out their credit cards is a way for the independent film companies, some of whom are owned by large conglomerates, to have all these unwitting investors doing their development of projects for them with no money and no financial risk on their part. They then can pick the cream of the crop from film festivals and film markets, which, in my opinion, they control or subsidize or unduly influence.

How to Get What You Need

Now that we've finished talking about raising money, remember, rule number one on an underground production is "Nothing is free!" What I mean by this is that everyone on your production will have to be paid something and it's up to you to decide what the currency will be. The most obvious currency is cold, hard cash, but if you are reading this book you obviously don't have enough of this. So when you have decided who you can pay with actual dollars and cents, what can you pay everyone else with?

Whether they are people you've known or worked with before or have just met, you have to find out what they want from you and your production. And if you listen carefully enough, they will usually tell you, but you may have to dig a bit when you are initially interviewing them. Now this is where the underground filmmaker really differs from the Hollywood model.

Remember how Jean-Luc Godard talked about being to talk with his crew about their life outside the production or how he wanted to know what they thought about what they were filming? On a guerrilla production, you must know everyone in your cast and crew because they are your main resource. What they contribute to you and your vision will far outweigh whatever money you may have. They become your main investment and the more you invest in them, the greater your return will be.

There is nothing worse on low-budget productions than when ego-centric "geniuses" believe that the world revolves around them and their only goal is to use and/or abuse their cast and crew in attaining their vision. Each one of you has something to offer your team and by talking with them as well as listening to them, you will find out what that is.

Are you telling a story that hasn't been told before? Are you dealing with characters who have never been dealt with before? Are you pushing new boundaries of filmmaking method or aesthetics? Are you giving your cast and crew opportunities to grow in new areas they have never worked in before? Are you bringing a certain excitement to someone's rather routine way of working? Is your film or video sexy, exotic, thrilling, dangerous, religious, calming or chaotic and are these qualities the ones that your cast and crew are attracted to ... searching for? You must find all this out and use it to your advantage — not to screw people over, but to make sure that it's a fair transaction benefiting both of you.

My cast and crew are my prime focus when putting together a production. Once I have cast my crew, as well as my cast, I share my goals, ambitions and strategies with them, asking for any ideas or assistance they can offer. Some people call this brainstorming, but I hate this term; however, if it helps you understand better, then fine by me. If you've never done this type of thing before, you'll be astonished by the results. I have discovered major locations, cast difficult roles, changed my script (when I had one), found free transportation, uncovered wonderful wardrobes, met collaborators, been introduced to great facilities and much, much more, all through listening to the people working with me on my films.

It is only after I have exhausted every lead from all my acquaintances (including family and friends) that I then begin filling in budget lines with people, goods or services that I will eventually have to pay for. But even then, I once again pass all my unfulfilled needs past my cast and crew, asking for any recommendations from their past working experiences. And just as with the freebies, you'll be astonished by the results.

Obviously, these recommendations shouldn't be taken non-judgmentally because, as you remember, just as everyone has a different currency, they will also have different agendas to go along with it. So when your lead actor recommends an actress, who just happens to be his girlfriend, you had better take that into consideration and if she's not right for the part, you better come up with very good reason why you can't use her.

And as you may have discovered by now, quickly coming up with reasons, answers and justifications is one of your most vital roles in being the director. They don't always have to be true, but like Aristotle said (notice how I bring in Aristotle when I'm telling you how to not necessarily tell the truth), they must be probable and they must be fast. If you're not good at this, you had better practice, because one of your largest responsibilities will be answering everyone's questions. You may not know all the answers, but you better *appear* to know all the answers.

What Do You Go After When You Get What You Need?

Now this doesn't happen too often on an underground film, but what happens if you find yourself with every element you think you need to successfully complete your production and you're still under budget? First of all, recheck all your figures. If they still check out, then go over any key element, whether it's your camera package, wardrobe or crew, etc., that you feel may be a bit "iffy." By "iffy," I mean something somewhere in the back of your mind that you're not entirely comfortable with. It doesn't have to be something concrete, it can be anything that just doesn't feel right.

Examples of this can be an actress, who though perfect for the part has seemed a bit reticent about certain aspects of her role, such as nudity or violence or her co-star or anything else which makes you feel less than 100 percent confident about her commitment. Or a director of photography whose style you love and you would really like them working on your project, but feel they may only be agreeing with your working methods until production begins and then they may try to exert more control than you're comfortable with.

These, and any other similar situation, call for Underground Insurance — that is, *options.* This is a valuable lesson I learned early on in production, when I needed a photograph for part of a dance video I was putting together. I didn't have access to the facility until the day of production, so I didn't know which of three or four photographs would look best on their graphic's camera. I brought all four and was thankful I did. Things will always go wrong and you must always give yourself options.

On one shoot I had an actress I had used before and whose previous performance I was very happy with. But when I cast her in the new production, I sensed a slightly defensive, uncomfortable quality that may have stemmed from her relationship with a stage director. Sensing this and realizing I had only six days to shoot a totally improvised feature, I decided to have another actress play a somewhat similar role, knowing that she could play the uncomfortable actress' role if there were any problems. There were and she did. The actress I had worked with walked off in the middle of shooting one night. Fortunately I was able to move the other actress into her role without losing any time.

If your DP is "iffy," have a back-up; if a location's "iffy," have another nearby; if an actor's "iffy," have someone waiting in the wings. Give yourself as many options as you can afford, making sure that most of them will not cost anything extra, while providing you with a certain peace of mind. Not that you will find too much of that once production begins.

Once you've put together your budget, it's time to begin rounding up your collaborators and all the things you'll need to make your dream a cinematic reality. I have touched on all these elements while going through the budgeting process, but now I will go into greater depth concerning these crucial elements.

10

Your Team

As I've been preaching throughout this book, films are made with people by people and for people, so it's no surprise that I consider the "team" to be the essential nucleus of your production. We've seen from past examples how all the Patron Saints of Underground filmmaking have formed a tightknit group of collaborators around themselves and to whom they returned picture after picture.

Not everyone working in this business is cut out to work on guerrilla-style productions and by this I'm not necessarily talking just about money, although it obviously enters the picture. The ideal team, cast and crew, will get their main satisfaction from a job well-done while simultaneously stretching creatively. Whereas there are an increasingly large amount of people entering this field only for the monetary results from the work, rather than the satisfaction of the work itself.

Your job is to sort these people out and find the ones who have a passion for just the kind of work that you're doing. Obviously this is not going to be 100 percent possible, so the next best thing is to find those people whose career needs, at that moment, coincide with what your production offers them (or, as the saying goes, one hand washes the other). This sort of transaction is probably the most frequent type of exchange you'll encounter, so it's very important for you to know what your production offers to other people, as well as what each prospective member of your cast and crew is looking for themselves.

Last of all is the "gun for hire," which doesn't have to be a bad thing, as long as they understand the limitations of your budget, schedule, etc. But there's nothing worse than a "pro" who has no sympathy for you or your work. Beware of the "pro" who needs a job to fill in a slow period from their higher paying jobs; they will probably spend every available moment telling anyone who will listen what they're used to and how lacking you and your production are in those regards.

This is why it's so important for you to know your priorities, enabling you to effectively communicate this to your prospective cast and crew, while searching for simpatico priorities in them as well. As Che Guevara advised future guerrilla leaders, the key to a successful operation is the solidarity of *all* those involved.

Your role in this process, whether you like it or not, is to be the leader. How you lead is something that you must find out for yourself. There is no one right way to lead, but there usually is only one right way for each one of us to lead. You have to discover that in yourself, because it's only then that you can effectively lead other people.

Personally, I came from a team sports background—high school and college football, to be precise. And I unconsciously carried this over into video and film production when I first started out. Now this works fairly well when everyone you're working with is a macho kinda guy, but not so well when you're working with practically anyone else outside that small sphere. So when I first started, I always picked an assistant director who had people skills in areas I lacked. They were my buffers with the more "touchy-feely" kind of people that make up a great deal of the people you'll deal with. Over the years, I've advanced so I no longer have to rely on an assistant to do this, but realizing early on that I had this leadership deficiency, definitely made my life easier.

As I stated earlier in the Lucca Theory of Negotiation, if you can't negotiate … don't negotiate. Find out what works for you and use it. If you're terrible at organizing things, make sure you have a trusted, key assistant who's extremely organized. If you're over-organized and lacking in people skills, have someone whose strength is in that area and delegate as much as you can to that person.

Are you an "inspirer," someone who can convince anyone to do anything? Then play that card. Are you someone who is attuned to the most intimate emotional nuances of the people around you, but can't push those people when you have to? Then find someone to be bad cop to your good cop. Look carefully and hard at yourself, then use your strengths and minimize your weaknesses by finding people who can make up what you lack.

What Actors Look for in Directors

While the dynamic of leading a crew normally tends to more assertive and macho, the dynamic of leading your cast can be much more elusive and ephemeral. Each and every actor or actress will bring something different with them and, in turn, will need something different from you. One of your most important tasks will be to find out what that is.

Some actors or actresses will approach a part intellectually and want to discuss various aspects with you; some only need to know the emotion that they should be striving for; some want to be told exactly what to do; others want only the barest indication; some need endless rehearsals; some do much better with no rehearsal at all; some love to improvise; some hate to improvise; some want to be disciplined while some want to be consoled or encouraged. Whatever they need, you need to be aware of. Of course, that doesn't necessarily mean that you will be capable of *giving* that to them, but at least you'll have a better idea of how to deal with them, if you take the time to find this out.

Once you have learned how to deal with each individual actor or actress, you then must develop an overall strategy that integrates the variety of different

Celia Hansen, the lead actress in *Daddy*, takes a quick break between scenes (photograph by Jamie Renning).

perspectives each member of your cast brings with them. Whether they love you or hate you, almost all of them will vie for your attention, and you will constantly have to juggle these rivalries and requests and demands for your attention.

Obviously, some actors will need your attention more than others; whether they are emotionally needy, miscast or just need the extra work to do a good job. But you must always keep in mind your priorities for the final production. For example, if your second female lead is envious of the time you're spending with your female lead (who is in almost every scene), then you either have to try and delegate to someone else the responsibility of giving her the attention she needs. If that fails, just expect a more difficult time from that particular actress.

And although it would be ideal if you were everything to everybody, that is not really possible. So based on the priorities that you've set, you must try and mediate between all the different members of your cast and crew. Every relationship will be different, every production will be different, but that's one of the unique features that makes this job so interesting and so demanding and why so many directors try and work with the same collaborators over and over.

And once again, this is where knowing your own strengths and weaknesses will be of great assistance. If you don't have the kind of personality to put up with certain types of actors or actresses, try and find that out *before* you cast them. Search for those qualities that you are comfortable working with at your auditions. Casting is such an integral part of your role as director, putting together the right person with the right attitude with the right role will make your life much easier and the production run much smoother.

But no one ever said your life was going to be easy and once again, it ultimately only matters what ends up on the screen. Some of the best actors and actresses I have ever worked with were the biggest pains in the ass. Where they worth it? Yes? Would I use them again? Yes. Just try and make sure that if you have to expend a lot of your time and energy on a particular performer, their performance is worth your extra effort.

What Crews Look for in Directors

First and foremost, the crew wants to be led and they want to have confidence that the person leading them knows what they're doing. Sounds simple, but it puts quite a bit of responsibility on your shoulders.

The crew wants to see that you are decisive, knowing exactly what you want at all times, because your main job will be answering their questions, hundreds and hundreds of questions about every aspect of the production. What size lens? Is this the right color for this wall? Is this the right fabric for this sheet? Where do you want this light? Can you do without this?

Now obviously, no one immediately has all the answers, but that is what almost every crew will expect from you. And I believe that appearing to be decisive and coming up with quick, confident answers to everyone's constant questions is the best way to instill confidence in your crew. You must always appear to be self-assured and decisive, even when you're not. But when you do have your doubts or misgivings or moments of crisis (and you will have hundreds of them), just don't have them in front of your crew. They want to believe in you; help them.

A very difficult but very important thing for the leader of a guerrilla production is to have some way of occasionally being able to get off by yourself and think

things over in quiet isolation. These moments will usually be few and far between, but they can be essential. Obviously on a Hollywood production you can lock yourself up in your trailer, but for the low-budget auteur, locking yourself into a bathroom can be a much cheaper (although more "fragrant") alternative.

Not all directors lead by being assertive and decisive; some have learned that by expressing their doubts out loud they can create sympathy for their plight by encouraging those around them to pitch in, helping to solve the problem at hand. In other words, make your problems *their* problems by involving them in the process. There's more than one way to skin a chicken and I have seen this method work extremely well with someone wise enough to use a supposed limitation to their advantage — something a good leader always does.

I have also seen a very decisive, confident director occasionally fake a moment of doubt to draw out sympathetic reactions from the cast or crew. On the other hand, I have seen directors fake anger to shake people up, or use the opposite tack of trying to get the cast or crew angry at the director himself, to take the heat off of a member of the cast who keep flubbing his lines.

And that's another of your duties as the leader: You have to make things work on the screen. Because ultimately there is only one test of the success of your endeavors: whether the audience is moved. They don't care about any of your problems, the crew's problems or the actors' problems; they only care about the result on the screen. So as your production's fearless leader, you have to do whatever you can to achieve the results you're after.

Using Your Team

Don't be afraid to use your team, to push them beyond where they're comfortable or used to. When I first started directing, I was so intimidated by the cast and crew that when they started grumbling about some things I asked them to do, I backed off. But after a couple instances of this, I realized that most casts and crews grumble and complain about being pushed beyond what they're accustomed to. And if you have a vision that is not the norm (what the hell is the "norm" anyway?), you will end up having to push your team in areas they may not be comfortable with.

One of the most successful ways of moving people beyond their self-imposed limits is by posing your challenge as a creative problem that you need their help in solving. Involve them, provoke their curiosity, stimulate their creativity, give them responsibility, create a spirit of unity, praise them when they succeed, encourage them when they fail, demonstrate concern for their safety, give them an example to follow and, if all else fails, push them to where you need them to go. Ultimately it's more important to be respected than to be liked. However, if you can do both, you'll be much better off.

Among filmmakers there are Traffic Cops and Leaders. Traffic Cops, who make up the vast majority of filmmakers, make sure everything runs smoothly by obeying the rules, while a Leader *leads* his team into uncharted territory, places unknown.

Obviously, this book is for Leaders and if you're willing to do what you ask your cast or crew to do, they will be much more likely to follow. Be the first one on the set in the morning and the last one off at night, go anywhere you ask them to go, endure what you ask them to endure and demonstrate what you want them to do. If you are fearless, they will be fearless, if you are timid they will be timid. Be fearless and they will follow … well, most of them anyway.

Being Used by Your Team

One hand washes the other, as the old saying goes, and if you ask your team to allow themselves to be used for your personal goals and ambitions, then it is only fitting that you allow yourself to be used for theirs. Now this doesn't mean that you have lie down at their feet and be their slave, but it does mean that you owe them something for working on your project. What do you owe them? Besides the money (if you are paying anyone), first and foremost, live up to your word by doing what you say. By doing this, you will inspire their trust and when things get rough, and I assure you they will, your team will be with you.

Always take the time to listen to what they have to say, even if you don't agree and go along with it. There has to be more give and take on a low-budget production and when there's too much take and not enough give, that's when problems arise. Give them your time, not only about the production, but their lives as well. I know this doesn't seem to be a very business like approach but it is, especially if you're in this for the long run and not to trying to be the next one-hit "indie" wonder, who exploits as many people as they can to get their *big break*.

Now I'm not saying that you aren't going to be using people to further yourself and your goals, but how you go about doing that will have quite a bit to do with how your career in this business proceeds over the long run, as well as how smoothly your current production runs right now.

Keeping Your Team Together

How well you follow the above advice will have quite a bit to do with how well you succeed in keeping your team together. Remember, almost all of the "Patron Saints of the Underground" Edgar Ulmer, Val Lewton, Roger Corman, John Cassavetes, Ed Wood and Jean-Luc Godard, as well as Che Guevara, stress the prime importance of a small but dedicated band who fully understand and agree with both the goals and methods of their leader.

This can and often times does extend to after the production is completed. For example, if you have offered copies of the finished production to those who want one, make sure they get one. If they need you as a reference on another job, take the time to do so in a timely manner. If they invite to a new show of theirs, make time to go see them and give them your response. If you have screenings of your film around town or at festivals, keep them informed. If you hear of other production they may be suited for, give them a call and let them know. If they need a demo reel cut together, see if you can help them out.

By staying involved and showing genuine concern, you will be on your way to forging long-term relationships that can be rewarding not only professionally, but

Daddy's home! Bevin McGraw, Katherine Petty, Celia Hansen and Cynthia Polakovich react as Daddy returns (photograph by Christopher Philippo).

personally as well. I have worked with a small group of collaborators for over 15 years. Of course, some have drifted away, but their overall consistency and generosity over the years has been one of the truly fulfilling aspects of working on my films.

Your Cast

Since the decision whether or not you pay your cast is one that always influences your finished film or video, it's imperative that if you cannot pay your cast, you spend the extra time and effort to find the very best people available. So go out and ask your fellow filmmakers which people they recommend (then watch them on film or tape), go to see local plays (let them know you're casting a movie and you'll probably get in for free!), ask some of the actors or actresses with whom you've had successful working relationships in the past to recommend people. Of course, last and least (at least in my eyes) is the open call, where you put an ad in a trade paper, secure a room and maybe a video camera, then hold onto your hats and see what turns up.

Open calls usually mean long hours of wading through tons of photos, extended casting sessions and callbacks as well as the depression of seeing so many hopeful people with so little talent. You will always be able to find actors and actresses who will work for free; however, whether they are good or not is another question.

That said, there *are* many good actors and actresses out there who will work for no money or deferred pay (let's not kid one another, it usually amounts to the same thing). But most will want something in return. This then becomes the currency you must work with.

What are these non-monetary currencies? At the top of the list is offering your prospective actors and actresses the opportunity to become an integral part of a project that involves and stretches their range as an actor. In other words, it's a great part in a challenging script and you have an interesting way of working, perhaps somewhat different from what they may be used to. The second is that their time is not going to be wasted in an amateurish and/or unorganized production. Nothing pisses actors or actresses off more than this, especially if they're not being paid. The third is that they will be treated respectfully and receive a copy of their work that will help them secure future jobs. You'd be surprised how many people making low-budget films or videos fail to treat their cast with respect and consideration, especially since they can just walk off the set at any time.

For some reason, quite a few low-budget filmmakers forget this power that their actors or actresses can hold — until, of course, they actually *do* quit and then the filmmakers are faced with gaping logistical holes in their schedule as well as myriad continuity problems, to say nothing of having to recast. Remember, in an underground film shoot, the power to walk off is the cast and crew's ace in the hole; whether they choose to use it will depend mostly on you and how you treat them. Ultimately, it's the actors and actresses up on the screen who will determine more than anyone else whether an audience responds to your work; remember this and treat them accordingly.

Last but not least, make sure that you have all cast members sign a performance release (including payment provisions) before production begins. I had to have a lawyer draw mine up because I improvise extensively, but they can easily be "borrowed" from the Internet or various filmmaking resource books. And if you are doing deferred payment, make sure every detail is written out and agreed to.

Auditions

Finding the right actor or actress for the part can be a daunting task, further complicated by the fact that during auditions, every actor or actress will desperately try and convince you that they totally understand you, your material, your approach, their character and anything else you ask them. And 90 percent of the time they're lying through their teeth. So you have to devise means to find out those things which will better help you find the right person for the role, thereby taking you a long way towards achieving your production's goals.

For me, the problem has always been two fold. The first and most difficult is finding actors and actresses who are comfortable working at the emotional extremes my work demands. The second is finding actors and actresses who are open to and adept at improvising.

I address both of these problems at my auditions. When talking to prospective actors or actresses, I always stress the emotional extremes that my characters will have to reach, In fact, I go out of my way to say the kind of things that will cause them *not* to take the role, figuring if I'm able to talk them out of taking the role at that early stage, they weren't right for it anyway. Secondly, I always pick a particularly troubling scene (at least emotionally) for their audition. If they flinch, they're out. It's that simple ... at least for me. The only problem, which I get better at with practice, is recognizing *the flinch*.

My second problem, of finding actors and actresses comfortable with improvisation, is solved by having them audition by improvising that particularly, troubling emotional scene, thus killing two birds with one stone. And I always make sure that the scene is between two people, one of whom is an actor or actress I have worked with before. With two unknown actors or actresses, it's always possible for a bad actor or actress to throw the other off, or for a particularly cutthroat, competitive one to purposefully sabotage the other's performance. Also since improvisation is so dependent upon cooperation between actors, I want to know that the auditioning actor is working with a competent partner, without a hidden agenda.

Last of all, it's very important to me that my actors and actresses listen to my direction and make appropriate changes. So after they've done the scene the first time, I will ask them to make some changes or adjustments and then see if they actually listen and *make* the adjustments. I like flexible, creative actors and actresses who will bring a lot with them to the role and this is one way of checking for that.

Now obviously, this is a rather odd way of auditioning actors and actresses, but it works for me. You should find out the way that you work best with your actors and actresses and set up your auditions to help you seek out and find those qualities.

To me, having hundreds of people walk in and do some kind of monologue to the camera or you is just a waste of everybody's time. The audition is becoming more and more like an audition for stand-up comics— that is, doing their routine (monologue) at the audience (*you*) with you having no idea how they *interact*, which to me is the most important aspect of acting.

But if you insist on going along with the traditional method (which is totally bound to staged theatrical productions anyway), put your ad in a trade paper, local alternative paper or acting school, rent (or hustle) an audition space, beg, borrow or steal (not really) a video camera (optional, but becoming more the rule), then sit back and watch. Then go through the tapes, find the ones you liked best and call them back to read or improvise with some of your other choices.

Or alternatively you can ask for headshots and résumés first (not that they even look like the people or can you really tell anything from them) and then only call in people you like the looks OF. But one word of caution: Most of the really bad casting mistakes I've made were because someone *looked perfect for the part*. They did *look* perfect, but they weren't particularly good or compelling actors or actresses. Try and find the actor or actress that *is* your character, not someone who only looks like your character.

Rehearsals

The rehearsal is generally the first time that your cast will meet one another. It should be used not only to go over your script or outline or whatever type of structure that you've decided to use, but it is also a valuable time for you to discover the various interpersonal dynamics that will play themselves out during your production. You should begin to find out who gets along with whom, who doesn't like whom, who's a snob, who's lazy, who's bossy and who's going to be a pain in the ass.

Even though rehearsals are some of the most important times you will spend with your cast before production begins, they are also the hardest things to get people to attend, especially on a low-budget shoot. Not necessarily because they don't want to, but because you are often in the position of paying little or nothing, they probably have to spend quite a bit of their other time earning the money that will allow them to do your production for little or no money. A Catch-22 that can only be solved by understanding and learning to juggle everyone's ever-changing and conflicting schedules.

More than anything else, I think rehearsals help your cast understand their characters' relationships with the other characters in your production. And unfortunately in this celebrity-driven world, where stand-up comics are often the role model for aspiring actors and actresses, there seems to be less and less films where you can actually believe the actors or actresses have relationships with the other members of the cast. Rather it seems as if everyone is doing some kind of personal stand-up routine *at* the other members of the cast.

At rehearsal, you can begin to see what works in your story, in terms of the relationships. And if certain relationships aren't working, you either have to find a way to make them work or somehow change your story to fit what you have. Because at each stage of your production, the preceding stage becomes irrelevant and only what you are working with in front of you at that moment has any relevance.

Watch what the actors bring with them, what they're giving you and then use that as the basis for your changes. Hopefully, the changes will be minimal, but to me, it's always better to change the things that are right in front of you and can be changed rather than insisting on any preconceived idea which is proving to be unworkable. If a relationship between two actors just doesn't seem probable or possible, even with lengthy rehearsals, change the relationship.

Example: I had an actor cast as a working class hustler who was attempting to scam a famous actress. But no matter how much we rehearsed, I never believed that he was working class and the relationship with the actress wasn't working either. But one day before rehearsal, I heard him talking to one of his friends over the phone. I changed his character to a slumming rich kid and he was the most pleasant surprise of all the actors in the film.

You will find that you get better results by not forcing people into situations that they cannot attain, rather than insisting that they conform to your preconceived ideas, no matter how good they may have been. Because ultimately, for your film, it's better to have a believable character that's slightly different from your original conception than any kind of unconvincing character.

Now for the specifics of rehearsing ... there are none. There are many and what they are determined by the priorities of your particular vision. I was rehearsing two actors for a scene in one of my recent films when the first, rather inexperienced actor, interrupted to tell me that I wasn't rehearsing the scene properly. He very politely informed me that we should sit down at a table and read through the script first, then block out the action. The other actor, who had worked with me before, was looking on in bemused silence.

The generally accepted way to rehearse *is* to have all the actors and actresses sitting around a large table, doing a "dry run," that is, reading their parts "cold," without any particular emotion or inflection. You are supposed to read through the entire script this way. That way everyone knows everyone else's part and it may be one of the only times, other than the actual production, where everyone gets together at one time, especially if it's a play, where this process originated.

Some directors do this and some don't. The increasingly competitive economics of today's film world make this method more and more difficult to achieve. But it is also, to my mind, totally rooted in a theatrical way of doing things and not necessarily of great help to me and the way I do things. A great many actors and actresses are comfortable doing this, a great many directors swear by this; I don't, so I don't do it. But if it works for you fine.

My main argument against this procedure is that play rehearsals are meant to produce a performance that will be repeated night after night, but for me, making my film, I want the actors and actresses to strive for spontaneous moments that can never be repeated, but *are caught forever* on film or videotape. This is to my mind one of the distinctive things that film or video can do that no other medium can.

Since I use improvisation to a great degree, I will quickly go over the way I use my rehearsal time, which may be slightly different than most. I usually rehearse scenes that *are not* in the actual film. The reason I do this is so that the cast can learn about their characters, maybe their characters' back stories and their relationships with other characters in the film. I don't want them to begin making choices in their actual scenes from the film, that's something I want them to do only at *the moment* they are on camera. This is my own particular little quirk about creating a series of totally unrepeatable moments that add a certain aspect of experiencing something for the first time, thus, hopefully adding spontaneity, uncertainty and risk.

The one thing to avoid in any type of rehearsal situation, no matter what method you choose, is to have your performers "leave" their performance at the rehearsal by over-rehearsing them. This was the main reason that I stopped rehearsing scenes from the actual film. I once had an actor and actress rehearsing one of the key scenes from the film while I videotaped it. After I had finished the film, I happened to be looking back over the rehearsal tapes for some reason and found that I much preferred the rehearsal to their actual performances in the film.

Problem Actors and How to Deal with Them

For a variety of reasons, ranging from lack of money to people backing out at the last moment, you will almost always be involved with problem actors or actresses. By the term "problem," I don't mean mean or nasty, even though that also may be true, but rather a professional without craft and/or talent or an amateur without any natural gift.

By far the worst to deal with is the "professional" lacking talent or craft. The problem actor invariably thinks they know more than they actually do and is more than willing to proclaim it to anyone who will listen. They demand more of your attention for less return than any other element in your production. Luckily, at least for me, they have been few and far between.

Obviously the best way of dealing with a problem actor is to spot them during the audition process and don't pick them. But for a variety of reasons, especially on a low-budget production, this may not be possible. The only thing you can do once you actually cast a problem professional actor is damage control, that is, to keep them from spreading their bad habits or attitudes to the rest of your cast.

The reason for this is that once you begin filming, especially if that actor or actress has a large part, they become a necessary part of your production. If they quit or back out, you're screwed, because you probably can't afford to reshoot their footage. So damage control becomes your only option. Now this may seem like an overreaction on my part, but almost every time I have felt "blackmailed" by a member of the cast or crew, it has been by a problem actor intimating that they could always back out or quit and then I'd be up the creek without a paddle.

This reminds me to repeat another very important point: Get all your releases, deal memos, agreements, etc., signed by both your cast and crew *before production begins.* Once the ball starts rolling and production begins, *you* become susceptible to being blackmailed by anyone with whom you do not have a written agreement, whether it be the writer, the DP, the actor or anyone else with a stake in your production.

The "blackmail" comes in the form of "I won't sign the release/deal memo/whatever until you give me [fill in the blank]…." *They* know and *you* know they have you by the short hairs. It's not pretty, but if you are absolutely vigilant about getting all your releases and agreements signed *before* production begins, you can avoid this very unnerving situation.

Back to problem actors or actresses. As I was saying, they will invariably attempt to spread their "problem" to the rest of your cast and crew, whether it's directly sabotaging you or your viewpoint with fellow cast members or badmouthing you behind your back to your crew. The bad actor or actress must be contained without antagonizing them, to prevent their leaving the production. This means attempting to simultaneously humor them while limiting their contact with other members of the cast and crew. Whether it's through clever scheduling or housing and meal assignments, you must somehow limit their access to the others.

Practically, what this means that you must patiently listen to whatever kind of nonsense they choose to go on about (often slowing down production), and maybe even outwardly agreeing with them, although without actually implementing their suggestions. If they want to do another take, let them — just don't run film or tape while they're doing it. If they want to discuss or suggest something, do so, but insist it be done privately. However, you cannot capitulate to their demands or they will gain the upper hand and you will suffer the consequences.

The worst case scenario would be if your problem actor or actress is having a noticeably detrimental effect on one of your lead actors or actresses (God forbid they are actually one of your leads!). You must then take all steps necessary, short of murder, to stop this, unless you are willing to give the reins of your production over to this person. So what I suggest is that you tell your "infected" lead how their performance is being sabotaged by this problem actor or actress and how it would be to their best advantage to politely ignore their advice.

However, if this polite approach doesn't work, then you must begin to sabotage the problem actor or actress in the same manner that they are sabotaging you. Play them off against one another or, if possible, write the problem actor/actress out of the script. As a last resort, get rid of them and reshoot their scenes. I have on occasion resorted to all of these, a fact of which I am not particularly proud.

If you are unfortunate enough to have cast the wrong actor or actress for one of your leads, I believe that drastic actions are called for. The moment you have this realization, you should recast, even if that entails pushing back a start date. But if there is any time left at all, recast, even if you can't possibly push back the start date.

If recasting is impossible, the next best (least worst?) thing is to rewrite the script, minimizing your problem actor/actress while building up one of your better actors or actresses in another role. I know this throws things off, but an unconvincing lead will kill your production.

And while you are in the midst of these drastic measures, continue studying your problem actor/actress, see if there's anything *you can use*. No one is totally without talent, so search out the things they can do (there must have been some reason you cast them) and play them up, while minimizing the bad. If they have a boyish charm, play that up even if they're supposed to be the toughest sonofabitch on the block. If they're attractive, pose them in nice light and give them some non-verbal business.

But if they are giving a particularly bad line reading, have them mumble it in a corner, or if they are doing an unconvincing gesture, have them do it in the shadows. If you have to do a close-up of them, put their eyes in the shadows.

Now a more benign but still troubling presence is the problem amateur actor or actress. But instead of containment, they need to be put at ease and encouraged, because their deficiency comes from a lack of confidence, or lack of craft or natural talent. Hopefully you have cast them in a role in which they already resemble the character you want them to play; if not, you should consider changing the character to someone like them, so they can more easily be themselves.

Also, you may want to let them make up their own lines, maybe even improvise a bit or run the camera when they think they're just rehearsing. Try not to repeat the scene from many different angles and limit their interaction to just one other actor or actress, hopefully one they like as a person. And *do not give them large emotions to portray*; keep things small and intimate and within the range of who they normally are as a person.

Once again I want to mention that the *how* of minimizing problem actors and actresses is something that you have to do in a manner consistent with your personality. If you can't confront people, don't, but have someone working for you who can; if you can't finesse, don't, but have someone who does it smoothly. Do things your way, but remember: *Contain* the "problem pros" and *encourage* the "problem amateurs."

Your Crew

The crew is an extension of you, allowing you to actualize what was only an idea or dream, but is now becoming a reality. The best crew relationship occurs when your crew knows what you want and agrees with how you want to achieve it. Most of the time, this comes about from using the same people over and over; that's why most of the "Patron Saints of the Underground" repeatedly used the same people.

Auditions

Just as you auditioned your actors or actresses, you should "audition" your crew. All too often, beginning directors will hire their crew solely by how much (or how little) they cost or what kind of equipment they own (or don't own) or on the basis of work they have done in another area of film or video production. Now all of these criteria have a place, and it seems (in today's ever-increasing cutthroat mentality) an ever-increasing place, but I firmly believe that your crew should be picked on the basis of what they know *and* how well they understand or have experience with the type of production you're planning.

If you're planning on shooting a down-and-dirty digital video feature in ten days, with verité lighting and hand-held camerawork, it probably isn't in your best interest to hire a crew who specializes in commercials or broadcast TV. They just aren't used to the low-budget, set-'em-up, shoot it, set-'em-up mentality. However, if you happen to be a director coming from those particular areas and you've worked with these people for a while, they may be just the ticket.

But if you're planning on doing a very visually stylized production, then that really cheap documentary crew probably isn't your best choice, even if they seem to be the only ones you can afford. You have time, that is your one luxury as a guerrilla filmmaker; use that time to your advantage to search out and find the sympathetic and skilled collaborators you need. All too often, I see projects rushed into production without proper preparation and, 90 percent of the time, it could have been avoided.

Talk things over with them, see if they flinch. Just like actors, most crew members will tell you they love your concept, understand what you're after and love doing just that kind of work. And just like the actors, they're probably lying. Hey, I do it when I'm hiring out as a line producer; it's part of the game, but learn to play the game. Ask questions. What other DPs does your prospective DP like and why? What film stocks does your DP prefer and why? What kind of camera and why? What do they think of hand-held? What kind of budgets have the productions your prospective crew members worked on had? What kind of schedules? How many set-ups in a day? Challenge them, prod them and, if they don't flinch, then seduce them once again with your vision.

Before moving on, let me once again remind you that you should have each and every crew member sign a deal memo that includes their terms of employment and payment (deferred or otherwise) conditions. As always, these can be found or "borrowed" from the Internet or filmmaking resource books and will go a long way in ironing out any disagreements about pay, working hours or schedules.

Rehearsals

Rehearsing your crew isn't something that's usually done, especially on low- to no-budget productions, but it is something that can be of invaluable help to you and your production. Usually the first couple of days of a feature shoot are spent with everyone getting to know one another, cast and crew. The footage usually reflects this and usually in a negative way. Some older Hollywood directors used to set aside time to reshoot the first couple of days of production due to this "getting acquainted" period.

I have found that *if* you can get your key production people to come to one of your rehearsals, even having them videotape it if possible, adds immeasurably to smoothing over those first few rough days of principal photography. It also allows you to check out how well everyone understands what you're after, how they work (or don't work) together, and gives indications of any possible personality conflicts that you may have to deal with during production. Try it, you'll like it!

Problem Crews and How to Deal with Them

Just as there are "problem" actors and actresses, there are "problem" crew members. And the same principles apply to them as to the problem professional actor/

actress. If you can replace them before principal photography, do so. But, unlike an actor or actress who appears in Scenes 1, 9 and 49, a crew member may be replaced at any time. So when most crew members act badly, you can afford to be a little harder on them than your actors.

But having said this, I want to say that I never have had crew problems, except on my very first independent production, where the entire crew came with the cameraman, who (once shooting began) turned out to be a total asshole. I have never made this mistake again and I have never had a problem with my crews since then. I have always asked more of my crews than they are normally asked to give, but once they see that I'm committed to do as much or more work as they do and that I'm prepared, they've invariably been extremely loyal. Without them, I would never have been able to achieve such beautiful results on such poverty-stricken budgets.

Back to problem crew members: If you can't replace them, contain them in the same manner you would a problem actor, but always try and find someone to replace them. On a guerrilla production, you should always have back-up crew members. Whether it's your DP who is "totally committed" until he gets a great paying commercial gig that he "can't turn down," or some flaky PA who doesn't bother to show up, back-ups should be in place for every position in your crew. It's just a case of guerrilla insurance.

I've had DPs with whom I spent weeks going over my visual approach towards the style of that particular shoot, loaning them books and videos, only to have them leave for another job after just two days of a 12–day shoot. I ended up having five cameramen on that feature, but it got done and no one looking at it can tell. So make sure you have your guerrilla insurance, but hope that you never have to use it.

For amateurs or those who are using your production to break into the business, the same applies as with the actors: encouragement. Unfortunately, I have never been able to put people who can't do their job at ease; I go at them like a pit bull. So I have found, over the years, that I would rather have fewer people on the crew, knowing that each one there is a skilled professional.

But if you have to use inexperienced people on your crew, you must have patience and be willing to spend at least part of your time being a teacher. Or have someone else who is willing to take on that responsibility. I have had some pleasant surprises in that category, but it's never been me who has had the patience to do the nurturing.

Working Relationships

Now comes the time when you must begin to implement your strategy for working with the crew. What better way to prepare for this than to peruse some very intriguing parallels between Che Guevara's strategies for guerrilla warfare and Roger Corman's tips to his new directors?:

CHE GUEVARA MEETS ROGER CORMAN ON THE
SET OF UNDERGROUND FILMS

GUEVARA: Win every battle	CORMAN: Never say die, never say can't, never say quit,
GUEVARA: Mobility	CORMAN: A quick disciplined pace on the set
GUEVARA: Keep moving	CORMAN: At least 20 set-ups a day
GUEVARA: Adjustability	CORMAN: Act decisively when unforeseen circumstances arise
GUEVARA: Invent	CORMAN: Reuse standing locations
GUEVARA: Take advantage of the enemy's weak points	CORMAN: Take advantage of accidents ... Steal shots

Your attitude will determine that of your crews. If you never say die, the odds are that they never will either. And if they see that your methods are working out, you can be sure they will be right behind you.

If you keep things moving, your crew will follow. If you dawdle and do film small talk (a really great time-waster on most sets) between set-ups, your crew will follow that. Move! Move! Move! At least 20 set-ups a day, more if you can. Actors and actresses used to sitting in trailers hours on end are known to really respond to a quickly paced production where there is less sitting around and more acting. And if you have the right crew, they will fall in line too. Momentum is contagious; create some and watch things move.

And if something's not working out, find a way to make it work. Adapt, adapt, adapt. Nothing is written in stone; where there's a will, there's a way. If you can't go through something, be flexible and go around it. Or go to your crew, ask for their suggestions, make them a part of your production, not apart from *your* production. Listen and involve them and you'll be amazed by the results.

If you find yourself needing something that you don't have or can't afford, invent it for yourself or have someone on the crew do it for you. I needed to light the entire countryside that appeared outside the car that my lead actor was driving down a dark country road. The truck driver–lighting equipment owner operator rigged up a 1K spotlight on the top of the car that ran off a generator we squeezed into the car's trunk. It was noisy, it scared the hell out of that peaceful resort community, but we got the shot and it looked great!

And make sure you are open to everything happening around you, so that you and your crew can take advantage of it. I had finished shooting a music video called "Danger" and we were on our way home when we noticed a huge conglomeration of flashing lights in the night at a large fire in midtown Manhattan. We got the lead singer next to the window and shot her with thousands of dollars of New York City's bravest and finest flashing 20 or 30 lovely red lights in the background, all for the price of being open to opportunity. Use whatever presents itself, just make sure you remain open to what is being offered ... often for free.

As I mentioned before, your crew wants to be led and with the proper preparation and motivation they will follow where you lead. Remember, as a guerrilla filmmaker you must be *mobile*, *agile* and *hostile*, at least to anything that stands between you and the completion of principal photography!

11

The Ambush

Now the time has come to begin shooting. Even though it's a worn-out cliché, it's still applies: Proper Planning Prevents Poor Performance. If you have planned your shoot well in advance, taking into account your way of working and those of your co-workers, while trying to have some kind of back-up for almost every line in your budget, then you should be ready to go. This doesn't mean that you've taken everything into consideration, that's impossible, but it *does* mean that you have a clear plan of what you want to achieve and how to achieve it. I hope you don't think that the many precautions I've been going over have only been there to pad out the pages of this book. In all probability, in one way or another, you'll probably run into some variation on all of them. And when you do … good luck!

This is also that point on your production where the person to whom you've delegated the logistical elements of the production, whether it's the producer or line producer or unit production manager, will more fully assume that role, thus allowing you to focus on what's happening in front of the camera. But it's still your responsibility to see that they're doing their job. They should have gotten contact lists out to everyone involved with the project, including all the relevant contact information — not only for every member of the cast and crew, but also for every location, every supplier, every film commission. In other words, anyone and everyone on the project you may need to contact during the shoot.

They also should have made sure that everyone has an up-to-date schedule and gone over the schedule with them to make sure they fully understand where and when they're needed. The schedule should include the date and location, when and where the crew call is and when and where each actor or actress will be needed. I try not to have my actors or actresses hang around needlessly all day; I try to schedule them only for the time of day that they will be on camera. Unfortunately, they sometimes have to hang around more than they might like, but it's usually due to some unforeseen event beyond my control.

I also like to have my schedule/breakdown reduced to one sheet of paper (see *Daddy* Full Schedule in the back of the book) even if I have to have it printed both sides, using two separate pages only when absolutely necessary. It includes not only the date, location and times of the scenes to be shot, but also includes the needed cast members, any additional crew needed, any special wardrobe needs, all props, any special equipment needs, where the equipment will be stored and any other pertinent information. Having it all on one sheet simplifies things tremendously and saves the time and extra paperwork necessary to do daily call sheets. And in this way everyone knows everything about the logistics of the entire project on just one sheet. And if they do lose it, it's easy to replace or borrow someone else's. And if there are changes, usually not *too* many, we just change the master for that one sheet and re–Xerox them. That way everybody's working on the same wavelength, which is the way I like it.

But if you've got a larger scale production to contend with, then you will probably need to hand out daily call sheets to everyone, including all the above information. Just make sure that the right sheets get to the right people. Some people also like to use those color-coded production books, which work well, but I find them to be just extra pain. With the advances in the laptop computers and programs such Movie Magic Budgeting and Scheduling, more and more laptops are finding their way onto the set. And while computers can save time and money in many areas, I find they actually generate more work than they save on a truly underground, guerrilla production.

One last crucial matter that must be taken into consideration is communications. Often, depending on the size of your production and the logistics involved, you will have your team in two or three places at the same time. Some of them may be setting up for the next scene, while others may be striking a previous scene or running around picking up props or actors or whatever else may be needed. A few years ago, walkie-talkies or beepers were the only way to solve this problem, but today with the advances in cellular phone technology, this seems to me to be the best solution. For communication over small distances, walkie-talkies may be more economical in the long run.

But I want to add one word of advice: moderation. Whether you decide to use walkie-talkies or cell phones or smoke signals, make sure that the only people using them are the people that absolutely need them and no one else. There's nothing worse than having everyone on their own cell phone between every take or someone's cell phone unexpectedly going off during a take. With a small guerrilla production, there should be no more than three and preferably only two cell phones. You and/or your line producer should have one, and your utility person who is going out in advance or getting meals or getting props should have the other. And if you have another person helping with this last responsibility, they might need one. But on set there should only be one.

Regarding walkie-talkies, the less the better, hopefully only two and no more than three. I have only been on one production where we needed walkie-talkies and that was only when we were out of town, with our lodgings quite a distance from some of our locations. It just seems that the walkie-talkie becomes a status item and that the people with them will increasingly use them when not absolutely necessary. Essential communications to the essential people is the rule.

And don't forget, hand signals are one of the oldest and most efficient means of communication across short distances, as long as there's a clear sight line. Develop a series of hand signals with your cast and crew for many of your commands such as stand by, roll camera, speed, action, cut, repeat the scene from the top and "That's a wrap." You can even station one of your PAs in the vicinity to relay your signals to the actor if necessary. If you make each of your signals clear and distinct, visible over wide spaces, you will amazed at the time and money you can save.

Last-Minute Reminders

All right, you've double-checked everything, people, equipment, locations, and everything seems to be ready to go. The best thing you can do at this point is to forget everything, set your alarm clock on its loudest setting and then get a good night's sleep. Now this seems like such an obvious thing, so why do I mention it? Because most of you will probably want to obsess over every detail of the next day's shoot; and then tomorrow night after the first day's shooting is over, you'll want to obsess over that day's shooting as well as the next day's.

You must try and resist that temptation, because as the production wears on, the one thing you undoubtedly will lack is sleep. The better and longer you sleep, the better you will be able to attend to complex multi-tasking that's necessary to run a guerrilla production. This is not something that's easy for most people, but the better you are able to sleep, the better you will be able to deal with everything the next day.

The next morning on your way to the first day's location, you should remember three fundamental strategies that should hold true for the duration of your entire production. The first is "The Wilder-Monroe Theory of Punctuality." The director Billy Wilder was once asked how he got along with/put up with Marilyn Monroe's erratic behavior (not knowing her lines, being constantly late and so on). His response was that he had an aunt back in Austria who could memorize everything perfectly and was always on time, but nobody wanted to see his aunt in the movies.

So, as you struggle to stay on schedule with all the seeming chaos and crises constantly going on around you, there can be a tendency to forget that the only thing that ultimately matters is what ends up on the screen. Everything else is only a means to that end. Never, never lose sight of that.

The second overriding strategy is "The Kubrick-Wood Theory of Priorities." What exactly is this? Well, if you know what Stanley Kubrick and Ed Wood. Jr., had in common as directors, you would be a long way towards knowing the answer. The answer is that they both played chess, which gave both the ability to shake off the distractions that are always close at hand and make their decisions based on the film's overall priorities rather than on a temporarily expedient solution.

As I mentioned before, your most time-consuming job as the director will be to answer people's questions, hundreds of questions a day from everyone around you. And you must have your project's priorities constantly in mind when you are making all of these decisions. You can't possibly make all the right decisions, but knowing your priorities and using them as the basis of all your decisions will go a long way to keeping you on track of what will undoubtedly be a long, arduous journey.

The last theory is none other than killing two (or more) birds with one stone. It's an absolute necessity on any guerrilla production and will save you both time and money, without diminishing the quality of your finished film. And now as they say in John Ford's *The Searchers*, "Let us go out amongst them!"

Arriving on Set

I always try to be the first one on the set in the morning and the last one off the set at night; it sets an example and you hope it will be contagious. It also demonstrates to everyone the value you place on punctuality, which is something that you want everyone involved to practice religiously. Those extra minutes lost when someone is continually late will cost you time that can never be made up. Make sure that you're always on time and the odds are everyone else will follow your lead. I also try, if at all possible, to go in with the DP, as it gives me some extra time to go over my plans for the day and discuss any other camera-related problems.

The first thing you should do after arriving on set is to begin setting the tone

Daddy (Aaron Renning) closes in on his next victim.

for the entire production. And this depends on what kind of person you are and how you want your production to run. If you want a casual, family-like atmosphere, then establish that right off the bat; if you are shy and feel more comfortable hiding behind a more formal set-up, let your key people know that from the beginning; if you like joking around, make jokes; if you're serious as a heart attack, frown a lot. No seriously, whatever tenor you want the production to take should be established from the get go.

Then jump right into your first shot, which to me is a crucial moment in any production, because it's on that first shot that everyone's first impression will be made and, as they say, there are no second first impressions. This is where you will set up the basic routine for every shot; how successfully you do that will go a long way to determining the success of your shoot.

My routine is to first set up the camera position. Some directors prefer to rehearse their actors and actresses first, then set up their camera position in response, while others will confer with their DP first. Any or all of these are fine; it just depends on your priorities.

Once I set up the camera position, I confer with the DP about the kind of lighting that I would prefer, then I go off and begin working with the actors building the scene. Normally I will block the action (non-verbal) scenes while only setting out general areas and letting the actors block themselves for the dialogue scenes. This is not normal, but as far as I'm concerned it's right for me.

I would like to add a word about (what *I* consider to be) the most efficient procedure for your camera and lighting set-ups. All too often I see the DP begin putting up the lights without knowing exactly where the camera is going to be. Then after they set up some lights, which invariably have to be moved because they were set up without a reference point, they set up the camera.

First decide on your camera position — exactly. Not approximately, but exactly where you want it, with what lens and whether you're going to move it. Then either block the cast or give them a general area to work within. Next you set up your lighting beginning with your key light, your main source of illumination.

And once you've begun setting up your lighting, you should never move your camera, so that everything is moved in relation to your camera's position. You should always have a constant from which you base all your lighting. That way, if there is a problem with the lighting, you are only working on one light at a time, starting with the key light, and any problem can be more easily distinguished and remedied.

The most important relationship to establish while lighting is that between your camera and your key light. This relationship must be exact, to a fraction of an inch, but once that is done, everything else falls naturally into place. It's then usually a simple matter of adding any extra lighting accents necessary to complete the scene.

And if there *is* a problem, it's simple to discover what it is by just turning each light on and off to see the effect. However, if this isn't followed, the lights and the camera are constantly being moved around, without a fixed point of reference. This is what leads to a constant tinkering with lights, trying this and that and the next thing, until something close to satisfactory is stumbled on. Because, as I've stated before, the camera has only one perspective, one point of view, and everything must follow directly from that one perspective. Change the perspective, even an inch, and you will change everything else. If you follow this procedure, you'll save time, money and have a greater creative control over the final look of your film.

For the "coverage" style of shooting, most directors will run through the entire scene with the actors and actresses, then pick their camera position, light it, rehearse the cast and then shoot the entire scene in a longshot or master shot which will be the basis for how the rest of the scene is "covered." Then after conferring with the DP and/or the actors, they will move the camera closer for two-shots or over-the-shoulder shots, then finally moving in for the closeups. Then if there any insert shots of the other actor's reactions or closeups of objects, they are usually done last or may even be done by stand-ins at the end of principal photography. On an underground production however, everything is usually done at that moment, as there's often no going back.

If you are shooting in this manner, you will probably need a continuity person and/or attentive script person, to ensure that all the actors and actresses are doing the same actions at the same time so that their actions will match up when it comes time to edit all the various takes together to make them appear seamless. If you're shooting film, you can rent a video tap on the camera for this purpose and if you're shooting on video ... pardon me, *digital* ... you can also play back tape for continuity purposes, although I don't recommend it as a habit. Also, on a film shoot, if you can't afford a tap on your film camera, you can have someone with a small video camera shoot everything for continuity purposes.

And don't forget, having the video tap or even someone with a video camera for reviewing your takes will slow you down. Your level of confidence in your DP and in your own ability to gauge performances without seeing them through a lens will go a long way to determining whether you should use this option.

Obviously, the coverage method of working is predicated on the dominance of dialogue and moving from the largest to the smallest. It's how most casts and crews are used to working these days. I hate it. But that's me. If you like and are comfortable with it, use it.

Another method of working is the so-called Jigsaw Puzzle method, which means that you only shoot the actual angles that you are going to use in the editing. This usually means that you've gone through the script or outline beforehand and indicated what each shot will be. You probably will modify your decisions once you are in the actual location, but you should stay relatively close to your original design. Unless of course you're one of those people who can "cut in their head," knowing how any shot will cut with any other shot without actually seeing them.

Using this method, you may start with a closeup, then as your actor moves out of the shot you go to a two-shot with another actor walking into frame, then follow them talking for awhile, then when the second actor leaves the scene and the frame, you end the scene with another closeup of the first actor. Your main continuity problems will be ensuring that the end of your last shot matches with the beginning of your next shot, which is much easier to follow than the coverage style.

One way to lessen this continuity problem is to have the actor fully repeat whatever action they were performing both at the beginning and at the end of each take.

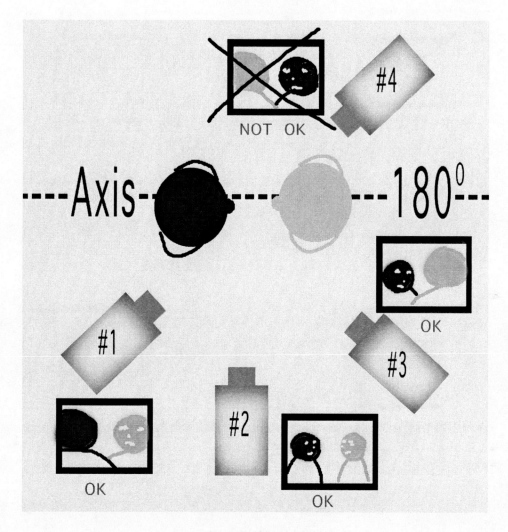

Axis or 180 degree line.

Overlapping your action will give you more options in the editing room just as it will give your cast members more performance options during each individual take. This method also works better with inexperienced performers who are not used to or trained to repeat the same motion at the same point in a series of shots in the coverage style of shooting. The danger with this method is that it leaves you with less choices in the editing room, so you had better be sure these are the angles that you want to use and that they cut together. If you don't know whether they cut together, ask your DP for advice.

The usual rule is that you can't "cross the line"—that is, an imaginary line drawn through the center of two people talking or along either right side or the left side of any action you are trying to film. Your camera must always keep to whichever side was selected not switching back and forth over this imaginary line. If you *do* cross

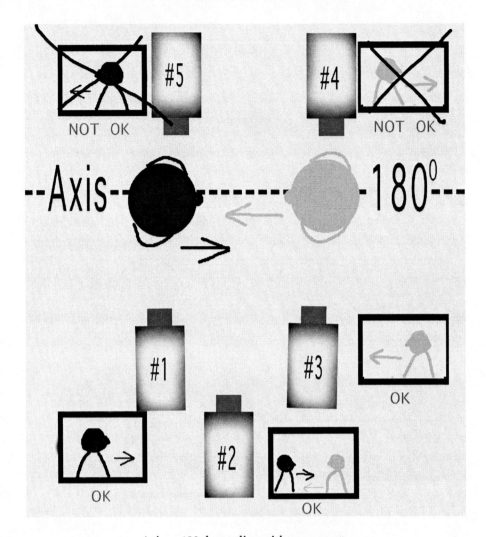

Axis or 180 degree line with movement.

the line, it will appear that the actors are not facing each other when they're talking, or that the action on the screen is going in two separate directions. Even this once seemingly unshakable rule is being broken all the time — but if you set out to break it, at least know why you're breaking it.

In addition, the actor's "eye lines" — that is, the level at which their eyes are looking at someone or something — should always be consistent, as well as the three-dimensional placement of people and objects in the scene. To put it in plain English, if a vase is on the right side of the table when the camera is on a long shot, it still should be in that position when the camera moves to another angle. The same thing goes about breaking these rules as with "crossing the line" — know why you're doing it.

In addition, many directors who shoot in this "Jigsaw" method will shoot additional cutaways, usually doing non-dialogue reaction shots of the actors or actresses, or alternative angles with different line readings or closeups of some physical action, all of which gives them more options when they go to the edit room. You only need one "motivated" cutaway during a dialogue sequence to be able to move from one take of that particular scene to another. Eric Rohmer is a master of this technique, making his dialogue sequences appear seamless through the use of motivated cutaways.

One last method of shooting a scene is the "Moving Master," where the entire scene is done in one take, but the camera and/or the actors are moving into the different types of shots, so that the camera may start on a long shot of two actresses sitting on a couch, then move into a medium two-shot, then follow them as they get up and walk into another room and finally moving out to another long shot to end the scene. This method offers you the least flexibility in the cutting room, so you better make sure the scene is exactly the way you want before you move on. There's a scene is Orson Welles' *Touch of Evil*, as well as one in Sam Fuller's *Pick-Up on South Street*, where the camera and actors work together in an amazing dance-like manner for over five continuous minutes. It can work, saving time and money ... if you know how.

Of course there are an infinite number of variations using all or part of these methods and an important part of your growth as a director will have to do with finding the method or combination of methods best suited to your own needs.

Once you've set up your first shot, then it's time to shoot it and here you should establish another routine that will continue through the shoot. The usual routine on a film shoot, once the shot is ready to be taken, is for the assistant director to ask for quiet. The director says to "roll sound"; then, once the sound recorder is up to speed, the sound person says "speed,"; then the director says "roll camera." And when the camera's up to speed, the DP says "speed." The director then says, "Mark it," and the person with the clapboard gives the scene and take number, then claps the clapboard. Finally the director says "Action!" when he wants the actors to begin. When the shot is over to the director's satisfaction, he says "cut" and the sound and camera stop recording and the actors stop acting.

For video shoots, after the AD asks for quiet, the director says "roll camera," the DP says speed when the camera's up to speed, then the director says "Action!" and later "cut" when the shot is over to the director's satisfaction. However, if you're still using a slate when shooting video, the slate person reads out the scene and take number before clapping the slate, just like a film shoot.

The reason I'm going through this in such detail is that you would be amazed how many shoots I've been on where this procedure or some variation *was not* being done. The rationale behind this is to allow the recording mechanisms a chance to get up to their proper running speed before beginning your action. If you don't do this, chances are those first few seconds will be out of sync or they may not even have been recorded. All these machines need a few seconds to get up to their proper running speed; let them. And at the end of a take I always wait a few seconds before saying "cut" to give me a little more leeway in the editing room. It helps.

The order in which you say to do these things should always be the same, but what you say or how you say it is up to you. Some directors love yelling "Action!"

while others will simply say "Begin"; my choice is, "Whenever you're ready, begin…," because I often find that actors or actresses are not really ready to begin when the machines are and that if you give them an extra second or two, it helps their concentration. And of course, on an underground production, you may not have all these people, so it's the director who asks for quiet and may even read out the scene and take number. But whoever does what, make sure you follow the proper sequence that you set up.

The camera (if you're shooting film) and sound logs are vital documents that must be accurately kept to ensure a smooth, well-functioning production. The camera assistant, if you have one, will keep the camera log, which should tell you how many takes you've done, how much film was used and if there were any particular problems with each take. The sound recordist should be doing a similar log as you go along. Some people shooting on video prefer to have camera logs as well, but I find they slow things done unnecessarily and can be more efficiently done later.

Make sure they are kept up-to-date, as they are sometimes apt to fall behind, especially if you're moving quickly. The logs are essential for your reference when you're printing or transferring your film, allowing you to print or transfer to video dailies only the good takes, thereby saving money. In addition to being useful during post-production, they come in handy during shooting, ensuring that you've covered everything that you were supposed to or allowing you to go back over a sound take to see if you think it has to be redone due to a borderline over-modulation.

In addition, you or your assistant should have some method of making sure that you've got all the shots you need at each location before you move on to the next. I just drag along my script and mark each section as we shoot it, but some productions have shot lists for each day or have a script/continuity person handling this aspect. Whoever does it, make sure that you *never* leave a location before you get everything you need for that particular scene. There's usually no going back.

One final note before leaving this section: The director should be the only person to stop a take once it has begun, and only once they have said "cut." No one else should say "cut" and no one else should ever stop a scene. The only exception to this is when there may be some danger unseen by the director that may cause injury to someone, but that's the only time anyone other than the director should stop the scene.

I have sometimes been on shoots where the sound recorder and/or camera operator will stop a take due to some technical problem that will probably ruin that particular take. But under no circumstances should you allow this to continue, because even if that particular take is no good, something wonderful and totally unrepeatable may be going on between the actors, so that even if you can't use all of the take, you could redub it later or cut away for a second or two that will mask the unusable part of the take.

Also, I believe it's important that the actors and actresses listen only to the director while a scene is going on. There is absolutely nothing worse and more amateurish than having everyone voicing their opinion on a set. The director is the only person who should be talking to the actors about their performances. It only confuses them if they begin to receive a variety of conflicting opinions; it's your vision, so make sure that you communicate it clearly. I don't mean that someone shouldn't necessarily make a suggestion, but they should make it to the director, who then should decide whether to pass it on or not.

There is a tendency for people who have never been on a set to voice their opinion when a problem arises, thinking they are only helping out. And although their intention may be good, the result is not. There must be some kind of order or a chain of communication, especially with a small cast and crew, otherwise every set-up will dissolve into a time-consuming debate; and in this way lies madness, as well as running over schedule and over budget. If you want to set up some informal suggestion system, that's fine and to be encouraged, but it should be set up within a framework that you provide and doesn't slow down or interfere with the momentum that you're trying to establish.

And make sure you set this out clearly at the very beginning; that way the routine is set and everyone knows what it is. It can be applied to any situation with everyone knowing in advance the role they are to play. But you have to be sure that you take the lead, guided by your priorities, which then makes it easier for everyone to contribute in a meaningful way.

Actors and Other Strangers

And now that you're on the set and the camera is rolling, your cast finally reveals their true selves, the ones they've been skillfully camouflaging until now. If you had inklings of problems before, you ain't seen nothin' yet. This is when the amount of time that you spend with each actor and actress will be measured to the minute and judged accordingly. This is when petty jealousies will become feuds, when friends become enemies and enemies become friends, when the only thing that seems to matter is how much time and how close they are *to the camera* when it's rolling. Okay, I'm exaggerating, but not by that much.

Now you will clearly begin to see the acting problems you have to solve to successfully complete your vision. The insecurities as well as the egos will break forth, running rampant, and you'll see who you must play understanding mother to and who you must play stern father to and who you must treat as your mistress and who you must treat as your slave. And once again, if you're not able to play one of these roles, you'd better hope you have someone you can hand that role over to, whether it's another actor or crew member.

But just as these are real problems that you must deal with, they are also possibly solutions in disguise, because you can just as effectively use someone's weaknesses as well as their strengths, if you keep your wits about you. Your job is to get the best possible results from those you have around you and if an actor can't remember their lines, *use that*, have them *use that*, if an actress has grown to dislike another actor, *use that*, have them *use that*, if an actress is shy about her body, *use that*, try and have her *use that*, if an actor is a macho creep, *use that*, have the other actresses *react to that*, if an actress can't scream convincingly, *gag her* so she mumbles convincingly by reacting against being gagged. You should train yourself to use *everything* around you to achieve your goals. Sometimes it's just your lack of perspective that keeps you from seeing the possibilities inherent in any situation, whether "good" or "bad," "positive" or "negative."

Remember that you are in the business of emotions and *all* emotions (if pushed far enough) can be turned into their opposites, by either pushing them even further or by using other people's reactions to them. And just as often as you get unpleasant surprises, you will also get pleasant surprises, like the actor who's terrible in rehearsals suddenly blooms on camera, or the actress who is shy and withdrawn in real life is an exhibitionist in front of an audience or the guy who was complaining about everything before you started shooting is really a sweetheart hiding his vulnerability behind the mask of a curmudgeon.

I just want to briefly touch on the subject of film/video shoot romances, which inevitably happen on most productions whether large or small. There's something about being thrown together in adverse situations that seems to facilitate affairs on a shoot. Most of these affairs last only as long as the shoot itself, but I did meet my wife on a shoot, for better or worse; better, better, better, I'm positive, really! This can be especially helpful if the actors who are supposed to be falling in love on screen are doing so in real life, because anything that makes your film better is good and the more open you are to that concept, the more you will be able to use the supercharged emotional states around you on your set and off, channeling them into your production and onto the screen where the audience will feed off them.

One very important aspect of directing actors on film or video is the necessity of making sure that they are all acting in the same film, that all their various acting styles have a unity which makes it appear they all live in the same world. And it doesn't matter what world that is; it just has to be the same one. Whether it's the "emote 'til you drop" world, or the "downcast eyes and monotone world," or the "strive boldly with declarative sentences" world or the "slapstick world of cartoon characters," all your actors and actresses should be at a similar emotional or non-emotional pitch. This inevitably means that some actors or actresses will have to be toned down (the most frequent occurrence) while others may have to be prodded towards more emotional displays or even cartoony exaggeration that you are striving for.

Another important aspect of this one consistent world is that you have to establish a certain rhythm which will extend throughout your entire production, affecting not only your actors' and actresses' performances, but also the way your crew records the action and right on through post-production, including how your editor will edit all those shots together and the tempo of the music your composer creates. Ultimately, it really doesn't matter which of those vastly different styles you use, just as long as you apply it consistently and create your own unique world within a world.

Working with Your Crew

I've never had as many problems with my crew as with my actors. That could say more about me than my crews or casts, I'm not sure. But I think because the actors and actresses use their emotions so much and that what they do is so much more ephemeral, they are more prone to emotional extremes.

This having been said, I find that crews have to be approached more as a unified group than as a conflicting set of individuals. If you piss off one member of the crew, you are more likely to get the whole crew down on you than if you piss off one actor.

Part of it may be that the crew must always be acting in unison and they always have to be aware of the other crew members and what they are doing at any particular moment. But mainly I think this difference has to do with the different kind of jobs the cast and crew are being asked to do. This doesn't mean that you don't try and treat your crew members as individuals, but rather that your range of responses will not be as broad as they must be with the cast.

And although on the larger, "Hollywood scale" productions there is a definite division or caste system that seems to separate the cast from the crew, I find on the guerrilla, underground filmmaker level that seems to be much less true. Which is something that I personally find very attractive about the smaller productions. It's one team, not a conflicting set of classes. Everyone is usually willing to help everyone else, there are no unions, no set roles, no set goals other than the successful completion of the task at hand. You will also find that the cast and crew on an underground, guerrilla production are much more alike in their interests. Intellectually and culturally, they are very much on the same wavelength, making for some very stimulating evenings of conversation, as well as some other activities that will go unmentioned.

Staying on Schedule

Now that you've set up the standard routine that will be repeated throughout your entire production, you must learn to apply that to an array of constantly shifting conditions. And how well you can adapt yourself to these changing conditions will to a great extent determine how successful you are in coming in on time and on budget.

There will be a constant conflict between what you want to achieve and the amount of time you have to achieve it. And *you will never have enough time*! No director has ever had or will ever have enough time; that's just the nature of the beast. So you should always be striving to achieve the very best that you can within the time set aside for that.

And this is the time when how well and realistically you've set up your schedule comes into play. If you anticipated your problems as well as your priorities and given yourself extra time to successfully create those crucial moments of your story, you should be all right. If you've deceived yourself in pre-production, now is the time to pay the piper. Since money (or the lack of it) is such an overriding reality on most underground, guerrilla productions, staying on schedule is extremely important.

The best way to stay on schedule is to keep moving! The only time any of your crew should be sitting still is on their meal break or if they are not actively involved on a shot that is in progress. Otherwise, everyone should be, as they say, "asses and elbows!" Once you are satisfied with a shot, the moment you say "cut," you and your whole team should be moving immediately to the next set-up. Remember, Roger Corman said at least 20 set-ups a day.

There is always a tendency to sit and chat after a take, so make sure you take the lead right after the shot is finished and begin walking over to the next set-up. And not only should you be moving toward the set-up, but anyone who wasn't absolutely necessary for the previous shot should already *be* working on the next shot or the shot after that. You have to be able to think in advance and have as many of your people as you can preparing for the next shot, the next scene, the next move, the next day. "Next!" is always the first word out of my mouth after "Cut ... good!"

Take advantage of any extra "down time" by preparing for the next shot. If you're still rehearsing the actors and the DP has everything set and is waiting on you, have them begin the next set-up after this one. If they don't have enough available lights, at least they can plan where they will put them and secure them and plug them in, as well as give some thought to any other problems they may run into. There's always something else that can be done, so get in the habit of thinking of it and then have someone begin working on it *now*. It's contagious; after a while, your team will start thinking like that on their own. But if *you* don't do it, they surely won't.

After the first day's shooting, one of your prime responsibilities is to access how smoothly things seem to be moving. Are you ahead of schedule with no problems? Are you behind schedule because someone didn't show up or was late? Are you on schedule but see the beginning of a feud between the DP and the lead actor?

Is your boom operator constantly letting the mic slip into the frame? Is your crew working smoothly together? Are your actors all acting in the same movie?

Obviously, it takes a few days before everyone gets used to everyone else and starts working as a smoothly functioning unit, but if there are any budding problems, they usually will start surfacing as soon as principal photography begins and the earlier you can discern possible problems, the quicker you can nip them in the bud. The longer you let any problem that interferes with the smooth running of your production go unattended, the more of a problem it will become. It's important to address any potential problem quickly, with tact and diplomacy at first and then more forcibly if that doesn't have any immediate effect.

Now, once again, that's my way of handling it, but any potential problems must be addressed as soon as they become apparent. How you accomplish that is something you will have to work out. If you're confrontational ... confront, if you're slick ... be slick, if you hate confronting people, use your producer or assistant director. But do it *now*!

This is also where you will begin to get some idea of how well your pre-production planning is coming along. Did everyone show up when they were supposed to? Or was there some confusion? Was all your equipment there? Were there any undue delays due to missing wardrobe or props? Did the scheduling of meals work smoothly and were the meals satisfactory for everyone? If you did need to get something at the last moment, was it done quickly and efficiently or did it take forever? Were your insurance permits close at hand when the police dropped by? And ultimately the two most important, are you getting the results you want and are you still on schedule?

Just as when there are problems with your people, if there are problems with your logistical arrangements, they must be fixed or changed as soon as possible. At the end of the day, have a talk with all your key production people, ask them how they thought the day went, do they see any possible problems or are things slowly shaping up? You shouldn't have to do this with your actors and actresses because this kind of feedback should be going on constantly between you and them. They must feel secure enough to be able to come to you about any problem. If you're not that kind of person, make sure there is someone working for you who is and consult with them often.

When Things Go Wrong

When things go wrong, and I guarantee they will, how well and quickly you adapt will determine whether your shoot turns into a long, hard haul through Hell or a bumpy but ultimately enjoyable roller coaster ride. And as I've been saying over and over again, having creative options at every stage of the process will be your best insurance against these problems overwhelming you and your dream.

Although no one wants problems to occur, they will, and perhaps somewhat in the order I list below. The reason is that these are the kind of problems that should be happening if you production is running relatively smoothly, because they usually happen on any production large or small, high- or low-budget.

Cast Problems

The most difficult problem you will ever have to face is when a member of your cast, for whatever reason, decides to walk out or quit, once production begins. And the less you are paying your cast below the minimum going rate, the more liable this is to happen. Hopefully, you've sensed their dissatisfaction and have arranged some kind of possible back-up.

If they leave before they have appeared in scenes that make them indispensable, just recast — quickly. However, if they leave after appearing in scenes where it would be difficult to either eliminate them or the entire scene, there are only two options. You can either rewrite the script by eliminating (if you haven't gotten a release) or changing (if you have their release) their character or by re-shooting all their scenes with their replacement. It's not a nice situation, but you have to make your decision and then carry it out immediately.

Although a disappearing performer may be the most unsettling cast problem you may face, the "difficult" actor or actress will be the problem you will probably face most often. I have found most so-called "difficult" actors or actresses are usu-

ally extremely talented, with much of their difficulty arising from the desire to do the best job possible. So when you have a difficult actor or actress, the best way to deal with it is to try and understand the source from which their difficulty arises.

And a very big part of their difficulty may be due to the fact that you're not giving them what they need to create a convincing character. As I mentioned before, every member of your cast will come from a different approach to acting and will need a different, maybe even unique approach from you; it's your job to find out what that is. Apart from having a working knowledge of every different school of acting, it can often be as simple as asking them what they need or want from you. Is it more character analysis? Or maybe just a simple emotional key to each scene? Is it to tell them when they've gone too far or not far enough? Is it some aspect of their character's back-story that unconsciously drives them? Do they need praise, a hug, a pat on the back after every take? Ask and you shall receive ... hopefully. Unfortunately, this amount of attention should only be given to your actors or actresses in key roles, because you just will not have the time to give everyone this time-consuming consideration.

If the performer doesn't respond to your efforts and remains a pain in the ass without giving a particularly good performance, then damage control is your next option. In fact, damage control is one of the key functions you will have to perform with a variety of possible issues arising from your cast that might include jealousy, backbiting, not taking direction, miscasting or just a plain bad attitude. Quite a few of these problems probably stem from some sort of insecurity; unfortunately, you will have neither the time, energy nor inclination to diagnose and attempt to treat all the insecurities your cast will bring with them to your shoot. So damage control is the best remedy.

For jealousy (usually regarding the amount of attention another cast member is receiving), the quick fix Band-Aid is to pretend to understand and give them a little extra time or have someone else from your cast or crew pay them more attention. This last option has accomplished wonders and also comes in handy with an insecure actor or actress who only needs a little more attention. This can work especially well if one or the other of these two people is in any way attracted to the other.

While miscasting is another matter (because in some way you caused this particular problem in the first place), so the only alternative is to work extra hard at building a performance out of whatever strengths that actor or actress has, while attempting to minimize their deficiencies. You can also change their character to be somewhat closer to your miscast actor's range or ability or real personality, making their part less of a stretch.

A word about the ham or over-actor: wear them out, do repeated takes (if you can afford the stock and the time) or repeated rehearsals with them alone. And after every take, take them down a tiny bit; you should be able to wear them down. Of course, if you like their "hamminess," then you just have to make sure you keep everyone else close to their level.

Another irritating problem can be lateness. Some of your cast are bound to be late at one time or another. When they are, you should shoot as much of the scene around them as you can before they get there, even if it throws off your planned coverage of the scene. You cannot hold up the entire production just because of one actor or actress. The best approach, especially if this is an infrequent occurrence, is not to say anything, but use their guilt about being late to your advantage by asking more out of them that particular day. It works much better than complaining to them, which may make you feel better but may set them against you.

If an actor or actress is consistently, late you have two options. The first regards a performer who is creating a unique and moving portrayal, a la the Wilder-Monroe theory of punctuality. If they're that good, try and change their bad habit, but if you can't and they're really worth it, learn to accommodate the best you can. So if an actress is consistently an hour late, give her an earlier call time than everyone else or plan on things that can be shot to cover that extra hour. If it's someone who's not doing that good a job, you should consistently prod them towards punctuality, possibly putting someone in charge of giving them a wake-up call or actually going to their place to pick them up. And shoot around them as much as possible or start cutting their part because of their consistent lateness. They may shape up.

Crew Problems

As with your cast, the most difficult problem you will face with your crew is if someone decides to leave or quit in the middle of production. And although this may not be as disastrous as losing an actor midstream (unless, of course, your DP walks with his camera), it still can have extremely damaging repercussions if they are not addressed immediately. And with more and more people not paying their crew anything, more and more people are leaving productions for a paying gig that suddenly comes up.

You should have a back-up. For crew members on a guerrilla-scale production, it's best if your back-up crew member is *already* a member of your crew. But if this is not practical or possible, have that back-up crew person's phone number readily available, whether it's someone your originally considered for the job or someone that another crew member has recommended. Ultimately, in a real pinch, it could turn out to be you. It may even be a trustworthy PA who is willing to give it a try. Usually finding a replacement for anyone but your DP can be done without stopping your production mid stream.

The problem you will probably run into most often on a film or video shoot is the "old pro/bad attitude/inertia/won't try new ways/back biting" crew member. They've been working in production for quite a while, have a certain way of working that they're comfortable with, and anything else is just "not the way it's done." Everything should be done "by the book," "the way it's always been done." Unfortunately for them and for you, that's probably not the way you'll be doing your production.

Most of these people will either be from an corporate, industrial or commercials-oriented background. They've probably taken your job in a slow period for them, with nothing else coming in. In other words, they're slumming and they need to let everyone else know that at every opportunity. From their limited perspective they may be correct but, for you, they can be a constant pain in the ass.

The best way to win them over is by trying to engage them on something that challenges them on a professional level, then continuing to do this throughout the shoot. Almost all of that corporate/industrial/commercial work is routine and unexciting, so excite them by challenging their professionalism — putting it to the test, so to speak. Come up with a complex camera move they would never dare try with so little time or resources. Have a shot where your boom operator has to follow a couple talking through some impossibly dense overhanging objects. And once you win them over, they are yours and will probably follow you just about anywhere. *However*, if you try some hare-brained stunt that backfires horribly, you will probably lose them forever, so you pays your money and you takes your chances.

There is always the possibility that no matter what you try, some members of your crew will attempt to subtly sabotage or blackmail you in various ways, whether by slowing down, or refusing to do something the way that you ask, demanding meal breaks before you want them, or spreading dissent among the rest of your crew or cast. And the same goes for this kind of crew member as an actor or actress who tries this approach. If you can rid of them, get rid of them, immediately! If you can't get rid of them for a variety of logistical or technical or financial reasons, damage control is the name of the game.

Do whatever you can to limit how many other members of your team they "infect," whether you isolate them by their work assignments, or having them eat a little earlier or later than everyone else, or by how you treat them, or by who you send to deal with them. As much as possible, you should attempt to keep these forms of containment from appearing to be any kind of reaction on your part to what they've been doing or saying. And you should always try and use whatever means they are using to sabotage you against them, to undermine them and limit their influence, while also adding any of your own particularly effective ones. This is not a happy situation and there are no happy solutions. But it is important for you to find one that works—and quickly.

I want to quickly go over problems with inexperienced crew members, as it seems more and more crews are containing more and more inexperienced (read non-paid) crew members. The inexperienced crew member can be your biggest help or your biggest hindrance, depending on how well you treat them. More than anyone else on your set, they will respond to encouragement — as well as being discouraged more by criticism.

This doesn't mean that they shouldn't be criticized or be expected to do their very best at all times. It just means that when you criticize them, it must be in a way that they learn through your critique and become a better crew member through it. If they continue learning, they should be encouraged. If not, they should be fired or their influence minimized by giving them non-essential functions such as glorified go-fers.

What's That Whispering Behind Your Back?

Before we leave the section on cast and crew, I would like to take a few moments to talk about the whispering behind your back that you will surely hear ... but only barely and never loud enough to understand what they're saying. It goes on behind all directors' backs, it's part of the job, and you have to learn to live with it. It's mostly second-guessing practically every decision that you make. (Considering how many decisions you have to make, that's probably quite a bit of whispering.) It's only when the whispering rises to a dull roar that you should begin to really worry. Everyone on a film or video set loves to second-guess the director, it's *the* favorite pastime. So get used to, but never ever let it get to you.

Equipment Problems

The biggest problem that you'll run into with the equipment is a malfunction without warning during production. And this is where how well you've selected your equipment and the people who run it will come into play. Either you got it from a reputable rental house, who will stand behind their equipment and either fix it immediately or get you a replacement, or the crew member working the equipment (that they possibly own) is able to quickly fix almost any problem that arises.

If there's a problem with rented equipment, call the rental house immediately and then go over with the equipment and your crew member who's been working with it. Most places should either try and fix the problem right then or give you a replacement. When it's equipment owned by the operator, they should be able to fix it immediately or be able to arrange a back-up at a reasonable cost. If you have insurance covering this, you're probably covered; if not, *c'est la vie, c'est la guerre!* And if none of these options work, you should immediately find a back-up at the cheapest price and then jump back into production as soon as possible; otherwise you may jeopardize the entire project.

Many of the equipment problems that do happen fall into the category of "intermittent." There is nothing more maddening than a recurring problem, which always seems to disappear just when you bring it in to be looked at. But for my money, on a guerrilla production, an intermittent problem is the same as a totally malfunctioning piece of equipment. It should be quickly fixed or replaced; you do not have the luxury of being at the whim of a piece of equipment that is having intermittent problems.

Another potentially critical problem regarding equipment is its being stolen during your shoot. Every single piece of equipment should have someone with it at all times; if equipment is left somewhere overnight, it should be in a location that you *know is secure*. A laxity on your part leaves you and your entire production open to disaster. Make sure everyone in your crew is on this same wavelength regarding this matter. This is obviously when it's advantageous to be renting your equipment from the person operating it, because they have a vested interest in its safety. But whether it's theirs or not, they should treat it like theirs for the duration of the shoot.

Since more and more gangs of professional thieves are specializing in film and video equipment, camouflaging your production equipment should be your first line of defense. I always carry all of my personally owned equipment in plain bags or cases. But if you're renting equipment that comes in marked cases, etc., try and tape over any brand names or logos with black gaffer's tape. Try not to make a big deal out of it when you're loading or unloading equipment into a location. Keep a low profile and resist the temptation to be a big-time film crew. Don't unload your equipment and leave it lying around outside while people come and go; it should go from the car, van or truck directly into your location. Treat the equipment like it's your own, because during your production *it is*. And it goes without saying, but I will say it anyway: Having equipment insurance can go quite a way in alleviating your anxiety.

Locations/Sets Problems

Whether or not you have liability insurance and permits will determine what your biggest problems on location will be. If you don't have insurance and permits, your biggest problem will be to avoid attracting attention from any governmental authority. Anyone who can "pull the plug" must be eluded. How do you do this? Most of the methods were mentioned earlier in the chapter on finding locations, but what happens when the authorities *do* come around?

The time-honored response is that you are only film students from some local college and you didn't know that you needed permits. It helps tremendously if someone has a valid college ID on them. And if they'll only let you finish this scene, you'll move on. Then, if they're nice enough to let you stay, you do so until they kick you out, shooting as much as possible.

The second most used excuse is that you're doing some local cable access show and they said there was no problem shooting on the streets without permits. Once again, if this works, you shoot as much as you can until they kick you out. I don't condone either method, but I've been told that they have worked in the past.

The method of last resort is the truth — that you are a starving artist who's put up their own money to do this thing and, while you understand their concerns, if they'll only let you finish this scene you'll move right away. I know this is sexist, but if you have a sympathetic and good-looking actress or crew member around, it helps. But once you've been sent away from a location, it's best if you can keep away from that area or any nearby ones for a few days. Try rescheduling and doing interiors or night exteriors in another precinct or city or town for a day or two.

Even when you have insurance, the biggest location-related problems will occur when you are outside in a crowded area during a busy time of day. The only difference is that, instead of hiding from the local authorities and keeping a low profile, now you just have to worry about keeping a low profile so that you can shoot without interruption, while using everything and everyone around you as (free) background.

Of course many things can go wrong, like people staring into the camera, some street hustler making a commotion, an angry neighbor or business person complaining about interfering with their life or business as well as any unanticipated event like an auto accident or any other "Act of God." Obviously, the best tactic is to keep a low profile, so that when you are actually filming, it still looks like you're just standing around. Learn to get the shot while appearing to rehearse or just moving around setting things up. Communicate by non-verbal hand signals and don't scream "action" and "cut." Hollywood gets its shots by controlling the streets; you should get yours by blending in with them.

And remember, the quickest and most expedient method of settling any disagreement with anyone about anything when you're out on location is cold, hard cash slipped into their greasy palms. Nothing works better or quicker than a good old-fashioned bribe, which is what most people causing a commotion are looking for anyway. And even if they aren't, it still works. Make sure you're always carrying cash with you when you're on location; you'd be surprised how well a quick 10 (maybe 20 now) bucks works. I know, I know, you're saying, "But I have a permit, I paid all that money for insurance, I can get the cops, why pay again?" The reason is that you save more time and ultimately more money doing it this way. It's always worked for me; however, if you insist on calling the police and waving your permit around, be my guest, but I told you so.

Most of this advice also goes for when you're shooting inside at someone's house or apartment: Keep as low a profile as possible. Try and make it seem as if nothing special is going on, but if you have to do any stunt or loud commotion, do it before people normally go to sleep or the very last thing before you clear out of that particular location for good. More productions have been kicked out of residential areas because they have pissed off someone's neighbor than for any other reason. And in the over 16 years I've been doing this, my productions have never been kicked out of a location. Keep a respectful, low profile; it works. Remember it, communicate it to your entire team and follow it religiously.

The last and least controllable element concerning locations is the weather. Start following that long-range forecast; the monthly ones aren't really that accurate, but they help. The ten-day ones are closer to the money and the five-day forecasts are usually pretty accurate, but you have to stay on top of the changing fronts that may bring unexpected weather your way. That way you'll have a fairly good idea about the viability of shooting exteriors on certain days and when it's in your best interests to start thinking about alternatives. Especially when rain is forecast as likely (70 percent or more) during a couple days of exterior locations, it's time to think alternatives.

Some exteriors can be done in the rain and you should know which ones they are when you're making up your schedule, so that when problems do arise, you can quickly make all your options available. This can be done by having a sheltered place for the camera and a relatively sheltered place for your actor or actress. You can all be under the same protection, whether it's an awning, park shelter or bus stop. Or you can be separated but both covered, with the camera under an awning shooting across the street at your actors standing underneath a bus shelter. Also, the effect of failing rain can add a certain emotional hue that can be very effective for some scenes. And since you can't control the weather, you should have some locations of last resort, if the weather turns totally against you for long periods of time.

Sylvia (Celia Hansen), alone and frightened deep in the woods, in *Daddy*.

Transportation Problems

Now that your production is beginning, the more dependent you will become on your chosen means of transportation. And any problems here can have a ripple down effect that can be crippling to your schedule. Since getting everyone and everything to the right place and the right time is so crucial, I always try and prepare a small, simple map of the areas where we'll be shooting so that everyone has a quick reference that shows exactly where they're supposed to be. It should illustrate how each location can be reached by car and/or public transportation.

And you should also make sure *before* you begin production that you go over the schedule with everyone to ensure they know where they're supposed to be and how they're going to get there. And if anyone expresses any doubt about being able to get somewhere or about getting back from somewhere, you should provide some means of transportation that will quell their doubts. Whether that means sending a car to pick up someone with a disability or personally driving someone home after a late night's shooting, every one of your cast and crew should feel secure about getting to and going back from every day of your shoot.

If you can't afford what they need, whether it's cab fare or tokens for the subway or giving them a ride home at night, then you should not cast them or you should reconsider cutting other areas of your budget to get the proper transportation. Nothing screws up a schedule like a lost or late cast or crew member.

If you do have insurance and are using permits, make sure you get all your license numbers on the permits and have your permits okayed well in advance of your shoot days. This can be especially critical in large cities, so make sure that you double-check with the person whom you've delegated this important task to.

One final note about transportation: Once you begin production, the more time you save transporting your people and equipment, the more time you'll be able to spend shooting. So now's the time, if you have to shell out a little extra for cabs or whatever, to do so.

Food Problems

As I mentioned earlier, there are two major problems you can run into with food, the quality and a lack of variety. But especially on a low-budget guerrilla shoot, food problems can turn into cast and crew mutinies and that's something you should avoid at all costs, especially since it can be devastating to morale and is relatively simple to avoid. Just make sure you delegate this to someone you *know* will take it seriously and do the best they can on the budget you provide. And don't skimp on this, if you can at all help it; it's just not worth the few dollars saved.

One other problem with food is the scheduling of meal breaks. Breakfast should be there when people arrive, not a minute after. And then you should have two main breaks during the day, whose timing should be dictated by the scenes that you're shooting that day, not by any set time. But if you start hearing a concerted grumbling from those around you, it's probably time to at least start taking orders or call your caterer, girlfriend, boyfriend or mother to bring on the chow.

Supplies Problems

In terms of supplies, your biggest problem will be running out of something on location that requires pulling one of your crew members to go and get it. And the best way to avoid this is by having options or anticipating anything that could possibly run out. It's always worth it to have more than you'll need (if you can afford it!) than to run out and then have someone run off in the middle of production. But once you do have to send someone, make sure they have enough cash and get back as soon as possible. And if this necessitates that you stop shooting a particular scene, find another scene to work on until your person gets back.

A quick note about faulty stock: If you think you have faulty stock, you should try and ascertain how much is bad and return it for an exchange as soon as possible, worrying about who's responsible after production is finished. If you're covered by insurance, they will in all probability cover the loss; and if you're not covered, you're at the mercy of the vendor anyway. And wasting your valuable production time will not make life easier. Remember, once you begin production, it's like a rollercoaster: It's impossible to get off until the end of the ride, unless you want to bail out and take a terrible spill in the process.

Another guerrilla insurance tip is to make up a small utility supply kit and have it with you at all times. It should include a variety of nails, tacks, push pins, straight pins, clamping wooden clothes pins, extremely thin "flying" wire (used by window designers to make clothing appear to fly, but is useful in invisibly altering all sorts of curtains or drapes in a matter of seconds), a flashlight with new batteries, needle and a variety of threads, a leatherman-type all-in-one utility tool, aluminum foil, clear wrap, large black plastic garbage bags and a small first aid kit, all packed together in one large duffel bag. I've used all of the above on all of my productions; they really do come in handy.

Wardrobe/Props Problems

Having a dedicated crew member in charge of wardrobe is the best way to avoid wardrobe problems while shooting, with the next best solution is having the cast be responsible for their own wardrobe. But even with these precautions, there are bound to be problems. The most frequent problem I've run into is when something that you bought a few weeks ago and looked great in the store, now looks terrible on camera. Most of the time, this is only a matter of a small alteration.

You only have to alter what appears on camera, so if you have an actress who's lost a few pounds in anticipation of being in front of the camera (a very common occurrence, as many of the actresses I've known have started on diets the minute they know they're going to be in a movie) and her skirt is now too big around the waist and she's only facing the camera, a clothespin at the back of the skirt's waistline will work fine and only take a minute rather than trying to sew the damn thing.

Gaffer's tape can be used for a wide variety of quick clothing alterations. Straight pins, which should also be part of your supplies, can more permanently hold up an annoying cuff or sleeve. And of course a needle and various kinds of thread should always be in your miscellaneous supply kit, as a last resort. Whenever you think you'll have any clothing and/or material that must appear pressed, you should have an iron or steamer with you. One last tip: The quickest way to remove or tone down a stain is a cold, damp cloth followed by a blow dryer, another handy, multi-use tool.

Yeah, yeah, yeah, I know it sounds like a young homemaker's club, but that's why so many amateur productions *look* amateur. You have to take the time to make the difference about what finally appears on camera. It doesn't take that much time, but it does make the difference.

Running Out of Time

Up until this point we've been talking about situations that were, for the most part, negotiable, not absolute. I now am going to discuss the two non-negotiable, brick wall realities of underground, guerrilla filmmaking: running out of time and running out of money. First, I will cover running out time, since (let's hope), that will be occurring more often than running out money.

You will always be running out of time on a low- no-budget shoot, no matter how well you've planned things in advance, but how well you react to the many different situations will have a major impact on ultimate success or failure of your project. The best way to successfully navigate these treacherous waters is to always have your priorities in mind and use them as the basis of your decisions.

When you step onto every set at every location, you should have a clear idea of the shots that you need to get and those extra shots that you would *like* to get. Your first priority should always be to get the shots that you need to get. Never get bogged down with a shot that is not necessary until you have finished every necessary shot on your list. (A necessary shot being one that, if you *don't* have it, you will not be able to have a complete film, it will leave an unexplainable gap or hole in your story.) Many of these shots are often the least interesting shots you may have to make that day, but get them done, then move on.

And this is where how well you've prioritized your schedule in advance will save the day or not. If you've taken the scenes you wanted to take extra time with into consideration when you made your schedule, you should have the time to do them. If not, then....

But if you are running out of time and it looks like you're not going to have time to even do your necessary shots, it's time to come up with an alternate plan that will allow you to get what you need. The main way of accomplishing this is by compressing and/or reducing the remaining shots into the least number of shots that will communicate those necessary story-based elements. However, if you keep running into this problem day after day, it reflects your unrealistic planning and now is the time to pay the price.

Practically, this means that if you have planned a complicated scene with ten set-ups and you only have an hour or two left, you must figure out how to shoot that scene in only one or two shots, one or two set-ups. Whether you accomplish this by doing it in a continuous take instead of the ten you planned or you use a hand-held camera to try and get all the shots with only one set-up or you rewrite the entire scene to accommodate the time remaining—that's up to you.

As a side note, this is also the point where some productions begin grinding their cast or crew into the ground by doing extremely long days with little or no turn-around and not allowing for proper sleep. This can work for short periods of time, but if it continues, it usually has an increasingly negative effect not only on morale, but also on everyone's performance, both cast and crew. And it will begin to show up on the screen, the worst mistake you can make. Also, other mistakes will begin to be made; people will get careless and people will begin to get hurt. This is not a happy situation and one to be avoided, if at all possible. This is another area on low/

no-budget productions where mutinies can begin to occur. Your cast and crew should not be asked to pay for your mistakes in under-budgeting or under-scheduling.

But this is a time when you should be consulting with your cast and crew for their suggestions, as they may have some experience in this area and come up with a solution that may be better or quicker than yours. It really doesn't matter who comes up with the solution, as long as the solution is a good one that allows you to get what you need. Don't be proud, be successful. But be on your guard against making compromises out of exhaustion, yours or others; they are often the most expedient, but seldom the best.

While these suggestions deal with running out of time during individual shoot days, there is also the remote possibility that you will run out of time on your schedule and not be able to shoot enough footage to make a complete film or video. Although this is not a particularly joyous moment, it is a crucial moment for you and your vision. Once again, your priorities should guide you.

You should immediately figure out how much you can accomplish with the remaining time and how much will be left to shoot. You should then figure out exactly who you will need to complete the remaining material. And make absolutely sure that you begin at once to secure their cooperation. If you've treated them well, you probably won't have to worry.

Another option is to see if there's a way to finish your film with the footage that you have, either by rewriting it or figuring out an editing strategy that allow you to stretch the material you do have. But whatever plan you devise, you should try and have your strategy in place within a day or two after your first realization that you're not going to be able to finish all that you've planned. Then set right out to begin building the foundation for what will be necessary to complete this next stage.

Running Out of Money

Okay, you've done it, you've run out of money and you haven't finished shooting — what do you do now? Beg, borrow or steal? Considering that you've probably done one, two or all of the above already, what you should be doing is figuring out how much it will cost to finish what you absolutely need to have a completed film, if you continue now. And then figure out how much it will cost you if you have to stop and begin again later to complete whatever you will need. Is it cheaper to borrow the money at some exorbitant rate or shut down and start again once you've raised the extra money? Hard questions.

Can you get the actors or actresses you need back again or are they already figuring out their blackmail demands? Can you get back into the locations or will new ones do? Will you actually be able to raise the extra money after what you went through to get this money? Do you want the hassle of doing this all over again or do you want to get it over with? If you borrow off your credit cards, will you have a way of paying them back or has personal bankruptcy always held a fascination for you? Who can you stall for money that might let you finish? These and probably a thousand other questions will probably being racing through your mind at this point, but it's important to make a somewhat rational decision, even though you're on one of the more irrational work-related paths anyone could think of at this moment.

Your main consideration should be whether you want to finish at all (and if you're reading this book, you'd better), then to decide what is the best for the project while being the least financially onerous solution for you. I would then suggest if there is any way that you can finish without putting yourself into undue financial jeopardy that you should do so. But you will have to define for yourself what is "undue" and what is "financial jeopardy." But it usually costs quite a bit more to start over again than it does to continue by borrowing from somewhere or someone. Just try not to make a deal that gives away too much of your ownership in the film, as some people in this situation have given away most of their rights and/or percentages, just in order to finish.

I detest taking credit card loans, although I have done so, but never more than I could comfortably pay back. And at the budgets and schedules I've been suggesting, your shortfall, at the most, should be a few thousand dollars. And if you must resort to credit cards or loan sharks (is there much difference any more?) because they are the only place that will give you the money you need quickly, I suggest that you look for a lower interest rate immediately thereafter. And the loan shark reference was a joke ... really.

You might try for a personal loan at your local bank or find those credit card deals with extremely low rates for the first few months and keep transferring around as much as you can to avoid paying their exorbitant interest rates. But the best way is to offer to pay a friend or relative a fraction of the percentage of the loan rate that the banks and credit card companies are asking you to pay and that will still probably be way more than they pay their depositors. Figure it out: The credit card companies will want you to pay 14 to 20+ percent, while the banks pay their customers less than 5 percent. You should be able to find a good deal with someone that benefits both of you. Try it, it's a lot better than the banks or credit card companies.

If it's more than a few thousand dollars, you should seriously think about shutting down until you can raise the rest of the money or rewriting/re-editing or making a short film out of what you have. No film or video in the budget range I've been covering is a sure thing for distribution and don't let anyone kid you to the contrary. In today's market, that's just not real.

12

Metamorphosis of the Ambush

Looking at Your Footage

Now that you've spent a few weeks or months of your life striving to hold onto some elusive yet strangely compelling vision, it's finished and in the can. Exhausted but proud of having endured this ordeal, you now want to begin looking at your footage, right? Wrong! The best thing you can do at this point is to take time off, rest, recharge your batteries and try, as much as possible, to forget everything to do with the shoot. *And don't look at the footage!* A break will give you a clearer perspective, allowing you to view the footage on its own merits, without associating all the difficulties you had in making it.

Another reason I suggest not looking at your footage for a couple of weeks, is because you are now entering the last distinct part of the filmmaking process and nothing that you have done up until this point is relevant, except the footage you now have before you. Your script is irrelevant. Your shoot is irrelevant. The only thing that matters at this point is the actual footage in front of you, not what you *should* have had or *could* have had or *would* have had, but what you have *now*! And the very best way to make the very best finished film with the footage you have, is by being able to view this material with a totally fresh eye.

My Editing Process

I will now spend a moment detailing my editing process, which (to be polite) would best be described as idiosyncratic. And the reason I'm putting it here is that I want you to start thinking of your own personal preferences and not the way it's supposed to be done, although I will cover that also.

The first thing I do is to throw my script away, because I'm now editing my film, not my script. And if I don't know my story by now, I'm in real trouble anyway! And I don't pick the "best" takes or selects, since I transfer all the film I shot to video, with the audio already synced. I then have everything I shot on three or four two-hour SVHS tapes, which I start to edit on a cuts only, SVHS edit system that I own.

With every bit of footage that I shot in front of me, I begin editing, constantly scanning (at 32x speed with stable picture) back and forth over the footage. This is how I "learn" my footage; I don't want to make any selects until I'm editing the actual scene. I then pick out only those shots that work for me in this particular scene and I put them together. They don't necessarily follow any continuity and the scene may not even work this way, but these are the shots I want to stay with and build my scene around.

If the scene works as is, I leave it. If it doesn't work, meaning it either doesn't make narrative sense or I don't like the narrative sense that it does make, I start looking for shots that will make it work. They can come from any scene, any take, bad or good, from any of the footage I'm constantly scanning through. Anything that will make the scene work. Since the scene is my building block, with my outline (instead of a script) as the overall structure.

Once I finish a scene, I attempt to see where it's leading me; usually it's to the next scene, but occasionally something visual will lead me somewhere else and I usually follow. Then I build the scene I've just been led to in the same way, seeing where that takes me. Usually it's close to my original outline but occasionally I've discovered editing elements or visual leitmotifs that weren't in the outline, but have entered some time during the shoot.

Once I have gone through my entire story this way, I look back to see how it flows. Where I feel it stops flowing, I look at that scene and try to decide whether it's just a bad scene that needs to be dropped entirely or if it just has to be placed somewhere else. Once I get to this point, it begins to become clear which scenes constitute complete sequences and should always stay together. Once I've got my scenes down, the main editing problem then becomes the placement of these sequences and the further elimination of any scene that doesn't work or gets in the way of the flow of sequences. The main problem remaining is to place my sequences in a structure or order that allows them to flow uninterrupted from one sequence to the other.

Dailies

Now back to the main road: If you shot on film, you will either be looking at your film dailies or most likely video dailies transferred from your negative; if you shot on video, you'll be looking at time-coded copies of your master tapes. Remember, play your master video only when absolutely necessary — that is, making these dubs and for the final edit. All the video should have time code to help you identify each take and the video dailies from film should also have the key code or the identifying edge numbers that are imprinted on all film these days.

The film dailies will also include the slates with their scene and take numbers, which should match up to your camera reports, allowing you to identify each take. When shooting film, I try and have video dailies made of everything I shot; it costs a little more, but I think it's well worth all the little extra things I have found in some of my n.g. (no good) takes over the years. At this point you may want to sync your audio with your video dailies, while your time-coded (from the video masters) ones are already in sync.

The Log and Your Selects

Then proceed to make a list of every take, selecting those that you think might work and those that definitely don't work, with their timings, in and out points and any other comments about that particular shot (see *Daddy* Sample Shot Log in back of book). Do you like take #3 and #4? Then highlight them. Is take #5 shaky but interesting? Mark that. This is the only first impression you will ever have of your footage, so make the most of it. Look for anything that moves you on an emotional or story level, not at how difficult it was to get this or that shot.

Another seemingly obvious, but very important point to remember is the main goal of the editing process is to edit out the bad or whatever doesn't work and leave in the good or whatever does work. And how ruthless and critical you are with yourself at this stage will largely determine how well your edit proceeds. Remember, one of Roger Corman's key pieces of advice to new directors was to be very tough with yourself when editing.

Try as much as possible to divorce yourself from the entire production process and look for those things that work now as you sit watching, those things that move you emotionally, intellectually or aesthetically. These moments should be your select takes, the key building blocks of your final edit. If they match what you believed the key moments of your script were, great. If not, think about throwing out your script.

This is the single biggest editing problem I see in independent films: They only edit to their script. For some unknown reason, they will not deviate from their original script. That's why the independent films that seem to be most successful are the well-written ones, even though they usually end up being not very interesting as films. If your script helps you put this footage together, great, use your script, but if things don't seem to be working out, change them until they do. You have absolutely no obligation to follow your script; your only obligation is to make the footage in front of you work as a moving picture.

Film Cutters and Film Editors

With the proliferation of non-linear computer-based editing systems, more and more people are calling themselves editors. To my mind, most of these people may be cutters, but they are really not editors. What's the difference? A cutter knows how to run the equipment efficiently, will cut your film together (usually the way you ask them) without making any creative editorial/content decisions that will help shape your material, and it will usually end up being boring as hell.

Real editors will help you shape your material, taking an active part in helping you decide what "works" and what "doesn't work," all the while offering creative alternatives to those sections that don't work. They will have the ability to totally restructure your material, if it needs it, or fine tune those elements that only need to be tweaked to gain their maximum effect. They will edit not only your material, but your story as well, helping you find and fix any slow spots, irrelevant scenes, bad performances, poorly placed sequences or overlong sections. They should also be able to suggest an editing solution to practically any problem you have, whether performance, ruined footage, missing scenes—even creating totally new scenes that never existed in your original script. A real editor will always contribute to the process; cutters will do what they're told.

Therefore, your editor should be as carefully "auditioned" as your DP or lead cast members. Ask to see what they've worked on, making sure that they were actually responsible for the creative editing decisions. Try to look at more than one feature that they've done. And ask for references; talk to the directors they've worked with, especially concerning the creative process that they went through. Did the editor contribute creatively or only punch the buttons?

The Rough Cut

Once you've chosen your editor or decided to go it on your own, the typical course is to begin your edit following your script, using your selected takes as you go along. This then gives you your first rough cut. Don't slit your wrists ... yet. First rough cuts almost always look horrible and last way too long. They are also usually missing most parts of an extremely important element—*the sound*—which makes them seem even more incomplete.

But once you have finished your first rough cut, you should have some idea of the monster you have in front of you. This is where you should begin to discriminate between those elements that need work and those elements that are bad and simply do not work. Lop out any and all things that do not work. I mean *everything* that doesn't work; whether it's a shot, a sequence or an entire scene, it's time to get ruthless. Quite often they are the pieces you may have worked the hardest or the longest to shoot, but if they're bad, get rid of them and find an editing solution around them.

Hope that, between the scenes that need work and those that just don't work at all are the ones that work relatively well right away. Don't meddle with what works right off the bat, just be thankful and hope that at some later point you're not forced to remove one of these sequences because they interfere with the overall shape of your finished film. Too much tinkering can be just as bad as not enough tinkering. Leave well enough alone ... for now.

But it's only after you've put all your individual scenes together that you can begin to see the overall shape of your film. Does it work? If not, what doesn't? Can you fix what doesn't work? If not, get rid off it! Will something work if you change its position? Try it! This is where you must think about rewriting/restructuring your film if what you shot is not successfully piecing together the way you have set out in your original script. I can't stress enough that if your story isn't working at this stage of your edit, you have to begin rethinking the ways in which the material you do have can be reshaped to work as a film.

Remember, it's always better to have an interesting 60–minute film that works than a boring 80–minute film that doesn't work. No one remembers bad or boring films, thank goodness! But a film that holds your interest for the entire running time, no matter how short, is not something to be dismissed.

Technical Options for Editing

Most films are now edited on video— hell, most films are now shown on video, but that's another story. If you shoot on film and decide to edit on video, it will probably be some sort of Avid, Final Cut Pro or Media 100. Whatever non-linear system you pick, your film will be transferred to video sometimes with your sync audio or sometimes with your synced audio added later.

Your selects (and maybe more if you have enough storage space) are then loaded into the non-linear system where you will do your edit, ending up with an edit decision list (EDL) that will be translated into key codes or edge codes of the film, allowing your negative cutter to cut your film negative from that list. Many people try and do as much of their mix as possible on the non-linear system, especially if they are on any kind of deferred deal, thus saving them time and money mixing at a separate sound facility. But this is half a dozen of one and six of the other.

If you decide to cut your film solely on film, you will have a work print made, usually a one light print — that is, the film will be exposed with a general overall timing for every scene. This work print will be used for your rough edit, working towards your final cut. Once you have locked your picture edit, you will have your negative cut, then have an internegative made from that and then a timed answer print, making each shot correspond to your visual ideal as much as possible, while correcting any variances of correct exposure. Your sound will be recorded and mixed to mag stock from this answer print. Then your mag track with the mixed sound will locked to your answer print, creating your picture with an optical track. At the end of all this will be your final print as well as a safety print for back-up.

Get a Second Opinion, or: Staying Open

During the process of editing, it's essential that you remain open, open to other viewpoints, open to anything that will make your film or video better. Don't shut yourself up in a room and only emerge after you've finished. Show your rough cut to other people; you'd be surprised how many things you never noticed will be picked up by others. This is the stage where you should be interested in anything that doesn't make sense to people, that bothers people, that interferes with their viewing experience, no matter how small or trivial. I'm not saying that you should be making thousands of changes based on anyone's and everyone's comments, but you should be listening, carefully.

You should want to know of anything that you were not aware OF, that is, your blind spots. And nothing is better at discovering these blind spots than showing your rough cut to people. But there are a few things you should be aware of, that may help you through the dense jungle of other people's opinions.

First of all, you have to be in film or video production to be able to watch a rough cut with any degree of critical accuracy. Anyone who is not involved in production has little or no chance of being able to watch a rough cut without being distracted by the missing or unfinished elements that all rough cuts have.

Second of all, even if someone is in the business, most people cannot intelligently watch a rough cut and make helpful critiques. If you can find four or five people you are doing pretty good (and this is something that can only be picked up over years of experience). This aspect is much harder to gauge because everyone in the business really thinks they can look at rough cuts and make accurate and helpful, critical comments without being distracted by the missing and/or unfinished elements.

This doesn't mean that it isn't helpful when someone starts scratching their ass at 45 minutes into the picture, but it does mean that not many people are able to effectively articulate what the problems are, let alone making helpful suggestions. Because too often the suggestions have less to do with your film and more to do with the film they would make if they were doing your film. They really need to be able to have a sense of your film, where it breaks down and how you might best correct those imbalances in the film you want to make, not the one they want to make.

Which leads us to the third and most difficult element to gauge and correct, and that is what is usually called "story editing," those structural elements that can make or break a feature film's chances for success. I find that even most editors, unless they have experience cutting only feature films, are not very helpful in this very critical area.

The majority of editors spend most of their time cutting pieces that run no longer than 20 minutes or even less. So they may be helpful in putting a scene together, but forget about sequences, let alone an entire feature. In fact, some of the best story editors aren't really editors in the physical sense, but the function they perform is most definitely an editing function. So when you're looking for an editor, try and find one who edits features, not on the side, but as their main focus.

Now that I've gone through those whose professional opinion may be of help, I'll try and cover some of the key aspects of having non-professionals viewing your rough cuts. Everybody will have some opinion about what they like and dislike about your film or video. And the one thing that most people will have a very distinct opinion about is the actors and actresses. Whether they like them or not, which usually has quite a bit to do with how much those actors or actresses match up with how they think of themselves. They will be looking for idealized versions of themselves. And everybody will love different actors or actresses while also hating different actors and actresses. There will never be a consensus and quite frankly there's not a lot you can do about this—nor should you.

But it will help you to know when and where you may be losing part of your audience and when and where your film may need some work. If everyone hates all of your characters all the time, you have a problem, a real big problem, but if there is only one character everyone dislikes, and I'm talking about their lack of conviction as an actor, as opposed to their character's personality, then their scenes need to be cut or beefed up. Look carefully at these performances and be ruthless. If they suck, cut out as much as possible and if that's not practical, try to minimize the damage, but choosing shots that favor another actor or actress.

Another area about which you can get accurate feedback is dull spots or places where the film is moving too slow or losing your audience's interest. This means that when you are viewing the film with any audience, professional or amateur, you should be watching the audience, not your film or video. Looking for any non-verbal reactions that will give you feedback on what works and what doesn't. So watch your audience, not your film.

Use What You Have ... Time

And then use what you have, the extra time, to make the necessary changes that will make your entire film work as one moving picture. Don't think that you have to rush your work out to make a certain festival or film market deadline. Because, here once again, your film will only make one first impression. Festivals, buyers, distributors, critics will only view your film or video once, so that the first time you present your work had better be the best shape it's ever going to be in.

Sound Advice

So keep cutting out the bits that don't work, then figure out something that does work, whether that involves adding new elements or restructuring sections or even the whole thing. And one of the most overlooked but useful tools in patching up or bolstering slow or dull spots is the creative use of sound. Not only music, but voiceovers, sound effects or subtle room ambiences can add that extra element that turns a humdrum scene into something special. Remember, just as every character has a specific wardrobe that reflects who they are, so every location in your film should have a specific ambience that gives your audience a feeling of actually being there.

And every sound effect should be treated as a unique occurrence, not the seventeenth time you've heard that same gunshot in the last two minutes, or every time one of your characters walks down the street, they have the exact same footsteps. Individualize your sound effects and add that extra dimension that will draw your audience into your story.

Sound can also add an extra dimension to your story that is missing in your visuals by being used contrapuntally, that is, working against the visual to create some completely different third dimension through the interaction of that particular sound and that particular visual.

An example, you have a long shot of a sunny country road one lazy summer day. If you have sync sound, it would probably be birds singing, bees buzzing and maybe the wind blowing. But what happens if you add some ominous, dissonant music rumbling in the background? Your visual is totally undercut by the sound. Something nasty is hiding somewhere, waiting to happen.

I once was editing a short film that was shot in an apartment whose walls were painted in muted warm tones that I thought worked against the ominous scenes taking place there. So to darken the mood without changing the color of the wall, which was way beyond our budget, I devised a series of low frequency ambiences that were barely audible under each scene. This added a definite creepiness to the action which you could feel, but could never define. Use sound to add new dimensions to your story that you may have missed when you were shooting.

And just as you have attempted to repeat various visual elements that together form your visual style, you should have audio elements that create an aural style. The German film director Leni Riefenstahl said that when her visuals weren't very interesting, she worked especially hard on building up the sound, so that there is a constant shifting of emphasis that ensures the audience's constant engagement throughout the entire film. Whether it's through the use of unusual ambiences like David Lynch or the subjective audio distortions that Alfred Hitchcock sprinkles through his films or the distinctive musical scores used by countless directors, creating a unique aural signature can only add to the richness of your film.

One other element to remember about your sound mix is that just as you should vary the relationship between sound and image, you should also try to vary all three ranges of audio frequencies, so that they play off one another like an instrumental trio. Making sure to use some kind of lower bass tones, mid-range, usually verbal mid-tones and accented with the higher frequencies, having them constantly working off of one another, or at times isolating one or the other. Don't have sounds of the same frequency going on simultaneously, as they will tend to cancel each other out.

By finding and building many of these sound effects yourself, you can save a considerable amount of editing time and money. All it takes is a quality audio recorder, a good microphone and time. I've found that if I went out with a portable, professional quality audio deck, analog or digital and a good shotgun mic with headsets, I can not only record many of the extra sounds I needed, but I could edit them together on my linear video edit system.

But this can now be better accomplished using many of the relatively cheap computer-based sound mixing programs. This will allow you to spend as much time as you like in the comfort of your home or office, getting your sound effects exactly right, then just dropping them into your edit, saving time and money.

Here's an example from my film *Death Desire*. I had an interesting scene where this actress went back to her old boyfriend's place to pick up her stuff. When she walks in, he wakes up from a drunken stupor and confronts her. I wanted her to seem more like a ghost than a real person and, although the scene worked on a visual level, it needed something to give it that extra dimension. I had tried music, but the only music that worked was too obvious and didn't fit in with the rest of the film. So I went out and recorded various noisy heating pipes which when mixed together created a disturbing, otherworldly aura. And it didn't cost a cent.

More Sound Advice

It's always cheaper to have original music done for your film than getting the rights (publishing and performing!) to previously recorded material. Your work will never be shown if you are "borrowing" copyrighted music. Do all those aspiring filmmakers from New Jersey really think Bruce Springsteen will let them use his music, just because they're from New Jersey too? To my ears, music composed specifically for a film is always better overall than a cobbled-together score, with my apologies to Kenneth Anger, Stanley Kubrick, Martin Scorsese, Werner Herzog and Quentin Tarantino, who are the only directors I can think of that make pre-recorded compilations really work in their films.

Make sure that you have a written agreement with your composer/songwriter/musician that includes the performing as well as the synchronization rights for their music, as you'll need both to use their work on your film. Sample agreements can be "borrowed" from the Internet or filmmaking resource books.

The hardest part of this process is finding that specific composer and/or musicians who are on a similar wavelength and who you can afford to pay for their efforts. But the monetary angle can often be negotiated by offering to do a music video for them or their band in return for doing your score. Or you may feature them or their band somewhere in your film or video. Or the person running the post-production sound facility maybe a musician or closet composer. There are many different avenues that you can explore when trying to negotiate deals with musicians and recording studios. They are usually much more flexible, when making deals, than most video or film facilities.

While the cheapest way to get a soundtrack may be to find a local band or two that have already recorded albums (CDs, tapes, etc.) that you like and then just pick and cut their songs to your film or tape, I almost always find this works to the detriment of the finished film or video. For my money, it's always best to find a composer who loves film music and work with them, but remember, the only people who can tell a composer what they want using words are other musicians.

Anyone else who tries to use only words is asking for trouble. The slippery shades of verbal meaning are never more slippery than when a non-musician is trying to explain what they want musically to a musician.

I suggest using music that arouses in you similar thoughts or emotions to those you want to convey to your audience and then play it for your composer. Give them music to listen to, to respond to, to work from. But make sure that your composer knows specifically what it is in the music that made you pick it out. Sometimes you may pick out a piece of music only because it's the right kind of instrumentation, but your composer hears that it uses only minor chords and writes something using minor chords but a totally different instrumentation. Try and be as precise as possible, giving more than one example of what you're looking for, then let them interpret that for you.

Suggest that they come back later with a couple of different approaches. Do it on an inexpensive medium, like a piano or synthesizer, which allows for a give-and-take process, while not running up your budget with studio and/or musicians costs at this early stage. But don't play a piece and expect them to spit it back for you, the same, but different. If that's the case, go out and find that music and pay for it. And remember, it also helps to tell them right up front how much you can spend on the music, letting them know if the budget includes everything, which usually includes the composer, the musicians and the recording sessions or if the budget includes only their services.

One last reminder: If you have music underneath your dialogue, make sure your composer is aware of the need to use sound frequencies other than that of the human voice or compose music that is so sparse that the dialogue can fall between the musical notes.

Obviously, the best thing is finding someone whose music you love, setting some sort of instrumental and/or monetary boundaries, then letting them loose. This is what Hitchcock did with Bernard Herrmann and you can hear the amazing results.

13

Presenting the Ambush

Screenings

Now that you've finished your film or video, who do you show it to? As I've been saying all along, your first responsibility is to your cast and crew, so as far as I'm concerned, they should be the first ones to view it. I always try to arrange a screening for the entire cast and crew, as well as any close friends of theirs. I also try and make it into some kind of celebration, with little gag gifts for various cast and crew members, as well as some sort of party afterwards. You are not only thanking them but (if you're in this for the long run) attempting to cement long-term relationships. In addition, this is probably the most positive reaction your work will receive and it's always nice to get a boost before having to go out and face the sometimes cruel realities of the outside world.

I always try and sit off to the side so that I can watch people's faces and reactions, because as you embark on the equally arduous task of selling your film, the more you know about how audiences react to your film, the better your ability to position your film to prospective buyers, festivals or critics.

Your first official public screening will have an important effect on how your film is perceived, so take care in where you screen and who you invite, as this will be yet another variation on making your only first impression. And in this business, the "buzz" (which is the hype generated — or not) is taken very seriously, occupying an increasing role in the promotion and sales of films, especially independent films. And even though it may be bullshit, it will actually affect how your film is perceived and treated, so take it seriously.

There are a variety of options available, all with their own positive and negative aspects, which I will now cover. One, you can hold a private screening by inviting distributors, festival programmers, sales agents, agents, other production people or anyone else who may be able to give your film or video that extra push it will need to be commercially successful. Two, you can wait until your film or video has accepted by a festival or screening series, then use that screening as your premiere while inviting prospective buyers, sales agents or other festival programmers *to* that screening. Three, you can enter one of the many film markets, with the Independent Feature Project being your best and often only bet. However, since I started writing this book, they have changed their entire set-up so that the event no longer resembles a true market, but rather someone's "curated" idea of what is worthy, leaving most of its members out in the cold where they were before the Independent Feature Project was formed. And, finally, you can mail out screening videotapes and/or DVDs directly to the distributors, festivals, agents or critics.

The first option (holding a private screening) is best if you can be sure that most of the industry people you invite will actually show up. And unless your film is being shown in Los Angeles or New York, and/or has some sort of commercial angle, i.e., some kind of celebrity attached to or involved with the project, the odds are not really in your favor of getting those distributors, festival programmers, sales agents or critics to come to your screening.

However, if you realistically think you can get these people to attend your screening, it is by far the most advantageous approach. And as an underground, guerrilla filmmaker you will want to find the most prestigious setting at the lowest possible cost, which obviously is free. The best choices would be a screening room, a local theater, a media access center, a school or anywhere you know someone and can get a great deal. I have a friend who works for an AV company that's located in hotels and through his extreme generosity I have had most of my screenings with top-flight equipment in great settings. Work whatever angles you can; try talking to your local movie theater, which may not be showing films in the afternoon or late night.

If you pull off such a screening and your film or video is well-received, you can be pretty well assured of creating a positive "buzz" about your project. However, if your screening is not well-received, you may have permanently damaged your film's commercial potential. So make sure that you've tested your work in front of audiences before attempting any private screening for "the industry." Then you "pays your money and takes your chances."

Now for most underground, guerrilla productions, I would say that having your premiere at a festival or screening series would be your best and most viable option. And although I do have many serious doubts about most film festivals (which I will enumerate a little bit later), they can be of immense benefit to you and your work. If your film or video has been picked by a prestigious (there aren't that many) festival, it has already passed one level of industry acceptance, which automatically puts you one step up. So by making distributors, sales agents, agents or critics aware of your screening, you have everything to gain and little to loose, *if* that particular festival is one that most of them will be attending. This is where picking the right festivals comes into play and I will also cover that in more detail.

As you may remember, the Eastwood Theory of Limitations states that a man (or woman) "has got to know" their limitations. And just as it was extremely helpful to know your limitations when shooting your film or video, it will be extremely helpful to know your projects limitations and strengths when trying to market it. Although the prevailing industry attitude is that you have to know how and to whom you will be marketing your film *before* you make it, it is absolutely necessary before you begin to market it, *after* you've finished making it.

No one wants to classify their work, it's unique, and while that may be true, that's not the way things work today. There are strictly defined genres, audience demographics and marketing strategies that offer little room for variations from the norm, whatever the hell that norm is. This will be true for almost all the distributors out there. However, if you're determined to do it on your own, then all power to you and you can do what you like. But no matter how you proceed, you should have an objective view concerning what kind of beast your film or video is. It's strengths as well as its weaknesses. So look long and hard at what your finished film is, not what you started out after, not what you wrote your script to be, not what would be easier to sell, but what your finished film or video *is*.

If it's any kind of love story with humor and has a happy ending, it's a romantic comedy, if it has an unhappy ending even with humor, it's a drama. If it has more gunplay and car chases than dialogue, it's action, if it has gangsters then it's crime, if it has vampires it's horror. If you have any doubts, just walk into any Blockbuster Video store and ask yourself, where would they put my film or video?

In order to best gauge which festivals to enter, which distributors to contact, which sales agents to approach, you have to know what you have and what each particular festival, distributor or sales agent has previously been interested in as well as what they are now looking for. You don't enter an underground festival with a subtle drama of middle-aged angst, any more than you would send your "beach and babes" film to Sundance.

Another option, whose viability for most underground, guerrilla filmmakers has recently been greatly diminished, is the Independent Feature Project Market in New York City. They were the only game in town, hell, in the *world*, for low- or no-budget films and videos. But be forewarned, they are becoming more and more restrictive in terms of the films or videos that they accept.

The only alternative to the Independent Feature Project Market is the American Film Market, which is located in Santa Monica and specializes in lower-budgeted films from Hollywood and other smaller companies not affiliated with the large studios. They specialize in genre pictures that are typically knock-offs of their larger-budgeted brethren. It's not cheap to attend and you have to sign an agreement not to try and sell your film, unless you're attending as a registered seller at an even higher fee, which is usually beyond the range of most underground, guerrilla productions. But one way some people get around this is by assigning their film to a registered seller to represent them during the market, usually for some percentage of any deal made there. And although this isn't the best deal, it is a way in without paying up front. But if you can afford to attend, it will really open your eyes, giving you a much more realistic look at the business of film in the "reel" world.

The last option is sending your VHS/DVD screener out to prospective buyers, agents, festivals, etc. This is where doing your homework can make or break you. You should have researched which companies or festivals or agents seem to be the most responsive to the type of material you're sending them, then find out the particular contact people in that organization who have the responsibility of going through submissions in your area. The more specific you can be, the better your chances of at least being seen.

Once you've sent it, you may want to do a follow-up in a few weeks, but don't keep bothering them with phone calls or e-mails. I've found that if companies or people are interested, they will call you back almost immediately and if they aren't, you will never hear from them. No one wants to say no, because they may want to say yes later and not have you remember they said no earlier. So the standard response is usually no response. But if you do get a response, be sure to follow up immediately.

One more bit of advice: When sending your VHS/DVD out, you should have two or three levels of companies or people that you want to approach. The first level should be those people you would ideally like to distribute or screen or represent your work, your very top choices. The next level are the ones you wouldn't mind handling your work. And if all those fail, any others who handle your type of material, good, bad or indifferent.

When sending VHS/DVDs out, it's best that you have some sort of "For Screening Purposes Only" or "For Preview Only" in small type across the lower third of your picture, to prevent unscrupulous people from copying and selling your film without your knowledge. Although not a commonplace event, it does happen. And if you can't afford to have that done, ask if the duplication place can make copies with the time-code burned in the lower third. It's not as classy, but it works and can save you the cost of making an extra master.

Of course, you should make sure that you get the best quality dubs done since, once again, this is the only first impression your film will be making with the companies or individuals you are sending your film to. And you will want it to be the very best that you can afford. You may also want to present any promotional material such as reviews, news of festival screenings, etc., that may help someone evaluating your work. And make sure everything looks professional. Most people in the business will not want to waste their time on an amateurish looking piece of material. Also putting your presskit on CD can save you quite a bit in photocopying costs.

The Press, or: You Gotta Have Friends

As the old saying goes; "Bad press is better than no press," so it's in your best interests to cultivate any kind of relationship with any of the different branches of the press, whether print, TV/cable, radio or Internet. These are the only outlets that will allow you to gain a measure of access to wider audiences without costing too much, other than your time and effort.

The best way of forming relationships is by sending your work out for review. Search out those publications, websites or critics who seem to like the same kind of work that you do and send them a DVD or VHS screener with a nice letter and you may be surprised at the results. People in the press are always looking to find the "next" thing, as well as building relationships with those who may become the "next" thing or actually building someone *into* the "next" thing. Everyone wants to *discover* someone, so help them discover you. The more your work gets out there and is known, the greater your chances of finding other like-minded individuals who might become future collaborators or supporters.

Quite a few of the smaller genre and/or fan newsletters, magazines and Internet sites are always looking for material, so an entertaining article you've written recounting the trials and tribulations of making your film may be just what they're looking for. But make sure you approach those people who have a definite feeling for the kind of work that you do. And once you have found a champion in the press, don't wear out your welcome by constantly asking for attention or coverage or favors. It's a delicate game that, if played correctly, can only benefit you and your work.

Festivals, or:

Give me your poor, your downtrodden, your dispossessed ... all for the entry fee of only $$$!

There was a time, not too many years ago, when acceptance at a film festival was something to be proud of, and would almost always be beneficial. Things have changed, in a major and mostly negative manner. Where ten years ago there may have been maybe 30 film festivals in the entire U.S., there are now 300 or more! And the reason for this is simple — money. Film festivals are becoming cash cows for their organizers, a way to make a lot of money with little or no risk.

It's very easy for a popular film to be shown at 25 film festivals around the world while bringing in money for everyone but the filmmaker, who never finds a distributor or even makes back a fraction of their movie's cost. Of course, part of the reason they can't find a distributor is that they've been over-exposed in all those film festivals. Another reason for this glut of film festivals is all those "indie" films being made that will never be picked up for distribution, but do provide free product for all these new festivals. And this all ties into the cynical fostering of the "indie" film movement, as a way to avoid development costs while simultaneously devaluing and freezing out foreign competition. But I digress.

So be careful about the film festivals that you apply to, because most of them aren't even worth one-tenth the entry fee that you pay them. This said, there *are* film festivals that can help your film, but due to the glut of independent product, they are becoming more and more difficult to get in, unless you have a "Dutch Uncle." So I will give you a list of the festivals which are supposed to be the ones that most distributors and industry people consider to be prestigious, must attend events. They include Cannes, Sundance, Berlin, Venice, Toronto, Telluride and New York.

There also is a hierarchy of festivals, some of which may demand a premiere screening in their country, so try to set up a prioritized listing of festivals, much in the same way I suggested setting priorities for sending out tapes to distributors. The most prestigious, most helpful festivals should be at the top of your list and then you gradually work your way down. There's nothing worse than being in some small festival which may disqualify you from attending that one big festival you believe necessary for your film's success.

There are other festivals which are covered by the trade magazines like *Variety* and *The Hollywood Reporter* and may garner you a review in their pages, making them worth the price of admission. You can find out which those are by going through back issues of these newspapers or maybe even sending an e-mail asking for a list of the festivals that their reviewers cover.

And whatever festivals you wind up at, make sure to network, as there's no better place or atmosphere to begin or cultivate friendships or working relationships than at the relatively, relaxed after-screening get-togethers. Take the opportunity that the festival offers to meet new people you might never have had a chance to come into personal contact with. An awful lot of business (as well as other things) can be conducted and/or consummated at the bar!

Distributors, or: You Gotta Get Screwed Some Time!

Almost all, first-time filmmakers will be screwed by their distributor in one way or the other. It's sort of a rite of passage in the film business. I don't say this to scare you away but to warn you of the reality. You will probably never see a full return on your investment on your first project, even if it is moderately successful. And for all the *Blair Witch Project*, *Brother's Mcmullen*, *Clerks*, etc., hoopla, there are thousands and thousands of filmmakers who have never seen any money back.

So if you are lucky enough to find a distributor, make sure you get an advance from them, because that's probably the only money you will ever see. However, with the glut of "indie" product out there today, it's becoming less and less viable to receive an advance on any film other than one with "bankable" elements such as name stars or some other name creative talent attached. Items which will probably exclude most of you who are reading this book.

If you are forced to take a percentage, you can expect around 50 percent with the "expenses" included as part of the distributor's 50 percent. Or you may be offered up 70 percent, but with this split the distributor's expenses are being taken out of your percentage. Since you will usually be screwed by the expenses taken or how they compute that figure, it's best to pick the percentage with the expenses already taken out, since they are set in advance. If that option isn't available, try to have some kind of cap set on expenses taken. Another distributor angle is when they lump your film with other films and take expenses out for the group, thus penalizing films that make money to pay for the ones that don't. You should also watch out for the length of the licensing agreement. Five-to-seven years is normal, with anything above that being relatively excessive.

Another negotiable area in distribution agreements regards the "deliverables," that is, what materials the distributor requires from you before you see any money from them and who will pay for them. I mentioned earlier that they can cost as little as a few hundred dollars or more than $100,000, depending on the distributor. I have included two vastly different deliverable budgets from the high and low end,

which you can refer back to in the budgeting section. Sometimes a distributor will pay for some of the deliverables, but they will usually take that amount out of any monies they owe you and they usually charge considerably more than if you do it yourself. So if at all possible, try and have as many of the deliverables as you can for your distributor.

Again, I will quickly recap this list of deliverable elements from two different distributor deals, letting you decide what you will need from what you may need. On the high end of the spectrum you will have to provide a Full List of Credits, Copy of Script, Director's Bio, 35mm Blow-Up for Theatrical Release, M & E Track, Stereo Mix, Film Prints, Low-Contrast Print for Video, Music Clearances, NTSC Digi Beta Master and Pal Digi Beta Master (Covered By Foreign Distributor), Trailer, Color Production Stills, Poster, Dialogue List, Errors and Omissions Insurance (not always necessary) and (only for theatrical distribution) an Internegative/Interpositive Print.

And for a smaller distributor who handles only video or TV, a Beta SP Master (NTSC), SVHS Master (NTSC), five or ten color photos, Full Film Credits, a synopsis and any press, reviews, etc. And of course everything between these two extremes is negotiable, usually to your disadvantage. Now let's go over some of the inexpensive ways to make sure you have those deliverables that your distributor will need.

The easiest as well as one of the most overlooked is production stills. All too often this is left to someone having little or no professional knowledge, resulting in their having to be redone after production, at a much greater expense and effort. It can be especially difficult to find and/or assemble your actors and actresses back and/or have them look the same as they did when you shot your film. So take the time to have the most professional photographer you can afford do this for you. And if you aren't paying for their services, make sure you at least pay for their supplies. It also helps if you have in mind the kind of promotional shots you want for your artwork. In this way, you can help direct your photographer to better achieve the exact look you're looking for.

You will also need an accurate script or dialogue list for dubbing or subtitling into foreign languages. If you've been improvising extensively without the benefit of a script person, then you may need to have your script sent to a transcriber for the actual dialogue used. Alternatively, you can just plunk yourself down and type it out all on your own.

The M & E (music and effects) track is all your music and sound effects on an audio track separate from all dialogue. This allows the dubbing of foreign languages without interfering with the music and effects. You can save yourself money by structuring your non-linear edit so that this can more easily be accomplished by isolating selected tracks, say only tracks one and two for dialogue and only three and four for music and effects. However you structure it, if done correctly it can save you considerable time and money.

You should also try to cut your trailer while you're doing your editing; it's another way to save money by not having to go back and edit more (or paying someone to do it). And once again, make sure you have the rights to all your music, which is made a thousand times easier when you have it done specifically for your film. But let me assure you that by the time you get to the distributor, you'd better have the rights to every little bit of music heard in your film or you may just lose any small profit you had hoped for or maybe even lose the deal entirely if you are unable to obtain or afford the necessary rights.

You may be able get a deal costing little or nothing for the artwork, one-sheet, poster and videocassette cover for your work. And this can be some of the most critical work after your film's production. Because your cover art may have more to do with whether some distributors pick up your work than the actual film itself. Certain distributors may insist on their in-house agency doing the work, but if you have great artwork going in, you may be able to avoid even that expense.

Look at the artwork that's out there and pick out the kind of things that you like in your genre. With today's computer graphics programs like Photoshop, professional artwork is within everyone's grasp. Then try and get the very best person you can find whose work reflects those very same qualities. It can be a photographer, graphic artist, computer artist, anyone who reflects a style that communicates your vision. Give them a little space and see what they come up with. Show them what material you've responded to, make suggestions. But remember, try and keep it simple, bold and striking. It can go along way in selling your work ... or not. Take your time and get it right.

The remainder of the deliverables are items will probably have to negotiated, in order to find the best price. So look around for the best deals. Sometimes if you include items like the masters or dubbing masters as part of your editing package and/or deal, you can find reduced rates. And with the insurance for Error and Omissions, you should shop around for the best price; it's a one-time payment, but different insurers will have different rates. Or negotiate with your distributor about whether they actually need this insurance; sometimes this may also be negotiable.

Now that we've gone over some hypothetical distribution scenes, let me give you an example of a bad distribution deal which I was actually offered but turned down. The company wanted the film for 15 years with a $100,000 advance for the first two years. Not bad so far, except that 15 years is kind of long. Their distribution fee would be $50,000 taken off the top. Still not too bad. But then came the clincher: They said they would need $70,000 to market the film "properly." So we would have ended up $20,000 in the hole to the distributor after the first two years, which just happens to be the two most profitable years for almost all films. And they then would have my film for 13 more years, and I would be highly unlikely ever to make back the $20,000. So in effect, I would just be giving away my film for 15 years without seeing a penny. Nice deal? Well, people are making this kind of deal every day just to get their films out there.

If you get into an agreement and find out after a while that your distributor is doing little or nothing to promote your work, try asking to dissolve your licensing agreement, allowing the rights to revert back to you. If they haven't given you an advance, they may just do so, as your agreement is not doing either of you any good. But you'll never know unless you ask.

And of course the distributor of last resort is always the do-it-yourself route, which many filmmakers have tried in the past. My experience in this area has been that you end up spending more of your time marketing and selling your films than you do making them, which is something I prefer not to do. But there are a few independent filmmakers out there who are making a go of it, especially in the low-budget horror genre.

This raises an interesting aspect of selling your own work, which is whether or not the rise of the Internet has made the prospect of selling your own work a viable solution. At this point, it seems obvious the Internet still isn't a place to make money showing your work, but it may be a place to make money selling your work. Only the future will tell and probably by then, it may become possible to actually make money showing your work over the Internet. But until then we'll have to wait and see.

Lawyers

And before we leave this section on distribution, I want to add a few words about lawyers. And once again:

Do you need a lawyer? No.

Will you get screwed without a lawyer? Yes.

Will you get screwed with a lawyer? Yes.

Then why have a lawyer? Hopefully, you will be screwed less.

There is no doubt that a lawyer can help you untangle and maybe even help negotiate the distribution agreement to your advantage. But whether the fee that they charge, especially on a low-budget project, is equal to what you may be losing without their help is another question. Again remember, anything I say is not intended as legal advice or the practice of law. Since some distributors are relatively honest and some are just plain dishonest, having a lawyer (at least one versed in entertainment law) will ensure that you don't enter into an agreement where you could, in effect, lose some, if not all of your rights.

Obviously, if you have a large enough budget and/or investors, you will need to have a lawyer, not only to protect your rights, but to also ensure that the legalities of your agreement with the investors is followed. But if paying a lawyer means the difference between seeing any of your money back or not, then you have to look real hard at your options.

You can act as your own lawyer, while remembering the old saying that anyone who acts as their own lawyer has a fool for a client. Then read the contract as carefully as possible, making sure that you understand everything in it. Remember the Eastwood Theory of Limitations and if you don't understand anything, no matter how small and seemingly insignificant, find someone who can explain it to you.

You may be able to pay an attorney a reduced rate to just "look over" the agreement or you may be able to qualify for the Volunteer Lawyers for the Arts, which is found in some of the larger U.S. cities and offers free or low-cost legal advice to artists who pass their financial guidelines. In addition, several of the independent filmmaker organizations offer consultations with entertainment lawyers as part of their services. And if all that fails, your lawyer cousin who only does wills and DWIs is better than no lawyer at all.

Other possible resources regarding distribution agreements are libraries which may have books on entertainment law or that contain sample distribution agreements. I know the AIVF in New York City has a very helpful library. But there are also a few books available covering distribution, which can provide sample contracts, allowing you to research and better understand anything that isn't clear to you. But never sign anything until you fully understand it — never!

14

Beware of the Bottom-Feeders

(or, how to keep your getting screwed to a minimum)

In the world of independent/underground/guerrilla filmmaking, the general rule is, almost everyone makes money *except* the filmmakers. Distributors, festivals, Internet sites, service providers, film organizations, critics and publishers all can and do make their living off the work of independent/underground/ guerrilla filmmakers. Very few truly independent filmmakers have found a way around this paradox. The main reason for this is that, no matter what they tell you, most of these people are in the business of film — a priority most filmmakers have the other way around. And this may indeed be one of the main reasons for the growth of the underground as well the proliferation of non-mainstream Hollywood videos and DVDs. So before moving on, I'd like to issue a few warnings to anyone beginning this arduous journey.

The "Fame Game" seems to be the only game in town these days. What I mean is that everything concerning film or video is primarily geared toward financial success and/or fame. It is more important to become successful and thus famous than becoming a competent filmmaker or having an intelligent and/or unique point of view. I'm not saying that you should be unconcerned about making money or maybe even being "discovered," but if that's your number one concern, you shouldn't be reading this book.

One of the key illusions being perpetrated is that the only way to become successful and/or famous is by having your work discovered by one of those "gate keepers" who has the ability to "make" you instantly successful or famous. And what follows from this attitude is that you have to be willing to give away your effort, your script, your film, your video, your ideas, all for the possible opportunity of being considered for the elevation to success, fame or celebrity.

What does this mean in practical terms to you as a beginning filmmaker? Number one, there is an entire industry that preys on aspiring filmmakers with little or no knowledge and/or experience. Don't be deceived, this book is part of that, although hopefully it's a little more honest (and cheaper) than most of the other "services" being offered.

What are some of these other services? The biggest rip-off/con job is anything that takes money from you for looking at/evaluating/presenting your work. Whether it's the website that charges money for listing your script/synopsis/finished film or a film festival with a hefty entry fee or an "agent" who charges for reading your script or an attorney who will show your script to certain stars for a "fee" or an "ex-studio" reader or executive who will "evaluate" your script for a fee or an organization that supposedly represents your interests while taking more money from the people they are supposed to be helping or film books that offer advice on how to become successful or production companies/equipment suppliers who offer inflated production packages to inexperienced but well-funded beginning filmmakers or any kind of film-related (especially scripts) contest that charges any entry fee. These are the most prevalent ones, but there are hundreds more. Watch out!

Listen, no legitimate ... well, *almost* no legitimate entertainment business person will take up front money from you to evaluate and/or represent you or your work. The reason for this is the legitimate people know they can make more money from you later when you are established, but the bottom feeders only want to get at whatever money you have *now* and the quicker the better.

The second biggest scam is giving your work away for free, with little or no hope of remuneration. And by your work, I mean working on someone else's production or letting someone shoot your script or giving your film or video to a distributor or Internet site without being paid. Of course *everyone* asking for your work without paying for it will be offering something in return and, as I mentioned earlier, you may be put in that very position to get your film or video completed.

This is a difficult question that is growing more and *more* difficult. If you remember back when John Cassavetes was making his films, he had to offer deferred payment to his cast and crew, which at that time was the only way he could make his very original but extremely non-conformist features. But what's happened along the way is that now everyone from the small non-conformist maverick moviemakers to the large media conglomerates have begun using similar tactics. And for a growing number of them, their only motivation is making more money, not taking creative risks.

You have to decide whether it's worth your while to become involved with these people, whether it's an "indie" production whose only "indie" element is their funding or some vast media conglomerate's "indie" division. Most of the ads now soliciting your free labor stress possible festival play, deferred payment, working on future paying gigs or making contacts. Out of all these, the only one that probably isn't bogus is making contacts; whether they are helpful or not is another story. If you believe the rest of these, your check's in the mail.

You should be as sure as possible that you can learn what you want (whether acquiring new skills or expanding those you already have) from working on each particular production or that you will be making the type of personal contacts that will be of benefit to you later. These are the only two things you can realistically gain by working on something without being paid. Anything else is possible, but remote.

The second most prevalent giveaway after your labor is your script, which is due to the vast number of unproduced and unproducable scripts being written. Everyone is looking for a free script (remember, deferred has a 99 percent probability of meaning free) on which to base their production. If you don't get the money up front, you will probably never see any. However, there are many scriptwriters, including professionals with a few of their scripts optioned but never produced, who will give their script away for no money or that elusive "after it's picked up."

Obviously, the allure of your script being made is very attractive to aspiring writers, but make sure that you're getting what you want and need from the transaction. In other words, is the company legitimate or are they a fly-by-night or totally amateur outfit? Will they be attentive to your needs, allowing creative input, or will they only take what they like and change anything they don't without your liking or permission? Find these things out and get everything in writing beforehand.

All too often, smaller companies will troll for scripts, having open submissions, only looking for ideas and/or entire scripts they can "borrow" for free. And the larger companies are not above this either, but remember —*ideas are not copyrightable*! And many of these companies are only looking for fresh ideas without having to pay for them and aspiring scriptwriters are their number one resource.

The larger companies now make this their legal right by having you sign releases before they will accept unsolicited scripts or material. These releases basically say that anything you submit can and will be stolen if they so choose. And on the off-chance they do like your work, they will probably screw you on the deal.

You also usually sign away any right to sue them at any later date for any kind of transgression on their part. Obviously, they have some very legitimate concerns arising from some past court cases, but they've used that excuse to give themselves unrestricted access to any submitted material by you signing their releases. So you must balance your ability to get your work read with the probability of it being stolen … I mean, "borrowed."

I was talking to an experienced screenwriter who has been in the business a while and had several scripts optioned and produced. He told me how one of the large studios "stole" a script of his for one of their weekly shows, even unofficially acknowledging this to him, but told then him that it wasn't in his "best interest" to sue them. He went to his agent who, in effect, told him the same thing, even though the agent knew the script was indeed stolen. This is the game, these are the players.

Last but not least are those entities looking to get your finished film or video for no money. As I mentioned earlier, in the section on distributors, most of them now will probably not give you an advance on your film or video unless you have what is considered "bankable elements," which most of you reading this book will in all probability not have. The most you can hope for is seeing some kind of percentage down the road, but to even get this, you need to do your homework by asking other filmmakers whose work the company distributes whether they are in fact receiving a far accounting. Does the company pay at all? Do they pay on time? Are they actively promoting the work? Do they take out inordinate expenses? Are their books open for inspection? Do they respond to filmmaker inquiries?

A number of distributors out there get their product for no up-front money and the filmmaker never sees one cent from them. They are the true bottom feeders, but if you do your research, you should be able to pick them out and avoid them. Know them by what they've done in the past and not what they are promising you now, especially if it's not in writing (and even *then* they know you probably don't have the resources to audit or sue them). So pick your distributor carefully, unless you are just desperate to get your work out there; in *that* case there will be plenty of people willing to take advantage of you.

The fastest growing group of nothing-for-something distributors are the Internet-based ones, who ask you to sign away many if not all of your work's rights in exchange for the privilege of being presented on their websites. I know of a couple of filmmakers who had films on these sites, only to find out that their work was being made available to other sites without their knowledge; it was because they had not read their agreement closely enough. Many of these sites are including some type of partial or entire ownership of rights "In Perpetuity"— that is, forever — well-hidden in their seemingly innocuous agreements.

Read everything carefully or you may not wind up owning all or part of your work any more. Some websites that will promote your film or video retain rights to any material you put on their site. In other words, if they allow you to put your trailer on their website to help promote or sell your film, they gain the right to do anything they want with your trailer. This would include selling all or part of it, recutting it and reselling it, cutting out shots or segments and selling that. Nice, huh?

There seem to be more and more companies and individuals trying to obtain as many rights as possible with the inadvertent consent of unsuspecting film or video makers. As I mentioned in the section about Lawyers and Distribution, make sure you read and understand *everything* in any agreement and/or contract you sign regarding the rights to your film or video, whether it's a distributor, film festival, promotional agent or website.

Even some rather well-known festivals have included the retention of certain rights to any films or videos they select, as part of their entry form agreement. When I mentioned this to a videomaker who was considering entering one of these festivals, he wasn't even aware of this possible loss of his video rights to a festival he was paying to enter. Now they take your money and your rights and you get the chance of winning a prize. Is this a film festival or a lottery? Or is this today's brave new world of supposedly media-savvy filmmakers actually being taken in brave new ways?

Before I quit my ranting and raving, let me remind you once again that your ideas and titles are not copyrightable. This means that if you tell your great story idea to someone, they can steal it with little you can do. To be copyrightable, your ideas must be in a fixed form, i.e., a script or detailed scenario; otherwise you are leaving yourself open to have your original ideas taken away at any moment. And all of the companies— I mean *all*, from the largest, multi-national conglomerate to the smallest, low-rent direct-to-video producer — they are all looking for good ideas. And if they can get them for free, all the better.

Comrades old and new: *Daddy* director DiPaolo (left) with leads Celia Hansen and David Shepherd (photograph courtesy Celia Hansen).

Why Bother?

Okay, if the world of low-budget filmmaking is so full of assholes and double-dealing, why would anyone in their right mind bother wasting their time and effort in the pursuit of such a difficult dream? A question I've been asked more than once and my first immediate response is that there's no bigger legal adrenaline rush than directing your own film. It's downright addicting. The moment I stepped onto my first film set as the director, the rush was immediate as well as permanently hooking me and I've been doing it ever since.

But beyond the immediate gratification, there's been something much more satisfying and long-lasting. I've really learned who to play with and a great many of those people with whom I began working, over 27 years ago, are still my close friends and/or collaborators. I'm still working with David Shepherd who gave me my first chance over 27 years ago and who just last year acted in my DV feature *Daddy*; Amy Wallin, the lead in my video feature *Requiem for a Whore* over 15 years ago, was my casting director on *Daddy*; and Marc St. Camille, who played the deputy sheriff in *Daddy*, has been with me since playing one of the leads in *Transgression* back in 1993. The list goes on and on, because if you treat the people you work with as trusted confidantes instead of just another sucker to screw over so you can get ahead, the rewards will many and long-lasting.

So before leaving, I'd like to invite you to visit me at my website, http://www.blackcatcinema.com, and then depart with a few words of encouragement from the French poet Stéphane Mallarmé: "For what is relative immortality—/especially since we are often immortal in the minds of idiots—/compared to the joy of looking on Eternity/and enjoying it within ourselves while we are still alive?"[29]

Appendix 1:
Daddy Timeline/Schedule

*Note: shots specify day(d), night(n), or
twilight(t), and interior(i) or exterior(e).*

Wednesday, July 31st 3:30 P.M. Sharp!!!

4 P.M. Leave for upstate
7 P.M. NYC caravan arrives upstate
7 P.M. John arrives upstate
7–10 P.M. Settle in, get groceries, do chores
10 P.M. Dinner
11 P.M. Movie
1 A.M. Sleep

Thursday, August 1st

10 A.M. Breakfast
11 A.M. Pickup meal worms
Noon Bring stuff to sheriff's house location
Noon Bevin, Aaron, Jamie, Chris arrive
1 P.M. Crew call ... set up at base
2–3 P.M. Shoot Alison visit at base sc#10(d/i)
4 P.M. Dinner
5–8 P.M. Shoot slumber party flashbacks sheriff's house sc#25a-i,28a-c(n/i),
8–9:30 P.M. Shoot cemetery flashbacks rd.sc#25j&k(n/e)
8–9:30 P.M. Pickup 4 × 4 at sheriff's house & remaining crew preps Alison's house
10 P.M. Break/ Cynthia & Katherine to sheriff's house-sleep
10 P.M. Aaron makes-up
10:30 P.M. Shoot sheriff into Alison's sc#5 (n/e)

11:30 P.M. Shoot Alison's attack sc#1,1a,2,2a (n/e&i)
1 A.M. Shoot sheriff inside Alison's crime scene sc#6 (n/i)
2:30 A.M. Wrap/sleep/Bevin home?

Friday, August 2nd

11 A.M. Bevin home
12 noon Breakfast
1:30 P.M. Pack up
2 P.M. Leave for victims 2&3 location
2:30 P.M. Arrive/set up at victims 2&3 location
4 P.M. Shoot talk with Jamie @ end sc#30(t/e), 31(t/i), 32(t/e)
5 P.M. Dinner
6 P.M. Set up night exterior lighting
9 P.M. Shoot Jamie's attack sc#14a(n/e) & 15(n/i)
10:30 P.M. Shoot Jamie's crime scene sc#18(n/e&i) & 19(n/e)
11:30 P.M. Shoot Sylvia & deputy talk @ Leslie's sc#24a(n/e)
12:30 A.M. Shoot Sylvia & Leslie talk sc#25(n/i)
2 A.M. Shoot Leslie's attack sc#26(n/i)
3 A.M. Shoot Leslie's aftermath sc#26(n/i)
4 A.M. Wrap
4:30 A.M. Back at camp ... sleep

Saturday, August 3rd

1 P.M. Deputy, Jamie & Leslie breakfast/back to NYC via Greyhound from Albany
2 P.M. Breakfast
3 P.M. Pickup generator
4 P.M. Leave for graveyard location
5 P.M. Set up night shoot ... lights/generator
7 P.M. Day for night zombie shots
8 P.M. Dinner
9 P.M. Shoot zombie out of grave shots sc#1(n/e),14(n/e),
11 P.M. Shoot sheriff/zombie final fight sc#33(n/e)
1 A.M. Shoot sheriff to grave sc#23a(n/e)
2 A.M. Shoot misc zombie shots 1(n/e-one shot),14a(n/e-oneshot),
    23(n/e),26(n/e-oneshot)
3 A.M. Wrap for day
4 A.M. Back at camp ... sleep

Sunday, August 4th

1 P.M. Breakfast
2 P.M.–4 P.M. Review tapes

5 P.M. Dinner

6–9 P.M. Shooting any re-takes

9 P.M. Base camp sc#11(t/e)

9:30 P.M. Shoot video store sc#12(t/i)

10 P.M. Snack

11 P.M. Skelton crew w/Sylvia & Daddy

11 P.M.–3 A.M. Shooting misc exteriors sc#1b(n/e-one shot), 11(t/e-one shot), 14a(n/e-one shot), 17(n/e), 23(n/e-one shot), 24(n/e), 32(t/e)

3 A.M. ... hopefully earlier ... sleep

Monday, August 5th

1 P.M. Marc and Murad back from NYC

1 P.M. Breakfast

2 P.M. Leave for sheriff's house location

2:30 P.M. Set up at sheriff's house location

3–6 P.M. Shoot Sylvia at home after attack sc#28(d/i),28d(t/i),29(t/i)

7 P.M. Shoot Sylvia out to lake sc#29a(t/e)

8 P.M. Dinner

9 P.M. Shoot Sylvia out to 4x4, returning with 4x4, sc#4(n/e),

9:30 P.M. Shoot Sylvia with Ed outside sc#21(n/e)

10 P.M. Shoot Sylvia with Phil sc#13(n/i)

11 P.M. Shoot Sylvia in bed w/John 1 sc#1a(n/i), 3(n/i)

12:30 A.M. Shoot Sylvia Russian Roulette sc#13a(n/i)

1:30 A.M. Shoot Sylvia alone in bed sc#16(n/i),21a(n/i)

2:30 A.M. Wrap ... back to base camp

3 A.M. Sleep

Tuesday, August 6th

11 A.M. Breakfast & David arrives from Mass.

12 noon Dress set and light at base camp

1 P.M. Shoot Sylvia, doctor, usher sc#22(d/i)

1:30 P.M. Shoot Sylvia, doctor, Usher & deputy sc#27(d/i)

2:30 P.M. Shoot Sylvia with deputy sc#9(d/i)

3 P.M. Marc & Murad back to NYC

3 P.M. Shoot Sylvia with Dr sc#8 (d/i)

5 P.M. Shoot Sylvia with Ed sc#7 (d/i)

6 P.M. Shoot Sylvia alone day for night (n/i)

6:30 P.M. *Wrap* & dinner

Appendix 2:
Daddy Script Excerpt

Scene 5

Isolated House
Exterior Night SYNC

Pulling up to an old house, which she seems to recognize, Sylvia gets out of her 4×4 and walks up to Richie, her deputy, who is already on the scene.

Sylvia
Calm down ... what exactly are the facts?

Richie
It's Alison Headly ... she's ... she's been
raped ... pretty bad ... looks like.

Sylvia
What do you mean 'looks like'?

Richie
Well, she's pretty beat up, can't talk,
an' appears to be in shock an' her
place is a god awful mess.

Sylvia
If she's unable to talk, how do
you know she's been raped?

Richie
Take a look ... you'll see ...

Sylvia
Where's Jack?

Richie
Over there ... he found her when
he got back ... supposta be
their Anniversary tonight.

Sylvia
Nice ... where's Alison?

Appendix 3:
Daddy Scenario Excerpt

She hurriedly throws on her uniform and races out of the house before her bed-mate can realize what's going on.

Sylvia gets in her car and, sirens blasting, takes off down the darkened country road.

Pulling up to an isolated old house, which she seems to recognize, Sylvia questions Ted, her deputy who is already on the scene, about what's happened. He informs her of a hideous rape, which has just occurred, leaving the woman unable to speak or communicate at all; it's obvious by the physical evidence that she has been brutally raped.

Attempting to see through all the physical damage done to the victim, Sylvia realizes that this is Alison, one of her childhood friends, and attempts to communicate with her, all to no avail.

The girl is then taken outside and whisked off in an ambulance, leaving Sylvia and Ted alone in the house to investigate.

They walk to the front door and follow the short trail of mud and worms to the rape scene on the couch. It is a disgusting mess of blood, mud and still writhing worms.

Unable to stomach the sight, Ted rushes over to the champagne bucket and vomits, which causes Sylvia to yell at him for messing up a crime scene, even though she can barely keep her supper down.

He gets up and begins wiping his mouth. Looking around at the mess they are confused ... very, very confused.

The next morning, sitting in her office having some tea underneath a calendar of semi-nude male dancers, Sylvia gets a call from Doctor Vance, who examined her friend Alison for the county. He needs to see Sylvia in person at his office, because he's afraid to say anything over the phone. Curious, she rushes out.

Appendix 4:
Daddy Outline Excerpt

9 Sylvia's House … Night Interior
Sylvia hurriedly throws on her uniform and races out of the house.

10 Sylvia's House … Night Exterior
Sylvia runs to her 4 × 4 and takes off with sirens blasting.

11 Sylvia's 4 × 4 … Night Interior
Sylvia drives to house in country

12 Alison's House … Night Exterior
Sylvia at Alison's, Victim # 1
Questions Deputy outside

13 Alison's House … Night Interior
Sylvia Inspects Crime Scene with Deputy
Attempts to Talk to Alison and her husband
Alison taken away in ambulance
Sylvia and Deputy talk, then exit crime scene

The Next Morning…

14 The Sheriff's Office … Day Interior
Sylvia talks to Dr. Vance on phone

15 Dr. Vance's Office … Day Interior
Sylvia confers with Dr. Vance about last night's attack
Dr. Vance warns her that town is talking about her affairs
She forces him to talk about case

16 The Sheriff's Office ... Day Interior

Upset by Doctor's findings returns to office, only to be greeted by call from State Police
which further upsets her.

Deputy attempts to comfort her ... doesn't succeed ... she leaves office.

17 Alison's House ... Day interior

Sylvia visits Alison who still appears to be in shock.

Appendix 5:
Daddy Budget

Cash	Budget	Projected	Spent
CAST			
Sylvia	$500.00		$500.00
Doctor	$200.00		$200.00
Deputy	$200.00		$200.00
Alison	$200.00		$200.00
Jamie	$200.00		$200.00
Leslie	$200.00		$200.00
Daddy	$200.00		$200.00
Casting		+100	$100.00
Subtotal	**$1,700.00**	1800?	**$1,800.00**
CREW			
Boom Operator	$400.00		$600.00
Gaffer	$400.00		$400.00
ProdMgr	$250.00	plus 150	$400.00
Music	$500.00		$500.00
Subtotal	**$1,550.00**	1,200?	**$1,900.00**
OTHER			
Locations	$700.00	*minus 550*	$180.00
Costumes	$100.00	**plus 100**	$295.22
Food	$200.00	**plus 400**	$362.97
Supplies	$200.00	**plus 100**	$594.79
Set	$100.00		$95.16
Transport.		**plus 100**	$165.08
Misc PC			$48.49
Subtotal	**$1,300.00**		**$1,741.71**
		Plus 400?	
Contingency	**$455.00**		
TOTAL	**$5,005.00**		**$5,441.71**

Appendix 6:
Daddy Full Schedule

THURSDAY—*DAY# 1 NIGHT*
AUG 1st — 2PM — Crew Call
1) Visiting Alison Base Camp — DAY
SCENE 10(d/i)
2)Slumber Party *Flashbks*— Sheriff's House
<DAY4NITE>
SCENES 25A (n/i), 25B (n/i), 25C (n/i), 25C
(n/i), 25D (n/i), 25E (n/i), 25F (n/i), 25G
(n/i), 25H (n/i), 25I (n/i), 28A (n/i), 28B
(n/i), 28C (n/i)
2A)Graveyard — Farm — NITE
SCENES 25J (n/e) & 25K (n/e)
3) Alison's Crime Sc — Base Camp — NITE
SCENES 5 (n/e) & 6 (n/i)
4) Alison's Attack — BaseCamp — NITE
SCENES 1A (n/e), 1B (n/e), 2 (n/e), 2A (n/i)
ACTORS — Sylvia, Alison, Jamie, Leslie,
Deputy, Daddy, Nurse, A's Hus, Ambul
Guys (2)
WARDROBE—#10— Sylvia — uniform,
Alison — dressing gown, nurse suit, FLASH-
BACKS — 4 × nightgowns, 4 × jeans, sneak-
ers, t-shirts, jacket/sweatshirt, mother's
dress, dad's suit
#s 5 & 6 — Sylvia/Deputy — uniforms, Ali-
son — Long translucent gown × 3,
panties/heels, blanket, A's husband — what-
ever, Ambul Guys— white shirts × 2
PROPS — Flashbacks— Magazines, Glasses,
Booze, Black Plastic, **Martini**, Hammer,
Rope, 3 × Flashlights, old Car
Alison's— CD player, flowers, vase, Hus-

band's Photo, Ice bucket & Champagne —
MARTINI, Cake, Knife, Table, Matches,
Perfume, Mirror, Mud & Worms,
VEHICLES—4 × 4, Red Pickup, Justin's,
One Extra?
FRIDAY—*DAY 2* (NIGHT)
AUG 2 — 2pm — Crew Call
All @ Tamborton Rd
1) Talk with Jamie @ end — TWILIGHT
SCENES 30 (t/e), 31 (t/i), 32 (t/e)
2) Jamie's Attack — NITE
SCENES 14A (n/e) & 15 (n/i)
3) Jamie's Crime Scene — NITE
SCENES 18 (n/e & i) & 19 (n/e)
4) Sylvia & Deputy Talk @ Leslie's — NITE
SCENE 24A (n/e)
5) Sylvia & Leslie Talk — NITE
SCENE 25 (n/i)
6) Leslie's Attack/Aftermath?— NITE
SCENE 26 (n/i)
ACTORS — Sylvia, Jamie, Leslie, Deputy,
Daddy, Nurse, Ambul Guys (2)
WARDROBE—#s 30, 31, 32— Sylvia — red
Jacket, blue jeans, blue T, sneakers, Jamie —
dressing gown/slippers, Nurse — uniform,
#s 14A, 15, 18, 19— Sylvia/Deputy — uni-
forms, Jamie — dress/heels & blanket, Ambul
Guys 2 × white Shirts
#s 24A, 25, 26— Sylvia — red hoodie, blue
jeans, blue training Bra, sneaks, Leslie —
mini skirt & top, pink panties
PROPS —#s 30, 31, 32—Canoe, tea,

#s 14A, 15, Grocery Bags, Keys, Couch Cover,
#S 18 & 19 Notepad, Pen, Blue Lights
VEHICLES — 4 × 4, Red Pickup, Red Subaru
SATURDAY — *DAY 3 (NIGHT)*
AUG 3 — 3PM — Crew Call
1) MISC. EXT'S — Farm — NITE
SCENES 1 (n/e — one shot), 14A (n/e — one shot), 23 (n/e), 26 (n/e — one shot)
2) GRAVEYARD — Farm — NITE
SCENES 1 (n/e), 14 (n/e), 23A (n/e), 33 (n/e)
ACTORS — **Sylvia, Daddy, Ed**
WARDROBE — Daddy — Deadwear,
Sylvia — Red Sweatshirt/Jacket, Blue Jeans, Sneakers, White T, Ed — Craven Yellow
PROPS — Mud & Worms, Fake Rocks, Saw, Shovel, Bag, Gun, Dad's Photo, Flash Light Lrge
VEHICLES — 4 × 4, Red Pick Up, Red Subaru
SPECIAL~EQUIPMENT — Bug Stuff, A/C Xtensions, Fog?
SUNDAY — *DAY 4*
AUG 4 — am — Crew Call 4PM
1) VIDEO STORE — COHOES — NITE
SCENES 11 (t/e) & 12 (t/i)
2) MISCELLANEOUS EXTERIORS NITE
SCENE 1B (n/e — one shot), 11 (t/e — one shot), 14A (n/e — one shot), 17 (n/e), 23 (n/e — one shot), 24 (n/e), 32 (t/e)
3) GRAVEYARD LEFTOVERS NITE???
ACTORS — **Sylvia, Daddy, Phil**
WARDROBE — #Daddy — Deadwear,

Sylvia — Uniform, Phil — Philwear
#s 23, 24 & 32 — Sylvia — Red Hoodie, Blue Jeans, Sneaks/BlueT
PROPS — Cigar, Blue Light,
VEHICLES — 4×4, Phil's Car
MONDAY — *DAY 5*
AUG 5nd — Crew Call — 2PM
SHERIFF'S *HOUSE* DAY & NITE
SCENES 1A (n/i), 3 (n/i), 4 (n/e), 13 (n/i), 16 (n/i) 21 (n/e), 21A (n/i), 28 (d/i), 28D (t/i), 29 (t/i), 29A (t/e)
ACTORS — **Sylvia, Deputy/John1, Phil, Ed,**
WARDROBE — Sylvia — Blue Nite Shirt, Uniform, Red Jacket, bluejeans, blue T, sneakers, Deputy — uniform, Phil — Philwear, Ed — CravenYellow
PROPS Sheets, Red Drapes, Cigarettes, Cell Phone, Blue Light, Cigar, Gun, Vodka Bottle, Canoe
VEHICLES — 4 × 4, Phil's Car, Red Truck?
TUESDAY — *DAY 6*
AUG 6th — Crew Call — 12NOON
BASE CAMP DAY
SCENES 7 (d/i), 8 (d/i), 9 (d/i), 20 (DFN — n/i), 22 (d/i), 23 (V.O.).27 (d/i)
ACTORS — **Sylvia, Deputy, Ed, Dr Vance, Usher**
WARDROBE — Sylvia/Deputy — Uniforms, Ed — Yellow, Dr.Vance — DressShirt/Tie/Glasses, Usher — suit/badge
PROPS — SHER office STUFF, Coffee Mug, Men's Muscle Mag, Newspaper, TLS, Report Folder, Aspirin, Report Folder 2, Gauze, Bandages/Tape, Notebook, Police ID
NO VEHICLES

Appendix 7:
Daddy Sample Shot Log

Shot Description	Timecode In	Timecode Out	E.T.	Sync	Comments
LS Lake Sheriff runs into house shot 17 take 1	01:13:10:23	01:13:56:02	45:09	Yes	Jiggle in middle of pan
LS Lake Sheriff runs into house, shot 17 take 2	01:14:20:03	01:14:53:22	23:18	Yes	Good
MS Sheriff in door, shot 18 take 1	01:15:00:23	01:15:10:23	10:00		OK
MS Sheriff in door, shot 18 take 2	01:15:22:17	01:15:30:27	08:10		Better
MCU Sheriff in door, shot 15A take 1	01:16:01:22	01:16:41:03	40:11	Yes	No Good Soft focus
MCU Sheriff in car, shot 15A take 2	01:16:55:03	1:17:41:24	45:19	Yes	Camera Jiggle
MCU Sheriff in car, shot 15A, take 3	01:17:51:23	01:18:22:24	31:01	Yes	Good

LS Victim 2, crime scene shot 19, take 1	01:19:02:13	01:20:05:20	1:03:07	Good
LS Victim 2, crime scene, shot 19, take 2	01:20:10:06	01:21:12:07	1:02:01	Very good

Notes

1. Roger Corman with Jim Jerome, *How I Made a Hundred Movies in Hollywood and Never Lost a Dime* (Random House, 1990) p. xiii.

2. Todd McCarthy and Charles Flynn, *Kings of the Bs* (E. P. Dutton, 1975) p. 377.

3. *Ibid.* p. 408.

4. *Ibid.* p. 408.

5. Corman and Jerome p. xiii.

6. Drawn from Corman and Jerome.

7. Ray Carney, *The Films of John Cassavetes* (Cambridge: Cambridge UP, 1994) p. 154.

8. John Cassavetes, "Special Issue: John Cassavetes," *PostScript: Essays in Film and the Humanities* 11.2 (Winter 1992), guest editor Ray Carney <http://people.bu.edu/rcarney/cassavetes/ http://people.bu.edu/rcarney/cassoverview/quotes/quote4.shtml>

9. Colin MacCabe, *Godard: Images, Sounds, Politics* (Indiana UP, 1980) p. 105.

10. McCarthy and Flynn p. 408.

11. McCarthy and Flynn p. 408.

12. Peter Bogdanovich, *Who the Devil Made It?* (Knopf, 1997) p. 217.

13. Stephen Rubello, *The Making of Psycho* (St. Martin's Press, 1999) p. 134.

14. *Ibid.* p. 93

15. Roman Polanski, *Polanski by Polanski* (William Morrow, 1984) p. 272.

16. Susan Dworkin, *Double DePalm* (W.W. Norton, 1984) p. 83.

17. *Ibid.* p. 83.

18. Clint Eastwood as Harry Callahan in *Magnum Force* (Warner Bros./Malpaso Production, 1973), script by John Milius and Michael Cimino.

19. Che Guevara, *Guerrilla Warfare* (Bison Books Corp., 2002) p. 107.

20. Corman and Jerome p. xiii.

21. *Ibid.* p. xiii.

22. Aristotle, *The Poetics of Aristotle*, trans. Stephen Halliwell (University of North Carolina Press, 1987) 39.

23. *Ibid.* p. 47.

24. *Ibid.* p. 47.

25. *Ibid.* p. 60.

26. Christian Metz, *Film Language*, trans. Michael Taylor (University of Chicago Press, 1974) p. 239.

27. Kevin Brownlow, *After the Parade's Gone By* (Random House, 1976) p. 270.

28. Drawn from Corman and Jerome and Guevara.

29. Stephane Mallarmé, *Selected Poetry and Prose by Stephane Mallarmé*, ed. Mary Ann Caws (New Directions, 1982).

Bibliography

Almodovar, Pedro. *Almodovar on Almodovar*. Faber & Faber, 1994, London.

Alton, John. *Painting with Light*. University of California Press, 1995, Berkeley, CA.

Antonioni, Michelangelo. *The Architecture of Vision*. Marcelo, 1996, New York, NY.

Aristotle. *Aristotle's Poetics*. Trans. S. H. Butcher. Hill and Wang, 1986, New York, NY.

_____. *The Poetics of Aristotle*. Trans. Stephen Halliwell. University of North Carolina Press, 1987, Chapel Hill, NC.

Auiler, Dan. *Hitchcock's Notebooks*. Avon Books, 1999, New York, NY.

Bergman, Ingmar. *Bergman on Bergman*. Simon & Schuster, 1970, New York, NY.

_____. *The Magic Lantern*. Viking, 1988, New York, NY.

_____. *Images: My Life in Film*. Arcade, 1994, New York, NY.

Bogdanovich, Peter. *Who the Devil Made It?* Alfred A. Knopf, 1997, New York, NY.

Bresson, Robert. *Notes on Cinematography*. Urizen Books, 1977, New York, NY.

Brownlow, Kevin. *After the Parade's Gone By*. Alfred A. Knopf, 1968, New York, NY.

Buñuel, Luis. *My Last Sigh*. Alfred A. Knopf, 1983, New York, NY.

Capra, Frank. *The Name Above the Title*. Macmillan, 1970, New York, NY.

Carney, Ray. *The Films of John Cassavetes*. Cambridge University Press, 1994, Cambridge.

Cassavetes, John. "Special Issue: John Cassavetes." *PostScript: Essays in Film and the Humanities* 11.2 (Winter 1992). Guest editor: Ray Carney.

Castle, William. *Step Right Up! I'm Gonna Scare the Pants Off America*. Pharos Books, 1991, New York, NY.

Chaplin, Charles. *My Autobiography*. Simon & Schuster, 1964, New York, NY.

Clair, René. *Cinema Yesterday and Today*. Dover, 1972, New York, NY.

Cocteau, Jean. *Beauty and the Beast: Diary of a Film*. Dover, 1972, New York, NY.

Corman, Roger, with Jim Jerome. *How I Made a Hundred Movies in Hollywood and Never Lost a Dime*. Random House, 1990, New York, NY.

Cronenberg, David. *Cronenberg on Cronenberg*. Alfred A. Knopf, 1992, New York, NY.

DeMille, Cecil B. *The Autobiography of Cecil B. DeMille*. Prentice Hall, 1959, Englewood Cliffs, NJ.

DeToth, Andre. *DeToth on DeToth: Putting Drama in Front of the Camera*. Farber & Farber, 1996, London.

Dmytryk, Edward. *It's a Hell of a Life, But Not a Bad Living*. New York Times Books, 1978, New York, NY.

Dovzhenko, Alexander. *The Poet as Filmmaker*. MIT Press, 1973, Cambridge, MA.

Dreyer, Carl. *Dreyer in Double Reflection: Translation of Carl Th. Dreyer's Writings About the Film (Om Filmen)*. E. P. Dutton, 1973, New York, NY.

Dworkin, Susan. *Double DePalma*. W. W. Norton, 1984, New York, NY.

Eisenstein, Sergei. *The Film Sense*. Harcourt, Brace, and World, 1942 (rev. ed. 1947), New York, NY.

_____. *The Film Form*. Harcourt, Brace, and World, 1949, New York, NY.

_____. *Film Essays*. Praeger, 1970, New York, NY.

_____. *Immoral Memories*. Houghton Mifflin, 1983, Boston, MA.

Eisner, Lotte H. *Fritz Lang*. Da Capo Press, 1988, New York, NY.

Farber, Manny. *Negative Space*. Praeger, 1971, New York, NY.

Field, Syd. *Screenplay*. Dell Publishing, 1979/1982, New York, NY.

Garnett, Tay. *Light Up Your Torches and Pull Up Your Tights*. Arlington House, 1973, New Rochelle, NY.

Godard, Jean-Luc. *Godard on Godard*. Viking Press, 1972, New York, NY.

Grey, Rudolph. *Nightmare of Ecstasy*. Feral House, Portland, Oregon.

Guevara, Che. *Guerrilla Warfare*. Bison Books, 2002, Lincoln, Nebraska.

Halliday, Jon. *Sirk on Sirk*. Viking Press, 1972, New York, NY.

Hawks, Howard. *Hawks on Hawks*. University of California Press, 1982, Berkeley, CA.

Hitchcock, Alfred. *Hitchcock on Hitchcock*. University of California Press, 1995, Berkeley, CA.

Huston, John. *An Open Book*. Alfred A. Knopf, 1980, New York, NY.

Kazan, Elia. *Elia Kazan: A Life*. Alfred A. Knopf, 1998, New York, NY.

Kurosawa, Akira. *Something Like an Autobiography*. Alfred A. Knopf, 1982, New York, NY.

Jones, Chuck. *Chuck Amuck*. Farrar, Straus and Giroux, 1989, New York, NY.

LeRoy, Mervyn. *Mervyn LeRoy: Take One*. Hawthorn Books, 1974, New York, NY.

Lewis, Jerry. *The Total Film-Maker*. Random House, 1971, New York, NY.

_____. *Jerry Lewis in Person*. Atheneum, 1982, New York, NY.

Lynch, David. *Lynch on Lynch*. Farber & Farber, 1997, London.

MacCabe, Colin. *Godard: Images, Sounds, Politics*. Indiana University Press, 1980, Bloomington, IN.

Machiavelli, Niccolo. *The Prince*. Penguin, 1995, London.

Mallarmé, Stephane. *Selected Poetry and Prose by Stephane Mallarmé*. Mary Ann Caws (Editor). New Directions, 1982, New York, NY.

McCarthy, Todd and Charles Flynn. *Kings of the Bs*. E. P. Dutton, 1975, New York, NY.

Metz, Christian. *Film Language*. University of Chicago Press, 1974, Chicago, IL.

Minnelli, Vincent. *I Remember It Well*. Doubleday, 1974, New York, NY.

Murch, Walter. *In the Blink of an Eye*. Silman-James Press, 1995, Los Angeles, CA.

Negulesco, Jean. *Things I Did and Things I Think I Did*. Simon & Schuster, 1984, New York, NY.

Parrish, Robert. *Growing Up in Hollywood*. Harcourt Brace Jovanovich, 1976, New York, NY.

Polanksi, Roman. *Roman by Polanski*. William Morrow, 1984, New York, NY.

Powell, Michael. *A Life in Movies*. Alfred A. Knopf, 1987, New York, NY.

_____. *Million Dollar Movie*. Random House, 1992, New York, NY.

Preminger, Otto. *Preminger: An Autobiography*. Doubleday, 1977, New York, NY.

Ray, Nicolas. *I Was Interrupted*. University of California Press, 1993, Berkeley, CA.

Renoir, Jean. *My Life and My Films*. Atheneum, 1974, New York, NY.

Riefenstahl, Leni. *A Memoir*. St. Martin's Press, 1992, New York, NY.

Rohmer, Eric. *The Taste For Beauty*. Cambridge University Press, 1989, New York, NY.

Rossellini, Roberto. *My Method*. Marsilio, 1992, New York, NY.

Rubello, Stephen. *The Making of Psycho.* St. Martin's, 1999, New York, NY.

Russell, Ken. *The Autobiography.* Bantam Books, 1991, New York, NY.

Schickel, Richard. *The Men Who Made the Movies.* Atheneum, 1975, New York, NY.

Scorsese, Martin. *Scorsese on Scorsese.* Faber & Faber, 1989, London.

Sennett, Mack. *King of Comedy.* Doubleday, 1954, New York, NY.

Siegel, Don. *A Siegel Film.* Farber & Farber, 1993, London.

Siegel, Joel. E. Val Lewton. *The Reality of Terror.* Viking Press, 1973, New York, NY.

Simmons, Garner. *Peckinpah: A Portrait in Montage.* University of Texas Press, 1982, Austin, TX.

Sturges, Preston. *Preston Sturges on Preston Sturges.* Simon & Schuster, 1990, New York, NY.

Tarkovsky, Andrey. *Sculpting in Time.* Alfred A. Knopf, 1987, New York, NY.

_____. *Time Within Time.* Faber & Faber, 1994, London.

Truffaut, François. *Hitchcock/Truffaut.* Touchstone/Simon & Schuster, 1967, New York, NY.

Vidor, King. *A Tree Is a Tree.* Harcourt Brace, 1953, New York, NY.

_____. *King Vidor on Film Making.* David McKay, 1972, New York, NY.

Von Sternberg, Josef. *Fun in a Chinese Laundry.* Macmillan, 1965, New York, NY.

Walker, Alexander. *Stanley Kubrick Directs.* Harcourt Brace Jovanovich, 1972, New York, NY.

Wajda, Andrzej. *Double Vision.* Henry Holt, 1989, New York, NY.

Walsh, Rauol. *Each Man in His Own Time.* Farrar, Straus and Giroux, 1974, New York, NY.

Warhol, Andy. *The Philosophy of Andy Warhol.* Harcourt Brace Jovanovich, 1975, New York, NY.

Welles, Orson with Peter Bogdanovich. *This Is Orson Welles.* Harper Collins, 1992, New York, NY.

Wellman, William. *A Short Time for Insanity.* Hawthorn Books, 1974, New York, NY.

Index

One final note: With today's increasingly fast (ASA–wise) film stocks, there is a real savings to be had by using less lighting and camera equipment and still achieve striking professional results. Some of the newer stocks cost a little bit more, but what they save in reduced lighting, transportation and crew costs may more than compensate for their extra expense. And don't forget extra take-up reels, film cans and changing bags!

For videotape, things are slightly different. Processing the tape is not necessary; only the actual cost of tape stock is to be considered. Although even here there are options. Once again, as with the film stock, I have my prejudices. I prefer Maxell, TDK or Fuji tape stock to all others, this being my own personal preference over years using practically all the brands out there.

The main thing you should be looking for in videotape is that it has as few dropouts as possible and that the adhesive used to stick the metal (usually) particles to the tape have a durability to adhere for as long as possible. This also means that you should always buy the professional stock; although it costs more, it will more than pay for itself over the long run. I've been able to play and actually re-edit some of my videotapes from over 15 years ago because I bought the top-of-the-line stock, which has lasted. If you're in this for the long haul, you should see quality tape stock as an investment, not an expense.

There are various studies out there and some of the technical video magazines will periodically do tests. Your DP probably has a preference and if he does, sound him out as to *why* he prefers what he does. If it sounds reasonable to you, I would probably go along with his decision, but if you have any reservations, you should conduct your own research.

Because tape stock is relatively inexpensive compared to film stock, there is a tendency to shoot way more than you need and sort it out in the editing. Unfortunately, most films that do that usually look just like that. But there are additional expenses that will come around if you use a lot of videotape, such as having to have them time-coded for your rough cut as well as having to have your editor sit through it all. Shooting a lot of videotape also takes up time and your actors' and actresses' energy. Know what you want or what you're after and use as much as you need, but don't run tape because of your indecision.

Also, a word on the smaller videotape stocks like Hi-8 and DV. Once you shoot with these tapes, ideally, you should never play them back until the final edit, only making window dubs for your rough cut. The reason of this is that the small gauge of the tape stock makes them especially susceptible to tape dropout — and dropout on such small tapes can look like golf balls. *Avoid playback.* I know there's no way to avoid it entirely, just try and keep it to the bare minimum.

BUDGETING AUDIOTAPE STOCK

Obviously, the amount of film or videotape stock for which you budget will determine the amount of audiotape that you need to budget for. Once again, as with the videotape, I prefer Maxell, TDK and Fuji for my audio stock; do your own research or ask your sound person.

A personal quirk of my own is that I like to have my sound person do "wild takes" of any ambient sound they think may contribute to the project's final sound mix. It can be anything from a noisy refrigerator, to hot water pipes banging and sizzling, to a bird singing outside the window. I want my sound person to feel free to explore the soundscape of the shoot in the same way a camera operator shooting a B roll camera would. And for this, I usually budget an extra roll or two of audio tape. I also add two or three rolls for the post-production period, as I often will go out to find supplementary sounds for the audio mix, as well as occasionally doing my own Foley work.

Film/Video/Audio Stock Considerations. Where do you buy your film or tape stock? For film stock, it is in your best interests that the film all come from the same batch to assure a certain uniformity of manufacture. (In film much more than videotape, this is a consideration that can show up on the screen.) So buy all your stock at the same time and from the same source. I usually get all my stock directly from the manufacturer, but reputable dealers in your area will probably have enough quality stock for your needs. If you plan on using a stock that is not commonly used, I would suggest checking with them in advance as to its availability in the amounts that you'll need.

Once again, organizations such as the Independent Feature Project and the AIVF have discount programs for the purchase of raw stock, both film and video. But some people swear they get better discounts on their own and those organizations' discounts also can sometimes be limited to specific types and/or amounts of stock. It may be more worth your while to buy a particular non-discounted stock that is better suited to your production's needs. On one of my recent films, my DP and I had decided upon a new, faster stock of 16mm film that wasn't available at the member discount, but because the new film was more light-sensitive than the discounted stocks, we figured it would more than pay for the difference in the discount by our having to use less lighting. We were right and the effects we achieved were well worth it.

If you're buying recanned film in any kind of quantity, you should do a test before filming, to ensure its quality. And always try to buy from a reputable reseller, not from someone you've never met who is offering a great deal over the Internet. And if you're using short ends, good luck.

I usually have my DP store the film and bring whatever he deems necessary on each day of the shoot, although it's something I discuss with them beforehand. You don't want to be stuck on location and run out of film. Once you've brought the stock home it should be kept in a refrigerator, but must be restored to room temperature a full eight hours before filming.

Once you've exposed your film, get it to the lab as soon as possible, making sure that it's on a camera spool or on a core and put in a black paper bag. Then in the film can, with the can being taped around the edge. Most labs will provide a film bag where you can put all your exposed stock.

You will probably have to set up an account with the lab beforehand and make sure that when your film is dropped off, it's labeled with the title of the production, a description of the film materials, the amount of footage, the services you desire and whether you will pick it up (usually) or have it sent somewhere. And if you only want selected takes printed or dailies made, you will have to provide a copy of the camera report with the selects clearly marked. Once it's been processed, have your processed stock and the film or video dailies picked up as soon as possible. You want to be able to look at your first results as soon as you can to check for any camera or film stock or processing problems.

When you buy your videotape for your shoot, you should also buy all of the tape at the same time from the same supplier, although this is not as crucial as it is with film stock. Stick with the brand that you've decided upon with your DP and always try and get the top-of-the-line product, as it's much more likely to withstand the test of time.

Like film stock, videotape should be kept in a dry, cool, dust-free space away from any strong electromagnetic fields. Unlike the film stock, I store it and bring along with me. And once we shoot the video, I take back it with me, to make window dubs and store at my place. I try never to screen my master tapes (except to make the window dubs from which I will run any other copies) until the final edit, as running a videotape always entails the risk of adding dropout and even occasionally getting stuck in a player. At this stage, that's not a risk I want to run, but that's up to you. However, if you must check something shot on videotape while on location, never scan the tape; fast-forward and rewind, but try to avoid running the tape over the heads, and only play back the take you need to see.

Budgeting Supplies

Go through your script, outline, whatever you're using, and make a list of *anything* that will be used up during production (that you can't beg, borrow or steal from family, friends, cast and crew), with its approximate price. Then go through your written plan again; anything else you will need to achieve or build or that will aid in your production gets added, along with its price, such as: photocopies, still photography film, stationary, batteries, paint, brushes, fuses, makeup, shoe dye, towels, blankets, nails, screws, hammers, light fixtures, fog machine rental, coffee maker, paper cups, AC extensions, paper, ink markers, fluorescent light fixtures and everything else that you (or anyone else) can think of.

Budgeting Wardrobe

Most wardrobe on low-budget films is provided by the actors and actresses themselves, in consultation with the filmmaker, the art director and possibly the DP. When you are figuring out your wardrobe budget, you should be looking through your written plans for any piece of wardrobe that is out of the ordinary. It could be a uniform, a special pair of shoes, a bizarre piece of lingerie, anything that may be ruined in shooting or that you may need multiple copies of due to special effects (for instance, what if you're going to shoot a stabbing from four or five different camera set-ups?).

Then either go out and price those items or, if you have someone on board like an art director or a particularly fashion-conscious production assistant, have them go out and price them. Obviously, second-hand stores or flea markets can be of great assistance, as well as buying things from clothing stores and then returning them — that is, if they haven't been too abused during shooting.

WARDROBE CONSIDERATIONS

Every piece of clothing that your cast wears is important. If it isn't important to you ... find someone to whom it is. I personally dress every member of my cast. No, I don't go with them into the bathroom and help them on with their socks and shoes, but I either pick out or approve everything that everybody wears in my films.

Sometimes this causes problems because the actor or actress doesn't personally like what I have them wearing, but I don't care, because I know what their character would be wearing and that's what's important. I also know that it will fit into my color scheme for the entire film, something they don't have to be concerned with.

If you're not this fussy about what your actors or actresses are wearing, then you should find someone who is. It can be your production designer/art director or a student from a nearby fashion school or a local artist. They should have a good eye for color and fabric, know what does and does not look good on camera and know where to go for bargains that look great. If they can't be there on set all the time taking care of the clothes, they should at least be available to go out alone or with you and the cast to help select their wardrobe.

You really have to see how the clothes look on someone, how they move on the actor or actress, before buying them for your film. On my first couple of films, I had too many unpleasant surprises by not going along when the clothes were picked out or made. In addition, before you actually buy the clothing, make sure you ask your actor or actress their opinion about the garment. How it feels, is it comfortable, does it fit, etc.? They may have a valid complaint that you should listen too or they may not, but you want to know how they feel before you get on set in front of the rest of the cast and crew.

And remember, any clothing involved in an action sequence where it might get dirty or soiled has to be bought in multiples of the exact same piece for as many takes as you anticipate or can afford. In addition, to save the expense of a wardrobe person, I assign the responsibility of their wardrobe's upkeep to the individual actor or actress. I'm more than willing to pay the occasional dry cleaning bill if I can cut down on an extra crew member.

On a low-budget production, your actors and actresses can be your best way to save money on wardrobe by using their own clothing, as long as it fits into your visual scheme. But you must be willing to reimburse them for anything ruined or any cleaning bills due to the shoot. It's generally not a good idea to have them risk their own clothes in any kind of action or stunt, due to the ill will it can create. Buy your own low-cost multiples for these scenes.

This is another area where the additional expenditure of a few dollars may make the difference between your movie looking like amateur hour and a professional pro-formed the Weavers. The group would score many hits including "Kisses Sweeter Than Wine," "Wimoweh," "Goodnight Irene," and "On Top of Old Smoky." The Weavers were instrumental in the folk boom which occurred a decade later. But before they could reap that success, they had to survive the early 1950s and the McCarthy communist hunt.

Seeger was sympathetic to the ideas of humanitarian socialism. He was brought before the House Un-American Activities Committee and joined those who were blacklisted. In 1962, a decade later, he was finally cleared of all suspicion. The spirited singer pressed on with his career. In 1958, he left the Weavers to become a solo artist, just when college campuses and coffeehouses across the country embraced the folk style.

The 1960s were a boom time for Seeger. The decade of protest needed a leader and he fit the bill perfectly. Long before his song "Waist Deep in the Big Muddy" became an important Vietnam War chant, Seeger was active in the civil rights movement, where his version of an old spiritual, "We Shall Overcome," became the anthem of the pursuit for racial equality. His third important song of the era was "Turn, Turn, Turn." With words taken from the book of Ecclesiastes, it became a classic for the Byrds.

Seeger organized marches and rallies throughout the country, but focused on the South, where the civil rights movement was hottest. He also performed at and helped arrange the Newport Folk Festivals. Bob Dylan, Joan Baez, Phil Ochs, and the rest of the politically active 1960s folksingers embraced the elder statesman and regarded him as a spokesman.

However, Seeger was a folk purist, and was genuinely disheartened with the combination of folk and rock and roll. He was one of the main protesters when Bob Dylan went electric. Seeger was also upset when the Byrds enjoyed a huge hit with his song, "Turn, Turn Turn." He seemed helpless to turn the tide of the folk-rock movement.

In the latter half of the 1960s, he focused his energies on the Vietnam War issue. He was an active antiwar protester and organized many rallies against America's military commitment in Southeast Asia. He heavily criticized President Lyndon Johnson on the comedy show *The Smothers Brothers*, which endeared him to his followers but not to the authorities.

Throughout the 1970s and 1980s, Seeger turned his attention to environmental causes, mainly pollution, and much of the material he wrote reflected these concerns. He performed with Arlo Guthrie on numerous occasions on the sloop *Clearwater*, located on the Hudson River, where environmental activists gathered for political rallies and speeches. He also remained active on the festival circuit, appearing at outdoor folk concerts and organizing rallies for labor union struggles.

After 50 years in the music business with many highs and lows, Seeger received national recognition in 1994, when he received the National Medal of Arts, as well as a Kennedy Award. In 1996, he was inducted into the Rock and Roll Hall of Fame and released a studio album that introduced him to a new generation of fans. That same year he won a Grammy for Best Traditional Folk Album. In 1999, he traveled to Cuba to receive the Felix Varela Medal for humanistic and artistic work in defense of the environment and fighting racism.

In 2007, Seeger appeared in concert with his sister Peggy, brothers Mike and John, his wife and several other family members. It was held at the Library of Congress to honor the Seeger family and proved to be very successful. A year later, he returned to television for only the second time since being blacklisted to appear on the *David Letterman Show*. He continues to record and perform.

Pete Seeger is a folk music icon. During his 60-year career, perhaps no one has done more to preserve, promote and orchestrate the power of the style. He has displayed a passion for major and minor causes; led political rallies, marches, and protests; and survived good and bad times to become the granddaddy of the genre.

Seeger's style is peaceful. There is passion in his music, but no anger or hatred. He never initiated change with violence but instead used pure honesty and gentle conviction. The songs "Turn, Turn, Turn" and "We Shall Overcome" are two classic examples of his good-hearted musical abilities. His easy instrumental skills and strong, even vocals have always been accessible.

In many ways, Seeger's innovations reinvented the role of the banjo in folk music. He modified the instrument with a longer neck which allowed him to play different chords and notes. His classic book *How to Play the 5-String Banjo* was a seminal work which influenced many to begin careers as banjoists.

He was also adept at the 12-string guitar, an instrument with its origins in Mexico. Although Leadbelly was hailed as the king of the 12-string, Seeger modified the instrument as he had done with the banjo. His custom-built guitar had a triangular sound hole and was tuned differently. He played with finger picks and used his thumb extensively to create a whole new dimension of music.

He is associated with a number of other songs including "Kumbaya," "Turn, Turn, Turn," "We Shall Overcome," "Sixteen Tons," "There's a Valley in Spain Called Jarama," "Viva la quinte brigada," "Moorsoldaten" ("Peat Bog Soldiers"), "Die Thaelmann-Kolonne," "Hans Beimler," "Das Lied Von Der Einheitsfront" ("Song of the United Front"), "Der Internationalen Brigaden" ("Song of the International Brigades"), "Los cuatro generales" ("The Four Insurgent Generals"), "If I Had a Hammer," "Beans in My Ears," "Where Have All the Flowers Gone?," "Waist Deep in Big Muddy," and "Little Boxes." While he didn't write some of these he brought them to public attention with his smooth banjo-vocal combination.

As well as being a solid composer, he was also a song collector. While making history, Seeger was also preserving it. He always had an eye toward posterity. Before the age of 20, Seeger began to amass folk tunes, roaming the country on the rails as well as hitchhiking to remote areas, displaying a wanderlust he shared with Woody Guthrie, Cisco Houston, Alan Lomax, Leadbelly and Burl Ives.

His passion for collecting the music of his country led to a two-year stint as an assistant in the Archive of Folk Song at the Library of Congress. His journeys with Alan Lomax also taught him much and, in turn, Seeger passed on this knowledge to everyone he encountered. The enthusiasm he displayed was infectious and many wanted to join him in his endeavors.

Seeger has shared the stage with hundreds of performers of every style. A partial list includes Eric Clapton, Bonnie Raitt, Lee Hays, Fred Hellerman, Peggy Seeger, Mike Seeger, Cisco Houston, Bob Dylan, Joan Baez, Judy Collins, Leadbelly, the Band, and Phil Ochs. Many artists consider performing with him to be a highlight of their careers.

He has won many awards and accolades. The tribute album *Where Have All the Flowers Gone: The Songs of Pete Seeger* was produced in 1998. It featured readings and songs from Jackson Browne, Eliza Carthy, Judy Collins, Bruce Cockburn, Donovan, Ani DiFranco, Dick Gaughan, Nanci Griffith, Billy Bragg, Richie Havens, Indigo Girls, Roger McGuinn, Holly Near, Odetta, Tom Paxton, Bonnie Raitt, Martin Simpson and Bruce Springsteen.

Some of the other awards bestowed upon the folksinger include the Grammy Lifetime Achievement Award, the National Medal of Arts from the National Endowment for the Arts, the Kennedy Center Lifetime Achievement Honor, the Harvard Arts Medal, induction into the Rock and Roll Hall of Fame, the Letelier-Moffittt Human Rights Award, the Eugene V. Debs Award and the Schneider Family Book Award for his children's effort, *The Deaf Musicians.*

Seeger always understood the power of song, which has enabled him to help bring about social justice and equality. He was a master at marshaling songs from different sources to support a particular cause. He was the twentieth century folk man.

DISCOGRAPHY:

Songs to Grow On, Vol. 2, Smithsonian Folkways 7020.
American Folk Songs for Children, Smithsonian Folkways 7601.
A Pete Seeger Concert, Stinson 57.
Frontier Ballads, Smithsonian Folkways 5003.
Frontier Ballads, Vol. 1, Smithsonian Folkways 2175.
Frontier Ballads, Vol. 2, Smithsonian Folkways 2176.
Goofing-Off Suite, Smithsonian Folkways 2045.

How to Play the 5-String Banjo, Smithsonian Folkways 8303.
Pete Seeger Sampler, Smithsonian Folkways 2043.
Bantu Choral & Folk Songs, Smithsonian Folkways 6912.
Birds, Beasts, Bugs and Little Fishes, Smithsonian Folkways 7610.
Birds, Beasts, Bugs and Bigger Fishes, Smithsonian Folkways 7611.
Camp Songs, Smithsonian Folkways 7628.
The Folksinger Guitar Guide, Vol. 1: An Instruction Record, Smithsonian Folkways 8354.
Love Songs for Friends and Foes, Smithsonian Folkways 2453.
With Voices We Sing Together, Smithsonian Folkways 2452.
American Ballads, Vol. 3, Smithsonian Folkways 2322.
American Industrial Ballads, Smithsonian Folkways 40058.
Gazette, Smithsonian Folkways Fm-2501.
Sleep Time, Smithsonian Folkways 7525.
Pete Seeger and Sony Terry, Smithsonian Folkways 2412.
American Ballads, Vol. 2, Smithsonian Folkways 2321.
American Playparties, Smithsonian Folkways 7604.
Folk Songs for Young People, Smithsonian Folkways 7532.
Carnegie Hall, Smithsonian Folkways Fn-2512.
Champlain Valley Song Bag, Smithsonian Folkways Fn-5251.
Pete Seeger at the Village Gate, Smithsonian Folkways 2451.
Song and Play Time with Pete Seeger, Smithsonian Folkways 7526.
Songs of the Civil War, Smithsonian Folkways 5717.
Champlain Valley Songs, Smithsonian Folkways 5210.
American Favorite Ballads, Vol. 4, Smithsonian Folkways 2323.
Story Songs, Columbia 1668.
Songs of Memphis Slim and Willie Dixon, Smithsonian Folkways 2385.
Indian Summer, Smithsonian Folkways 3851.
American Favorite Ballads, Vol. 5, Smithsonian Folkways 2445.
American Game and Activity Songs for Children, Smithsonian Folkways 7674.
The Bitter and the Sweet, Mobile Fidelity 873.
Broadside Ballads, Vol. 2, Smithsonian Folkways 5302.
Children's Concert at Town Hall, Columbia/Legacy 46185.
Broadside, Folkways 2456.
Strangers and Cousins, CBS C-2334.
Little Boxes and Other Broadsides, Smithsonian Folkways 9620.
I Can See a New Day, CBS 2257.
God Bless the Grass, Columbia 65287.
Dangerous Songs?, Columbia 65261.
Abiyoyo and Other Story Songs for Children, Smithsonian Folkways 45001.
Pete Seeger Sings Woody Guthrie, Smithsonian Folkways 31002.
Waist Deep in the Big Muddy and Other Love Songs, Columbia 57311.
Pete Seeger Now, CBS 9717.
Pete Seeger Sings Leadbelly, Smithsonian Folkways 31022.
Pete Seeger Sings and Answers Questions of Ford Forum Hall Boston, Smithsonian Folkways 5702.
Tell Me That You Love Me, Junie Moon, CBS 3540.
Pete Seeger Young Vs. Old, Columbia 9873.
Rainbow Race, Columbia 30739.

Banks of Marble, Smithsonian Folkways 31040.
Fifty Sail on Newburgh Bay, Smithsonian Folkways 5257.
Circles and Seasons, Warner Bros. 3129.
Sing-A-Long, Smithsonian Folkways 40027.
Sing-A-Long Demonstration Concert, Smithsonian Folkways SF 40027.
Sings Traditional Christmas Carols, Smithsonian Folkways 40024.
A Fish That's a Song, Smithsonian Folkways SF 45037.
Sing-A-Long: Live at Sanders Theatre, Cambridge, Massachusetts, 1980, Smithsonian Folkways 40027.
Pete Seeger's Family Concert, CBS 48907.
Live at Newport, Vanguard 770082.
Stories and Songs for Little Children, High Windy Audio 1207.
Pete, Living Music 32.
Kisses Sweeter Than Wine, Collector's Edition 8.
Live in Lisbon, Movie Play 374.
Ao Vivo Em Lisboa, Movie Play 30174.
In Prague 1964, Flyright 68.
Brothers and Sisters, Discmedi Blau 4203.
At 89, Appleseed 1113.
Activity Songs, Smithsonian Folkways 45025.
America's Balladeer, Olympic 7102.
Ballads, Smithsonian Folkways 2049.
Broadside Ballads, Vol. 3, Smithsonian Folkways 5302.
Folk Music Live at the Village Cafe, Smithsonian Folkways 9013.
Folk Songs by Pete Seeger, Capitol 2172.
Folk Songs of Courting & Complaint, Smithsonian Folkways 2049.
Folk Songs of Four Continents (Liberia, India, Bahamas, Chile/Norway), Smithsonian Folkways 6911.
Folk Songs of Pete Seeger, Prestige 7375.
Freight Train, Capitol 2718.
How I Hunted the Little Fellows, Smithsonian Folkways 7527.
In Person at the Bitter End, CBS 1916.
Lonesome Valley, Smithsonian Folkways 2010.
Pete Seeger at Carnegie Hall, Smithsonian Folkways 2351.
Pete Seeger on Campus, Smithsonian Folkways 9009.
Songs of Selma, Smithsonian Folkways 5595.
Songs of the Lincoln and International Brigades, Stinson 52.
The Guitar Course: 12 String As Played By, Smithsonian Folkways 8371.
The Rainbow Design, Smithsonian Folkways 2454.
The Story of the Nativity, Smithsonian Folkways 35001.
Where Have All the Flowers Gone, Smithsonian Folkways 31026.
Wimoweh (And Other Songs of Freedom and Protest), Smithsonian Folkways 31018.
American Favorite Ballads, Vol. 1, Smithsonian Folkways 31017.
Pete Seeger's Greatest Hits, CBS 09416.
The World of Pete Seeger, Columbia 31949.
The Essential Pete Seeger, Vanguard 97/98.
Clearwater Classics, Pair 1076.
Carry It On, Songs of America's Working People, Flying Fish FF 104.

Essential Pete Seeger, Vol. 2, Vanguard 73112.
We Shall Overcome: The Complete Carnegie Hall Concert, Columbia 45312.
Folk Music of the World, Legacy 342.
Clearwater Classics, Sony Special Product 17865.
20 Golden Pieces of Pete Seeger, Bulldog 2011.
Darling Corey/Goofing-Off Suite, Smithsonian Folkways 2003.
Essential # 1, Vanguard 73111.
Pete Seeger Concert/Pete! Folk Songs and Ballads, Collectables 5608.
Classical Folk Songs, Fat Boy 274.
Sing Out, Magnum 008.
Link in the Chain, Columbia 64772.
Seeger & Hester: Members Edition, United Audio 3030.
American Favorite Ballads, A World of Music 12504.
Best of Pete Seeger, Vanguard 501.
Birds, Beasts, Bugs and Fishes (Little & Big), Smithsonian Folkways 45039.
For Kids and Just Plain Folks, Sony Wonder 63424.
If I Had a Hammer: Songs of Hope & Struggle, Smithsonian Folkways 40096.
Headlines and Footnotes: Collection of Topical Songs, Smithsonian Folkways 40111.
Pioneer of Folk, Prism 500.
American Folk, Game and Activity Songs for Children, Smithsonian Folkways 45056.
Round and Round Hitler's Grave, ABM 1321.
Folk Singer, Masterson 503662.
Best of Pete Seeger, Music Club 462.
American Favorite Ballads, Vol. 1, Smithsonian Folkways 2319.
Greatest Hits, Legacy 5060362.
Pete Seeger's Greatest Hits, Columbia/Legacy 65711.
The House Carpenter, Hallmark 70196.
It Takes a Worried Man, Traditional Live 1387.
American Favorite Ballads, Vol. 2, Smithsonian Folkways 40151.
Seeds: The Songs of Pete Seeger, Vol. 3, Appleseed 1072.
Which Side Are You On?, Acrobat 167.
Collection, EMI 576125.
If I Had a Hammer: 1944–1950, Naxos Folk 8120737.
American Favorite Ballads, Vol. 3, Smithsonian Folkways 40152.
The Essential Pete Seeger, Sony 92835.
Genius of Folk, Genius of Folk 6586.
We Shall Not Be Moved, Prism 1414.
We Shall Not Be Moved: 40 Original Recordings, Prism 2269.
Folk Songs, Ballads and Banjo, Golden Stars 5420.
Pete Seeger: The Weavers, Goldies 25455.
The Legend, Cherished Classics 3017.
Canciones de Las Brigadas Internacionales, Discredi Blau 4231.
Una Leyenda, Disc Medi 426302.
Talking Union, Xtra 26575.
Hard Travelling: The Best of Pete Seeger, Music Club 638.
Golden Slumbers, Caedmon 1399.
The Bitter and the Sweet, Mobile Fidelity 873.
Sing-a-long at Sanders Theatre, 1980, Smithsonian/Folkways 40027.
Precious Friend (with Arlo Guthrie), Warner Brothers 3644.

Fred Hellerman (1927–)

The Little Cowboy

The importance of musical groups is not judged on their longevity, but rather on the impact they have on others. The Weavers were a powerful folk band because they influenced a wealth of folkies with their politically charged tunes. One of the members was known for his role within the foursome, as well as for his career as a solo artist, where he earned the nickname "Little Cowboy." His name was Fred Hellerman.

Hellerman was born on May 13, 1927, in Brooklyn, New York. His father was a Latvian immigrant and worked in the rag business. The young Hellerman spent his formative years in the shadow of the Great Depression, which taught him several lessons. He knew that he never wanted to experience such economic hardship again.

Although he listened to the popular music of the day, Hellerman didn't take up music until a stint in the Coast Guard, when he taught himself how to play guitar. He enjoyed finding the right chord and note, which relieved tension. Although not the greatest instrumentalist, he managed to develop an accessible style that was acceptable within the folk framework.

After the war, Hellerman led a double life. By day, he was a student at Brooklyn College, majoring in English, with ambitions to be a teacher. On the side, he performed with a group called American Folksay. His musical activities attracted the attention of People's Songs, an organization devoted to union and other causes, who utilized folk music to broadcast their message and help the downtrodden.

Lee Hays, singer, songwriter, union activist, and political idealist, was the secretary of People's Songs and invited Hellerman down for a visit. The two struck up a friendship. Some time later he met Pete Seeger, a major figure in folk activism. Years before, Ronnie Gilbert and Hellerman had met at a summer camp, working as counselors. The energy which surrounded the group of young liberals was infectious and Hellerman was drawn into their world.

In 1948, Hellerman made "The Little Cowboy," his first recording for Young People's Records. Will Geer and Ernie Lieberman were in on the session, but the song did not become popular. Despite the lack of attention, Hellerman forged ahead and continued to develop a musical career.

Later that year, he joined forces with Hays, Seeger and Gilbert to become a member of the Weavers. The group started at a hootenanny. They sang a medley of folk songs they called "Around the World." The magic among the four members was evident from the very beginning and they decided to stay together.

The audience enjoyed the blend of the four distinct voices harmonizing in unison. The quartet continued to rehearse and the group dynamic strengthened with the increased time members spent practicing. It was Hellerman who suggested they call themselves the Weavers, a title taken from a German play he was reading at the time.

On January 2, 1949, the Weavers made their radio debut on Oscar Brand's WNYC program Folksong Festival. It was a successful event and proved that the four talented artists possessed something special. Although they had occasional gigs, each member had other commitments and couldn't give the group the attention it deserved to achieve any kind of sustained progress.

Later that summer, Hellerman performed at a resort in the Catskills Mountains, where Gilbert worked as a secretary. The two found time to harmonize and on occasion shared the stage. That year, in September, at a Paul Robeson concert held in Peekskill, New York, Gilbert, Hellerman and Pete Seeger managed to escape the anti–Communist vigilantes who rioted after the event.

This experience fueled commitment to the group effort as well as its first single, "The Peekskill Story, Parts 1 and 2." While the song did nothing to boost their career, the Weavers forged ahead and recorded "Wasn't That a Time," followed by "Dig My Grave." The group gained some momentum with the Seeger-Hays composition, "The Hammer Song." Later, the title was changed to "If I Had a Hammer." On the flip side was the tune "Banks of Marble."

Despite the brisk recording activity, the Weavers were not very successful. In fact, the group was in the process of disbanding. Hellerman was headed toward a graduate degree at the University of Chicago. Gilbert, Seeger and Hays were also busy pursuing their own interests.

But the Weavers were not finished. Seeger managed to secure a gig at the Village Vanguard in Greenwich Village. They were such a success that the engagement kept being extended. They played their last show in June of 1950, the initial two weeks having lasted six months.

During their stint at the Village Vanguard, a representative from Decca sat in one night and signed them to the label. The group recorded "Tzena, Tzena, Tzena" and "Good Night Irene," a Leadbelly staple. While the first song did well; the second became a major hit and spent three months at number one on the charts. The success positioned the group as one of the top draws on the folk circuit.

Just as it seemed that the Weavers were on the verge of true stardom, politics intervened. Anti-Communist feeling during the McCarthy era classed them as radicals and a TV contract was cancelled. Blacklisting halted the incredible momentum that the quartet had built up over the past year.

But the group refused to quit. A national tour scheduled for a series of night clubs and theaters was enhanced when Hellerman recorded the anti-nuclear song "Old Man Atom." Despite using a pseudonym, he was still recognized as the singer, which caused a major sensation. The Weavers continued to record and toured as often as possible.

The Weavers had perfected arranging existing folk tunes to fit their quartet sound, with major changes to melody and lyrics. Many of the traditional songs had no real author and the group claimed the reworked versions with new names as their own in order to collect royalties. "Suliram," "Hush Little Baby/I Know Where I'm Going," "Follow the Drinking Gourd," "Darling Corey," "Wimoweh," "Greensleeves," "Easy Rider Blues," and "Kisses Sweeter Than Wine" were among their hits.

However, this flush of success proved to be brief. The anti–Communist hearings falsely implicated the group's members in left-wing politics, and they found it nearly impossible to find a gig. Their record sales fell drastically and that spelled the end of the Weavers. In 1952, they officially broke up.

Hellerman began teaching guitar, arranging music and composing original material for others to record. Don Williams, the Band, Sam Cooke, Ronnie Lane, and Bobby Vinton all recorded their own versions of "I'm Just a Country Boy." The song was one of seven which Harry Belafonte included in his debut album, *Mark Twain and Other Folk Favorites.* It was a generous boost for the struggling songwriter whose career had been so hard hit.

In 1955, Hellerman and Hays recorded a song entitled "Goodnight Sweet Dreams." Later on, the Weavers reunited for a show at Carnegie Hall, which sparked a rebirth of the group. Although each member was too involved in solo projects to give the group proper attention, they managed to perform on weekends. While they got live gigs, television and radio opportunities remained unavailable.

In 1957, the album *The Weavers at Carnegie Hall* was released and Hellerman delivered a solid version of "Sixteen Tons," the song Tennessee Ernie Ford had made famous. Later they recorded *The Weavers on Tour,* which received a hearty welcome from listeners as the McCarthy reign of terror faded. Within a year, they would be hailed as important trendsetters responsible for the folk boom.

Pete Seeger left the Weavers around the time that *The Weavers on Tour* was recorded, and Erik Darling filled in for him. The group's repertoire around this era included "Every Night" and "Come Little Donkey." However, many Hellerman compositions such as "The Way I Feel," "Fare Thee Well, "I Never Will Marry," "Green Grow the Lilacs," and "Walking on the Green Grass" were found on the albums of Harry Belafonte.

Hellerman moonlighted as a conductor on Theodore Bikel's *Bikel Sings Jewish Folk Songs* and *Theodore Bikel Sings More Jewish Folk Songs.* But his main focus remained with his solo work and the Weavers' irregular activity. In 1959, they recorded *Travelling On with the Weavers,* which included "I Never Will Marry," another original Hellerman composition. The group's longevity seemed tied to his productivity.

In 1960, The Weavers recorded another live album at Carnegie Hall and it reached the *Billboard* charts. There were two numbers credited to Hellerman on this release including "There Once Was a Young Man Who Went to the City" and "Tapuach Hineni." As the major songwriter for the group, he provided them with first-rate material which kept their name vibrant on the folk circuit.

While his career continued with the Weavers, others began to recognize his talent. Harry Belafonte continued to record Hellerman's songs including "Chickens," "Who's Gonna Be Your Man," and "Long About Now." Joan Baez asked him to sit in on her debut album for Vanguard as a guitarist. He also guested on Judy Collins's release, *Maid of Constant Sorrow,* and the Chad Mitchell Trio's *At the Bitter End.*

In 1963, the Weavers released *The Weavers' Almanac,* which included Hays, Hellerman, Gilbert and Darling, as well as Frank Hamilton, who would eventually leave; Bernie Krause would provide a fine replacement. Their shows at Carnegie Hall were recorded for two more albums and included the anti-war "Come Away Melinda." The song became a folk standard as Judy Collins, the Big 3, Kenny Rankin, Tim Rose, Bobbie Gentry, Uriah Heep, UFO and Harry Belafonte all recorded their own versions.

In 1964, the Weavers disbanded and went their separate ways. Hellerman pursued his solo career and continued to write songs, often collaborating with partner Fran Minkoff. They were a productive duo. Other groups recorded their material, including the Kingston Trio, one of the most popular groups on the folk circuit, who produced a version of "Poverty Hill."

Harry Belafonte continued to draw on the Hellerman/Minkoff partnership for material, including "In My Quiet Room," a re-release of "I'm Just a Country Boy," "The Honey Wind Blows," "Our Time for Loving," "In the Beginning," "The First Day of Forever," and "Sunflower." The Jamaican entertainer brought the songs to life.

In 1967, Hellerman produced Arlo Guthrie's smash hit *Alice's Restaurant,* as well as the 1968 *Arlo,* and later, *Last of the Brooklyn Cowboys.* In 1969, he would assume the role of musical director for the movie version of *Alice's Restaurant.* His involvement in this project elevated his status throughout the musical community.

In 1968, Hellerman and Minkoff wrote two songs, "A New Waltz" and "The Girl in the Mirror," which were part of the Broadway musical revue *New Faces of '68.* Although it had a short production run, the show released an album. It emphasized Hellerman's and Minkoff's range of abilities and ensured they would get more work in the future.

In the early 1970s, Hellerman moved to Weston, Connecticut, where he built a new recording studio. He composed the score for the film *Lovin' Molly.* The political songster remained active throughout the decade, and in 1979 produced the album *Circles and Seasons* with Ronnie Gilbert. Hellerman sang backup. The entertainer proved that he had not lost his magical touch.

In 1980, at the end of the year, Seeger re-formed the Weavers for concerts at Carnegie Hall. Hellerman, Gilbert, and an ailing Lee Hays all participated in this historic event. Despite the fact that they had officially disbanded many years before, the group still commanded much respect throughout the folk community. The concert was filmed as a documentary, *The Weavers: Wasn't That a Time!* This was their final appearance before Hays passed away.

Throughout the 1980s, Hellerman continued to produce and write film scores, but his solo career seemed finished. He oversaw the release of a concert album, *Together Again,* getting more mileage out of the Weavers. In 1982, he composed the score for the TV movie *The Rainmaker.* Later, when tapes of the Weavers were unearthed, they would be released, which enhanced Hellerman's career.

In 1995, he joined Peter, Paul & Mary on their *Live Lines* album. A few years later he performed at a tribute concert when Woody Guthrie was inducted into the Rock and Roll Hall of Fame. An album, *'Til We Outnumber 'Em,* was recorded for the occasion. His participation proved that he still possessed a strong voice and was capable of contributing in any situation.

In 2003, he returned to do more Weavers tribute material at a concert, which led to the filmed documentary, *Isn't This a Time!* In 2004, he rejoined Seeger, Gilbert, Darling and Eric Weissberg for a performance. Finally, a year later, Hellerman, who had written for so many others, released his first solo work, *Caught in the Act.* The collection of vaudeville songs from the turn of the twentieth century appeared on his label, Honeywind. He continues to record, perform and write.

Fred Hellerman has been an integral part of the folk movement for a long time. His participation in the Weavers, his songwriting abilities, his production credits, his film scores, and his participation in Broadway musicals show him off as a complete entertainment artist. He performed many roles and excelled in each one.

Hellerman was a singer and guitarist, but like most folk musicians, he was not a great virtuoso. He could hold his own live and in a recording studio. But instead of distinguishing himself as a great instrumentalist, he played simple lines suited to his overall delivery. His rhythms are heard in many of the Weavers' songs as well as in the studio work of others.

He was not a great vocalist. Hellerman sounded best when he could blend in within a group, as in the Weavers. He added depth and balance to the overall projection. However, his voice was good enough to be included in a variety of projects over the years in different situations.

He was a strong arranger who had learned from the best, including Pete Seeger, Woodie Guthrie, and Lee Hays. Hellerman had a knack of juxtaposing the right note to the right lyric. His skills would extend to producer and his most famous work was Arlo Guthrie's *Alice's Restaurant*, which became a classic and continues to draw audiences more than 40 years after its release.

His writing skills extended to the motion picture industry as well as the theater. Again his most famous project was the movie version of *Alice's Restaurant*. The film became an underground cult favorite while the song remains an integral part of the U.S. Thanksgiving tradition. Involvement in this project was crucial to Hellerman's career because it shed light on his writing and production talents.

However, Hellerman's forte was songwriting. A partial list of the songs he wrote alone or in collaboration includes "The Little Cowboy," "Around the World," "The Peekskill Story, Parts 1 and 2," "Wasn't That a Time," "Dig My Grave," "Suliram," "Hush Little Baby/I Know Where I'm Going," "Follow the Drinking Gourd," "Darling Corey," "Wimoweh," "Greensleeves," "Easy Rider Blues," "Kisses Sweeter Than Wine," "I'm Just a Country Boy," "Delia," "Goodnight Sweet Dreams," "Every Night," "Come Little Donkey," "The Way I Feel," "Fare Thee Well, "I Never Will Marry," "Green Grow the Lilacs," "Walking on the Green Grass," "There Once Was a Young Man Who Went to the City," "Tapuach Hineni," "Chickens," "Who's Gonna Be Your Man," "Long About Now," "Come Away Melinda," "Poverty Hill," "In My Quiet Room," "The Honey Wind Blows," "Our Time for Loving," "In the Beginning," "The First Day of Forever," "Sunflower," "A New Waltz," and "The Girl in the Mirror."

As a member of the Weavers, Hellerman played a vital role in the pre–folk-boom era. In the late 1950s and 1960s, he laid down the groundwork for the eventual explosion. He benefited greatly from the folk boom, performing with Judy Collins, Joan Baez, and others. Many of the younger generation of folk artists had a tremendous respect for his abilities because he had been a pioneer and paved the way for them to succeed.

Fred Hellerman is a folk music institution. As a solo artist, a member of the Weavers, and a songwriter for films, theater, and special concerts, his impact was enormous. There was a defiance, strength and urgency in his material which inspired two generations of entertainers. The Little Cowboy displayed a wealth of talent throughout his entire career.

DISCOGRAPHY:

Caught in the Act, Honeywind B0009J8QB2.

PART FOUR

Folk Around the World

Every country has its folk music. The indigenous sounds of each nation are crucial to the survival of a particular culture. Although many believe that the term "folk music" refers only to American music or that of Great Britain, Ireland and Scotland, to ignore the ethnic music of other countries would be a disfavor to the genre.

Canada, with its rich and diverse history arising from its vast geography and migration patterns, developed a strong contingent of folk musicians. On the East Coast, known as the Maritimes, the Celtic style was established long ago and remains a dominant, vibrant form to this day. Quebec, predominantly French-speaking, possesses its own 500-year history of music from travelers, fur traders, religious figures, and others. Ontario, a cultural hodgepodge of nationalities, demonstrates a proud folk heritage and an influence from the United States. The western provinces boast a strong collection of cowboy and prairie tunes. And native people who once roamed the land have a strong musical tradition attached to dance.

South America has indigenous music also closely associated with dance, including dozens of major styles, each with their own subgenres. Brazil, Peru, Argentina, Colombia, Ecuador, Venezuela, Uruguay, Chile, and Bolivia each boast several styles that stand on their own and intertwine with each other. The richness of the folk music in this region has never been broadcast to its fullest potential.

The Caribbean is home to a wonderful mixture of calypso, reggae and other styles from Africa and Europe. The Dominican Republic, Haiti, Puerto Rico, Turks and Caicos, St. Lucia, Trinidad and Tobago, the Virgin Islands, and all of the other nations that make up the region are proud of their musical heritage. The Bahamas and Bermuda, both non–Caribbean nations, share some similar styles, instruments, and dance rhythms. Jamaica is a special case because of its dominant reggae sound, which broke through internationally. Beginning in the 1950s and extending into the 1960s, music from the West Indies would assume a more powerful position on the world stage.

European folk music is a vast richness of textures, melodies, and rhythms with a documented history that dates back at least 1000 years. Each culture has different features, including Russian and Greek folk dances, Bulgarian tunes, French secular hymns, German drinking chants, Italian opera, Jewish melodies, hot Spanish rhythms, Austrian waltzes, Czechoslovakian peasant songs, Polish polkas, Dutch jigs, Hungarian classical elements, Portuguese swing, and Romanian and Ukrainian stomps. Every country has a strong ethnic flavor which was interchanged with those of many other nations.

Northern Europe has an interesting musical legacy which includes the Swedish sagas of Vikings, conquerors, explorers, and gods and goddesses. There too are powerful, breathtaking Finnish folk dances, Norwegian ballads and dance tunes and Danish fiddle/accordion/guitar groups who play fiery, high-tempo numbers. The Scandinavians exchanged musical innovations and ideas but each retained an original element.

In Asia, folk was preserved mainly through dance. In India, there is a 5000-year-old musical tradition where the practitioners play for pennies rather than prestige. In China, ethnic music was played in the courts of the great imperial dynasties. In Japan, a strong folk heritage descended from one generation to another.

The Middle Eastern nations were great innovators and introduced many musical elements into European culture which the settlers brought over to the New World. One of these was the *oud* or *ud,* which was a predecessor of the lute and the guitar. The entire Arab community has a music of tradition, ceremony and distinct tones. The Egyptian civilization, which dates back thousands of years, always boasted a strong folk strain. In Iran, the folk style was linked to the unique brand of classical music.

In Africa, the land of rhythm, are hundreds of subgenres of folk music, because of the diverse languages and ethnic groups. The seventh century Arab invasion reached the northern part of the continent and influenced tribal dances and songs. Today, Africa boasts dances and tunes committed to memory from thousands of years of practice. The rhythms transported to America and every other corner of the globe helped spread African influence.

Like the United States and Canada, Australia built its folk tradition on that of England, Ireland and Scotland. However, over the years, a unique strain evolved which could truly be called Australian. Also of importance is the primitive sound of the Aborigines, who developed their own musical language long before the arrival of any white settlers.

Each country in every continent produced music on a variety of instruments. Many of them were homemade, particularly in the poorest regions, and consisted of material that was unique to that area. Ideas for new types of strings, horns or drums were exchanged among nations. In the post-modern era, these include the acoustic guitar, banjo, accordion, fiddle, harmonica, rhythm devices, dulcimer, dobro, and piano.

The individuals included in this book represent their countries in a variety of roles including singer, collector, and musician. This section, "Folk Around the World," provides examples of many of the folk music styles of the world. The musical history of just one country, one region, or one territory could fill volumes. But the following are representative of their cultures.

Béla Bartók was a Hungarian classical composer who united classical music with the peasant folk music of the Carpathian basin. Udi Hrant Kenkulian was a Turkish *oud* player of superior ability. Atahualpa Yupanqui was an Argentinean folksinger who ushered in the modern movement. Luiz Gonzaga was a passionate accordion player who wrote hot dance tunes which catapulted him to stardom.

Edith Fowke was a Canadian folklorist and tireless champion of bringing the songs of her country to national attention. Vassilis Tsitsanis was a Greek folkie whose powerful instrumental skills and compositional abilities made him a star. Amália Rodrigues was a Portuguese singer who was an international star and the greatest exponent of the fado style.

Buddy MacMaster is a classic example of the Canadian East Coast/ Cape Breton musical tradition. A serious fiddler, he has a dedicated following. Hamza El Din of Egypt earned his fame by collecting a repertoire of Nubian folk tunes of the Sudan region. Severino Dias de Oliveira was a Brazilian folk artist who preserved the hundreds of years of tradition from his country.

Béla Bartók (1881–1945)
The Hungarian Ethnomusicologist

In the twentieth century, the term "ethnomusicologist" was coined when individuals began to collect, organize and preserve folk tunes. The term is usually applied to the study of the music of different cultures, especially those considered non–Western. At the turn of the century, one figure would embark on a journey to educate himself and the world on traditional ethnic sounds. His name was Béla Bartók.

Béla Bartók was born on March 25, 1881, in the small town of Nagyszentmiklós in Austria-Hungary. It is now known as Sînnicolau Mare, Romania. He was a musical prodigy and by the age of five could play the piano with a definite expertise. He understood rhythms, melodies, patterns and dance years ahead of his age. When Bartók's father died two years later, music became the young boy's solace and private world.

His mother moved her small family (Bartók and his sister) to the Ukraine, then Germany, and later Slovakia. Along the way, Bartók would perform his first public recital and receive rave critical reviews. The young genius had began to compose his own material and it was this music he often played to interested audiences. By the time he began formal piano instruction, he had already written a short but entertaining piece entitled "The Course of the Danube."

The period between 1899 and 1908 marked his early musical career. Bartók finished his studies, which included private tutors and an education at the Royal Academy of Music in Budapest, where he studied composition. During this period, he met Zoltán Kodály, a fellow Hungarian who also became a composer and ethnomusicologist as well as an educator, linguist and philosopher. They began a lifelong friendship.

In 1903, he composed his first major orchestral work, a symphonic poem, which honored Lajos Kossuth, the hero of the Hungarian revolution of 1848. At the time, the work of Richard Strauss, the waltz king, had a profound influence on Bartók, however the young musician would develop a unique, distinct sound. Bartók's rise in classical music was swift and permanent.

However, in 1904, he was exposed to Transylvanian folksongs, which ignited a lifelong dedication to the folk style. Meanwhile, his orchestral movements featured the influences of Claude Debussy, the great French composer, as well as Johannes Brahms, along with Strauss. In 1908, he performed the *String Quartet No. 1,* which contained many folk-like elements — a stark departure from his previous work.

In 1907, Bartók began a career as a piano teacher at the Royal Academy. There was a positive side to this engagement because he was no longer forced to tour Europe. It provided him the opportunity to dabble in traditional music collection, a hobby in which he had developed a keen interest.

In 1908, Bartók and Kodály embarked on a life-changing experience when they ventured through the countryside to collect and research old Magyar folk melodies. These were mistakenly categorized as Gypsy material, but the two explorers discovered that was false. With their superior musical training, the duo quickly realized that the music was based on Oriental traditions as well as those of Siberia.

The two composers incorporated the elements they had unearthed on the expedition into their respective compositions. This strong dose of Magyar peasant music shocked the purists when it first appeared in four volumes of *For Children* for solo piano. The work contained 85 tunes which combined folk, classical and modernism. Although he was not the first to mix traditional sound with classical music, Bartók's effort was unique because of his individuality.

Later discoveries included Romanian folksongs with a strong melodic and harmonic element. He also explored the rich vein of Hungarian peasant tunes, which provided a solid foundation for future works. Another source was the powerful rhythms of Bulgarian dance music. Bartók was a man of many talents, who had suddenly become a world musician with the inclusion of many different styles in his work.

In 1909, Bartók married, and later had a son. In 1911, he wrote his only opera, *Bluebeard's Castle*, which he dedicated to his wife. When it failed to win a Fine Arts Commission prize, he rewrote it. It received its premiere a few years later, but not before the government intervened and forced him to rework the piece. Although he obliged, the great Hungarian composer developed a distaste for the authorities.

During this period, he continued to collect folk tunes from a variety of sources, including the Hungarian, Slovakian, Romanian and Bulgarian countryside. Later, he extended the study to the ethnic songs from Wallachia and Algeria. However, the First World War forced him to end his expeditions and he concentrated on compositions like the ballet *The Wooden Prince* and *The String Quartet No. 2*. The former would earn him some international attention.

In 1918, at the end of the First World War, Bartók worked on another ballet, *The Miraculous Mandarin*, a sordid tale which dealt with the life of the most common person. Because of its sexual content, the piece would not make an appearance for another eight years. In between he wrote his third and fourth string quartets. Once the war was over, he was able to indulge again in his hobby of collecting folk music.

In 1923, he divorced his wife. A year later, he married one of his former students and they had a son. Throughout the decade he continued to fuse classical works with peasant folk tunes from his own country and neighboring nations. Later works included *Divertimento for Strings, Music for Strings, Percussion and Celesta*, and *String Quartet No. 5*. In 1936, he traveled to Turkey to collect and study folk music.

In the 1930s, like many other Europeans, he lived in uncertain times. Béla Bartók understood that war was imminent and spent his last few years running from it. As the escalation of conflict and tensions increased, his refusal to acknowledge Nazism caused him trouble. He had no performances in Germany after Hitler came to power and broke all ties with the country. In 1939, by the time his *Sixth Quartet* appeared, he had left his beloved Hungary to live in Turkey. However, fearing for the safety of his family, he emigrated to the United States.

In New York City, he found the adjustment difficult. In many ways,

Bartók was a European. He was well known as a good pianist, as well as an ethnomusicologist, and teacher, however his compositions had not penetrated the American market. He and his wife Ditta gave concerts, but also focused their energies on collecting Serbo-Croatian folk tunes.

In 1940, he had begun to experience health problems and four years later Bartók was diagnosed with leukemia. His last composition was *Concerto for Orchestra*, which enjoyed unbounded popularity. However, he never lived to see the impact of this final work because he passed away on September 26, 1945.

Béla Bartók was a folk music student. Although he was known for his classical compositions, the keen musician was constantly evolving and his thirst for the peasant sounds of the countryside of Eastern Europe never ceased. His use of Hungarian ethnic melodies enabled him to become a world musician.

Bartók was a first-rate pianist who was able to organize and arrange any style of music into a coherent package. Although he acknowledged his major influences as the masters Brahms, Debussy, and Strauss, among others, his other heroes were the unknown street musicians who were strict practitioners of folk music.

He utilized many different techniques to achieve his goals including atonality, bitonality, attenuated harmonic function, polymodal chromaticism, projected sets, privileged patters and different scales such as the octatonic, diatonic, and heptatonia seconda seven-note. Bartók was a master technician and, like a painter, blended all the elements together to create impressive finished products.

Bartók was an innovator. His compositions reflected the two trends of music in the twentieth century: the breakdown of the harmony system that had existed for 200 years and a generous dose of nationalism. Throughout his career, his music evolved from the late romantic style with new influences such as Strauss, Debussy, and peasant music. Bartók's compositional methods and performances changed as he allowed the different ideas to flow into his own creativity.

Bartók created the ethnomusicologist's blueprint. He undertook many expeditions to listen carefully, with genuine interest, to the music of the countryside. There was a sincerity in his approach and a pure devotion to bringing that sound to the international stage. His superior musical training and sensibility enabled him to compare folk sounds and draw out the best elements.

He was an exceptional teacher on many levels. A few of his most notable students were Fritz Reiner, Sir Georg Solti, György Sándor, Lili Kraus, and, after Bartók moved to the United States, Jack Beeson and Violet Archer. Each incorporated much of the same philosophy as their instructor, blending classical strains with folk ideas.

Béla Bartók has been honored many different ways. He is on a Hungarian bank note which was eliminated in 1983, making it a collector's item. In Brussels, Belgium, there is a statue of the famed composer situated in the central train station in a public square. Another monument to him is in London, opposite South Kensington Underground Station. And a Bartók museum stands in Budapest.

Bartók was not the first composer to mesh folk with the classical style. Joseph Haydn was the first, followed by Ludwig van Beethoven, Liszt, Brahms, Tchaikovsky, Dvořák, Percy Grainger, Ralph Vaughan Williams, Malcolm Arnold, and Benjamin Britten. In the modern era, it became a standard practice.

Bartók left behind two sons, Peter and Béla II. For the former, he wrote a six-volume primer comprising more than 150 pieces, that proved a valuable learning tool in various techniques, including melody, harmony and rhythm. Neither of his offspring followed in their father's footsteps.

Béla Bartók was a modernist and used his talent and skills to create a style of classical music which the world had never heard before. His integral emphasis and application of folk rhythms and melodies gave his sound a keen edge. He was an excellent student who studied and compared every strain to become an Hungarian ethnomusicologist.

DISCOGRAPHY:

Béla Bartók — A Portrait, Naxos 8558200.
Masters of the Piano Rolls — Mahler, Bartók, Del Segno 6712176.
Bartók: Concerto for Orchestra, Phantom Sound & Vision 7706105.
Bartók: String Quartets 1–6, Simax Records/Premiere 7477904.
Bartók: Strings Quartets Nos. 1–6, Phantom Sound & Vision 7634764.
Bartók: Tanzsuite/Ungarische Baue, Phantom Sound & Vision 7686918.
Bartók: Violin Concertos, Phantom Sound & Vision 7606934.
Béla Bartók (1881–1945), Phantom Sound & Vision 7706536.
Bartók at the Piano, Hungaroton 1115166.
Bartók for Orchestra, Nimbus 1123026.
Bartók in the Desert—The Art of Irén Marik, Arbiter 143.
Bartók Plays Bartók, Urania 340.
Bartók Plays Bartók-Mikrokosmos, Pearl 179.
Bartók Recordings from Private Collections, Hungaroton 1115167.
Bartók: 44 Duos for 2 Violins, ECM New Series 3674514.
Bartók: Bluebeard's Castle, Naxos 2560845.
Bartók: Choral Music, SOMM 216.
Bartók: Choral Works, Hungaroton 31047.
Bartók: Complete Solo Piano Music, Vox Box 3610.
Bartók: Complete String Quartets, Erato 679190.
Bartók: Complete String Quartets, Electra 2075.
Bartók: Duos & Folksongs, Hungaroton 32516.

Udi Hrant Kenkulian
(1901–1978)
The Oud Master

In Turkey and other Middle Eastern countries the oud has been the instrument of choice for many folk performers throughout the past few centuries. There have been many great players whose careers were never properly documented. They lived before a recording industry was established and their contributions were lost to time. However, in the twentieth century, one gifted practitioner of the oud stood out to be the acknowledged modern master. His name was Udi Hrant Kenkulian.

Udi Hrant Kenkulian was born in 1901, near Istanbul, Turkey. Blind at birth, he developed a great love of music as a young boy. His first professional experience was in the choir of an Armenian Apostolic church. In 1915, the family fled to Konya in order to escape genocide, and it was there, in his new hideaway home, that young Kenkulian picked up the oud for the first time.

Although he benefited from having an instructor, the blind teenager was soon plucking out national standards and original songs. Kenkulian remained faithful to the study of the oud as the family moved to Adapazari, a city in northwestern Turkey, and upon their return to Istanbul.

During his travels, several attempts at restoring his eyesight had failed. Now in his early twenties, he earned a living in a variety of ways by playing in cafes, giving music lessons and selling instruments. Although he enjoyed some of the best teachers, the self-taught element in his blossoming style separated him from others.

In 1927, he may have made his first recordings, although some claim that he accomplished this feat much earlier, while still a teen. The material was a mixture of original compositions and the folk tunes which formed part of every oud player's repertoire.

In 1928, he fell in love with a beautiful girl, but her parents forbade the young lady to marry a musician. However, years later, they met again and were secretly wed. In the years between, the desire to be with this woman inspired him to write powerful, mournful songs of lost love. It was during this period that he developed and reached his full potential, and would garner widespread attention.

In the 1930s, he continued to record and many of his songs were made available internationally through a series of labels including one in the United States. He joined a group, enabling him to break into radio, which greatly enhanced his career. Kenkulian continued to entrance all with his ability on the oud, which by this time had reached impressive virtuoso status.

During the war years, his activity was curtailed, as he maintained a low but productive profile. Kenkulian played at every opportunity that came his way as a solo artist as well as within a group. Much of his material reflected a point of view on the war which raged around the globe. Although the decade was not the best for his career, Kenkulian survived and further developed his unique style.

In 1950, an unsuccessful voyage to the United States to have his sight restored led to a series of concerts in East Coast strongholds like New York, Boston, and Detroit, as well as in the West, in Los Angeles and other points in California. At these events he played Turkish classical music as well as his own folk/blues compositions.

Upon his return home, Kenkulian was accorded more respect. He performed regularly on Istanbul radio as a solo artist and then with a small group he formed. He returned to the United States where he made some recordings and gave lessons to serious Armenian-American students of the oud.

His difficulty in recording in the United States was to find musicians of the same caliber who understood Turkish music and could blend their abilities with his, which were usually far superior. Often, he was backed by musicians with inferior skills. However, one session included Şükrü Tunar on clarinet, Ahmet Yatman on kanun and Ali Kocadine on drum. The quartet sounded good and the three musicians provided adequate support for the oud player, who by this time was on a level few could match.

Although he remained very well known in Istanbul and had many opportunities to perform and record, he enjoyed life on the road. In 1963, he embarked on a world tour that took him to Paris, France; Beirut, Lebanon; Greece; throughout the United States; and to Yerevan, at the time the capital of the Armenian Soviet Socialist Republic.

He was able to divide his time between performing in his native Istanbul and around the world. With each successive tour, his star appeal in his homeland was magnified. He did much radio work and taught young disciples who eagerly wanted to learn from the master. His devotion to ambitious youths only enhanced an already strong reputation.

In 1977, many of Turkey's most renowned singers and musicians assembled to honor Kenkulian's 60-year career. A year later, on August 29, 1978, Kenkulian passed away after a courageous battle with cancer. It was a day of mourning for millions of his fans across the world.

Udi Hrant Kenkulian was a Turkish folk master. He played the oud with more heart, expertise and imagination than anyone in the documented history of the instrument. The blind virtuoso possessed a special touch and selflessly taught many students over the years. He accompanied his refined playing with a soulful, plaintive voice and used first-rate material. His innovations were many.

He introduced the left-hand pizzicato, a technique of plucking the instrument with emotion and economy of style. Kenkulian played with as much expertise as a roomful of aspiring musicians. While the tradition had been to downstroke, he picked with the precision of a Piedmont blues figure from the United States.

He also used double stops, which created spaces in his playing that were breathtaking. Kenkulian never settled for standard tuning, and introduced a novel approach to changing keys on the oud. He used open tunings which allowed him to pair strings in octaves, much in the same way as the gifted jazz guitarist Wes Montgomery.

He was the master of the taksim, a mode of improvisation that allowed him to deviate from the normal progression. He was able to move around freely like the avant-garde and free jazz players. Because of his unique style, he was able to connect with the spiritual world and carry the listener along on the journey.

His vocal delivery was one of powerful, deep emotion which moved people. Very few folk artists of any country could match the depth of the soulful lyrics he delivered with such force. There was a definite yearning in his singing that drew comparisons to many of the greatest blues singers, especially the early Mississippi Delta players.

Although he recorded dozens of songs, his most famous remains "Hastayim Yasiyorum," which translates to "I Am Sick, Yet I Am Living." It has since passed into the Turkish folk canon, as dozens of modern artists have covered the song. The song has been translated into various languages, making it possible for others to learn and add the number to their respective repertoires.

It is difficult to get a proper perspective of Kenkulian and the impact he made on Turkish folk. The best method is to compare him to well known American figures. His innovations and improvisational techniques and expertise on the oud have drawn comparisons to the shadowy Robert Johnson and old-time stalwart Doc Watson.

Robert Johnson is the acknowledged king of the Delta blues singers. His stark expressionism, innovative guitar skills and first-rate material continues to fuel popular music 70 years after he died under mysterious circumstances. Doc Watson is one of the most influential folk/country artists of the latter half of the post-modern era and has had a huge impact on all the current players.

Some of Kenkulian's best known songs include "Parov Yegar Siroon Yar," "Siroon Aghchig," "Anoosh Yaren Heratsa," "Khrjit," "Rast Taksim," "Dilerim Sen (Rast Sarki)," "Hicaz Taksim," "Hüseyni Taksim," "Suzinak Saz Semai (Kemani Tateyos Efendi)," "Hicaz Sarki/Karslama," "Mahur Saz Semai (Kemençeci Nikolaki)," "Nihavent Taksim," "Saba Taksim," "Hüzzam Taksim," "Hicaz Saz Semai (Yusuf Pasa)," "Kurdilihicazkar Pesrev (Kemani Tateyos Efendi)," "Armenian Dance," "Hüzzam Sarki/Hoknadz Durtmadz," "Srdis Vra Kar Me Ga." Many artists have covered his songs around the world.

He influenced a number of oud players from his own country as well as those around the world. A list includes Richard Hagopian, John Berberian, Harry Minassian, Şükrü Tunar, Udi Yorgo Bacanos, and Tanburi Cemil Bey. He also had a profound effect on others playing stringed instruments. Any new artist who hears Kenkulian is usually overwhelmed with his supreme artistry.

Udi Hrant Kenkulian is a legendary figure of Middle Eastern music and is acknowledged as the greatest modern stylist. He was the entire package. Because of his many innovations, his textured vocal delivery and his skill level, he remains the undisputed master of the oud.

DISCOGRAPHY:

The Early Recordings, Vol. 1, Traditional Crossroads 4270.
The Early Recordings, Vol. 2, Traditional Crossroads 4271.
The Early Recordings, Vol. 3, Traditional Crossroads 4272.

Atahualpa Yupanqui (1908–1992)
Modern Argentine Folk King

Argentina — like all other countries — boasts a deep, rich history of traditional music which is part of the nation's psyche. While there have been many important figures in the genre's long history, few matched the singer in the twentieth century who became the modern Argentine folk king. His name was Atahualpa Yupanqui.

Atahualpa Yupanqui was born Héctor Roberto Chavero Aramburo on January 31, 1908, in Pergamino (Buenos Aires Province). The town, part of the Argentine pampas, was about 100 miles from the capital, Buenos Aires. His parents relocated to Roca, a small province where young Yupanqui became enchanted with the traditional music of the local culture. Although he took up the violin at first, he eventually made the guitar his instrument of choice.

By the age of ten, now a resident of Tucumán, he had greatly improved his guitar skills. Yupanqui had begun to write material which reflected the struggle of his people and to learn the traditional music of his country. Although proud of the family name, he adopted the stage moniker Atahualpa

Yupanqui in honor of two Incan kings. With all of these vital pieces in place, the blossoming musician was ready to become a folk artist.

Yupanqui traveled throughout northwest Argentina and the Altiplano high plateau studying the cultural history of his people. However, because it was extremely difficult to make a decent living as a musician, he moonlighted as a muleteer. Later, he found work as a journalist, which spurred a desire to be a novelist. His most famous book was *Cerro Bajo*, but music was more predominant in his heart.

As a young man, Yupanqui formed a political and social philosophy which leaned to radicalism. He joined the Communist Party of Argentina. In 1931, Yupanqui became involved in the politics of Uruguay and learned some important life lessons before returning to his homeland. The determined young man realized that in order to bring about social change and equality for the Argentine people, he would need to utilize the strongest weapons: his musical talents.

In 1935, he ventured to Buenos Aires, armed with a number of original compositions which had spread through the populace by word of mouth. He was building a national following with a precise, dedicated plan and took a giant step toward this goal by appearing on the radio. It was also around this time that Yupanqui met and befriended the piano player Antonieta Paula Pepin Fitzpatrick, whose stage name was "Nenette." They became lifelong companions as well as musical collaborators under the pseudonym "Pablo Del Cerro."

In the 1940s, Juan Perón ruled Argentina. He disliked communism, which led to Yupanqui's music being censored on the radio. Despite Yupanqui's popularity, he was treated badly by the ruling government and was a frequent inmate of state prisons on a variety of trumped-up charges. Throughout the decade, Yupanqui found it increasingly difficult to maintain a career.

In 1949, he left his home to escape the rigid government scrutiny and settled in France. With the help of the famous singer Edith Piaf, he was able to perform in Paris as well as secure a recording contract with the Chant Du Monde label. In 1950, his first record released in Europe, *Miner I Am*, was named best foreign disc in the Contest of International Folklore.

He became an international star overnight. Yupanqui performed throughout the continent and appeared at the most prestigious venues. He also recorded prolifically, adding to his burgeoning reputation. There was something very moving about his native folk sound which appealed to different cultures. With his partner Nenette, he was a smash throughout Europe.

But Yupanqui was first and foremost an Argentinean. In 1952, he returned to his native country and denounced communism, which enabled him to perform more frequently on the radio. He and his life partner Nenette built a house which became a must-see stop for tourists. The duo toured the country often. They were considered genuine national treasures with their concerts acknowledged as events.

The 1960s were Yupanqui's golden period. Many of his compositions became popular. They appealed to the Nueva Canción artists such as Mercedes Sosa and Jorge Cafrune, who recorded them. This increased his appeal among younger musicians. By this point he and Nenette were two of the most recognized figures in Argentina, where they caused a commotion every time they appeared in public.

In 1963–64, he embarked on the kind of world tour reserved for true superstars. He delighted fans in Colombia, Japan, Morocco, Egypt, Israel and Italy with his inimitable style, which focused heavily on patriotic songs of his native Argentina. Despite the cultural and in some instances language barriers, Yupanqui was a seasoned veteran who knew how to excite all audiences.

In 1967, he toured Spain and then settled in Paris for some time, returning to Argentina on several occasions. However, when the military dictatorship of Jorge Videla came to power, the visits became less frequent. Once again, Yupanqui was a victim of internal strife and politics which threatened to destroy his career. He became an even stauncher supporter of nationalistic rights for the common folk.

In 1968, the French Ministry of Culture named him a Gentleman of the Arts, in honor of his 20-year-plus contribution to French literature. Although he was a well-known musician, Yupanqui was also an excellent writer. While many musicians have written articles on folklore, few have also been novelists.

In 1973, he appeared in *Argentinisima II*, an Argentine musical documentary film which celebrated singers and musicians of the nation. As one of the country's most visible performers, Yupanqui had a starring role and provided some music for the soundtrack. The film opened in the summer to enthusiastic audiences and cemented his star status.

Eventually, Yupanqui left his native Argentina forever and returned to France, where he spent the rest of his life. In 1989, the University of Nanterre commissioned him to write lyrics to commemorate the bicentennial of the French Revolution. The piece "Sacred Word" was released to much fanfare. The man who had delivered to the world a wealth of pure Argentinean music died in Nimes, France, on May 23, 1992. His remains were eventually dispersed on Colorado Hill in his native country.

Atahualpa Yupanqui was an Argentinean folk icon. For more than half a century, he forged songs which celebrated the life and times of his people. Although he would call several different places home — especially France — there was always a nationalistic presence in his books. His heart always belonged to the people of Argentina.

He was a fine guitarist. Yupanqui was able to pick out notes with precision and meaning. His sound was a mixture of classical elements and deeprooted folk. He used a simple yet effective style which he made famous. Nenette always supported his guitar playing with her solid piano abilities.

Although Yupanqui didn't have an overpowering voice, he was able to project the meaning of his songs with a straightforward delivery. But there was also an edge to the music, a hypnotizing catch to the words composed with such great delicacy. Nenette and he formed a powerful duo.

He gave the world a number of songs including "Los Hermanos," "Viene clareando," "El arriero," "Zamba del grillo," "La añera," "La pobrecita," "Milonga del peón de campo," "Camino del indio," "Chacarera de las piedras," "Recuerdos del Portezuelo," "El alazán," "Indiecito dormido," "El aromo," "Le tengo rabia al silencio," "Piedra y camino," "Luna tucumana," "Los ejes de mi carreta," "Sin caballo y en Montiel," "Cachilo dormido," and "Tú que puedes, vuélvete."

He was also a noted novelist. Some of his more important books include *Piedra sola, Aires indios, Cerro Bayo, Guitarra, El canto del viento, El payador perseguido* and *La Capataza.* Many were translated into English, French and other languages. The dual career as a writer and musician only enhanced his strong reputation.

Atahualpa Yupanqui was an Argentine artist who celebrated the richness and simplicity of life through his songs. He was able to touch a nerve in Argentine audiences and throughout the world as the modern Argentine folk king.

DISCOGRAPHY:

Die Andengitarrem, Pläne 839883.
El Canto del Viento, Pampa Music 17.
La Pampa de Antes, Pampa Music 96.
Para Rezar en La Noche, Pampa Music 89.
Canto de la Tierra, Music Hall 10061.
Don Ata, Tropical Music 68956.
Amistad, Ans 15252.
Quisiera Tener un Monte, Pampa Music 52.
Y Su Guitarra, International Music LAT3004.
Testimonio, Vol. 1: Vivo en Alemania, DBN 51396.
Ultimo Recital [live], Last Call 3049052.
Zamba de Vargas, Continental 88031.
El Alazan, International Music 82065.
El Poeta, ANS 15561.
Buenas Noches, Orchard 5973.
Cancion de Abuelo, Orfeon 16157.
Testimonio III Rastros, DBN 51596.
Tierra Querida, EMI 837428.
Viajes por el Mundo, Orchard 802937.

Live Mar del Plata 1982, Fremeaux & Associes 439.
Basta Ya, Le Chant Du Monde 2741392.
Soy Libre, Le Chant Du Monde 2741391.
Buenas Noches Compatriotas, MBB 7798010675549.
El Legado, DBN 801944115207.
El Payador Perseguido, Warner Bros. 077779819225.
El Poeta de la Guitarra, Epsa 605457260627.
Folklore del Sur, Sony BMG 5099749384729.
La Guitarra, Acqu 712730031420.
La Palabra (Grabaciones Ineditas), Melo 712730028123.
Lo Mejor De, Sony BMG 71797.
L' Integrale, Vol. 1, Le Chant Du Monde 274948.
L' Integrale, Vol. 2, Le Chant Du Monde 274949.
L' Integrale, Vol. 3, Le Chant Du Monde 274950.
L' Integrale, Vol. 4, Le Chant Du Monde 274951.
L' Integrale, Vol. 5, Le Chant Du Monde 274952.
Camino del Indio, Blue Moon 2010.
La Zamba Perdida, Blue Moon 005.
Se Poblaban de Musica Los Andes..., Blue Moon 006.
Piedra y Camino 1936–1947, Discmedia 457219.
20 Grandes Exitos, Microfon 478971.
Los Esenciales, Sony International 493954.
Solo lo Mejor de Atahualpa Yupanqui, Major Label 5284.
From Argentina to the World, EMI 7863.
Coleccion Aniversario, EMI 72439966321.
Mis 30 Mejores Canciones, Sony BMG 5099749368828.
40 Exitos, EMI 162220.

Luiz Gonzaga (1912–1989)

Forró Folk

Every country has its own folk music and many nations boast an incredible array of talent. However, despite the best efforts of folklorists like the Lomaxes and others, the music of many regions remained in obscurity. However, some musicians around the world have exposed the beauty of national music, like a Brazilian entertainer with a special take on the forró style. His name was Luiz Gonzaga.

Luiz Gonzaga was born on December 13, 1912, in Caiçara, Brazil, in the northeastern part of the country. His father was an accordion player and a poor farmer. Gonzaga began to work in the fields at a very young age and had a limited formal education. It seemed that the young boy was doomed to toil for very little money the rest of his life.

The opportunity to escape this existence came via his natural curiosity, which combined with a love of Brazilian folklore. Various legends glorified a figure named Lampiao, a South American Robin Hood, who was a hero to the poor, working class. More importantly, this mythical figure was known as a great accordion player who enjoyed playing for hours, entertaining audiences with his special talent.

In an effort to imitate his hero, Gonzaga picked up the accordion and found solace practicing after a long day of hard labor in the fields. Later, he added the zambubma, a type of Brazilian drum, and honed his skills until he was proficient enough to play in front of an audience. As a teenager, Gonzaga played at local dances and parties, sounding much like the sophisticated professionals who were his heroes.

In 1930, he joined the army, spending time there developing as a musician. During his nine-year stint in a military band, the aspiring artist learned how to play the coronet. Eventually, Gonzaga decided he needed a change of career and left the army for the life of a busker in the streets of Rio de Janeiro.

He became a street performer in the 1940s and began to connect with the people and their cherished folk music. At times, he sang in clubs. His material included waltzes and tangos. The talented Brazilian might have remained in obscurity for the rest of his career, but caught a break when he met the legendary Ary Barroso, who was regarded as the greatest bossa nova composer in the country. More importantly, he had a radio show and invited Gonzaga for an audition.

The radio show exposed Gonzaga to a wider audience, which eventually led to a contract with RCA Records. His first song was "Baião," a strong rhythmic dance number which swept the country. After years of struggle, the former field hand and military man was a noted national musical hero who had fused several elements together to create a new style of Brazilian folk.

During the 1950s, his popularity reached its greatest heights. He was listed as a first-rate musician and performed in the most prestigious national venues throughout Brazil and in other South American countries. His brand of folk music consisted of forró, a rapid, danceable style played by a trio consisting of a triangle, a drum and an accordion. Despite the simple setup, there was an intricate interplay among the three musicians, who relied on execution, timing and rhythm to entertain enthusiastic audiences.

In the 1950s, forró was one of the most popular types of Brazilian folk music and Gonzaga was the acknowledged king. His tours concentrated in the large metropolitan centers of Rio de Janeiro and Sao Paulo. He recorded the song "Asa Branca," a pure example of the genre he had helped create with the help of Humberto Teixeira. Since the latter played an important in Gonzaga's rise to fame, a quick biographical sketch is in order.

Humberto Teixeira was born in 1915 in Ceará, in northeast Brazil. He began to study music as a child, learning to play the flute and the mandolin. As a young man, he decided first on a medical career, then a career in law, while continuing to compose and publish music. In 1945, he met Gonzaga. Working together they established the baião style of music. As a team, they wrote "Baião," "Qui Nem Jiló," "Baião de Dois," "Assum Preto," and the greatest hit of all, "Asa Branca." The pair, who understood dynamic textures, eventually parted ways.

In the 1960s, the rock and roll craze swept through Brazil, particularly among younger audiences, and Gonzaga was considered passé. The accordion master continued to record and perform, but the decade proved to be far less successful than the previous one. His fan base was an older crowd, those who had grown up dancing to his tunes.

In the 1970s, when young Brazilian musicians such as Gilberto Gil, Caetano Veloso, and Gal Costa began to champion Gonzaga's past efforts, he regained a measure of his previous popularity. Gonzaga had paved the way for new styles of Brazilian music by taking old forms and infusing them with new rhythmic ideas, something all of his disciples understood and wholeheartedly practiced.

Gonzaga took full advantage of his upswing in popularity. He performed at venues frequented by younger fans and proved that he wasn't passé. Although he recorded new material which appealed to all ages, he did not dominate the charts as he had done in his heyday. The aging accordion master cultivated a strong group of disciples and worked with newer northwestern artists who acknowledged their mentor's experience and abilities.

Gonzaga enjoyed his newfound celebrity status for the next few years and reveled in the attention. On August 2, 1989, at the age of 77, he passed away. It was a day of mourning across Brazilian urban centers, especially among the young musicians who were aware of his vast contributions to Brazilian folk music, in a career which spanned some five decades.

Luiz Gonzaga understood the complicated textures of the country's myriad musical styles and was able to mesh certain elements together to create something new and fresh. The accordion master's popularity soared because he created a folk sound which people could dance to.

Gonzaga brought the accordion to life. He could perform any style of music, but concentrated his efforts on forró. Many of the lively, fast-paced Brazilian styles required a powerful instrumental talent, a challenge he took on, met and surpassed. He brought the traditional instrument a tremendous amount of respect and raised its status on a national and international level.

He enjoyed a number of great hits. A partial list includes "Vozes da Seca," "Algodão," "A Dança da Moda," "ABC do Sertão," "Derramaro O Gai," "A Letra I," "Imbalança," "A Volta da Asa Branca," "Cintura Fina," "O Xote das Meninas," "Juazeiro," "Paraíba," "Mangaratiba," "Baião de Dois," "No Meu Pé de Serra," "Assum Preto," "Légua Tirana," and "Qui Nem Jiló." The biggest smash of his career was "Asa Branco," which ushered in an entire new dance craze. Fifty years later, much of Gonzaga's music sounds fresh and continues to create excitement among audiences.

He recorded and wrote with different artists including Ary Barroso, Ze Dantas, Humberto Teixeira, Onildo de Almeida, Joao Silva and Miguel Lima, among others. Arguably, Teixeirea was his most important collaborator. Later, he would work with younger musicians, including Gilberto Gil, Caetano Veloso and Gal Costa. Nearly every Brazilian singer of the modern era shared the stage with Gonzaga at one time or another.

The younger enthusiasts whom Gonzaga influenced went on to greater fame. Gil was a leader of the tropicalia movement, fusing samba, bossa nova, salsa and rock and roll. He had learned much from Gonzaga and proved to be a keen student. Eventually, the guitarist, drummer, trumpeter and accordion player would be recognized as a world musical figure.

Although Veloso was not the disciple of Gonzaga that Gil was, he nevertheless borrowed many traits from the master. The keen student would mesh the rich influences of Caribbean and African music and North American pop into a coherent sound to become one of the most important and popular Brazilian artists. Their distinct use of rhythm links the two musicians together.

A third student was Gal Costa. She became a recognized singer in her native country as well as on an international level. After studying Gonzaga's compositional style, she proceeded to imitate her teacher. She would eventually join forces with Veloso. Their marriage formed a strong musical union.

Luiz Gonzaga was an important member of the Brazilian community and continues to exude a strong influence long after his death. There was a sincerity to his music, as well as a fire and passion. In a country with dozens of intricate styles and hundreds of musicians, he reached the pinnacle with his forró folk.

DISCOGRAPHY:

Marchinhas e Quadrilhas Juninas, Sony BMG/RCA 74321216622.
Do Jeito Que O Povo Gosta, BMG Brazil 10144.
Acervo Especial, Vol. 4, BMG Brazil 60050.
Espetaculo Das Seis & Meia [live], BMG Brazil 60016.
Forro Do Comeco Ao Fim, BMG Brazil 120003.
Olha Pro Céu, BMG Brazil 10078.
Quadrilhas e Marchinhas Juninas, BMG Brazil 60054.
A Triste Partida, Sony BMG/RCA 74321568092.
Luiz Lua Gonzaga, Sony BMG/RCA 74321568082.
O Nordeste Na Voz de Luiz Gonzaga, Sony BMG/RCA 74321568102.

O Rei Volta Pra Casa, Sony BMG/RCA 74321568142.
Óia Eu Aqui de Novo, Sony BMG/RCA 74321560862.
Pisa No Pilao, Sony BMG/RCA 74321568132.
O Sanfoneiro do povo de Deus, Sony BMG/RCA 74321568112.
Sua Sanfona E Sua Simpatia, Sony BMG/RCA 74321568122.
Kamego, Sony BMG/RCA 74321568072.
No Meu Pé de Serra, Reviv 087.
Sanfona Dourada, Reviv 051.
Sabido, Iris 76.
Canaã, Sony BMG/RCA 74321762562.
Xodó, Reviv 151.
Testamento de Caboclo, Revivendo 167.
Eu So Quero Um Forro, BMG 74321753232.
90 Aninhos, Revivendo 184.
2 Em 1, EMI 5837492.
Veronica, Revivendo 132.
Eterno Cantador, BMG International 156815.
Eu E Meu Pai, BMG International 195022.
Quarque Dia, Revivendo 226.
Samarica Parteira, Revivendo 238.
Brasil Popular, Sony BMG 82876844332.
Canta Seus Sucessos Com Zé Dantas, BMG International 176257.
Capim Novo, BMG International 188359.
Duetos Com Mestre Lua, RCA/BMG Brasil 190036.
O Veio Macho, BMG International 176258.
Sanfona Do Povo, BMG International 176259.
Sao João Do Araripe, BMG International 176260.
Volta Pra Curtir, BMG International 185543.
Eta Cabra Danado de Bom, Reviv 029.
Focus, BMG Brazil 69061.
Forrobodó Cigano, ABW/Copacabana 99061.
Para Sempre, EMI 3305341412.
Performance, EMI Latin 42314.
Raizes Nordestinas, EMI 3235206582.
São João Na Roca, BMG 6261.
Serie Identidade, EMI 3295401502.
50 Anos de Chão, BMG 74321294162.
Luiz Gonzaga E Fagner, BMG Brazil 120010.
O Melhor de Luiz Gonzaga, BMG Brazil 10032.
Serie Aplauso, BMG Brazil 30548.
Asa Branca, Globe 137.
Meus Momentos, EMI 852340.
Serie Retratos, EMI 866361.
Maxximum, Sony BMG 515759.
Nova Bis, EMI 337103.
Monumento Nordestino, Sony BMG Europe 708252.
Seu Canto Sua Sanfona E Seus Amigos, Vol. 4–6, Revivendo 9914.

Edith Fowke (1913–1996)

Canadian Folklorist

The performers and folksongs native to each country are national treasures. Each nation needs people to catalog and preserve its folk music. In Canada, one woman was instrumental in preserving what she felt was important, Edith Fowke.

Edith Margaret Fulton was born on April 30, 1913, in Lumsden, Saskatchewan. On the vast prairie, she developed an interest in people and their social interaction. The young girl was a keen student of everything Canadian and loved the songs she heard in school, at Christmas time and during other celebrations.

Fulton remembered the songs she heard as a child and they formed the foundation of a very small, but growing collection. Because western Canada was only recently settled, it did not have a deep and strong folk tradition. In the Maritimes, Quebec and among the scattered native people, the regional folk styles were vibrant.

Fulton decided on a teaching career and studied literature and history, then continued her education at the Saskatchewan College of Education. She taught at the high school level and also worked very briefly for the Co-operative Commonwealth Federation (the CCF), a grassroots organization which represented western farmers and laborers.

The CCF party eventually swept through Saskatchewan, Alberta and British Columbia and became a force to be reckoned with in Canadian politics. They represented the interests of Westerners like none had ever done before. This fueled Fulton's interest in prairie socialism, which would eventually lead to a career in folk music.

In 1938, she married Frank Fowke and they moved east to Toronto, far from the lonesome prairie. Once established in the capital of Ontario, she began to devote time to her first love, the folksongs of the ordinary people. The lack of an archive forced her into action. Fowke devoted the rest of her life to collecting and protecting Canadian traditional material.

Throughout the 1940s, Fowke researched the roots of Canadian folksongs, which included native music, and the tunes imported by the various nationalities who settled the country. These included English, Scottish, Irish, German, Ukrainian, French, Russian, Chinese, Japanese, Dutch, Italian, and other immigrants. She observed a lack of published and recorded material.

She assembled a strong song catalog. Fowke was convinced that the great number of classic Canadian folk tunes should be assembled into one coherent package. A tireless worker, she gathered hundreds of songs with impressive skill and ability.

Fowke was given a golden opportunity when CBC radio allowed her to host a show called "Folk Song Time." She used the years of gathering material, the deep knowledge of Canadian music history, and the field trips she had made throughout Ontario. On the program, she championed the folksongs of her native country like no one had done before.

From 1950 to 1963, the show gained in popularity, aided by the roots revival in the United States. Fowke interviewed the few successful Canadian folksingers at the time and played their music and featured the work of unknown writers. During this period, she did more for folk music in Canada than anyone had ever done.

Fowke found a wealth of material in Ontario, particularly in Guelph, the Ottawa Valley and the Peterborough area. She "discovered" O.J. Abbott, Tom Brandon, and LaRena Clark, among others. For once, Canadian folksingers had a true fighter on their side who was tenacious in her devotion. Her efforts covered an enormous amount of territory.

In 1963, she began a new series for CBS entitled "Folk Sounds," which lasted until 1974. The show was another undisguised effort to promote the folksongs of Canada as well as the performers who sang them. The program proved to be very popular and coincided with the explosion of the Canadian music scene. Simultaneously, Fowke also hosted "Folklore and Folk Music," as well as "The Travelling Folk of the British Isles."

Back in 1956, she had become a founding member of the Canadian Folk Music Society (CFMS), which would evolve into the Canadian Society for Musical Traditions (CSMT). The organization began as the Canadian branch of the International Folk Music Council. In 1973, Fowke became the editor of the *Canadian Folk Music Journal*, a position she held for years. Eventually, it turned into an annual, then a quarterly, and is known today as the *Canadian Folk Music* magazine.

In 1967, Fowke and Barbara Cass-Beggs compiled a bibliography entitled *A Reference List on Canadian Folk Music*. Fowke also found time to edit *The Western Teacher*, and contributed articles to the *Journal of American Folklore, Midwest Folklore, Western Folklore, Ethnomusicology, Sing Out!* and the *Canadian Forum*. That she was involved in so many projects and excelled at all of them was proof of her skills.

In 1971, she returned to teaching at York University, educating eager students in a course on folklore. It was an exciting time because of the recent folk boom and the development of the Canadian music industry. In the 1960s, folk luminaries Gordon Lightfoot, Joni Mitchell, Neil Young and Buffy Sainte-Marie all enjoyed strong careers which continued for the next two decades.

In 1970, Fowke's work *Sally Go Round the Sun: 300 Songs, Rhymes and Games of Canadian Children* won a bronze medal from the Association of Children's Librarians. She was a prolific writer and her many books only enhanced her sterling reputation. Her tireless efforts would pay off as she won a number of awards.

Throughout the 1970s and into the 1980s, she continued to dedicate her time and energy to preserving folklore and folk music. She authored a number of books including *Folklore of Canada, Ring Around the Moon, A Bibliography of Canadian Folklore in English, Songs and Sayings of an Ulster Childhood by Alice Kane,* and *Singing Our History.* Fowke also wrote a number of articles for different publications.

She continued to promote folklore and folksongs until her death on March 28, 1996, in Toronto. The loss was a severe blow to the music industry in her native country, as well as internationally.

Edith Fowke was a Canadian folk champion. She worked tirelessly to promote musicians and their music within and outside her native country. The dedicated folklorist firmly believed that Canadian artists were as good and often better than those of other nations. She was a well-known collector, teacher, ethnomusicologist and writer. Interestingly, unlike many others in the genre who preserved traditional material, she was never a performer.

She was a collector who managed to mine the rich vein of Ontario folksongs, as well as those from across Canada and other countries. Fowke had a keen eye for spotting ethnic material as well as talent, and was able to spark interest in the most obscure artists. Many of the works she assembled were published in books or on records.

She had a direct and indirect hand in promoting the careers of many Canadian folksingers. A short list includes O.J. Abbott, Tom Brandon, LaRena Clark, Gordon Lightfoot, Joni Mitchell, Heather Bishop, John Allan Cameron, Murray McLaughlan, Anna McGarrigle, Kate McGarrigle, Ian and Sylvia Tyson, Kathleen Yearwood, Heather Dale and Faith Nolan. There is scarcely a folksinger from Canada who has not benefited from her behind-the-scenes work.

She was the author of a great number of books. A short list includes *Songs of Work and Protest, Folklore Canada, Sally Go Round the Sun, Tales Told in Canada, A Bibliography of Canadian Folklore in English, Lumbering Songs from the North Woods, Singing Our History: Canada's Story in Song, Folklore in Canada, Ring Around the Moon, Legends Told in Canada,* and *Folk Tales of French Canada.* She was one of the most prolific writers in the field.

She collaborated on books with others, including Joe Glazer, the American laborist/folksinger, with whom she wrote *Songs of Work and Freedom.* With Carole H. Carpenter, she wrote *A Bibliography of Canadian Folklore in English.* Fowke and Richard Johnston wrote *Songs of Canada* and *More Folk Songs of Canada.*

In 1978, she was appointed a Member of the Order of Canada and later, in 1983, she was named a Fellow of the Royal Society of Canada. She was also the first Canadian to receive a Lifelong Achievement Award from the Folk Alliance Conference. After her death, Fowke's archives were held at the University of Calgary, while her field recordings were deposited at the Canadian Museum of Civilization in Ottawa.

Fowke was a tireless champion for the folk music of Canada and her efforts were acknowledged across the country and globally by scholars and musicians. While she never played a note, she contributed more to the genre with her background work than many others. She was truly the Canadian folklorist.

DISCOGRAPHY:

Sally Go Round the Sun (companion to a book by the same name). T-46494–95.
Far Canadian Fields (companion to *The Penguin Book of Canadian Folk Songs*).
   Leader LEE-4057.

Vassilis Tsitsanis (1915–1984)
Urban Greek Folkie

Every European country developed its own brand of folk music and Greece was no exception. The musical legacy of the nation is as diverse as its history and dates back to ancient times. In modern times, traditional music is performed throughout every region thanks to the efforts of such notables as urban Greek folkie Vassilis Tsitsanis.

Tsitsanis was born on January 18, 1915, in Trikala, Greece. His father was a bouzouki player, but forbade his children to touch the pear-shaped stringed instrument. However, when the elder Tsitsanis died, his son picked up the mandolin look-alike and began to play it. He honed his skills quickly and was soon creating magic.

He practiced hard and immersed himself in the local music scene, acquiring songs from various sources and musicians as well as attempting to write his own material. Over a period of time he became very good on the bouzouki and started to play professionally, building a small but dedicated local following. Because of the strong ties between Greek folk and dance, Tsitsanis concentrated on a style which moved audiences.

Despite a reputation as a skilled player, a career in music seemed nothing but a distant dream. Instead, Tsitsanis prepared for a life as a lawyer. However, he continued to perform at amateur clubs as a solo artist and as a member of various street folk groups. His main style was dimotika, a type of folksong practiced extensively in the Greek countryside, but he didn't limit himself to one particular genre. Tsitsanis was a musical chameleon and equally adept on the bouzouki, mandolin and violin.

In 1936, he left for Athens to pursue his ambitions in law, but a year later had finally given in to his first love — music. In 1937, he moved to Thessaloniki, and fulfilled his military service as the approach of the Second World War loomed like a dark shadow over the country. However, Tsitsanis managed to record his first song, "This Is Why I Wander the Streets of Athens," which became a regional hit.

From 1936 to 1940, he wrote and recorded more than 100 sides, many of which fueled his quick rise to fame. Unfortunately, in 1941, the industry was completely shut down and Tsitsanis enlisted in the army while still writing songs, which he performed in secret under the German occupation. Although the war had stalled his career, it gave him an opportunity to hone his material. It also afforded him time to improve on his impressive bouzouki skills.

In 1946, with the war over, he resumed his career. Tsitsanis returned to Athens to record the songs he had written during the past few years but had been unable to record. A number of these sides featured his accomplished bouzouki playing. At this point, he was one of the best instrumentalists in all of Greece.

In the second phase of his career, Tsitsanis specialized in the rebetiko style of Greek folk music, which featured a more urban sound. Rebetiko combined a myriad of European influences as well as Middle Eastern folk elements. It was a type of blues music, with themes of poverty, alienation, crime, drink, drugs, prostitution and violence.

In many ways, the Greek "blues" sound mirrored that of the American South, especially in lyrical content. Both grew from the unrest and struggle of a minority people. The major difference was that the Greek version was more urban while the United States blues sound was, in its inception, predominantly rural. However, in the post-war era, the blues took on a distinct amplified and urban appeal.

In the 1950s, the pace of Tsitsanis's career accelerated tremendously. He performed extensively throughout the country delivering the hard-driving rebetiko material to enthusiastic audiences. Although he recorded infrequently, it was during this period that he established a reputation as a serious folk musician.

He rolled on through the 1960s. As one of the main proponents of Greek folk, his excellent material was just part of what made him popular. He was a physically intimidating bouzouki player in the manner of the electric rock-blues guitarists of the same decade. This instrumental virtuosity would cement the Tsitsanis legend among the tens of thousands of patrons who witnessed his emotional, intense performances. When other artists began to record his music, they only enhanced his solid reputation.

In the 1970s, Tsitsanis slowed down considerably. He recorded his last commercial offerings and his performance schedule was limited to selective dates. However, to his legions of fans, he remained a powerful symbol of modern Greek urban folk music. His legacy lived on through the countless young musicians who tried to imitate Tsitsanis's muscular instrumental skills, often with mixed results. Interpretation of his music required a solid command of the bouzouki and emotional passion.

After three decades in the spotlight, the career of one of the greatest exponents of Greek folk music came to an end. On January 18, 1984, at the Royal Brompton Hospital in London following a lung operation, Tsitsanis died. It was a national day of mourning across Greece.

Vassilis Tsitsanis was a Greek folk hero. He took a style which had evolved through hundreds of years and molded it into something modern and exciting. Although regarded as a first-rate bouzouki player, he was also known for his compositional skills. There were many sides to his illustrious career.

Tsitsanis was a spectacular bouzouki player and played the instrument in ways it had never been played with his innovation, imagination, and superior skills. As a young boy he had yearned to play the bouzouki, but was denied. When he finally got the chance it was as if all the secrets of Greek folk music had been bottled up inside him and they came pouring out.

He modernized the rebetiko style of Greek folk. Tsitsanis approached the subgenre with a different attitude and superior skills. He took an underground music and turned it into the most popular style throughout the land. Tsitsanis created material about tough characters down on their luck, drinking, gangsters, and world-weariness. His first hit, "Zembekika," was about hashish.

There was a freshness, a universality in the songs he created which have survived the test of time. Although much of his material was recorded before the start of World War II, his music had a modern touch which new generations of musicians have discovered and embraced. Because Tsitsanis constantly updated versions of his songs, they remained fresh.

While Tsitsanis has been credited with more than 500 original compositions, some scholars question this. However, a short list of his best known songs includes "Oso Me Malonis," "Antilaloune Ta Vouna," "Pikros Ine O Ponos Mou," "Apopse Stis Akrogialies," "Archontissa," "Sinefiasmeni Kiriaki," "To Poukamiso," "Gia Kita Kosme," "Neo Minore," "Chorisame Ena Dilino," "Arapines," "Gioul Bachar," "Baxe Tsifliki," "Apopse Kanis Bam," "Akrigialies Dilina," "Peftoun Tis Vrochis I Stales," "Paliose to Sakaki Mou," "Otan Simvi Sta Perix," "Ta Alania," and "Pexe Christo to Bouzouki." The musical structure of many of these songs was based on popular dance rhythms.

Although Tsitsanis created songs mainly in the rebetika style, he did not limit himself to this lone genre. His material was also based on Anatolian dance rhythms including zeibekikos, aptalikos, hasapikos and servikos, as well as tsifteteli, karsilamas, and syrtos. Most were of Greek origin except for tsifteteli, which was from Turkey and dates back to the Ottoman Empire.

Many important Greek singers of the post-war era would catapult to fame on the strength of Tsitsanis's compositions. Sotiria Bellou, born in 1921, turned professional at about the same time that Tsitsanis was recording his post-war material. She paid her dues performing in a variety of low-paying venues and was working as a waitress when she was discovered. The two would work together closely for years. She brought his compositions to life with her powerful, melodic voice.

Marika Ninou was another singer who greatly benefited from Tsitsanis's compositions. She was born in 1922, on a ship that arrived in Greece. She started to sing at a young age and learned how to play the mandolin in the school orchestra. The range of her vocal skills also allowed the talented artist to perform in churches. In 1949, she met Tsitsanis and started working with him at one of Greece's most famous clubs, Fat Jimmy's. They formed a powerful duo, incorporating his instrumental and writing skills and her high-pitched, precise tonality. In 1951, they went their separate ways after making a profound impact on the Greek folk scene.

Tsitsanis was one of the great exponents of Greek urban folk. The modern touch in his songs, virtuoso skills and vocal delivery separated his repertoire from the docile sounds of the countryside. His was the music of fire, passion, bawdiness, power, and volume. These elements enabled Tsitsanis to become a major musical hero to the young people who danced to his music throughout countless steamy nights.

Vassilis Tsitsanis was a major musical figure who took a different approach to the music of his homeland. He was a superior Greek bouzouki stylist and more importantly a unique songwriter who had a huge hand in shaping the nation's modern tastes.

DISCOGRAPHY:

Arhontissa, Minos/EMI 4807062.
40 Hronia Tsitsanis, Minos/Emi 711042.
Afieroma Ston Vasili Tsitsani, Minos/EMI 8221.
Ta Klassika, Minos/EMI 489772.
I Ellada Tou Tsitsani, EMI 478184.
Sinefiasmi Kiriaki, EMI 480009.
Concert at Herakleio Crete, Minos MCD-486/7.
1936–1946, Rounder 1124.
Best, Vivid Sound 908.
Greek Composers: Vassilis Tsitsanis, FM 17001726.

The Original Hits, FM 17001912.
The 22 Best Songs, FM 17003451.
Rembetika 3: Vassilis Tsitsanis 1936–1940, JSP 77111.

Amália Rodrigues (1920–1999)

Voice of Portugal

Every country cherishes its own branch of the folk tree. In France, the troubadours reigned, while in England, sea chanties were very popular. In Russia, the music which accompanied the peasant dances was energetic, dynamic and intricate. In Quebec, Canada, the French population treasured its home-grown singers. In another part of the world, fado, an emotional, intense style with a deep history, was preserved through the efforts of Amália Rodrigues, the voice of Portugal.

Amália da Piedade Rebordão Rodrigues was born on either July 1 or July 23, 1920, in Lisbon, Portugal, into a musical family. Her father was a trumpet player and cobbler. Her mother abandoned the young girl, who was forced to live with her maternal grandmother. It was a childhood of hard, menial work, religion and music. The latter helped her survive an otherwise tough period.

As a teenager, Rodrigues began to concentrate on developing her singing talent, particularly in the Portuguese folk strain of fado. The emotional style dated back to the early nineteenth century and was a mixture of lively, erotic dances, poetry and literature. During the 1920s and 1930s, the genre would evolve and become incredibly popular, appealing to a wider audience.

While Rodrigues was in her teens, fado began its dramatic rise, and she wrapped her skills around that style. She had the talent and passion to take the music to unexplored heights. Rodrigues was able to emote intensely in the same manner as many of the American female blues singers from the 1920s such as Bessie Smith, Sippie Wallace, Victoria Spivey, Ida Cox, Alberta Hunter, Memphis Minnie, Trixie Smith and Ma Rainey.

After years of peddling produce in the streets as well as toiling as a seamstress, Rodrigues became a tango dancer, a somewhat dangerous occupation considering the seedy places where she worked. At this point, her parents had returned into the blossoming singer's life. Despite family objections, Rodrigues had full intentions of becoming a famous singer.

She combined a soaring vocal style with sultry, suggestive dance moves which excited audiences. The potency of her emotional output touched a nerve in people. Her success enabled the fiery singer to graduate to a more fashionable night spot, where she shared the stage with her sister Celeste. Rodrigues's career progressed rapidly and within a couple of years she had become a star.

In 1939, many changes occurred in her career which proved to be pivotal. Among her growing legions of fans was Frederico Valério, a classically trained composer who began to write material specifically for Rodrigues. The songs, penned in the fado style, stretched the established parameters and even included orchestral accompaniment.

During the war years, while conflict raged across the world, in Lisbon, Rodrigues was the hottest singer and considered a national treasure. Her popularity was so great that she began to travel, and performed in Spain, among other centers. In 1944, the talented vocalist ventured to Brazil, where she quickly established a second, large fan base.

In Brazil, she often appeared at the Copacabana Casino and became a showstopper. Some time after that, Rodrigues made her first recordings in Rio de Janeiro. However, she only cut a handful of numbers, believing that buying albums would discourage people from attending her concerts. This strategy would eventually change.

In 1950, she performed at the Marshall Plan international benefit shows and introduced new songs that flowed from the imaginative pen of lyricist David Mourão-Ferreira. It was a new phase in her career. Rodrigues concentrated on material drawn from the country's greatest poets, which enhanced her star appeal in Portugal as well as around the world. During this era, the popularity of the fado style was at its greatest level.

In 1951, she was finally able to record the songs which had made her such a sensation. Far from diminishing attendance at her shows, the album releases brought audiences in greater numbers. The live appearances and studio material built up incredible momentum.

Her post-war career brought greater fame. She toured outside South America and scored an international hit with "Coimbra," which was given its world debut at the Olympia Theatre in Paris. France was just one of the many countries Rodrigues conquered with her powerful voice and excellent material.

Like other artists, Rodrigues utilized vocal talents as a springboard to expand her career. With her stunning good looks, she was a natural for feature films. In 1954, the talented actress appeared in *The Lovers of Lisbon* in a supporting role, and sang on screen. By the end of the decade, the multidimensional artist boasted three major markets aside from her own country of Portugal — the U.S., England and France.

In 1957, her popularity in France soared and culminated in a concert at the famous Olympia Theatre in Paris. Eventually a live album, *Portugal's Great*

Amália Rodrigues Live at the Olympia Theatre in Paris, was released. Because of this and similar recordings, the expressive singer would perform nearly all over the world including in the Soviet Union (which was closed to most artists), as well as in Israel.

In 1962, after taking a sabbatical year, Rodrigues returned with a different, more mellow style. The album *Amália Rodrigues* signaled her first collaboration with Alain Outmain, a French composer who would supply the singer with material throughout the decade. Like his predecessor Valério, Outmain wrote songs clearly suited to Rodrigues, which enabled her to expand her style as the fado craze began to fade. She maintained her momentum with steady concert appearances and a stream of new recorded output.

In 1964, she appeared in *The Enchanted Islands*, a performance many critics considered the only real highlight of the entire movie. In 1968, Rodrigues recorded the single "Vou Dar de Beber à Dor," a massive hit. Two years later *Com Que Voz* was released. Many critics believed it to be her finest achievement, which, considering the volume of her recorded work, was quite an accolade. The album would go on to win an unprecedented number of awards.

In the 1970s, she continued to build on her legendary status with impressive live performances. But she ran into obstacles. For instance she suffered heavy scrutiny when she was accused of being a member of the PIDE, a secret police and tool of repression. She was cleared of all suspicions.

In 1977, she countered those who claimed her career was finished with the release of *Cantigas Numa Lingua Antiga*. In 1983 she released *Lágrima*, her last studio recording of new songs. After this, lost and unreleased material would have to satisfy her fans' demands for fresh product. Later, an official biography, TV documentary, and a film, *The Art of Amália*, brought her increased fame.

In her seventies, after surgery, Rodrigues retired from public performances. Sadly, her last few years were spent in seclusion, but she managed one last public appearance at the opening of Lisbon's Expo in 1998. A year later, on October 6, 1999, the queen of the fado style passed away. The prime minister of Portugal declared it a great loss and three days of national mourning followed.

Amália Rodrigues was the undisputed queen of fado. She not only popularized the style in Portugal, but brought it to the international stage. With a striking voice, the brilliant singer was able to turn material written specifically for her into a string of gold records. Many of her performances became legendary events.

Although Rodrigues is acknowledged as the greatest exponent of the fado style, she constantly experimented with different forms. She had the talent to create something more than just a love song. She explored different themes about the lives of the common folk, making them universal in flavor.

Rodrigues had a vocal delivery that was powerful, sexy and sentimental. She added a passionate, romantic and bittersweet element which enabled her to touch everyone in the audience in a different way. Within the first couple of notes, her voice was instantly recognizable. Her earnest, yearning tone pleased listeners, especially in Portugal, where they regarded her as a national treasure.

In some circles, Rodrigues's voice has been compared to that of folk icons Joan Baez and Judy Collins. Rodrigues had a major influence on other fado singers, including the group Madredeus, Dulce Pontes, and Marisa dos Reis Nunes, among others. Her sister Celeste was another well-known Portuguese artist who performed in her sibling's shadow.

Rodrigues gave the world a number of great songs. A partial list includes "Lisboa a Noite," "Saudade Vai-Te Embora," "Cuidado Coração," "Barco Negro," "Uma Casa Portuguesa," "Coimbra," "Gorrioncillo," "Que Deus Me Perdoe," "Cabeca No Ombro," "Cama de Peidra," "Foi Ontem," "Nao Quero Amar," "Solidão," "Petenera Portuguesa," "Antigamente," "Grão de Arroz," "Anjo Inutil," "Marcha Do Centenário," "Sem Razao," "Trepa No Coqueiro," "Toiro! Eh! Toiro!," "Job," "Faia," "Lisboa Não Sejas Francesca," "Ni Niña Bonita," "O Namorico da Rita," "As Rosas de Meu Caminho," "Raizes," "Cansaço," "Fadista Luoco," "Lar Português," "No Me Tires Indiré," and "Por un Amor." Although considered a Portuguese artist, she performed songs all over the world and captured the hearts of citizens in every country.

Rodrigues has been continuously honored since her death. She is ranked as one of the top Portuguese figures of all times and appears in national polls with regularity. In 2008, a film about her life was released and proved a critical and commercial success. Her house became a museum. She was buried at the National Pantheon, where the country's notables are interred.

Amália Rodrigues was more than just another Portuguese singer. She was a wonderful artist who celebrated her country's folk music and made it known to the world. Undoubtedly, she was and remains the voice of Portugal.

DISCOGRAPHY:

Live at the Olympia Theatre, CTX 40–113.
Com Que Voz, Monitor 737.
Fados e Guitarradas, Festival 401132.
Fado, Celluloid 6147.
Sings Portugal, Celluloid 6146.
Queen of the Fado, Huub 90107.
Plus Beaux Fados, Alex 2633.
American Songs, Celluloid 6148.
Cantigas Numa Lingua Antiga, Ced 6149.
Coimbra, A World of Music 12502.

Fado: Amália Volta a Cantar Frederico Valério, EMI 781037.
Surun Air de Quitare, Alex 3716.
Raizes, Planet 6005.
Amália Rodrigues, O Melhor Dos Melhore 37002.
Enlightenment, Celluiod 6150.
At the Olympia Theatre [live], Monitor 63442.
Fado Lisboeta, Sounds of the World 90114.
Queen of the Fado, Sounds of Music 90107.
Amália in Italia, EMI 1403332.
Segredo, Valentim De Carvalho 23686.
Obsessao, Drg 5572.
Ai Mouraria, Movie Play 376.
Fado Amália, Movie Play 379.
Fado Malhoa, Movie Play 378.
Triste Sina, Vol. 2, Movie Play 377.
Musica Do Portugal: O Fado, A World of Music 12561.
Rainha Do Fado, Movie 90107.
A Dama Do Fado, Reviv 013.
Live at Town Hall, DRG 5576.
Fado, EMI 7810372.
Live in Japan, Musica Latina 51106.
Triste Sina, Alpha 005.
Amália/Vinicius, EMI 5317452.
Fado Amália, Sony International 501257.
Lisboa a Noite, Planet 6002.
Reina del Fado Canta Fados, Rancheras, Yoyo Music 12022.
Amália Rodrigues with Don Byas, Blaricum 102828.
Uma Casa Portuguesa, Intense 223614.
Fado Português, Sounds of the World 90208.
The Queen, CNM 184.
Art Os Amália, Vol. 1, Som Livre/EVC 1094.
Amália at the Paris Olympia [live], CNM 206.
Plus Belles Chansons de Amália Rodrigues, EMI France 829084.
Best of Fado, Double Gold 53026.
First Recordings, EPM Musique 995782.
Amália Rodrigues, DRG 5571.
The Best of Amália Rodrigues, Import 26194.
Art of Amália, Blue Note 95771.
Semplicemente il Meglio, Simply the Best 88274.
Fado Amália, Musica Latina 51101.
Uma Casa Portugesa, Musica Latina 51102
Yesterday and Today, Double Gold 53060.
Early Recordings, Nostalgia 3621.
Estranha Forma De Vida: O Melhor De, EMI 83444220002.
Fado Português, Vol. 1, EMI 7940912.
Fado Português, Vol. 2, EMI 7921112.
Queen of the Fado, Sounds of the World 70069.
Birthday Tribute, Movie Play 6848.
Amália Rodrigues, Movie Play 850481.

Fado, Movie Play 31001.
Abbey Road 1952, EMI 81195.
Amália No Cafe Luso, EMI 99652.
Asas Fechadas, EMI 92671.
Encontro, EMI 90874.
Folclore à Guitarra e à Viola, EMI 90873.
No Olympia, EMI 91259.
O Melhor de, Vol. 2, EMI 530078.
The Very Best of Amália Rodrigues, Very Best 7705.
Damo Do Fado, Proper 939.
The History of Fado, Proper 94207.
Le Meilleur d'Amalia, EMI 5356692.
The Voice of Fado, Sounds of the World 90202.
Best Recordings, Import 58003.
Amália Absolue, EMI 5357632.
A Rainha Do Fado, Vol. 1, Blue Moon 553.
O Fado, Atoll 8923.
The Best of Amália Rodrigues, EMI 25299.
Soul of Fado, Goldies 25453.
Legend, Next Music 50.
The Abbey Road Recordings, Sounds of the World 90206.
Le World ... Fado..., Suave 6942086.
Complete Recordings 1945–1952, Blue Moon 99911.
A Rainha Do Fado, Vol. 2: 1951–52, Absolute Spain 554.
The Soul of Fado, Deluxe 00023851.
The Art of Amália Rodrigues, Vol. 2, Narada 60983.
On Broadway, Blaricum 90392.
Melodias 1951–1952, Epm Musique 99622.
Tudo Esto E Fado, Alma Latina 006.
Semplicemente il Meglio, Disky 488274.
Amália Rodrigues, Suave 6943039.
This Is Gold, Disky 902351.
Queen of Fado, Disky 901908.
The Essential Collection, Manteca 59.
As Primeiras Gravações, CNM 1397002.
And So It Began/Amalia's Earl, CNM 5232012.
Anthology of Portuguese Music, Anthology Of World Music 020.
Amália Rodrigues, CNM 183.
Essential, CNM 185.
Fados & Flamencos, Vol. 1, CNM 190.
Fados & Flamencos, Vol. 2, CNM 191.
BD World, Vol. 3, Nocturne 11317.
Amália Rodrigues, Movieplay 30366.

Buddy MacMaster (1924–)

Dean of Cape Breton Fiddlers

Like the United States, Canada boasts a host of various folk styles. Canada has native dance songs, cowboy tunes from the West, Inuit contributions, and deep, rich French music from Quebec. Also prominent is the traditional music of the Maritime provinces, each region with its own champion. While there were many impressive Maritime players, none were better than the dean of Cape Breton fiddlers, Buddy MacMaster.

Hugh Allan "Buddy" MacMaster was born October 18, 1924, in Timmins, Ontario, into a Gaelic-speaking family. His father played the fiddle, but it was his mother who taught him the words to go with the tunes and how to appreciate the music of his ancestry. As a young boy, MacMaster started to mimic the sounds he heard around him until the music became a force inside ready to explode.

When he was four, the family returned to Cape Breton and settled on a farm. In the small town of Judique, an isolated community, rapid changes in communications and transportation opened up the area to the rest of the country and the world. Because of these changes, rigid regional styles would fade as barriers broke down. Prior to this, the musicians of the various isolated areas had always been identifiable through their inimitable techniques.

The small town that the MacMasters had settled in was a crossroads for traveling musicians, and young MacMaster proved a keen listener. He absorbed the different approaches of the pipers and fiddlers that passed through, incorporating their stylistic elements into his own developing artistry to create something unique. Although he came up with his own licks, there was no mistaking his playing as that of someone with Cape Breton roots.

MacMaster began to fiddle at the old-time parish picnics, dances and other venues. He learned much from older pipers and fiddlers who could turn a crowd into a dancing frenzy with their brisk attacks. This element of showmanship was something he carried on for the rest of his career.

While the cultural happenings were an important part of his development, the music that went on in his own household was of even greater impact. A handful of Scottish fiddling families such as the MacEacherns, MacQuarries, MacDonells, and MacDonalds visited the MacMaster home on a regular basis. They shared their repertoires and expertise with young MacMaster, who listened carefully in order to absorb their influences. Despite these influences, he retained a personal sound.

Although he could have played the pipes, become a lilter or played the fiddle, it was the latter he selected as his instrument of choice. MacMaster worked hard at establishing a trademark sound like the older musicians. He combined the gentle sound of his mother's music with that of the lively dance songs which echoed across halls and other venues.

As a teen, he started to perform at the dance halls and auditoriums in which those before him had begun their careers. Even at this point, he impressed many seasoned players with his old-time values as well as a unique tone and sound. He had a gift and understood the style for its rich depth and beauty. MacMaster would eventually build up a large repertoire that incorporated almost three centuries of Scottish fiddle music.

It was extremely difficult for musicians to make a living at this time, so MacMaster found work on the railroad. He served in different capacities including as telegrapher and station agent, among others. Although his job paid the bills, his heart belonged to music. Eventually, MacMaster found a way to combine the two.

MacMaster brought his fiddle to work to play between train arrivals and departures. During slack times, he worked on his material in the offices and sometimes entertained waiting passengers. Word spread throughout the Maritimes, and many enjoyed hearing MacMaster deliver unique renditions of old classics. Sometimes other musicians who worked for the railroad would arrive to jam with him.

Eventually, MacMaster developed a regular performance circuit which included dances in small local communities like Glendale, Dunvegan, Scottsville, Strathlorne, Southwest Margaree, and West Mabou. He also played benefit concerts, which endeared him to a wider audience. Although MacMaster established a solid reputation around Judique and its environs, other regions of the world were eager to hear him.

For 30 years, MacMaster remained an employee of the railroad while pursuing life as an amateur fiddler, despite being qualified to be a professional performer. Eventually, he began to devote more time to his musical career and as a result new doors were opened to him.

In 1970, MacMaster traveled to Scotland and performed at the Gaelic Mod in Oban, where he established a name for himself. He would return to Scotland regularly over the ensuing years. Back in Canada, he toured as part of the *John Allan Cameron* and *Ceilidh* television shows, as well as with the Cape Breton Symphony. In every situation, MacMaster added something special to the sessions.

Throughout the decade, MacMaster continued to build on his reputation. He rose among the Cape Breton fiddlers and eventually became one of the best. It was now his turn to educate the aspiring musicians who were eager to learn from one of the masters. MacMaster was a keen teacher and never disappointed his students. A selfless performer, he was always ready to play for a benefit concert or a community event.

In 1983, he traveled to the West Coast to appear at the Fiddle Tunes Festival in Port Townsend, Washington. He made a strong impact, as Cape Breton fiddlers were a rare treat. His reputation would spread across the vast territories of Oregon, California and into British Columbia in western Canada. MacMaster entertained new fans with the same exciting attack which had captivated the people back home.

In 1987, he performed at the Maybelle Chisholm in Philadelphia, where his talents were exposed to Irish-American audiences, who appreciated the Canadian fiddler's magic. MacMaster held his own against a number of excellent musicians. This drive to travel and play far away from his Maritime home enabled him to enhance an otherwise very strong, but regional career.

Up to this point, his reputation was based solely on live performances. However, two years later, MacMaster was able to record for the first time. His initial effort, *The Judique Flyer*, won him many new fans. While MacMaster was 61 years old when he cut that first recording, he instilled an energy in each track that young players could not duplicate.

The subsequent recordings *Judique on the Floor* and *Glencoe Hall* enabled MacMaster to raise his reputation internationally. His concerts in North America supported these recordings, as well as ventures into Great Britain, Scotland, and Ireland. In 1988, he retired from the railroad, which allowed him to continue to record and perform, which he does with no signs of slowing down.

Buddy MacMaster is a folk fiddler proponent. Specifically, he has concentrated on preserving the music of Cape Breton and has done it in spectacular style. Despite an international reputation, he remains very much a small-town fiddler, with the community dance at the heart of his sound.

MacMaster has always had a unique wholesomeness to his life and approach to music. A big-hearted artist who oversees many workshops and classes in Cape Breton, MacMaster has given more than he has ever taken from the music industry. He has passed on to a younger audience a passion for the style that lives in the very depth of his soul.

His fiddle playing is robust, alive, and fresh. He slides down the strings and executes a crisp, delicate run of notes in a precise, direct manner. MacMaster has always demonstrated a mastery of the instrument. Fire, control and dynamics are part of the total package.

The songs found in his repertoire include a variety of titles, most of them old-time Scottish classics. A partial list includes "Farewell to Glen," "Boston Life," "The Burning House," "Spin 'N Glow," "The Yetts of Muckart," "Warlocks," "Tarbolton Lodge," "Buddy's Detour," "The Duchess of Buccleuch," "The Lass O'Corrie Mill," "The Forth Bridge Strathspey," "Upper Denton Hornpipe," "Margaret's Waltz," "The Rosewood Jig," "Judique Jig," and "Happy-Go-Lucky Clog," among others. He has the ability to bring any tune to life.

The humble practitioner is a national star in Canada and an international attraction in the United States, the U.K. and Scotland. In the Maritime home of his ancestors, MacMaster is regarded as one of the prime keepers of the faith. Through his valiant efforts, MacMaster has ensured that the Cape Breton style did not disappear, but that it thrived and flourished.

A number of musicians have attempted to follow in his footsteps, including Dave MacIsaac, Hilda Chiasson, and Tracey Dares. All three appear on various MacMaster releases. MacMaster has also influenced Jackie Dunn, Glenn Graham, Rod MacDonald, the Rankin Family, Ashley MacIsaac, Joey Beaton, Betty Lou Beaton, Doug MacPhee, Mac Morin, Marie MacLellan, Howie MacDonald, and Natalie MacMaster. The latter is a niece who boasts a strong career of her own.

Buddy MacMaster is a small-town musician with an international appeal. He has made people of various nationalities in different parts of the world dance for more than 70 years. His special phrasing, impeccable timing, and danceable rhythms have enriched the lives of millions. The old master has proven that he is undoubtedly the dean of the Cape Breton fiddlers.

DISCOGRAPHY:

Cape Breton Tradition, Rounder 7052.
Glencoe Hall, Traditional Music TM042C.
The Judique Flyer, Stephen McDonald.
Various Artists—Heart of Cape Breton: Fiddle Music Recorded Live Along the Ceilidh Trail, Smithsonian Folkways, UPC 093074049129.

Hamza El Din (1929–2006)

Nubian Folk Master

The North African region of the world boasts a deep, rich musical history that has produced a great number of folk enthusiasts. Many of these individuals were accomplished oud and tar players, as well as incredible poets who drew upon the wealth of material from their roots to create magic. One of these figures was Hamza El Din.

Hamza El Din was born on July 10, 1929, in Toshka, a village near Wadi Halfa in southern Egypt. Although he was surrounded by music from an early age and it was an important part of his life, El Din concentrated his efforts on other endeavors. He trained to be an electrical engineer and worked for the Egyptian national railroad for a few years.

When he discovered that the Aswan High Dam project would destroy his boyhood home, he decided to do something about it. Since music was in his soul, he left behind a promising career as an engineer to move in a different direction. El Din began to delve into the music of his native country at Cairo University and continued his pursuit at the Academia Nazionale di Santa Cecilia in Rome.

By this time, he had picked up the oud and began the long, intricate process of mastering the instrument. Later, he would add the tar, the single skinned drum that originated in the Arabic world. El Din would add to his studies at Ibrahim Shafiq's Institute of Music and the King Fouad Institute for Middle Eastern Music.

El Din was also completing a different kind of education on his own time. He was collecting and amassing a repertoire of Nubian folk music, some of which dated back hundreds of years. He learned these songs and arranged them to give them a modern sound, while retaining the beauty of the original pieces. He also began to write his own material based on the legends and stories of his home.

Once his formal education was complete and he had a solid repertoire of songs, El Din was ready to carry out his true ambition: to preserve the Nubian music of his people before they were dispersed. He traveled from village to village, usually on donkey, to absorb and deliver the traditional folk of the Sudan region.

During his trek throughout the villages of Egypt, he blossomed as a musician. He shared with his people the beauty and starkness of the ethnic sounds which had been part of their culture for centuries.

Later, the government recognized his developing talent and awarded him a grant that allowed El Din to collect folksongs. Although he had already been pursuing this hobby, the money allowed him to expand his search. He had honed his skills on the oud so that he was able to perform in front of larger and more sophisticated audiences.

By the time the folk boom began in the United States, El Din had earned a reputation as one of the most promising folk musicians in his native Egypt. But the ambitious oud player wanted more than regional attention; he wanted to be known internationally. Through a series of concerts where he was usually attired in spectacular flowing white robe and turban, El Din began to attract the kind of attention he wanted.

In the early 1960s, two events would occur which would enable him to achieve world stardom. The first was the completion of the Aswan High Dam project, which flooded his hometown of Toshka and much of the Nubian Egypt, bringing it to the attention of the world. El Din sang about it and the rising stars of the American folk movement, Bob Dylan and Joan Baez, understood his concern.

In the 1960s, El Din relocated to the United States, eventually settling in Berkeley, a hot center for student revolt during the tumultuous decade. In 1964, with a solid reputation as an aspiring ethnic musician, and with the support of Dylan and Baez, El Din performed at the Newport Folk Festival. This opened many doors, including a recording contract with Vanguard Records.

Although he had departed from Nubia, El Din had not abandoned his musical roots. His first album on his new label, *Music of Nubia*, demonstrated his loyalty to the rich folk music of his ancestors. Some of its highlights include the public domain songs "Fegir Nedan" (Call to Worship), and "Shahadag Og" (Believe!). There were other high points such as "Desse Barama" (Peace), "Aiga Denos Ailanga" (Give Back My Heart), "Hoi to Irkil Fagiu" (The Message Bearer), and "Nubala" (Nubiana).

The eight pieces were more than just a collection of Nubian folk tunes. They carried a message of hope, peace, love and belief. Recorded in the mid-sixties, the work had a profound influence on musicians across the globe. It featured El Din's expert oud playing, a sound rarely heard in North America and other parts of the western hemisphere.

While his first recording proved to be groundbreaking, his second was exceptional. *Al Oud* was one of the first world music recordings to have an international impact. It featured a mixture of original compositions based on Nubian folk traditions and El Din's masterful oud, as well as his impressive vocal skills. A few of the highlights include "Childhood" (Assaramessuga), "Grandfathers' Stories" (Annun Sira'), "The Gondola," "Call for Unity" (Nuban Uto), and "The Fortune Teller" (Kogosh).

By this time, El Din had established a well-deserved reputation as one of the prime Egyptian/African folk artists. With every new concert appearance and album release, his reputation was enhanced. He inspired many to pick up the oud and the tar. In many ways, El Din opened the doors for other world musicians, including Ravi Shankar, who would perform at the Monterey Pop Festival and Woodstock.

While the first two albums had earned El Din much attention, his third effort, *Escalay: The Water Wheel*, proved beyond a doubt he possessed exceptional skills and was a potent musical presence. Although it had only three songs, the first, an original 21-minute piece entitled "The Water Wheel," became what many consider to be his true masterwork.

The album was released as part of the popular Nonesuch Explorer series, resulting in more than the usual amount of attention. The recording also featured the contributions of the gifted Egyptian Mohammed Abdel Wahab, who wrote "I Remember." Because of the composed element many argued that *Escalay: The Water Wheel* was not pure or traditional folk, but recognized it as a great document of musical traditions of Egypt. However, others argued that tracks such as "Song with Tar," in which El Din accompanied his playing on the tar with hand clapping, showed a true ethnic touch, weaving a hypnotic spell.

While many in the folk community understood his passion and recognized his talent, the members of the Grateful Dead would introduce El Din to the rock world. Mickey Hart was a huge fan and Jerry Garcia, the talented guitarist and leader of the band, jammed with El Din on numerous occasions. The San Francisco rock act boasted a fanatic fan following known as "Deadheads," who rarely acknowledged other performers. But they embraced El Din as a gifted musician.

In 1978, during one of their world tours, the Grateful Dead appeared at Egypt's Great Pyramid of Giza. El Din was their unofficial host and link to the crowds. Later, at the Winterland in San Francisco, El Din opened for the Dead on their own home turf. Garcia and other members jammed with the oud player, blending their blues/acid rock with his Nubian folk strains to the delight of the crowd.

Because he was a star in many regions throughout the world, El Din was able to market more albums. *Eclipse* featured five songs which underlined his mastery of the oud and the simple, yet effective, tar. Many of the tunes were original compositions and with a strong Nubian folk flavor. Mickey Hart produced the album.

In the 1980s, Joan Jeanrenaud, a cellist who was a member of the Kronos Quartet, entered El Din's magical musical realm. She was enchanted with many of his compositions including "Escalay: The Water Wheel," which truly inspired her. The string chamber ensemble often performed with El Din, and the combination of their classical style with his Nubian folk tradition proved to be an interesting musical collaboration.

El Din was also a teacher at various institutions, including Ohio University, the University of Washington and the University of Texas. A true student of world music and an expert in ethnomusicology, he was able to present to his interested classes a wealth of experience. El Din moved to Japan for some time in order to study the biwa, a Japanese, short-necked, fretted lute. He taught there and the Asian culture absorbed his oud playing, soulful singing and poetic lyrics.

El Din continued to record and release albums which had far-reaching effects on other world musicians. In 1982, he issued *A Song of the Nile,* which illustrated the many similarities and differences in the music of the same Middle Eastern and North African regions. The Sudan had a distinct sound which he was able to bring to life with his strong musical abilities and enchanting story-telling prowess.

The album had mostly original material, Nubian in origin. However, he included "Samai," by Greek composer Tatyoth. This marked an expansion in

El Din's musical style from a regional performer into an international one. Although in his fifties, he showed no signs of slowing down.

His next studio effort, *Lily of the Nile*, was another strong attempt to teach the world about the depth and beauty of Nubian traditional music. The five songs came from El Din's roots. The album featured the compositional skills of Muhyi Al-Din Sherif, an Egyptian composer/lyricist.

Despite his advancing age, El Din continued to produce exceptional albums. While the *Available Sound: Darius* effort received a lukewarm reception, *Muwashsha* proved that he had not lost his touch on the oud. The release also featured more of his singing abilities, especially on the outstanding cuts "Assaramessuga," "Gala 2000," and "Bint Baladna."

His last studio release, *A Wish*, included contributions from many individuals such as Shizuru Ohtaka's vocals, Joan Jeanrenaud's cello and W.A. Matheiu's piano. There were many highlights such as "Sunset," "Greetings," "Samai Husainj" and the title song. This final effort proved to be an outstanding example of his musical abilities.

Sadly, on May 22, 2006, the worldwide oud and tar player who had inspired so many died from a gallbladder infection. He was 76 years old.

Hamza El Din was a celebrated Nubian musician who was capable of fusing Arabic and Nubian musical elements into one cohesive unit. He enthralled audiences in his native country as well as around the world. Long after moving to the United States, he continued to promote the roots music of his childhood on an international stage.

He had a master's touch on the oud, the precursor of the lute. He was able to draw a wealth of music from the fretless instrument with a precise, concentrated attack. There was a delicacy to his approach to the instrument which balanced the more frenzied dimension of his playing. This duality enabled him to present a piece differently each time it was performed.

He was also more than adept on the tar, the single-skinned drum of Nubia, along the upper Nile. His understanding of rhythmic textures was strong, and he excelled at the subtle dimensions of beats and measures. El Din was able to play melodies and weave a hypnotic spell with his storytelling ability.

His warm, reedy voice merged seamlessly with his instrumental overtures to create a complete musical package. There was something catchy in his vocal delivery that touched people. His vocal expression was accessible, a soothing, homespun element.

He often appeared on stage in a white turban, dressed as a bedouin. His white stage costume juxtaposed against his shiny black, honest face created an interesting, yet very strong visual presence. When this figure of contrasts delivered his gentle music it captured the imagination of audiences around the world.

He was an incredible storyteller. Many of his songs flowed with a lyrical sweetness as El Din recounted personal incidents as well as Nubian and Arabic folklore. All cultures have an immeasurable number of tales to tell that are interesting and exciting to other societies if they are presented properly. El Din had the gift.

He gave the world a number of great songs. A short list includes "Fegir Nedan" (Call to Worship), and "Shahadag Og" (Believe!). Other high points include "Desse Barama" (Peace), "Aiga Denos Ailanga" (Give Back My Heart), "Hoi to Irkil Fagiu" (The Message Bearer), "Nubala" (Nubiana), "The Water Wheel," "I Remember," "Song with Tar," "Escalay: The Water Wheel," "Samai," "Assaramessuga," "Gala 2000," "Bint Baladna," "Sunset," "Greetings," "Samai Husainj" and "A Wish." Many of these were derived from traditional sources, or were written by El Din, Muhyi Al-Din Sherif and Tahru Ueda.

There were many dimensions to his talent. He wrote the film score for the movie *The Black Stallion*. El Din taught ethnomusicology at a variety of universities in the United States, as well as abroad. His many musical gifts explain his popularity in so many different centers around the globe.

Although he performed with a number of musicians, El Din is best known for his association with the Grateful Dead, particularly drummer Mickey Hart. The Dead percussionist learned many rhythmic subtleties from the Nubian master. El Din appeared on a number of Dead recordings, including *Grateful Dead Rocking the Cradle Egypt 1978*, *Grateful Dead Shakedown Street* and *Grateful Dead Beyond Description 1973–1989*.

He influenced a number of musicians including the oud players Abdel Aziz el Mubarak, Abdel Gadir Salim, and Ali Hassan Kuban. He touched the careers of Sandy Bull, Farid el Atrache, as well as Kronos Quartet performers Joan Jeanrenaud, David Harrington, John Sherba, Hank Dutt, and Jeffrey Zeigler. Others such as the composer Terry Riley learned much from the time he spent with El Din.

Hamza El Din was one of the most important figures in the history of the Middle Eastern/North African folk idiom. He left behind a solid and educational catalog that many have delved into from all corners of the globe. He was a tireless champion in bringing awareness of his Sudanese musical roots to the world.

DISCOGRAPHY:

Music of Nubia, Vanguard 79164.
Al Oud, Vanguard 79194.
Escalay: The Water Wheel, Nonesuch 72041
Eclipse, Rykodisc 10103.
A Song of the Nile, JVC 5007.
Lily of the Nile, Waterlily Acoustics 11.

Available Sound: Darius, Lotus 9621.
Muwashshah, JVC 5416.
A Wish, 110.

=====

Severino Dias De Oliveira
(1930–2006)

Sivuca

Brazil's special brand of unique traditional music remained a secret to the rest of the world until the arrival of Europeans, who were amazed at the complex native dances. In the twentieth century, a number of individuals dedicated their careers to promoting different national styles, including the man known as Sivuca. His true name was Severino Dias De Oliveira.

Oliveira was born on May 26, 1930, in Itabaiana Paraíba, Brazil. He grew up listening to the rich and varied music of his native country. The country was big, and each region developed a different style boasting African, European and Amerindian roots. In half a millennium of evolution the styles of choro, sertanejo, brega, fooró frevo, samba, and bossa nova prevailed.

Oliveira took up the accordion at a very early age and within a few short years he had mastered the instrument. He played indigenous songs of his ancestors in several different styles, but all of the material contained a folk element. Before he was ten, the aspiring artist was already playing at fairs and parties, earning the regular wages of a professional musician and in the process developing a strong following.

At 15, Oliveira left home to embark on establishing a professional career and moved to Recife, in the Pernambuco (northeast) region, performing as a solo artist as well as a member of a small group. His big break occurred with a radio appearance, which enabled him to reach a wider audience. Eventually, Oliveira was hired at a different station where he was able to host his own program.

Oliveira increased his fan base and was popularly known by the nickname Sivuca throughout the listening audience. In 1948, Guerra Peixe, a renowned maestro, recognized commercial talent in the 18-year-old and became his mentor. For the next two years, the instructor taught his pupil arrangement and composition. Oliveira proved to be a keen student and absorbed all the lessons until he was on par with the orchestra leader. In 1949, Peixe's band traveled through various parts of the country.

While Sivuca was on tour with Peixe, Carmelia Alves, a native singer with a good reputation spotted the impressive young musician and hired him to back her in the recording studio. In São Paulo, his career changed with the opportunity to make his first solo album. Over the years, Oliveira had amassed an incredible catalog of folk tunes in addition to his original material.

By this point, Oliveira was a multi-instrumentalist, on the guitar, keyboards, piano, acoustic guitar and accordion. He also sang, arranged and composed material at a professional level. In 1950, he recorded his first album, which contained the hit, "Adeus, Maria Fulô." He recorded with partner Humberto Teixeira, who was a rhythm master and specialized in the baião style.

Oliveira continued to record with Alves in 1951. He also made a second solo album. Brazilian music boasts many genres and subgenres, but at the beginning of the decade, baião, a popular dance style, emerged as a dominant force. Oliveira, with the contribution of Teixeira's rhythmic expertise, wrote songs which fit the baião groove perfectly. He gained fame throughout the Spanish-speaking world, as far away as Portugal.

Oliveira's reputation was so great that the nationwide network Diários Associados hired him to work on radio and television in Rio de Janeiro. In 1955, Oliveira relocated to Rio, where he remained for the next four years. During this time, he made three more successful albums. He had become one of Brazil's best-known musicians.

In 1958, he embarked as a member of the group Os Brasileiros on an international tour called the Music Caravans, which the government sponsored. He shone on the international stage where he mainly played the accordion touring Europe's greatest cities. Guio de Morais conducted the band and it was well-received. Oliveira was fired by the Rio television company for participating in a strike.

In 1959, he moved to Europe, where he became a member of the Brasilia Ritmos, which included Waldir Azevedo. He later found work in a Portuguese club and built up a solid fan base before relocating to Paris. He remained in France for the next few years and continued to record on a regular basis, including the album *Rendez-Vous a Rio.*

In 1964, he returned briefly to Recife and reconnected with the Brazilian population. Soon after, Oliveira moved to New York and toured the United States with Carmen Costa, a noted Brazilian singer. Later the capable guitarist backed the vocalist Miriam Makeba for the next four years. Together, they wrote the huge hit "Pata, Pata," and on the strength of the single were able to perform all over Africa, Europe, Asia and the Americas. Oliveira enhanced his world reputation during his time with Makeba.

In 1969, he settled in New York and became the director of the musical *Joy.* He also worked with Brazilian musicians Hermeto Pascoal, Airto Moreira and Glorinha Gadelha. He eventually married the latter and together they wrote the song "Feira de Mangaio," which became a classic in the forró style. He also united with Chico Buarque on "João e Maria," and Paulo Tapajós on the songs "No Tempo dos Quintais" and "Cabelo de Milho."

In 1971, he joined Harry Belafonte with whom he toured for four prolific years. Oliveira played guitar and keyboards, and also arranged music for Belafonte. He appeared on a few of Belafonte's albums, adding an extra dimension to his exciting sound. Oliveira still found time to continue his solo career, performing and recording, including the smash album *Live at the Village Gate*, which received excellent reviews.

In the late 1970s, Oliveira added the Scandinavian countries to his list of tour venues. He recorded three live albums and toured extensively throughout Northern Europe, where he became a star. With his deep versatility, the Brazilian musician was able to please all sorts of crowds, cutting through language and cultural barriers.

In 1977, he returned to Brazil after a long absence and performed at a variety of venues. Although Oliveira had not been in his native country for a long time, the old master was welcomed as an international star. He recorded with Rosinha de Valença at the famous Teatro João Caetano in Rio de Janeiro. The subsequent album *Sivuca e Rosinha de Valença* was a huge hit in a number of global markets.

In 1978, Oliveira added to his long list of top hits with the song "João e Maria," a collaboration with Chico Buarque and his sister Miúcha. That Oliveira could record and perform with a multitude of artists of all skill levels and cultural backgrounds was a tribute to his flexibility as a singer and instrumentalist.

In the 1980s, Oliveira began to slow down, as he toured and recorded with less frequency. In 1984, he teamed up with Chiquinho do Acordeon on a work entitled *Sivuca e Chiquinho*, which received enthusiastic reviews from a variety of sources. In 1987, he collaborated with Rildo Hora. A decade later, in Paris, he performed with Baden Powell. The concert was recorded for posterity.

From this point on his concert appearances and recordings became infrequent but genuine treats for fans. However, Oliveira continued to do what he loved best until near the end. On December 14, 2006, in João Pessoa, Paraíba, Brazil, the master musician passed away.

Severino Dias De Oliveira was a Brazilian musical force. He was a noted composer, arranger and musician. He not only became famous in his native country, but built an international career which helped other folk artists from Brazil succeed in other countries. Oliveira was beloved in his homeland, as well as in dozens of cities across the world.

There was an earthy, passionate element in his music which made him accessible to a cross-section of listeners. Although famous as a practitioner of the baião and forró style, he was comfortable with any groove. His joyous, good-natured repertoire endeared him to a large swath of the Brazilian population.

To understand Oliveira is to acknowledge his three greatest influences. Ernesto Nazareth was one of the most recognized composers of Brazilian national music. He had a major impact on the popular and classical forms. Luiz Gonzaga was probably the greatest oral folklorist in the history of modern folk music. Art Van Damme was a jazz accordion master who was a national hero. Each one made an impact on Oliveira which could be found throughout his catalog.

Oliveira wrote a number of classics which other artists continue to record and perform. A partial list includes "Adeus, Maria Fulô," "João e Maria," "Feira de Mangaio," "No Tempo dos Quintais," "Tico-Tico no Fubá," "Carioquinha no Flamengo," "Frevo dos Vassourinhas Numero 1," "Sivuca no Baião," "Entardecendo," "Chroo Balixo," and "Feijoada." He also sang songs from a wide range of artists including Americans such as Bill Withers.

Oliveira collaborated with an impressive number of artists. A partial list includes Humberto Teixeira, Chico Buarque, Glorinha Gadelha, Clara Nunes, Paulo Tapajós, Paulinho Tapajós, Paulo César Pinheiro, Luíz Bandeira, Armandinho, Hermeto Pascoal, Chiquinho do Acordeon, Carmelia Alves, Zequinha de Abreu, Waldir Azevedo, Matiás da Rocha, Luiz Gonzaga, Hervé Cordovil, Gabriel Migliori, Baden Powell, Toots Thielemans, Radamés Gnattali, Rosinha de Valença, Harry Belafonte, and Miriam Makeba.

Oliveira was a brilliant artist. He understood the complex textures of the music as well as anyone else and had the ability to excel in every style. Although many musicians made a large splash on the national and international stage, few had the magical touch of "Sivuca," the Brazilian folkie.

DISCOGRAPHY:

Sivuca e Rosinha de Valença Ao Vivo, RCA 107.0269.
Sivuca, Vanguard 79337.
Pau Doido, Kuanup 052.
Crazy Groove, RCA 35641.
Swedish Groove, P-Vine 5169.
Enfim Solo, Kuarup 092
O Desmatelo Continua, Sonzoom 311.
Raizes Nordestinas, EMI 5207822.
Terra Esperanca, Kuarup 206.
Sinfonico, Discmedi 4291.
Sivuca E Quinteto Uirapuru, Kuarup 186.
Cada Um Belisca Um Pouco, Biscoito Fino 583.
Som Brazil, Gazell GP 2001.
Cabelo de Milho, Movieplay 832000.
Norte Forte, Tropical 68959.
Samba Nouvelle Vague, Universal 9813077.
Sivuca & Rosinha de Valença, RCA 107–269.

PART FIVE

The Pre–Folk Boom Era

While folk music existed for thousands of years and in its twentieth-century form for at least 50 years, it hadn't gained mainstream popularity. The material had been sung and played in the parlors of homes, on back porches, while doing hard physical labor, and in every other human situation. But it remained neglected to some degree even after a recording industry was established. The hot records were jazz, blues, and country, then big band, and later, in the 1940s, R&B.

Many factors led to folk's failure to capture the imagination of the populace the way other styles had done since the 1920s. Traditional tunes were simple and didn't create much excitement in the United States or Great Britain. The recording industry quickly categorized many folk artists such as Robert Johnson, the Carter family, Blind Lemon Jefferson, the Stanley Brothers, Jimmie Rodgers, the Reverend Gary Davis, Bill Monroe, Earl Scruggs, Lester Flatt, Uncle Dave Macon and Mississippi John Hurt as either blues, bluegrass or country. And while many good amateur musicians played folk music, the genre had no leading figure. This all changed with the emergence of Woody Guthrie.

Woody Guthrie, from Oklahoma, lived through the dust bowl days of the Great Depression. He began his career singing the simple folk tunes which were commonplace, then started to write his own material. About the same time, Pete Seeger, the son of musicologist Charles Seeger, arrived on the scene and made a strong impact. Others, like Cisco Houston, Burl Ives, Josh White, and Leadbelly helped shape a strong, vibrant folk industry.

The new folk had new attributes. Simple tunes became political anthems, powerful ammunition against a government working its way out of a depression. The written material provided fuel to those who raged against the authorities for better conditions. Criticism through song was a tool.

The folksong also became attached to the union efforts. These disrupted service and incurred heavy commercial loss. The unions which had survived bloody battles at the turn of the century embraced the folksong as a weapon for equality. The labor movement would grow stronger after World War II.

The style also became the voice of social justice. In a segregated United States, blacks and other minorities voiced their interest in a share of the American dream. Folk and blues were employed to help bring about racial equality. The simple song "We Shall Overcome" became the anthem of the civil rights movement.

One of the greatest marks against the emerging folk artists of the early years was that many supported left-wing politics. In the 1950s, during the McCarthy era, blacklisting hurt the careers of many of folk's key leaders.

Despite folk's lack of commercial success, few recording opportunities, left-wing political views, and union ties, the music survived. Bridge artists such as Jean Ritchie served as a link between decline and revival. The anthologies of recorded material of the 1920s and 1930s played a key role. These fueled the folk boom.

In England in the early 1950s, A.L. Lloyd and Ewan MacColl ignited the roots revival in Great Britain. They opened the Ballads and Blues Club, later the Singers Club. Although their time together wasn't long, their influence proved extremely important over the next two decades.

A key figure not profiled in this book is Huddie "Leadbelly" Ledbetter. Although he made enormous contributions to the pre–folk-boom era, Ledbetter was better known as a bluesman. He was profiled in my earlier book, *Blues Singers: Biographies of 50 Legendary Artists of the Early 20th Century.*

This section is dedicated to the other pivotal figures who bridged the gap between early folk traditions and the boom which brought the style to the international stage. They laid down the foundation for what occurred soon after the McCarthy era ended, and include the following.

Hobart Smith was a solid musician and singer whose style would be greatly copied during the folk boom era. Moses Asch was neither a singer nor musician. He was the founder of the Folkways label and dedicated his work to recording folk performers. A.L. Lloyd was a British collector who managed to bring a scholarly approach to his work. Richard Dyer-Bennet was a musician, songwriter and interpreter whose work proved a solid foundation for later exploits. Alan Lomax was a prime musicologist who traveled thousands of miles to record authentic folk music in the United States and abroad.

Ewan MacColl was an English musician, activist, and songwriter who did much to bring about the folk revival in his native land. Oscar Brand was a Canadian who ended up in the United States where he became a radio personality with a long-running show. His contributions are enormous. Jean Ritchie was part of the famous Ritchie clan from Kentucky. They were excellent musicians with a repertoire that dated back hundreds of years and contained countless folk classics. Harry Smith was an eccentric visionary who assembled the Anthology of American Folk, a landmark collection vital to the revival of the late 1950s.

Hobart Smith (1897–1965)

Blue Ridge Legacy

Like other styles, folk music boasts heroes, cult figures, superstars and neglected musicians, who despite their contributions remain in obscurity. In the Appalachian hills were dozens of able performers who were overlooked because of poor recording techniques and the regional flavor of their sound. One of these forgotten individuals achieved recognition posthumously. His name was Hobart Smith.

Smith was born on May 10, 1897, in Saltville, Smyth County, Virginia, into a deep musical tradition that dated back several generations. The authentic Appalachian sound was all around him and it was only natural that he would master a number of instruments, including the guitar, fiddle, mandolin, piano and organ. Like Jean Ritchie, Aunt Molly Jackson, Woody Guthrie, Buell Kazee, Libby Cotten, and Dock Boggs, he learned his folk music at someone's knee.

While still a teenager, Smith formed a string band which played at local functions including auctions and prison camps. He also moonlighted on the minstrel circuit, performing as a solo artist. He could easily entertain because of his multi-instrumental abilities. He built a local following, but because he wasn't able to record, his fan base was developed through word of mouth and constant performing.

Although a straight Appalachian folk artist, he infused his tunes with a good dose of blues. Smith learned his blues from African American railroad workers who had enjoyed the company of Blind Lemon Jefferson. They taught the young, apt pupil the rudiments of the style.

In 1918, Smith met Clarence Ashley, another hard-driving Appalachian musician, and the two developed a deep respect for one another. While both had enough talent for musical careers, they worked menial jobs to make ends meet. Smith found employment as a farmer, wagoner, house painter and even a butcher.

Like those of so many others, Smith's musical career suffered in the Great Depression. He retained his dexterity and talent while he waited for economic prosperity to return. By 1936, his repertoire was more commercial-sounding. He appeared with his sister Texas Gladden at the Whitetop Festival in Southwest Virginia at the request of Eleanor Roosevelt. Later, he and his sibling performed at the White House.

In 1942, in a comeback attempt, he recorded a number of tracks for Alan Lomax and the Library of Congress. His set included English ballads, Virginia murder ballads, rags, blues, and traditional numbers performed on a variety of instruments including the banjo, fiddle, and guitar. Smith was perhaps one of the few old-time performers who was still able to maintain some momentum in his career.

The introduction to Alan Lomax opened doors and led to a friendship with Moses Asch, the founder of Folkways Records, one of the most important companies in folk history. Smith recorded for one of Asch's defunct labels, but the songs burned with an unusual intensity which eventually fueled the musicians of the boom period.

Smith continued to record for the Library of Congress. In-depth interviews were taped and the virtuoso shared his thoughts about the history and legacy of Appalachian folk music. These sessions provided an invaluable source of information for scholars and were preserved for future generations. Lomax had special connections in the music business and ensured that Smith performed at several folk festivals.

For years, Smith had carried the folk flag, proud to perform even at the simplest venues in order to promote the music. Eventually, his dedication paid off as a whole new generation of folkies discovered his music, including the New Lost City Ramblers, Tom Paley, John Cohen, Mike Seeger, Jody Stecher, Hank Bradley and Fleming Brown. This new respect swept him into the recording studio at Folk Legacy.

In 1963, he met with fellow banjo player Fleming Brown, and together they taped hours of his repertoire. As the afternoon stretched into night, Smith demonstrated his skill on many instruments. He played the blues, dance tunes, hymns, hoedowns, rags, and love songs of his youth. It was a meaningful interchange and, like the Library of Congress interviews, provided scholars and fellow musicians with a treasure trove of history.

Many folk artists from the 1920s and 1930s who had watched the Great Depression destroy their momentum benefited from the folk boom. Clarence Ashley, Dock Boggs, Buell Kazee and Smith enjoyed second phases to their careers. In the 1960s, at the height of the revival, Smith was experiencing a true renaissance. Sadly, his health began to fade and he passed away on January 11, 1965.

Hobart Smith was a folk vessel. He had a wealth of talent on several instruments, a deep knowledge of traditional music, a wide catalog and showmanship ability. His music lives on because he touched so many. A good example is the 2001 release, *Blue Ridge Legacy*, which a new generation discovered and embraced.

Smith was one of the best folk virtuosos in history. He produced high-energy, complex sounds on the 5-string banjo, and had a deep, gritty, country-blues touch on the guitar, with precise, intricate chord and note patterns. He danced with rhythmic magic to the run of fiddle notes he charmed out of the instrument with relative ease, and pounded out merry, rolling tunes on the piano.

Like many other performers, Smith had a dual personality. Off stage he was a quiet, shy man, but on stage he became a larger-than-life character. He was a prime showman with hard-driving songs and a storyteller's talent. The driving emotion attracted the new generation of musicians.

His huge repertoire included "Coo-Coo Bird," "The Banging Breakdown," "Jinny Put the Kettle On," "Golden Slippers," "Coming Around the Mountain," "Jimmy," "Wayfaring Stranger," "Hangman Swing Your Rope," "The Little Schoolboy," "Graveyard Blues," "Drunken Hiccups," "Claude Allen," "Railroad Bill," "Poor Ellen Smith," "Hawkins County Jail" "Chinquapin Pie," "Last Chance," "Sourwood Mountain, "Going Down the Road Feeling Bad," "Pateroller," and "What Did the Buzzard Say to the Crow?" Smith was able to take any old folk tune and bring it to life.

Like every other musician, Smith had his influences. They included his father; his mother; John Greer, a banjo player; Jim Spencer, an African American fiddler; Horton Barker; Dave Thompson; and Richard Chase, along with countless relatives. He was able to take some musical element from each musician and incorporate that into his own unique style.

In turn, Smith influenced many, including Fleming Brown, Pete Seeger, Joan Baez, Dave Van Ronk, Bob Dylan, Clarence Ashley, the New Lost City Ramblers, John Cohen, Mike Seeger, Jody Stecher and Hank Bradley. Scarcely a musician who emerged in the past 50 years has not been touched by some aspect of Smith's music.

Despite his vast contributions to the Appalachian folk form, Smith has often been overlooked. It took far too long for his material to be released in CD form, and others gained greater fame because of their recordings. But in the last few years, people have come to recognize Smith for his vast and deep talents.

Musicians of his caliber and spirit come along very infrequently. He had star quality, but never reached that status. His virtuosity, his deep knowledge of old-time tunes and his passion allowed him to leave behind a Blue Ridge legacy.

DISCOGRAPHY:

The Blue Ridge Legacy—The Alan Lomax Portrait Series, Rounder 611789.
In Scared Trust: The 1963 Fleming Brown Tapes, Smithsonian Folkways 40141.

Moses Asch (1905–1986)

Folkways Founder

A number of different figures played a vital role in the emergence of American folk music as a powerful style. Many were musicians with the ability to write and execute a catchy tune. Collectors helped preserve the songs so they would not be lost. Others recorded the music for posterity, including the Folkways founder, Moses Asch.

Asch was born on December 2, 1905, in Warsaw, Poland. As a boy, he relocated to New York and quickly adjusted to life in the United States. Like most American schoolchildren, he developed a love of music and sang the songs of Stephen Foster. However, his family forbade listening to jazz.

In his late teens and early twenties, he studied electronics in Germany. This opened the doors of the music business. In the mid–1920s, Asch returned to New York City and found work as a radio technician. Radio was booming and his financial prospects appeared solid.

The enterprising young man began to record radio programs destined to be aired at private and public events. He extended his efforts to include music and speech issued on commercial recordings by a few record labels. Asch noticed that his clientele consisted of artists who specialized in obscure styles. Because of the niche music they performed, these musicians would never attract the interest of the big labels.

Asch saw an opportunity to record ethnic musicians and promote their art even if it were not commercial enough for the mainstream market. The ambitious audiophile realized that folk artists were severely under-recorded, because of their left-wing politics and because folk didn't generate the same excitement as hot jazz and screaming blues.

In 1941, Asch recorded the legendary Leadbelly at the Asch Recording Studios. He would later focus on folk and jazz stalwarts, including Burl Ives, Sonny Terry, Woody Guthrie, Josh White, Pete Seeger and Mary Lou Williams. While he was not an avowed communist, his penchant for recording protest songs brought him in contact with left-wing politics.

In the mid–1940s, he founded Disc Label as an outlet for his collection, which was growing to be more valuable and diversified. However, his gamble nearly failed when he slipped into bankruptcy, jeopardizing his life's ambition. Asch, more determined than ever, recovered from the financial setback and, in 1948, founded Folkways.

Unlike other popular record companies at the time, which concentrated on blues (Chess), R&B (Atlantic), and mainstream (Capitol), Folkways became primarily associated with folk. Although Brunswick, Columbia,

Decca, Okeh, Vocalion and Victor were heavily into roots music, none concentrated exclusively on folk. During the volatile 1950s, which saw both the McCarthy era and the folk boom later in the decade, Asch's company survived and became a top label.

Asch released hundreds of folk and ethnomusicological recordings. His catalog grew into an incredible collection, one of the most valuable in the entire industry. Although he was criticized for some of his recording techniques, many forgot that he was a businessman rather than a folklorist. However, this didn't stop him from capturing on vinyl some very non-commercial material that other labels showed no interest in.

Throughout the 1950s and 1960s, he continued to record some of the heavyweights of the folk world, including Pete Seeger. Asch reached into bluegrass to capture the exciting sounds of Bill Monroe. But Folkways also delved in the poetry of African American writer Langston Hughes. Ella Jenkins, an acclaimed children's singer, was on the label's list of artists. He even recorded environmental albums with frogs and other wildlife.

He made money on many of his recordings, which enabled him to accept other, less profitable projects. He understood that ethnic and world music records might not be great sellers, but the music should be preserved for posterity. This vision enabled Folkways to become a leader and separate itself from other commercial labels.

Asch was a stubborn individual. In the 1950s, when the McCarthy era had wiped out a good section of the entertainment industry, he continued to record folk artist Pete Seeger. This was considered political defiance, but because he was not an avowed communist, no one stopped him. He never underwent scrutiny.

In the 1960s, during the height of the folk revival, Asch started up the Broadside label, as an outlet for topical songs. Phil Ochs and Bob Dylan recorded some songs for this offshoot of Folkways. But by this time Vanguard, Elektra and Columbia had begun to delve into the folk idiom, and with better recording techniques and an eye for emerging talent, they were able to surpass Folkways.

By the late 1960s, Asch was recording less material and his company began to decline. Many of the new releases were of an obscure nature, which made up the majority of the label's catalog for the next two decades. However, the company which recorded all of the early, great folk artists remained a power because of its incredible archives. With the deaths of Cisco Houston and Woody Guthrie, the Folkways collection proved even more valuable.

In 1986, an era came to an end when the entire Folkways catalog was sold to the Smithsonian. The institution began almost immediately to release all of the old material on CD. Moses Asch died later that same year on October 19, in New York City. Although he had never sung or played a note, he had made enormous contributions to folk and world music.

Asch turned his tiny label into an incredibly significant empire and brought the music of the common people unprecedented respect. He expanded the parameters of his business to include many types of music no other company would ever record. His dedication and preservation of folk music makes him one of the most important contributors to the genre in its entire history.

The company's catalog included Klezmer music, traditional drumming and dances of Ghana, bedouin music of the southern Sinai, vocal music of contemporary China, Temar dream songs from Malaya, music from South New Guinea, six Toronto poets, Creole songs of Haiti, Indian music of Mexico, song and dance of Brittany, Lappish folksongs from northern Norway, Polish concentration camp songs, ritual music of Ethiopia, and songs and ballads of the Scottish wars.

The eclectic label also recorded tribal sounds from remote Amazonian villages as well as New York avant-garde music and poetry. There were unaccompanied ballad singers, bluegrass, urban music, Greek literature, Soviet poetry read in Russian and the writings of an African American from Harlem. The variety of styles included American folk and traditional music, from field calls of the rural deep South to modern bluegrass, cowboy songs, Anglo-American ballads, New England whaling songs, string-band music, early country, hymns, sea chants, political and topical tunes, rhythm & blues, zydeco and Native American music.

There were other dimensions. Asch foresaw the environmental movement and recorded sounds of nature which would eventually be dubbed New Age music. He documented human aspirations for justice and freedom from the United States, Ireland, Poland, Africa and other struggling regions of the world. His efforts proved to be brilliant, educational and entertaining.

Although many of the Folkways recordings were found in public libraries instead of on the shelves of record stores, their importance cannot be overstated. Remarkably, no matter how poorly they sold, all the recordings remained in print. This availability separated Asch's company from other labels.

Folkways Records preserved the culture and heritage of people from around the world and societies that were often overlooked. The collection is eclectic and reflected Asch's diverse taste and philosophy. He was willing to document and save anything which he thought was interesting and vital. He would never exclude any form of music the way jazz had been forbidden in his childhood home.

Asch was a huge fan of folk music and believed that the style was the expression of the people, which is the general common definition of the genre. He had a very strong interest in the careers of Leadbelly, Woody Guthrie,

Sonny Terry, Brownie McGhee, Josh White, Richard Dyer-Bennet, Hobart Smith, Frank Warner, Pete Seeger, Cisco Houston and Texas Gladden.

Other notable roots artists associated with Folkways are the Rev. Gary Davis, Big Bill Broonzy, Harry and Jeanie West, Elizabeth Cotten, the New Lost City Ramblers, Doc Watson, Jean Ritchie, Mike Seeger, Frank Wakefield, the Country Gentlemen, Peggy Seeger, Dock Boggs and Clarence Ashley. The label recorded famous names as well as lesser-known artists who never would have been able to record with a major label.

The Folkways pressings were thick and packaged with two pockets, one for the LP and the other for program entries that accompanied each album. The liner notes, detailed and precise, provided texts, extensive background information and the history of the songs. Releases included bibliographic and discographic data as well as photographs. The label put out a truly wonderful product.

Asch believed that all music was international. For instance, blues was not strictly promoted in African American communities, but throughout all markets. There was a world flavor to each record and Asch wanted audiences to appreciate the music as global.

One of the most important recordings the label released was the Anthology of American Folk, which would become a audio-bible to the folk music revival artists. Many of the songs had been recorded between 1927 and 1932 and revitalized the careers of those forgotten artists, including Clarence Ashley, Buell Kazee, the Carolina Tar Heels, the Carter family, Frank Hutchison, Charlie Poole, Mississippi John Hurt, and Furry Lewis, among others. While some had passed on, interest in their work was rekindled.

Folkways was also a major resource for academics, research institutions and libraries. The Voice of America, the American Museum of Natural History and the Library of Congress all needed the materials the label released. They were of immense value to scholars. Hundreds of thoughtful music books would never have been possible without the Folkways assets.

After Asch's death, the Smithsonian took over the entire catalog. Eventually, Anthony Seeger was named to oversee the whole collection, and he made difficult decisions in order to keep the wealth of music intact, modern and accessible. Arguably, the Smithsonian was the best custodian for the catalog.

Eventually the massive collection would be organized and divided into different categories: CDs, cassettes and videos. A reading of the entire list is a journey through musical history from the early 1940s to contemporary times. With a list that includes the Stoneman Family, the Country Gentlemen, Dock Boggs, Gordon Tanner, Pete Steele, Rufus Crisp, the New Lost City Ramblers and so many others it is easy to understand how imperative it is to make the recordings available.

Moses Asch was a prime architect of the folk revival of the 1950s and 1960s, as numerous artists drew inspiration from the many recordings he made in the 1940s. His decision to concentrate on folk music helped preserve and promote it at a time when few other labels were interested in the sounds of the common people. He was a curious, devoted and energetic individual whose efforts reverberate throughout the industry 60 years later. The Folkways founder was the ultimate world music worker bee.

A.L. Lloyd (1908–1982)
Father of English Folk

Arguably, Great Britain is the mother of the modern folk sound. From the earliest days of such songwriters as Thomas D'Urfey, through colonization in the New World where pilgrims took their cherished songs from their homeland across the Atlantic and until the end of the late nineteenth century, England was at the forefront of traditional music. The decline of the style spurred on many to revive it, including the man who would be called the father of English folk, A.L. Lloyd.

Lloyd was born Albert "Bert" Lancaster Lloyd in 1908, in London. He was the son of a jack-of-all-trades, and his father had a fine singing voice. This was Lloyd's introduction to English folk music. The elder Lloyd died from injuries suffered in World War I. In 1923, Lloyd's mother succumbed to tuberculosis, leaving him an orphan at 15. In an effort to escape from the painful events in his life, he relocated to New South Wales, Australia.

From 1924 to 1933, Lloyd worked as a sheep and cattle hand. Bored, he purchased a gramophone and obtained records from a mail-order catalog. To complete his education, he raided the public library for books on art and music. But the songs of his fellow workers, the shearers, sheep tenders, swagmen and lumberjacks, truly inspired him to learn more.

Lloyd bought a copy of *Old Bush Songs* and it inspired him to forge his own notebook of material. He wrote down the words to several hundred songs in order to learn them. By the time he left Australia, Lloyd had collected enough material to fill several volumes, and spent the rest of his life interpreting them for the stage and the radio.

In 1934, he left Australia to tend sheep in Transvaal, South Africa. He returned to England, and later that winter encountered Leslie Morton, a Marxist historian. The two became friends. Lloyd was introduced to an informal group of left-wing intellectuals and impressed them with his facility for languages.

In 1936, unemployed, Lloyd utilized his time to learn more about folklore, Marxism, and England's social history. When Morton published *People's History of England*, Lloyd read it with keen interest. It enabled him to expand his social-historical perspective, which helped in the research on folksongs. Around this time, he stumbled upon the works of Francis Child and Cecil Sharp, which greatly influenced him.

England had enjoyed a folk revival around the turn of the twentieth century. It faltered about the time of the Great Depression. In 1935, the BBC started to make field recordings of English folklore, and around the same period a magazine called *English Dance and Song* commenced publication. In 1937, the first authentic recording of traditional music was released, but by this time Lloyd was on a whaling ship.

The seven-month trip to the Antarctic provided a wealth of material for the collector. There were a number of Welshmen aboard who sang hymns and popular songs including film-hits, Victorian and Edwardian tear-jerkers, sea chanties, and, of course, whaling tunes. It was an invaluable experience for the blossoming folklorist who absorbed everything he learned and saved it for future reference. Once his days on the sea were over, he concentrated on making a living as a radio journalist.

Lloyd had acquired writing experience publishing articles in newspapers and magazines, as well as contributing to anthologies and translating poets of different languages into English. In 1938, his first radio script, "The Voice of the Seamen," derived from his experiences on the whaling ship, was accepted. The BBC enjoyed the popularity of the program and hired him on as a broadcaster and journalist.

In the late 1930s, he developed as an amateur folklorist and singer with a steadily growing repertoire of Australian bush songs, American cowboy tunes, English ballads and folk lyrics and international sea chanties. He also performed industrial, occupational and political ditties. By this point, Lloyd boasted more than 500 collected numbers.

In 1939, Lloyd recorded Velvet "Jumbo" Brightwell at the Eel's Foot Inn, a pub where folk performers gathered to sing English standards such as "The Foggy Dew," "The Blackbird," "Indian Lass," "Poor Man's Heaven," "Little Pigs," "There Was a Farmer in Cheshire," and "Pleasant and Delightful." The songs were later broadcast before the outbreak of the war.

Lloyd left the BBC when his contract was not renewed and found employment as a journalist working for the *Picture Post*. An anti-fascist long before it became fashionable, Lloyd joined the army and trained as a tank gunner. However, the Ministry of Information rescued him from front-line action by posting him as an Anglo-Soviet liaison officer. In his free time, he continued to collect English and American folksongs.

In 1944, he published *The Singing Englishman: An Introduction to Folk*

Song. The book was Lloyd's Marxist attempt to write a social history of English folksong. It was a scholarly work unique for its time and cherished by some while loathed by others. Three years later, Lloyd ignited his singing career by winning a national folk singing contest. The first material he recorded was "The Banks of the Condamine"/"Bold Jack Donahue."

The 1950s were truly Lloyd's heyday. He collaborated with Ewan Mac-Coll and the pair performed authentic English folk material in out-of-the-way clubs. Alan Lomax, escaping persecution by McCarthy in the United States, discovered the pair and joined them. Later, Lloyd and MacColl would open a folk club in England which enabled many unknown artists to begin their careers.

In 1952, he published *Come All Ye Bold Miners,* his personal collection of folksongs and ballads. Also that year, he assembled the series, *Ballads and Blues,* which included performances from diverse artists, including American blues singer Big Bill Broonzy, musicologist Alan Lomax, folklorist Jean Ritchie and MacColl.

Lloyd conquered all media. In 1956, he had a role in the film *Moby Dick,* where he sang in the role as a shantyman. He also performed live throughout England, drawing material from his collection of folk tunes. Lloyd bolstered his acting credentials with television appearances and continued radio work. At this point, many considered him to be the leading figure of English folk music and folk dance.

By the 1960s, Lloyd was the granddaddy of the English folk scene and provided an important boost to the careers of Martin Carthy, Dave Swarbrick, Anne Briggs and Frankie Armstrong, the new generation of British folksingers. Fairport Convention and Steeleye Span, two groups who combined rock with folk, also owed a debt to Lloyd. They all delved into his collection of old drinking songs, sea shanties, labor tunes, and other numbers from Australia and his sea journey.

In the prior decade, Lloyd, like Alan Lomax, had roamed the world to make field recordings of native singers and their ethnic music. He ventured to Romania, Bulgaria and Albania to capture authentic folk tunes; however, it took 10 years before the collections were released. In 1967, he collaborated with composer Ralph Vaughan Williams on the *Penguin Book of English Folk Songs,* which became the standard reference in the field.

Throughout the 1970s, Lloyd continued to record, collect and promote English folk music with all of his knowledge and skill. He shared the stage with a number of other artists, who respected the elder statesman of the style because of his encyclopedic understanding of the textures of the music. By the end of the 1970s, he was as celebrated as the American Lomaxes for his vast contributions to the genre.

As the 1980s beckoned, Lloyd could look back on a very exciting and fulfilling career. He had made enormous historical contributions to the preservation of the English folksong. He remained a popular performer until his death on September 29, 1982.

Lloyd's endless search to collect the songs of native people catapulted him to a place of respect and honor. His name is synonymous with the genre and his contributions continue to reverberate long after his death.

Although there were many sides to Lloyd's career, the most important aspect was his folksong collection. He collected sea chanties, drinking songs, whaling tunes, songs of bitter love lost and gained, personal dirges, dance anthems, hymns, mountain ballads, and arias. The variety of material was staggering and featured music from all over the world.

He roamed the world to collect the songs and overcame many obstacles. He preserved material from a number of languages including Romanian, Spanish, Albanian, German, Hungarian, French, Greek, Bulgarian, and Turkish, and from dozens of local dialects such as Tosk and Gheg. He understood that the beauty of the song existed in the native language.

A complete list of all the songs he collected would fill several books. A short list includes "Farewell to Tarwathie," "The Foggy Dew," "Blood Red Roses," "The Lover's Ghost," "Flash Jack from Gundagai," "Weaver and the Factory Maid," "I Wish I Wish," "Jack Orion," "John Barleycorn," "Skewbald," "Talcahuano Girls," "Cockies of Bungaree," "Byker Hill," "Young Girl Cut Down in Her Prime," "Short Jacket and White Trousers," "Sovay," "Reynardine," "Farewell Nancy," "Fanny Blair," "Two Magicians," "The Demon Lover," "Roll Her Down the Bay," "Tam Lin," and "The Widow of Westmoreland's Daughter." This is a small example of the depth, wealth and breadth of the total diversity of Lloyd's collection.

Lloyd dedicated his life to maintaining an interest in and enthusiasm for the folk music of his native England as well as other countries. He was a leading musicologist and deserves the title of the father of English folk.

DISCOGRAPHY:

Traditional Songs, Fellside LC5382.
The Shooting of His Dear / Lord Bateman, HMV B.10593.
Down in Yon Forest / The Bitter Withy, HMV B.10594.
Bold Jack Donahue / Banks of the Condamine, Topic TRC84.
The Columbia World Library of Folk and Primitive Music — Vol. III: England, Columbia SL-206.
The Singing Sailor, Topic TRL3.
Australian Bush Songs, Riverside RLP 12–606.
English Street Songs, Riverside RLP 12–614.
Street Songs of England, Washington WLP 737.
English Drinking Songs, Riverside RLP 12–618.
The English and Scottish Popular Ballads, Volume I, Riverside RLP 12–621/622.

The English and Scottish Popular Ballads, Volume II, Riverside RLP 12–623/624.
The English and Scottish Popular Ballads, Volume III, Riverside RLP 12–625/626.
The English and Scottish Popular Ballads, Volume IV, Riverside RLP 12–627/628.
The English and Scottish Popular Ballads, Volumes 1–8, Washington WLP 715 — WLP 722.
Great British Ballads Not Included in the Child Collection, Riverside RLP 12–629 / Washington WLP 723.
Convicts and Currency Lads, 7" EP, Wattle B2.
Banks of the Condamine and Other Bush Songs, 10" Wattle C4.
Singing Sailors, 10" Wattle C5.
Shanties and Fo'c'sle Song, 10" Wattle C6.
Row Bullies Row, 8" LP, Topic 8T7.
The Black Ball Line, 8" LP, Topic 8T8.
Chants de Marin Anglais No. 1, 7" EP, Chante du Monde LDY 4155.
Chants de Marin Anglais No. 2, 7" EP, Chante du Monde LDY 4157.
Thar She Blows!, Riverside RLP 12–635 / *Whaling Ballads*, Washington WLP 724.
Across the Western Plains, Wattle D1.
Bold Sportsmen All, Topic 10T36.
Champions and Sporting Blades, Riverside RLP 12–652.
Rumanian Folk Music, Topic 10T12.
The Foggy Dew and Other Traditional English Love Songs, Tradition TLP1016.
Blow Boys Blow, Tradition TLP1026.
A Selection from the Penguin Book of English Folk Songs, Collector JGB 5001.
Outback Ballads: Songs from the Australian Bush and Outback, Topic 12T51.
All for Me Grog: English Drinking Songs, EP, Topic TOP66.
England and Her Folk Songs, EP, Collector JEB8.
Haul on the Bowlin', Stinson SLP 80.
A Sailor's Garland, Prestige INT 13043 (USA, 1962), Transatlantic XTRA 5013.
Gamblers and Sporting Blades, EP, Topic TOP71.
Whaler Out of New Bedford, Folkways FS 3850.
Off to Sea Once More, Stinson SLP 81.
Blow the Man Down, EP, Topic TOP98.
A Hundred Years Ago, EP, Topic TOP99.
The Coast of Peru, EP, Topic TOP100.
The Iron Muse: A Panorama of Industrial Folk Song, Topic 12T86.
English and Scottish Folk Ballads, Topic 12T103.
Folk Music of Bulgaria, Topic 12T107.
The Bird in the Bush: Traditional Erotic Songs, Topic 12T135.
First Person, Topic 12T118.
The Best of A.L. Lloyd, LP, Prestige PL-13066 Transatlantic XTRA 5023.
Folk Music of Albania, Topic 12T154.
Folk Songs: An Anthology (Topic Sampler No. 2), Topic TPS145.
Men at Work (Topic Sampler No. 3), Topic TPS166.
Leviathan! Ballads & Songs of the Whaling Trade, Topic 12T174.
Folk Songs: A Collection of Ballads & Broadsides (Topic Sampler No. 6), Topic YPS201.
The Great Australian Legend: A Panorama of Bush Balladry and Song, Topic 12TS203.
Fairport Convention, Babbacombe Lee, LP, ILPS 9176.
Sea Songs and Shanties (Topic Sampler No. 7), Topic TPS205.

The Valiant Sailor: Songs & Ballads of Nelson's Navy, Topic 12TS232.
Sea Shanties, Topic 12TS234.
Electric Muse—The Story of Folk into Rock, Island/Transatlantic Folk 1001.
The Transports, Free Reed FRRD 021/022.
Seven Creeks Run: Songs of the Australian Bush, Larrikin LRF 118.
Chants de Marins IV: Ballades, Complaintes et Shanties des Matelots Anglais, Le Chasse-Marée SCM 005.
Voices: English Traditional Songs, Fellside FECD87.
Ballades et Shanties des Matelots Anglais, Le Chasse-Marée SCM 030.
Classic A.L. Lloyd, Fellside FE098/FECD098.
The Old Bush Songs, Larrikin LRF 354.
Troubadours of British Folk — Vol. 1: Unearthing the Tradition, Rhino R2 72160.
The Bird in the Bush: Traditional Songs of Love and Lust, Topic TSCD479.
English & Scottish Folk Ballads, Topic TSCD480.
Bold Sportsmen All: Gamblers and Sporting Blades, Topic TSCD495.
English Drinking Songs, Topic TSCD496.
Leviathan! Ballads & Songs of the Whaling Trade, Topic TSCD497.
Round Cape Horn: Traditional Songs of Sailors, Ships and the Sea, Topic TSCD499.
World Library of Folk and Primitive Music — Vol. 1: England, Rounder CD1741.
The Ballad of John Axon (The Radio Ballads Vol. 1), Argo DA 139.
Song of a Road (The Radio Ballads Vol. 2), Topic TSCD802.
Singing the Fishing (The Radio Ballads Vol. 3), Argo DA 142.
The Big Hewer (The Radio Ballads Vol. 4), Argo DA 140.
The Folk Collection, Topic TSCD707/8.
Sing Christmas and the Turn of the Year, Rounder 11661–1850–2.
And We'll All Have Tea... English Folk Anthology, Proper / Retro R2CD 40–106.
Voices in Harmony: English Traditional Songs, Fellside FECD158.
The Acoustic Folk Box, Topic TSFCD 4001.
England & Her Traditional Songs, Fellside FECD173.
Classic Maritime Music, Smithsonian Folkways SFW 40053.
Sailor's Songs and Sea Shanties, Highpoint HPO6007.
Folk Songs and Ballads, Cheapolata LATA 574.
Ten Thousand Miles Away: English and Australian Folk Songs, Fellside FECD219.

Richard Dyer-Bennet
(1913–1991)

Renaissance Man

In the late 1950s, American folk music enjoyed a revival and entered its golden age. The fever spread to every corner of the globe including England. Much of the groundwork for the explosion in traditional music had been established prior, during, and after the Second World War. In Great Britain, one of the main figures instrumental in spearheading a resurgence in English folk was renaissance man Richard Dyer-Bennet.

Richard Dyer-Bennet was born on October 6, 1913, in Leicester, England. His future path would be shaped by the many times his family relocated, first to British Columbia, Canada, and then, in 1923, to Berkeley, California. During his travels, he discovered music and began to pay his dues singing in a children's choir. Later, he acted in a production of *Hansel and Gretel.*

In 1929, the adventurous teenager desired to see the world and traveled to Germany, where he remained for a couple of years. While there, Dyer-Bennet taught himself how to play guitar and developed his skills until he was proficient enough to play in front of an audience. More importantly, Dyer-Bennet saw first-hand emerging Nazism, which tainted his view of politics and government. In 1931, he returned to the United States.

At the University of California, Berkeley, he took courses that would help him form his political ideology into accessible and commercial material. Dyer-Bennet performed around the coffee houses and other local venues, honing his skills while writing new songs. While studying voice, he made a career decision and journeyed to Sweden, where he met Sven Scholander.

Scholander not only tutored Dyer-Bennet, he also provided him with a large number of quality songs to begin a solid folk music career. The young scholar left Sweden but stopped in South Wales to support unemployed miners. It was a life-changing experience. Once he saw the plight of the downtrodden, he quit school.

Dyer-Bennet began to perform whenever possible with a growing repertoire derived from the quality songs his mentor Scholander had given him and others collected during his travels. Eventually, the young musician boasted a strong catalog of American and European material. He also injected a healthy dose of quality original material.

In 1938, a concert at a club in San Francisco brought him to the attention of critics. This made Dyer-Bennet realize that he should go to New York to enhance his career. The blossoming musician ventured to the Big Apple several times and made numerous important contacts. In 1941, his hard work finally paid off when he recorded for the Keynote label. A successful performance at Le Ruban Blue, an Upper East Side nightclub, led to his radio debut on NBC.

By this point, the exciting and driving live performances served as the main pulse of his career. Dyer-Bennet played at the Village Vanguard, where he became a fan favorite. In 1944, he performed at New York's Town Hall and later at Carnegie Hall, becoming the first solo folk artist featured at a major venue. This achievement would pave the way for a number of future acts during the folk revival a decade later.

The Second World War fueled Dyer-Bennet's songwriting passion and he composed a number of ballads and propaganda tunes written for the Office of War Information. Dyer-Bennet would later perform at a USO tour of the Philippines and become a hit with the soldiers. At this point in his career, he boasted a deep, entertaining repertoire and sharply honed musical skills.

In New York, he became part of a diverse package tour that included the popular African American contralto, Marian Anderson, and the legendary classical guitarist, Andrés Segovia. In 1947, Dyer-Bennet and his wife moved to Colorado, where they opened an experimental school devoted to keeping the tradition of minstrels alive. However, career demands forced him to commute to New York on a regular basis.

During this time he became a target of the House Un-American Activities Committee. He was blocked from radio and television appearances, but survived with live performances, mainly at the Village Vanguard. In 1955, he and Harvey Cort formed their own recording company, which allowed Dyer-Bennet to record his material the way he desired, and to circumvent the blacklisting.

His first recording, *Richard Dyer-Bennet #1*, was a tremendous success. There would be more than a dozen albums released in this series. Others included: *Songs of Stephen Foster, Scottish and Irish Songs, Mark Twain's 1601, Fireside Conversations in the Time of Queen Elizabeth*, and *Songs in the Same Free Spirit*. The diversity of the material proved that he had a wide and imaginative musical vision.

When the folk boom began, performers such as Dyer-Bennet quickly reaped the benefits. They were acknowledged as keepers of the faith, because many had struggled for years in obscurity when folk music wasn't popular and performers were blacklisted. In the late 1950s, the pace of his career accelerated.

The momentum continued in the 1960s. He recorded on a regular basis and became a popular performer at large folk festivals. Many of the younger artists admired Dyer-Bennet's experience and he shared the stage with a number of acts including Joan Baez, Judy Collins, Bob Dylan, Tom Paxton, the Kingston Trio, and Peter, Paul and Mary, among others.

In 1972, Dyer-Bennet suffered a cerebral hemorrhage which spelled the end of his musical career, since he was no longer able to play guitar. However, he remained active, working on various projects including a musical adaptation of Homer's *Odyssey*. This and other ventures were never completed because on December 14, 1991, Dyer-Bennet died of lymphoma.

Richard Dyer-Bennet was a folk enthusiast. Despite being targeted during the McCarthy era and struggling for years, he never lost his passion for the music. He was one of the instrumental figures in the groundwork that enabled folk to enjoy unprecedented popularity in the 1950s and 1960s.

Dyer-Bennet was probably not the most original performer and wasn't an earthshattering guitarist, but his shows were cohesive and that was the secret to his success. He presented a united product of voice, instrumental ability, knowledge, story-telling charm and defiance. The combination of everything — especially the solid voice and economic guitar patterns — enabled him to present his original and traditional material.

He composed nearly 100 songs, but Dyer-Bennet's true talent was as an interpreter. The engaging folkie boasted a repertoire of more than 500 songs, including English sea chanties, spirituals, cowboy songs, French love ballads, American traditional songs, and European material, some of which dated as far back as the thirteenth century.

He gave the world a number of great songs. A short list includes "As I Was Going to Ballymore," "Agincourt Song," "Brigg Fair," "Flow My Tears," "Sweet Love," "Old Gray Goose," "Australian Girls," "Gentle Annie," "Leprechauns," "Sweet Little Pigs," "Oh Sweet Were the Hours," "Come Live with Me," "Lass from the Low Country," "Again, My Lyre," "Fox and the Geese," "Le Joli Tambour," "Venezuela," and "Eddystone Light." He boasted hundreds of diverse songs.

Dyer-Bennet laid the groundwork for future folk icons. He paved the way for Joan Baez, Bob Dylan, Judy Collins, Phil Ochs, Peter, Paul and Mary, Tom Paxton, and Gordon Lightfoot, among others. He did it through dedication and by breaking new ground with solo performances at prestigious venues such as Carnegie Hall and New York's Town Hall.

Richard Dyer-Bennet enjoyed a long and prosperous career despite many challenges and overcame various obstacles to play the music to which he was so strongly devoted. He was a courageous performer and became a seminal figure in establishing the folk rebirth. He was, in every sense of the word, a renaissance man.

DISCOGRAPHY:

Lute Singer (78 rpm), Keynote #108.
Ballads, Stinson 364.
Love Songs (78 rpm), Keynote 609.
Minstrel Songs of the USA, Vox Records 632.
Twentieth-Century Minstrel, Decca dl79102.
Richard Dyer-Bennet, Dyer-Bennet Records d45.
Folk Songs, Continental Records CST-2011.
Richard Dyer-Bennet Sings Olden Ballads, Mercury 2007.
Scottish Songs, Concert Hall, CHC-13.
Six Irish Songs, Concert Hall, Remington, RLP-199–34.
Richard Dyer-Bennet, Vol. 1, Dyer-Bennet Records DYB 1000.
Richard Dyer-Bennet, Vol. 2, Dyer-Bennet Records DYB 2000.
Richard Dyer-Bennet, Vol. 3, Dyer-Bennet Records DYB 3000.

Richard Dyer-Bennet, Vol. 4, Dyer-Bennet Records DYB 4000.
Richard Dyer-Bennet, Vol. 5, Dyer-Bennet Records DYB 5000.
Richard Dyer-Bennet, Vol. 6, Dyer-Bennet Records DYB 6000.
Richard Dyer-Bennet, Vol. 7, Dyer-Bennet Records DYB 7000.
Richard Dyer-Bennet, Vol. 8, Dyer-Bennet Records DYB 8000.
Richard Dyer-Bennet, Vol. 9, Dyer-Bennet Records DYB 9000.
Richard Dyer-Bennet, Vol. 10, Dyer-Bennet Records 10.
Richard Dyer-Bennet, Vol. 11, Dyer-Bennet Records 11.
Richard Dyer-Bennet, Vol. 12, Dyer-Bennet Records 12.
Richard Dyer-Bennet, Vol. 13, Dyer-Bennet Records 13.
More Songs by the 20th-Century Minstrel, Stinson Records SLP 60.
A Richard Dyer-Bennet Concert, Stinson SLP 61.
1601, Dyer-Bennet Records DYB 1601.
Ballads, Stinson SLP 35.
The Essential Richard Dyer-Bennet, Vanguard VSD 95–96.
The Lovely Milleress (die schoene muellerin), Dyer-Bennet Records 33674–33675.
With Young People in Mind, Smithsonian Folkways 45053.
The Art of Richard Dyer-Bennet, Vanguard Classics 6007.
Richard Dyer-Bennet, Smithsonian-folkways SF 40078.

Alan Lomax (1915–2002)

Folksong Revivalist

There is in every person's life strong influences which help shape their point of view and philosophy, and directs them on a definite path. John A. Lomax was an instrumental figure in the preservation of folk music and passed on this passion to his son, Alan, who would extend his father's work and become a folksong revivalist.

Lomax was born on January 15, 1915, in Austin, Texas. From an early age, he helped his father collect cowboy songs and therefore grew up with an appreciation of American music. It was an eagerness that would serve him well throughout his entire lifetime. The younger Lomax understood that folk music of the United States and the world needed careful study and preservation.

In 1931, his mother passed away and the family went through an emotional crisis. When John Lomax lost his job at a bank, the Lomaxes sank deeper into trouble, but rebounded when he decided to embark on a series of lecture tours. The family camped to save money and Alan Lomax and his brother John Jr. were drivers and assistants. It was in many ways a life-changing experience for the 17-year-old folk music enthusiast. It led him to a desire to follow in his father's footsteps.

In 1935, Alan Lomax traveled to the Georgia sea islands with folklorist Mary Barnicle to uncover the rich music of that area. It was here that one of the most heavily recorded yet mysterious bluesmen, the legendary Blind Blake, was rumored to have lived. To avoid confrontation with some of the local vigilantes, the two collectors often blackened their faces.

In 1937, Lomax ventured to eastern Kentucky in the Appalachian foothills and encountered people living in primitive conditions who could produce magic on instruments that were largely homemade. The area was a veritable gold mine of authentic American folk and Lomax recorded a great deal of it. He would tape what would become more than 200 record sides on his first solo trip, and would unearth a wealth of music that would be preserved for future generations.

In 1938, he set out again and headed to New Orleans, the cradle of jazz. Here he interviewed the legendary Jelly Roll Morton, a colorful character who had worked with every important jazz artist of the early era. The session produced a book, *Mr. Jelly Roll*, and an off–Broadway show. Although jazz had been around for better than 50 years and had been recorded for at least a dozen, no one had researched it as deeply as Lomax.

In 1939, he took to the airwaves and produced a 26-week broadcast entitled *American Folk Songs*, which was very well received. He would utilize his radio show to promote the war effort. He was very anti-fascist, which was common among folk artists at the time. Despite his patriotism, Lomax's left-wing politics conflicted with conventional thinking. However, it led him to meet and record Woody Guthrie, Burl Ives, Pete Seeger and Leadbelly.

In 1941, he ventured to Mississippi to record a little known, yet powerful singer on the Stovall Plantation named McKinley Morganfield. Years later, the young man with the commanding voice would be known as Muddy Waters, and would rule as the dean of Chicago electric blues for decades. The contrast between this early work and his later gritty style is of interest. Lomax helped document the progression.

Lomax continued his blues mission in 1946 when he recorded Sonny Boy Williamson I, Memphis Slim and Big Bill Broonzy, three key figures in the first wave of Chicago blues singers. Later, they would be included in the sessions on *Blues in the Mississippi Night*. The three were steeped in history and their views were preserved for posterity.

In 1948, Lomax hosted and wrote the series *On Top of Old Smoky* for the Mutual Broadcasting Network. Although his career in America was solid, the McCarthy communist witch hunt was looming. Because of his association with those considered to be communists such as Woody Guthrie, Pete Seeger, Cisco Houston, Fred Hellerman and Lee Hays, among others, Lomax decided to take a sabbatical in England.

In 1950, Lomax met A.L. Lloyd and Ewan MacColl, two highly talented individuals playing authentic English folk music in a small, out-of-the-way club. The trio realized they had much in common and Lomax encouraged the pair to continue their careers. They did, and opened another night spot which would spark the roots revival in England.

In Great Britain, he was able to research English folksongs and extended his work to include Spain and Italy. In 1955, he published the 18-volume set, *World Library of Folk and Primitive Music*. Lomax would broadcast for the BBC with a series that had a huge influence on the evolution of skiffle, the precursor to rock and roll. His work overseas was as effective as his work at home.

In 1959, Lomax returned to the United States and continued to do field work in the Deep South, most notably producing the recordings of Mississippi Fred McDowell. He would also record a number of prisoners as his father had done years earlier. This session discovered James Carter, whose song "Po Lazarus" would be featured in the film *O Brother, Where Art Thou?* some 40 years later.

Although not one of the original founders of the Newport Folk Festival, Lomax would eventually be one of the main figures organizing the event. The celebrated happening launched the careers of Joan Baez and Bob Dylan. As well, it popularized different types of traditional music including blues and country. During the revival years, both Howlin' Wolf and Johnny Cash would make appearances at the festival.

In 1962, Lomax spent six months in the West Indies, where he recorded the indigenous music. It was another successful mission, as Lomax caught on tape the magic of the racially mixed population, blending English, French and Spanish cultural threads. He also ventured to Trinidad to document the musical riches unheard by the rest of the world.

In 1967, he teamed up with old friends Woody Guthrie and Pete Seeger to produce the book *Hard Hitting Songs for Hard-Hit People*. It was a monumental project and was completed just before Guthrie's death. Despite Guthrie's controversial later years, Lomax remained a friend, understanding the enormous contributions that the dust bowl balladeer had made.

In 1968, Lomax published the book *Folk Song Style and Culture*. It was a summation of his many years traveling the world to study global music. He had covered more territory than his father and therefore had recorded a greater variety of singers. Lomax had not only surpassed his famous dad, he had established his own name among musicologists around the globe.

In the 1970s, Lomax reworked old territory. The invention of more sophisticated recording equipment allowed him to return to the South and to record more newly discovered musicians. In 1977, he released *Georgia Sea Island Songs* and *Roots of the Blues*. The former had been collected on separate trips in the previous two decades, while the latter featured a variety of singers working out standard material.

Lomax continued to travel in the 1980s to areas he had already explored, but found new talent to record. In 1986, his lone film, *The Longest Trail*, a study of the Amerindians of North and South America, appeared on television. The advent of the video camera spurred him to make numerous journeys back to points in the South. In 1990, he put together a series for PBS radio called *American Patchwork*, another triumph for the folklorist.

He continued his work and concentrated on academic writings while based at Columbia University in New York. Lomax would write and publish many books, including *The Land Where the Blues Began*, which would earn the non-fiction National Book Critics' Circle award. It would eventually blossom into a multi-media project entitled *Global Jukebox*. He resumed lecturing, writing and working on various projects, founding the Association for Cultural Equity.

Meanwhile, Rounder records compiled a 100-CD series of Lomax's global recordings. Not long afterward, on July 19, 2002, Alan Lomax passed away and an important chapter in American music came to an end.

Alan Lomax was a folk music traditionalist of the highest order. His extensive travels to the back roads, honky tonks, and work camps of the Deep South to collect and record an unequalled treasure of songs and singers is unparalleled. Through his efforts a range of traditions from the Delta blues to Appalachian folk to early Creole jazz to field songs was preserved. He depicted an era that otherwise would have disappeared from the pages of history.

Although best known for his forays into the South, he also traveled to New England, Michigan, Wisconsin, New York and Ohio. Outside of the United States, he recorded in faraway places such as Haiti, the Bahamas, and Trinidad, among others. He spent time in England, as well as other parts of Europe, including Spain and Italy.

Lomax recorded a number of musicians long before they became famous. The list includes McKinley Morganfield (Muddy Waters), Huddie "Leadbelly" Ledbetter (a credit shared with his father), and Woody Guthrie. He also captured Aunt Molly Jackson in her amateur days.

He enabled Lee Hays and Cisco Houston to attain greater heights. Lomax eventually turned his attention to jazz and delivered the definitive portrait of the enigmatic Jelly Roll Morton. He also boosted the careers of the first transplanted wave of Chicago bluesmen, Memphis Slim, Sonny Boy Williamson I, and Big Bill Broonzy.

He also recorded Maire O'Sullivan singing "An Cailin Aerach," the Irishman Seamus Ennis with his "The Banks of the Roses," Sean Moriarty performing "The Brown Thorn," and Elizabeth Cronin with "Dance to Your Daddy," and Ballinakill Ceili doing "Sack of Potatoes & Maid of Mount Kisco." He unearthed Kitty Gallagher's "An Mhaighdean Mhara," Mickey

Doherty's "The Fox Chase," Maggie McDonagh's "Amhrán Fosuíochta," Mary Joyce's "Connia" and Margaret Barry's "She Moved Through the Fair." He also recorded Kate Moynihan's "Mo Ghrádh-Sa an Jug Mór Is É Lán," Maire Keohane's "Cois Abhainn Na Séadd," Gubnait Cronin's "Innsin Bhéil Átha'n Ghaorthaidh," and Johnny McDonagh's "The Death of Brugh."

He collaborated with writer Zora Neale Hurston as well as musicologists Mary Barnicle and John Work. But his most famous partner was his father, and together they wrote a number of books including *American Ballads and Folk Songs, Negro Folk Songs as Sung by Leadbelly, Cowboy Songs* and *Our Singing Country*. Their efforts were instrumental in preserving the folk tradition.

Lomax was a pioneer in many respects. He was at the forefront of the archival study of world music, which many would undertake in the following decades. He developed an appreciation for the culture of people around the globe and awoke it among other nations. He was a global person long before the world became a "village."

Lomax was a historian. He added a great number of recordings to the catalog of the Library of Congress, preserving a very important part of American history for future generations. With each new recording in some remote region in America or the world, he was creating history. But he just didn't collect archives, he documented them in an organized fashion for others.

It is impossible to list every song that Lomax recorded. The number is simply too vast. However a partial list includes "London Bridge," "I've a Sweetheart in America," "Harry Lauder and Mussolini Are Dead," "Little Sally Walker," "All the Boys in London," "In and Out the Windows," "My Father Bought the Little Coat," "In and Out the Dusty Bluebells," "Mother, Mother, I Am Ill," "Queen Elizabeth Lost Her Shoe," "Jelly on the Plate," "The World Must Be Coming to an End," "Paddy Knight," "Geese, Ducks, Stones, Fires and Rain," and "The Donkey/The Croft/The Policeman." These field recordings included a cappella ballads, rugged fiddle tunes, jigs, reels and other treasures.

Alan Lomax perfected the role of musicologist and it is the blueprint he set down which all others have followed. He had an unbridled enthusiasm for his work, as well as a spirit that separated him from others, including his father. The folklore revivalist was instrumental in preserving the history of music on a global level.

DISCOGRAPHY:

Cowboy Songs of the Old West, Legacy 392.
Texas Folk Songs, Arian 64173.
Island & Southern Folk Music, CBS 91A-02025.
Unfortunate Rake, Smithsonian Folkways 3805.

Afro-American Blues and Game Songs, Library of Congress 4.
Prison Blues of the South: Live at the MS & LA Penitentiary, Laserlight 17026.
Sing Christmas and the Turn of the Year, Rounder 611850.
The Spanish Recordings: Mallorca—The Balearic Islands, Rounder 11661.
The Spanish Recordings: Ibiza and Formentera—The Pityusic Islands, Rounder 1770.
Southern Prison Blues and Songs, Collectables 0850.
Heather and Glen, Acrobat 309.
Gaelic Songs of Scotland: Women at Work in the Western Isles, Rounder 1785.
1951 Edinburgh People's Festival Ceilidh, Rounder 1786.
Italian Treasury: Lombardia, Rounder 1871.
Italian Treasury: Abruzzo, Rounder 611811.
Caribbean Voyage: The French Antilles—We Will Play Love Tonight!, Rounder 1713.
Singing in the Streets: Scottish Children's Songs, Rounder 1795.
The Spanish Recordings: Basque Country—Navarre, Rounder 1773.
Italian Treasury: Piemonte and Valle d'Aosta, Rounder 1807.
The Spanish Recordings: Basque Country—Biscay and Guipuzcoa, Rounder 1772.
Italian Treasury: Puglia: The Salento, Rounder 1805.
Alan Lomax: Blues Songbook, Rounder 1866.
World Library of Folk and Primitive Music, Vol. 7: India, Rounder 11755.
The Spanish Recordings: Extremadura, Rounder 11763.
Caribbean Voyage: Nevis and St. Kitts Tea Meetings, Rounder 11731.
Deep River of Song: Bahamas 1935, Vol. 2—Ring Games and Round Dances, Rounder 11832.
Deep River of Song: South Carolina—Got the Keys to the Kingdom, Rounder 11831.
Caribbean Voyage: Martinique, Rounder 611730.
Caribbean Voyage: Tombstone Feast, Rounder 611727.
World Library of Folk and Primitive Music, Vol. 5: Yugoslavia, Rounder 611745.
World Library of Folk and Primitive Music, Vol. XVII: Romania, Rounder 6117591.
Deep River of Song: Georgia, Rounder 611828.
Popular Songbook, Rounder 1863.
The Deep River of Song: Alabama, Rounder 611829.
Caribbean Voyage: Grenada—Creole and Yoruba Voices, Rounder 611728.
The Spanish Recordings: Aragon and Valencia, Rounder 11762.
The Spanish Recordings: Galicia, Rounder 11761.
Classic Ballads of Britain and Ireland, Vol. 1, Rounder 611775.
Classic Ballads of Britain and Ireland, Vol. 2, Rounder 611776.
Songs of Seduction, Rounder 611778.
Songs of Seduction, Vol. 2, Topic 158.
World Library of Folk and Primitive Music, Vol. 8: France, Rounder 11836.
The Ballad Operas: The Martins & the Coys, Rounder 611819.
Deep River of Song: Big Brazos, Rounder 611826.
Deep River of Song: Virginia and the Piedmont, Rounder 611827.
The Caribbean Voyage: Trinidad, the 1962 Field Recordings, Rounder 611725.
Italian Treasure: Liguria-Baiardo and Imperia, Rounder 11816.
Italian Treasure: Liguria-Polyphony of Ceriana, Rounder 11817.
The Italian Treasury: Sicily, Rounder 1808.
The Italian Treasure: Emilia-Romanga, Rounder 611804.
Caribbean Voyage: Saraca, Funerary Music of Carriacou, Rounder 611726.
Italian Treasury: Calabria, Rounder 611803.

Italian Treasury: The Trallaleri of Genoa, Rounder 611802.
World Library of Folk and Primitive Music, Vol. 4: Spain, Rounder 611744.
Black Appalachia: String Bands, Songsters, Hoedowns, Rounder 611823.
Bahamas 1935: Chanteys & Anthems from Andros & Cat, Rounder 611822.
Black Texicans: Balladeers & Songsters, Rounder 611821.
Caribbean Voyage: East Indian Music in the West Indies, Rounder 611723.
Carriacou Calaloo, Rounder 611722.
Caribbean Voyage: Caribbean Sampler, Rounder 611721.
Caribbean Voyage: Dominica — Creole Crossroads, Rounder 611724.
Cajun and Creole Music, Vol. 1: 1934/1937, Rounder 611842.
Cajun and Creole Music, Vol. 2: 1934/1937, Rounder 611843.
Deep River of Song: Mississippi — Saints and Sinners, Rounder 611824.
Deep River of Song: Mississippi — The Blues Lineage, Rounder 611825.
Calypso at Midnight!: The Live Midnight Special Concert, Rounder 611841.
Calypso After Midnight!: The Live Midnight Special Concert, Rounder 611840.
Negro Work Songs & Calls, Rounder 1517.
Italian Treasury: Folk Music & Song of Italy, Rounder 1801.
World Library of Folk and Primitive Music, Vol. 1: England, Rounder 1741.
World Library of Folk and Primitive Music, Vol. 2: Ireland, 1743.
World Library of Folk and Primitive Music, Vol. 3: Scotland, Rounder 1743.
Caribbean Voyage: Brown Girl in the Ring, Rounder 1716.
The Land Where the Blues Began, Rounder 1861.

Ewan MacColl (1915–1989)
English Folk Revivalist

Throughout the history of English/Irish/Scottish folk music many important contributors have made an impact with their musical abilities, while others have done so as collectors. Ewan MacColl earned his place in the community as a folk revivalist.

MacColl was born James Miller on January 25, 1915, in Salford, Lancashire, England. His Scottish parents were both singers. His lowland father spoke English and his highland mother spoke Gaelic. At 14, he quit school to begin a career as an entertainer.

He busked in the street for some time before the BBC discovered his talents. He sang and wrote programs for the radio which were well received. He was an avid member of the Young Communist League and a socialist amateur theater troop called the Clarion Players. In the 1930s, he was active in the unemployed workers' campaigns, for which he wrote one of his best-known songs, "The Manchester Rambler."

In 1931, he and other out-of-work performers formed a radical theater group called the "Red Megaphones." Later, they changed the name to Theatre of Action and it was here that MacColl met his future wife, Joan Littlewood. The couple settled in Manchester and formed the Theatre Union where, they later staged a production that incurred the wrath of the authorities.

Because of his beliefs and actions, the British Secret Service had an open file on MacColl, which caused the BBC to reject some of his songs. He further angered the authorities when he deserted the British Army six months after enlisting. This rebellious nature endeared him to a legion of admirers who saw the defiant MacColl as their rightful leader.

In 1946, after the war, members of the Theatre Union formed the Theatre Workshop. They toured England, concentrating on the northern part, where by this time Miller had changed his name to Ewan MacColl. He assumed the role of art director and dramatist while his wife became the lone producer. Although the troupe struggled financially, it slowly built up a loyal following. Some saw the troupe as innovators and others saw them as radicals and troublemakers.

MacColl was an all-around entertainer, not just a dramatist and actor. In the late 1940s and early 1950s, he began to devote more time to his singing career, particularly in the folk idiom. When the Theatre Workshop settled in the Stratford section of London, MacColl left to promote and perform material he had worked on for some time with the intention of becoming a recording artist.

He had been involved with Topic Records for a long period and the label released his composition, "The Asphalter's Song." MacColl's enthusiasm for folk ballads ignited a desire to collect them and he soon amassed hundreds of tunes derived from a variety of sources. He performed many of these songs, giving them a more modern sound to appeal to current tastes.

Eventually, his passion for folk material united him with A.L. Lloyd, the man known as the father of English folk. In 1950, the two performed together at clubs throughout England, and released a series of records. Their collaboration would ignite the British folk music revival a few years later.

In 1956, MacColl, no stranger to controversy, shocked the entertainment world when he began a relationship with Peggy Seeger while still married to his second wife, dancer Jean Newlove. He wrote the song "The First Time Ever I Saw Your Face" for Seeger. Many have recorded it including Elvis Presley, the Pogues, Dick Gaughin, and Roberta Flack, who took the song to number one. She earned a Grammy for Record of the Year, while MacColl won Song of the Year.

Because of his communist activities, MacColl was unable to enter the United States, which put a strain on his relationship with the much younger Seeger. However, the two managed to release a few collaborative albums. They enjoyed a hit with "Dirty Old Town," which the Spinners, Roger Whittaker, the Dubliners, Rod Stewart, the Pogues, the Mountain Goats, Simple Minds, Ted Leo and the Pharmacists and Frank Black all covered.

Although he wrote songs of love, MacColl also displayed his political conscience with songs such as "The Ballad of Ho Chi Minh," which was popular in Vietnam, home of the communist leader. Also political was "The Ballad of Tim Evans" (also known as "Go Down You Murderer"). It told the story of a man who had been executed for a crime he had not committed.

MacColl began a radio career in the 1930s that continued 20 years later. When assigned to do a feature program on the death of train driver John Axon, MacColl produced a script that contained the true voices and created a new form which became known as the radio ballad.

In the 1960s, his Ballad and Blues Club would be renamed the Singers Club, where he performed often with Peggy Seeger. It was a showcase for folk artists and launched the careers of many unknown singers, including the members of Steeleye Span and Fairport Convention. It was also a hub of socialist activity which the authorities watched closely.

In 1965, he was a founding member of the Critics Group and later they organized an annual event called the Festival of Fools. Despite his success as a songwriter, MacColl would never leave life as an actor behind. The well-seasoned performer thrived on the demands made upon him by various roles, which he played with great dramatic ability.

Throughout this period MacColl and Seeger collected a number of traditional songs of British origin. They produced two anthologies entitled *Travellers' Songs from England and Scotland* and *Doomsday in the Afternoon*. Their efforts to preserve the old songs was an important part of their activities, as imperative as singing and playing.

In 1979, MacColl suffered the first of a series of heart attacks. But he continued to tour, lecture and write songs. In 1980, his last play, *The Shipmaster,* appeared. A few years later, he began his autobiography, which was never completed. He died of complications following a heart operation on October 22, 1989.

Ewan MacColl accomplished much in the world of folk music. For 60 years, he collected and wrote songs, fought political battles, and produced plays and scripts on such subjects as apartheid, fascism, industrial strife and human rights. He also helped lay the foundation for the English folk revival.

Certainly one of the strengths of MacColl's career was his songwriting. He composed more than 300 pieces, many with strong political themes. A diverse array of artists recorded from his catalog, including Planxty, Dick Gaughan, The Clancy Brothers, Roberta Flack, the Pogues, Elvis Presley, and Johnny Cash, to name a few. His talent as a tunesmith was widely appreciated.

MacColl's songs featured a variety of themes, but often praised the working person. He featured railway workers, road builders, fishermen, coal miners, families, Gypsies, travelers, and Irishmen. His songs and radio ballads were about unions, love, war, peace, politics, society, racism, and apartheid. Because of this, common laborers embraced MacColl and his music in whatever forms presented.

His material fueled the folk revival in England. Throughout the 1960s and 1970s, MacColl inspired many acts, including John Roberts and Tony Barrand, Matt McGinn, Norma Waterson, Mike Waterson, Frankie Armstrong, Cyril Tawney, Sam Larner, Peter Bellamy, James Raynard, Al Jones, Brian Peters and Maddy Prior. He also helped the career of Irish singer-songwriter Dominic Behan.

He produced many television programs, including *Sing in the New, An Impression of Love, The Irishmen, The Stewarts of Blairgowrie,* and *The Ballad of Ewan MacColl,* among others. This was a dimension of his career that is sometimes overlooked. MacColl had a take-charge personality, therefore the role of producer was one he truly enjoyed and excelled at.

He was a first-rate dramatist. Some of his scripts include *John Bullion, Last Edition, The Flying Doctor, The Long Winter, Johnny Noble, Hell Is What You Make It, Uranium 235, Rogues' Gallery, Operation Olive Branch, The Other Animals, Landscape with Chimneys, The Good Soldier Švejk, You're Only Young Once, So Long at the Fair, St. George and the Dragon, Ours the Fruit,* and *The Shipmaster.* George Bernard Shaw, the famous English wordsmith, praised MacColl for his skills as a playwright.

One of the most interesting aspects of his career was his longtime professional relationship with Peggy Seeger. They were together for more than 35 years, and as a duo recorded a number of albums. They also performed at numerous venues and were well received. They formed their own record company called Blackthorne, which issued a lot of new folk material, giving many struggling artists their initial break.

In 1991, Peggy Seeger established an archive of her relationship with MacColl at Ruskin College, Oxford. It contains recordings, correspondence, play scripts, photographs, videos, books and other memorabilia. Also included are radio and television broadcasts and published material.

MacColl promoted equality, peace, harmony and socialism. A plaque dedicated to his memory is located in Russell Square in London. In 2001, the University of Salford awarded him a posthumous honorary degree. Another tribute to his talent was his daughter, Kirsty MacColl, who also enjoyed a musical career until her death in Mexico in 2000.

Ewan MacColl was a great folklorist, but he was also a poet, playwright, activist, actor, producer, and radio host. His contributions were many during a career which spanned some 60 years. The English folklore revivalist was one of the main driving forces behind the folk explosion.

DISCOGRAPHY:

English/Scottish Popular Ballads, Riverside 621–629.
The Big Hewer, Topic 804.
Bad Lads and Hard Cases, Riverside RP-12–632.
Bless 'Em All, Riverside RP-12–642.
Champions and Sporting Blades, Riverside RP-12–652.
Blow Boys Blow, Tradition 1024.
The Ballad of John Axon, Topic 801.
Singing the Fishing, Topic 803.
The Fight Game, Topic 807.
The Angry Muse, Argo ZDA 83.
The Wanton Muse, Argo ZDA 85.
Travelling People, Topic 808.
Solo Flight, Topic 810.
Scottish Drinking & Pipe Songs, Legacy 346.
Freeborn Man, Rounder 3080.
75th Birthday Symposium, Cooking Vinyl 2.
Folk on 2: Ewan MacColl, Cooking Vinyl 002.
The Body Blow, Topic 805.
Bagpipe Tunes, Smithsonian Folkways 3559.
Bothy Songs, Smithsonian Folkways 8759.
British Industrial Folk Songs, Stinson 79.
Broadside Ballads, Vol. 1: London 1600–1700, Smithsonian Folkways 3043.
Broadside Ballads, Vol. 2, Smithsonian Folkways 3044.
Child Ballads, Vol. 1, Smithsonian Folkways 3509.
Child Ballads, Vol. 2, Smithsonian Folkways 3510.
Child Ballads, Vol. 3, Smithsonian Folkways 3511.
Folkways Record of Contemporary Songs, Smithsonian Folkways 8736.
Popular Songs, Smithsonian Folkways 8757.
Scots Street Songs, Riverside 12–612.
Singing Streets, Smithsonian Folkways 8501.
Songs of Robert Burns, Smithsonian Folkways 8758.
The New Briton Gazette, Vol. 1, Smithsonian Folkways 8732.
The New Briton Gazette, Vol. 2, Smithsonian Folkways 8734.
Traditional Songs & Ballads of Scotland, Smithsonian Folkways 8760.
Whaler Out of New Bedford/Other Songs of the Whaling Era, Smithsonian Folkways
    3850.
Classic Scots Ballads, Tradition 1015.
The Real MacColl, Topic 463.
Black and White: The Definitive Collection, Green Linnet.
Antiquities, Recall 149.
Chorus from the Gallows, Topic 502.
Naming of Names, Cooking Vinyl 036.
The Definitive Collection, Highpoint 6006.
Classic Scots Ballads: Tradition Years, Empire Musicwerks 0754.
Blow Boys Blow: The Tradition Years, Empire Musicwerks 450849.
Van Diemen's Land/Lord Randall, HMV B10259.
Sir Patrick Spens/Eppie Morrie, HMV B10260.
Alan Lomax and the Ramblers, Decca DFE 6367.

The Asphalter's Song; I'm Champion at Keepin' 'Em Rolling.
Four Pence a Day; Barnyards of Delgaty, Topics TRC19.
The Four Loom Weaver/McKaffery, Topics TRC40.
As I Went Out One May Morning/Keach in the Creel, Topics TRC46.
Collier Laddie/Johnny Lad, Topics TRC48.
The Brewer Laddie/Johnny Lad, Topics TRC49.
Poor Paddy Works on the Railway, Topics TRC50.
Moses of the Mail, Topics TRC51.
The Ballad of Stalin, Topics TRC54.
The Coalowner and the Pittman's Wife/Jamie Foyers, Topics TRC55.
Dirty Old Town/Sheffield Apprentice, Topics TRC56.
Browned Off/The Union of the Fire Brigade, Topics TRC57.
Ballad of New Poland/Trafford Road Ballad, Topics TRC71.
Girl at Stzalinvaroz/It's Only Propaganda, Topics TRC75.
Johnny Breadiesley/Henry Martin, Topics TRC77.
Johnny Todd/Cosher Bailey's Engine, Topics TRC78.
Wull Cayrd/The Swan-Necked Valve, Topics TRC79.
The Iron Horse; Four Pence a Day; The Wark o' the Weavers, Topics TRC93.
Sixteen Tons/The Swan-Necked Valve, Topics TRC97.
The Banks of Sweet Dundee/Fitba' Crazy; The Wee Cooper O Fife, Topics TRC102.
Poetry and Song, Vol. 1, Argo DA 50.
Poetry and Song, Vol. 2, Argo DA 51.
Poetry and Song, Vol. 3, Argo DA 52.
Poetry and Song, Vol. 4, Argo DA 53.
Poetry and Song, Vol. 5, Argo DA 54.
Poetry and Song, Vol. 6, Argo DA 55.
Poetry and Song, Vol. 7, Argo DA 56.
Poetry and Song, Vol. 8, Argo DA 57.
Poetry and Song, Vol. 9, Argo DA 58.
Poetry and Song, Vol. 10, Argo DA 59.
Poetry and Song, Vol. 11, Argo DA 60.
Poetry and Song, Vol. 12, Argo DA 61.
Poetry and Song, Vol. 13, Argo DA 62.
Poetry and Song, Vol. 14, Argo DA 63.
The Long Harvest, Vol. 1, Argo 66.
The Long Harvest, Vol. 2, Argo 67.
The Long Harvest, Vol. 3, Argo 68.
The Long Harvest, Vol. 4, Argo 69.
The Long Harvest, Vol. 5, Argo 70.
The Long Harvest, Vol. 6, Argo 71.
The Long Harvest, Vol. 7, Argo 72.
The Long Harvest, Vol. 8, Argo 73.
The Long Harvest, Vol. 9, Argo 74.
The Long Harvest, Vol. 10, Argo 75.
Saturday Night at the Bull and Mouth, Blackthorn BR 1050.
Cold Snap, Blackthorn BR 1057.
Hot Blast, Blackthorn BR 1059.
Kilroy Was Here, Blackthorn BR 1063.
Freeborn Man, Blackthorn BR 1065.
Items of News, Blackthorn BR 1067.

Oscar Brand (1920–)

The Can-Am Folklorist

Although they share many of the same immigrant cultures, the United States and Canada saw different patterns in the evolution of folk music. Despite the differences there was often collaboration between artists on either side of the border. Some took it one step farther, including the Can-Am folklorist Oscar Brand.

Brand was born on February 7, 1920, in Winnipeg, Manitoba. He came into the world with a missing calf muscle in his right leg, which caused him considerable pain and embarrassment. He was taken to the most qualified doctors in New York City where he received the necessary help. The long train trips were a favorite part of Brand's childhood memories, but his parents decided that it would be wise if they relocated to New York. They settled in Chelsea and Brand adapted quickly to his new home.

He joined the war effort and found himself doing latrine duty. Brand, a quick-thinking fellow, boasted that he was a solid musician and was allowed to join the army band. In truth, about the only instrument he had ever studied was the kazoo. But he was determined to follow through with his deceit so he borrowed a banjo and bought a book to learn to play it. When Brand showed up with his five-string, an anomaly for a military band, he was given the cymbals instead.

After his discharge, he returned to New York in search of work. Brand had no marketable skills, aside from his experience in the military band. Unfortunately, there were few job openings for a cymbals player. He walked the streets and showed up at WNYC one cold December day and offered to sing a song. He came off well and was asked to return. He landed a radio show.

Brand realized that he might be taken more seriously as a musician if he knew how to actually play an instrument, so he taught himself the rudiments of guitar. His previous study of the banjo was an asset and he developed a good, but simple style. He had been singing for some time and the combination of his playing and vocal delivery blended together perfectly.

He settled in Greenwich Village and became a part of the artistic, Bohemian community. While not the most talented musician or singer, he was able to forge a stable career and wholeheartedly embraced the free-flowing, expressive lifestyle. Brand raised his three children there, as well as a stepson from a second marriage.

Like so many other folk singers, Brand was blacklisted during the McCarthy era. Ever the rebel, he refused to testify before the House Un-

American Activities Committee. Despite this defiance, his radio show did not suffer because in the Village, there was no blacklisting. He started banking royalties from his song "A Guy Is a Guy."

The one constant in his life was his radio show, *Folksong Festival*. It survived battles with those who tried to take it off the air because of some bawdy lyrics and stances Brand took on controversial subjects. But while his show might have been under scrutiny, his guests made up for any shortcomings. Performing on the program were the elite of the folk world — Bob Dylan, Joan Baez, Burl Ives, Judy Collins, John Denver, Arlo Guthrie, Woody Guthrie, Leadbelly, Pete Seeger, Bill Monroe, Harry Belafonte, Odetta, Merle Travis, B.B. King and Harry Chapin.

Brand continued to record his ballads on a fairly regular basis and concentrated on theme albums featuring bawdy tunes, animals, presidential campaigns, and seasonal and military numbers, among others. He found additional work as a playwright, as well as a producer. Later he became curator of the Songwriters Hall of Fame.

In the early 1960s, Brand returned to Canada with his TV program *Let's Sing Out,* broadcasted from university campuses across Canada. Some of the featured guests included pioneers Malvina Reynolds, the Womenfolk and the Weavers, who revived their careers after appearing on the program. It also brought to attention a struggling singer-songwriter from Alberta named Joni Mitchell.

Brand performed at various Canadian outlets including the Charlottetown Festival, Eton Auditorium, the Calgary Stampede, the O'Keefe Center, countless coffee houses, and dozens of folk festivals. His simple brand of homespun music entertained crowds of all ages and cultures. He played the banjo and guitar in a funny, easy manner, and boasted a great rapport with his audience.

In 1968, he created the score for the off–Broadway show *How to Steal an Election*, which had a huge impact on the election campaign that year. During the decade, his recording output dropped off substantially from his prolific pace of the 1950s. In 1961 he issued *Sports Car Songs, Every Inch a Sailor, Oscar Brand Sings for Adults, Tell It to the Marines,* and *Out of the Blue.* But eight years would elapse between releases when, in 1969, Brand surfaced with *Pie in the Sky.* He spent much of his time working on other dimensions of his career such as performing and writing.

In the 1970s, Brand's radio show celebrated its thirtieth anniversary. It remained a potent vehicle for introducing new folk artists and dealing with topics of the day, including Watergate, Richard Nixon's resignation, the oil embargo, and of course the American bicentennial. He released three albums, and spent much of his time performing at hundreds of venues across the country.

Brand started the 1980s collaborating on an album with noted folklorist Jean Ritchie, and ended the decade with the double release *Sing-A-Longs: I Sing, You Sing, We All Sing, Volumes 1 & 2*. It featured some traditional songs including "Yankee Doodle," "This Old Man," "The Alphabet Song," "Twinkle, Twinkle Little Star," "I've Been Working on the Railroad," "London Bridge," "The Itsy Bitsy Spider," "Skip to My Lou," "Old Macdonald," and "She'll Be Coming 'Round the Mountain." Although he continued to perform, his main activity remained his radio show, which would reach its fortieth anniversary in the middle of the decade.

Brand rolled on through the 1990s. His recorded output included *I Love Cats, Get a Dog, Bawdy Songs Rides Again,* and *Presidential Songs,* which covered every president from 1789 to 1996. It featured clever titles such as "If the Johnnies Get into Power Again" (James A. Garfield), "Get a Raft with Taft" (William H. Taft), "If He's Good Enough for Lindy" (Herbert Hoover), and "Buckle Down with Nixon" (Richard Nixon). He continued to perform despite his advanced age.

In 2000, Brand celebrated his eightieth birthday and continued to build on an incredible career. He saw many of his previous efforts including *Pie in the Sky* and *Four Albums of Military Song from Oscar Brand* reissued in a CD format, which enabled a new generation of fans to discover his music. His radio show rolled on and enjoyed its golden anniversary, entering the *Guinness Book of World Records* for the longest-running radio program on the air. He continues to record and perform.

Oscar Brand is a folk enterprise. For more than 60 years he has made major contributions as a radio host, singer, musician, recording artist, author, actor, and writer. Throughout the years, he has always championed the music and those who created it with a tenacious enthusiasm. His many offerings are deep and assure him a special place in folklore history.

Any discussion of Brand's career begins with his radio show. Since 1945, Oscar Brand's *Folksong Festival* has aired continuously and is a landmark achievement in folk annals. There have been hundreds of guests including Bob Dylan, Arlo Guthrie, Joan Baez, Huddy Ledbetter, Joni Mitchell, Pete Seeger, Harry Chapin, Burl Ives, Harry Belafonte, John Denver and B.B. King, to name a few. It has served as a platform for his own music and given him a free voice on the hottest topics of the day. He has never stepped away from controversy during his long reign as a host.

With his show, Brand was a prime architect of the folk revival. Many of the personalities who fueled the boom, as well as those who basked in the spotlight, were guests on his radio program.

Brand is a noted songwriter and many have recorded his songs. Doris Day and Ella Fitzgerald covered "A Guy Is a Guy," his signature tune. Harry Belafonte, the Smothers Brothers and the Mormon Tabernacle Choir are just a few of the acts who have included his work on one of their albums. In reality, nearly every folk musician during the last 60 years has taken one or more of Brand's songs into their repertoire.

Brand is the author of more than 300 songs and has recorded at least 100 albums. His recordings include Canadian patriotic songs, songs of the U.S. Armed Forces, sea chanties, presidential campaign songs and songs of protest. He wrote catchy, thematic folk tunes.

And many of his albums are thematic. For instance *Bawdy Songs & Backroom Ballads* included "Roll Your Leg Over," "Chandler's Life," "Rollin' Down the Mountain," "Winnipeg Whore," and "Black Eyed Susie." His *G.I. American Army Songs* included tracks like "The Freaking Fusiliers," "The Raw Recruit," "Old Soldiers Never Die," "The Regular Army," "Don't Want No More of Army Life."

In the studio, Brand always kept things very simple. He accompanied himself on the guitar and the banjo and used few backup singers. His sound was direct, raw, and loose. Because he was able to reproduce on stage everything he recorded, the live performances sounded fresh. No matter what his subject, he always had a folk slant.

In addition to songs, Brand authored a number of books on folksong and traditional collections. A short list includes *The Ballad Managers: Rise of the American Folk Song, Song of '76: A Folksinger's History of the Revolution* and *Bawdy Songs & Backroom Ballads*, a four-volume work. He also penned a number of plays: *The Education of H*Y*M*A*N K*A*P*L*A*N, A Joyful Noise, In White America, How to Steal an Election, Sing America Sing, It's a Jungle Out There, Thunder Bay, Fun and Games*, and *Second Scroll*. Although he never made a huge impact on the theater, it was always a special passion for him.

He was a fine actor and made several television appearances in, among others, *A Diet That Really Works, The Editor, Whistlestop, The Kate Smith Hour, Americana, Draw Me a Laugh, Presidential Timber, The Longines Hour, The Bell Telephone Hour, The Right Man, Let's Sing Out, Brand New Scene, American Odyssey*, and *Touch the Earth*. Like his interest in the theater, acting helped balance his career.

Because of his many contributions to the world of folk music it is only understandable that he has received many awards including the Peabody (twice) for broadcast excellence. In 1997, Brand shared the Peabody with Oprah Winfrey. He won the Valley Forge Memorial, Golden Reel, Scholastic, New York Critics, and National Council of Christians and Jews awards. He also got the Brooklyn College Community Service award, and the Thomas Alva Edison award. He received accolades at the Edinburgh and Venice film festivals.

Oscar Brand has been a folk music enthusiast for six decades. Although known primarily for his radio show, he has had a hand in every medium, including songwriting, plays, concert performances, and producing TV shows over a long career. No other Can-Am folklorist has done as much.

DISCOGRAPHY:

Absolute Nonsense, Riverside 12825.
Backroom Ballads, Crest 101.
Bawdy Songs & Backroom Ballads, Vol. 1, Audio Fidelity 5960.
Bawdy Songs & Backroom Ballads, Vol. 2, Audio Fidelity 5806.
G.I. American Army Songs, Riverside 12639.
Bawdy Songs & Backroom Ballads, Vol. 3, Audio Fidelity 5824.
Bawdy Songs & Backroom Ballads, Vol. 4, Audio Fidelity 5847.
Bawdy Sea Shanties, Audio Fidelity 5884.
Rollicking Sea Shanties, Audio Fidelity 5966.
Bawdy Hootenanny, Audio Fidelity 6121.
Bawdy Songs Goes to College, Audio Fidelity 5952.
Sing-Along Bawdy Songs, Audio Fidelity 5971.
The Wild Blue Yonder, Elektra Speciality 168.
Bawdy Western Songs, Audio Fidelity 5920.
Pie in the Sky, Tradition 1022.
American Drinking Songs, Riverside 12630.
Laughing America, Tradition 1014.
Sing-A-Longs: I Sing, You Sing, We All Sing, Vol. 1, Peter Pan 192860.
Singing Holidays, Caedmon 1505.
Oscar Brand/Jean Ritchie, Everest 207.
Oscar Brand Celebrates the First Thanksgiving in Story & Song, Caedmon 1513.
Billy the Kid in Song & Story, Caedmon 1552.
Trick or Treat, Caedmon 1624.
Singing Is Believing (Songs of the Advent Season), Caedmon 1658.
My Christmas Is Best, Caedmon 1776.
American Dreamer, Biograph BP-12067.
100-Proof American Drinking Songs, Caedmon 6534.
I Sing, You Sing, We All Sing, Vol. 1, Peter Pan 83.
Singalongs: I Sing, You Sing, We All Sing, Peter Pan 8082.
I Sing, You Sing, We All Sing, Vol. 2, Peter Pan 84.
Get a Dog, Alcazar/Alacazam! 125.
I Love Cats, Alacazam!/Alcazar 2002.
A Folk Concert in Town Hall, New York City, Smithsonian Folkways 2428.
Your Birthday Party, Caedmon 1782.
Give 'Em the Hook! Songs That Killed Vaudeville, Riverside 12832.
Four Albums of Military Song from Oscar Brand, Collectors' Choice Music 679.
Best of Oscar Brand, Tradition 2053.
Presidential Campaign Songs: 1789–1996, Smithsonian — Folkways 45051.

Jean Ritchie (1922–)

Mother of Folk

The folk music tree includes branches from different regions and styles. One of the most influential and important of these in America is Appalachian music. Many have carried on that tradition, including a woman whose efforts would earn her the nickname "the Mother of Folk," Jean Ritchie.

Ritchie was born on December 8, 1922, in Viper, Kentucky, into a musical family. The large clan prided itself on its repertoire of more than 300 songs, including hymns, love songs, ballads, children's songs and a dozen other types. As a child, Ritchie committed many of the compositions to memory while she developed her musical skills. From the start, her dedication to learning the music was an effort to preserve and maintain its incredible historical value.

She grew up singing songs associated with tasks and seasons. On holidays, seasonal hymns were an integral part of the celebration. When the snow melted and the spring was in full bloom, songs ushered in the new season. Ritchie found the beauty of nature reflected in music. All this fueled her desire to be an itinerant folksinger.

Ritchie took a giant step in reaching her dreams when she started to perform at local dances and country fairs. Ritchie was able to reel off the many songs in her repertoire and quickly established a solid reputation as a talented artist. These tiny venues enabled the blossoming musician to hone her skills and prepare for later concerts in front of massive audiences.

One of the highlights of her childhood occurred when she met Alan Lomax, who was scouring the Kentucky countryside looking for genuine folk talent to record for the Library of Congress collection. The musicologist stumbled upon the singing Ritchies and he interviewed Jean's parents as well as the 14 children in the family. The experience further fueled her desire to become a folksinger.

By the time of her high school graduation, Ritchie had honed her singing and playing abilities and was an integral part of numerous family jam sessions. She attended Cumberland Junior College in Williamsburg, Kentucky, and, in 1946, graduated from the University of Kentucky. Throughout her post-secondary education, she continued to add to her impressive folk music knowledge, and shared that wealth with schoolmates.

At school, Ritchie extended her musical skills. She was an outstanding member of the glee club, teaching fellow students many Appalachian standards. She also learned how to play the piano, adding another dimension to her musical talents. Although Ritchie became well known for her uncanny ability on the lap dulcimer, piano playing stood her in good stead.

Richie graduated with a B.A. in social work and, after gaining experience at an elementary school, relocated to New York City, where she found work at the Henry Street Settlement. Years of developing her music and learning the songs of her forebears paid off handsomely, because it allowed the caring teacher to reach out to the children. This connection enabled her to share with hundreds of students an enthusiasm for and understanding of the Appalachian tradition. Like all good folk artists, she played and sang to her classroom of eager youngsters.

In New York, Ritchie made important contacts in the folk world, including Oscar Brand, Leadbelly, and Pete Seeger, among others. She impressed her new friends so profoundly that she became part of their inner circle and began to perform with them. In 1948, Ritchie shared the stage at the Spring Fever Hootenanny with Woody Guthrie, the Weavers, Oscar Brand and Betty Sanders.

There was a genuine honesty, beauty, and charm in every song that she played and sang. Ritchie was determined to show the world the beauty of Appalachian music. Her voice was best suited to old ballads and combined well with the lap dulcimer, a traditional folk instrument. Although she was content to sing to the children, word spread about her talent and she was soon performing in various coffee houses.

In the early 1950s, Jac Holzman, founder of Electra Records, a company dedicated to folk music, had a keen eye for talent and signed Ritchie to the label. Three albums would be released including *Jean Ritchie Sings, Songs of Her Kentucky Mountain Family* and *A Time for Singing*. The latter appeared at the height of the folk revival and cemented her place as one of the most important aspiring figures on the scene. She shared her talent, enthusiasm and dedication with the new generation of singers and players.

During this era, Ritchie won a Fulbright scholarship, an award which enabled her to trace the links between American ballads and the songs of Ireland and England. She began with more than 300 songs and added significantly to the collection through interviews with Seamus Ennis, the McPeakes, Leo Rowsome, Sarah Makem, and a host of others. Ritchie's husband accompanied her and took many pictures, adding another dimension to the overall venture.

Her importance could not be measured in popularity. She would never reach the star status of Joan Baez, Bob Dylan, Peter, Paul & Mary, Judy Collins or the Kingston Trio during the folk boom. But the younger generation developed a strong respect for Ritchie because they understood that her diligence was second to none. Her efforts at preservation and scholarship in Appalachian music made her an integral part of the history of folk music in the United States and a favorite during the revival.

Ritchie was a constant figure on the coffee house and festival tour circuit. At many of the larger events she was revered as a pioneer, someone who had struggled and championed the music when it was not as popular. Her wealth of experience was esteemed by the new artists. She was referred to as the "mother of folk."

She continued to release albums including *Ballads from Her Appalachian Family Tradition* and *Child Ballads in America*. Long after the folk boom had subsided and been overshadowed by rock and roll, Ritchie remained devoted to her roots. In 1977, *None But One* won a *Rolling Stone* critics award. *High Hills and Mountains, Kentucky Christmas,* and *The Most Dulcimer* were all of excellent quality.

Ritchie continued to perform and boasted a strong, devoted fan base. Her focus as a musician was not for political ends or to bring about social justice, but to teach the history and the beauty of folk music, particularly the Appalachian strain. In the 1970s, her long-time husband photographer George Pickow joined forces with her to establish their own label, Greenhays Recordings Imprint. It re-released much of her previously recorded material.

In the 1980s, Ritchie began to slow down. She became more selective about concert dates and record releases. In 1995, a fiftieth anniversary album, *Mountain Born*, appeared, and featured her two sons, Peter and Jonathan. In 1996, the James Hardiman Library acquired the Ritchie Pickow Photographic Archive, and it was preserved at the National University of Ireland, Galway. Ritchie continues to record and perform sporadically.

Jean Ritchie preserved the music of her ancestors and broadcasted it throughout the world for others to enjoy. Her memory, musical skills, performances, and field trips all make her a legend. She made many contributions to the genre.

She was a first-rate lap dulcimer player. The instrument wasn't well known, but in her hands it enjoyed a revival. Ritchie's skills distinguished her from other folk artists. Later the Ritchies produced and sold lap dulcimers.

Ritchie had a charming voice to go along with her skills on the lap dulcimer. It wasn't powerful or forceful, but had a convincing element. The most important element in her vocal delivery was her authenticity. There was no mistaking the fact that she had been born and raised in the Appalachian region of Kentucky.

There was a homey appeal to her live concerts. She wore worn flannel shirts, sat with the dulcimer on her lap, and proceeded to deliver 300 years of musical history in an hour or two set. Her wholesomeness, passion and beauty moved the folk crowd.

One of Ritchie's best assets was the hundreds of songs learned as a young girl during family jam sessions. She preserved these songs by broadcasting them to the world, and she was regarded as an important historian. As others discovered the richness of her catalog, they added the material to their own repertoires, in turn passing them to the next generation.

Many artists delved into Ritchie's songbook. Linda Ronstadt, Dolly Parton and Emmylou Harris cut a version of "My Dear Companion," for their album, *Trio*. Judy Collins added "Tender Ladies," and "Pretty Saro" to her repertoire. Other tunes such as "Pretty Polly" and "Wintergrace" were recorded by countless other musicians. Johnny Cash became enchanted with "The L&N Don't Stop Here Anymore" after he heard his wife, June Carter Cash, sing it. With a scholarly collection of some 500 songs, not counting another hundred she wrote herself, Ritchie had an astonishing number of performers who covered her music.

Ritchie was a bridge figure. When interest in folk traditions declined, she helped inspire a renaissance. For more than 20 years, the talented Appalachian singer plugged away at ensuring that the music of her childhood would not be lost and forgotten. As one of the prime architects of the pre–folk-boom, she would receive her proper due during the revival.

She has been recognized for the many achievements of her long career. In 2002, Ritchie was presented with a National Heritage Fellowship, a rare honor in the folk field. A year later, she became a Kentucky Woman Remembered for her devotion to preserving Appalachian songs. In 2007, she was inducted into the Long Island Hall of Fame.

She influenced a number of singers. A partial list includes Linda Ronstadt, Dolly Parton, Lorraine "Lee" Hammond, Cousin Emmy, Aubrey Atwater and Elwood Donnelly, Alice Gerrard, Margaret MacArthur, Doc Watson, Peter Pickow, Jon Pickow, Oscar Brand, Nick Castro, Gillian Welch, David Schnaufer, Judy Collins, Phil Ochs, Pete Seeger, Bob Dylan, Tom Paxton and countless others. Scarcely one folksinger in the past 50 years has not crossed paths with the legendary mother of folk.

Jean Ritchie contributed more to the folk tradition than she ever drew from it. As a musician, singer, collector, recording artist, scholar, humanitarian, teacher, author, and performer, her gifts are bountiful.

DISCOGRAPHY:

Traditional Songs of Her Kentucky Mountain Home, Elektra EK-2.
Kentucky Mountain Songs, Electra EK-125.
Field Trip, Greenhays 726.
American Folk Tales and Songs, Tradition 1011.
Children's Songs & Games from the Southern Mountains, Smithsonian Folkways 7054.
Songs from Kentucky, Riverside RP-12–646.
The Ritchie Family of Kentucky, Smithsonian Folkways 2316.
Riddle Me This, Riverside RP-12–648.
Carols for All Seasons, Tradition 1058.
British Traditional Ballads, Vol. 1, Smithsonian Folkways 2301.
British Traditional Ballads, Vol. 2, Smithsonian Folkways 2302.

Ballads (2003; Vol. 1 and 2 above, issued on a single CD).
Ballads from Her Appalachian Family Tradition, Smithsonian Folkways 40145.
Precious Memories, Smithsonian Folkways 2427.
Jean Ritchie and Doc Watson at Folk City, Smithsonian Folkways 2426.
The Appalachian Dulcimer: An Instructional Record, Smithsonian Folkways 8352.
Marching Across the Green Grass & Other American Children's Game Songs, Smithsonian Folkways 7702.
Clear Waters Remembered, Sire 97014.
None But One, Greenhays 0708.
The Most Dulcimer, Greenhays 70714.
Mountain Born, Greenhays 725.
High Hills and Mountains, Greenhays 0701.
Childhood Songs, Greenhays 0723.
Lucky Christmas: Old and New, Greenhays 0717.
As I Roved Out, Smithsonian Folkways 8872.
Music Instruction: Dulcimer, Homespun Tapes 11D-802.
None But One/High Hills and Mountains, Greenhays 70708.
Mountain Hearth & Home, Rhino Handmade 778672.
The Tradition Years, Empire Musicworks 50858.

Harry Smith (1923–1991)
The Anthologist

In the 1920s, the first recordings of folk music provided a foundation for future generations. However, the Great Depression obliterated the careers of many of these early recording artists, including Buell Kazee, Dock Boggs, Clarence Ashley, Dick Justice, Uncle Eck Dunford, Kelly Harrell, Sleepy John Estes, and Henry Thomas, among others. One man assembled the works of these forgotten artists, Harry Smith.

Smith was born May 29, 1923, in Portland, Oregon. His Bohemian parents passed on ideologies that would influence Smith for the rest of his life, including an interest in spiritualism. Another of their passions was the plight of Native Americans and the pair spent a lot of time on reservations. Smith was initiated into the mysticism and culture of Native Americans and understood the importance of rituals. He experienced the power of music within the tribes and learned the special role which each musician played.

While still a boy, he started to collect religious objects, and this drive would mark his destiny. Eventually Smith left home to make his fortune armed with an interest in travel, a collector's interest in history, a deep appreciation for native culture, and an artistic bent.

During World War II, he scoured the used record shops to rescue the blues, jazz, folk, country and Cajun source material which had been recorded in the 1920s and 1930s. Smith amassed an incredible collection which would serve as the basis for his groundbreaking anthology. This valiant effort saved much obscure music that would have long been forgotten.

His obsession was important because at the time, no one thought much of preserving these cultural riches. Many records were being used as shellac for the war effort and rare recordings were being sacrificed. It was a race against time and Smith poured his energy into the challenge.

In the 1940s, he relocated to the San Francisco Bay area and continued to build his record collection. Throughout the decade Smith rescued hundreds of obscure records, preserving history and the otherwise forgotten artists. Smith also worked feverishly on his art and film projects, often moving from one apartment to another because of financial difficulties. The reclusive collector followed the Bohemian lifestyle inherited from his parents.

In the early 1950s, Smith relocated to New York City with his massive record collection, which now numbered in the thousands. He made a living as a painter and pieced together animated films, which did little to supplement a meager income. Short of cash, he approached Moses Asch of Folkways Records in hopes of selling some of his albums for money.

Asch was impressed with the collection and urged Smith to assemble his favorite tunes from the 1920s and early 1930s. He would create an anthology of folk, blues, Cajun, country, and old-time material. The process was difficult because of the thousands of works to choose from. Finally, in 1952, three volumes were completed, edited and published.

The anthology breathed life into the sagging careers of bluesmen Blind Willie Johnson, Henry Thomas, Mississippi John Hurt, and Furry Lewis. Old-time folk acts like the Cannon's Jug Stompers, Clarence Ashley, Uncle Dave Macon, Buell Kazee, Prince Albert Hunt's Texas Ramblers, Eck Robertson, Uncle Eck Dunford, and Dock Boggs all benefited from the three-volume effort. Country pioneers like the Carter Family and the Stoneman Family also found themselves on the collection, as well as the early Cajun artists Joseph Falcon and Cleoma Breaux.

Smith was instrumental in the selection of tracks on the anthology, but was also responsible for the editing and the cover art design. He wrote short synopses for each track, which were both serious and funny, a folksy touch unlike other records. He presented the notes with flair, like newspaper headlines.

The anthology wasn't an instant hit. However, a few years later, an informed few showed a keen interest in the collection, including Dave Van Ronk, John Fahey, Eric von Schmidt and John Cohen. Others such as Bob Dylan, Joan Baez and Jerry Garcia, lead guitarist for the Grateful Dead, would benefit from a later release.

Because of the sheer size of Smith's collection, many more anthologies were planned, but they never materialized. In 2000, the fourth volume celebrating American roots music was finally released on Revenant Records. If Smith had continued to issue these very introspective anthologies, his contribution to folk music would have been of greater importance.

Instead, Smith returned to painting and film to earn a living. However, he approached Moses Asch one more time in order to record the Fugs debut album. He was very enthusiastic about the group. Throughout the 1960s, as the folk boom made musical headlines for at least the first half of the decade, the anthologist knew that he was one of the figures who had helped ignite the process.

In the early 1970s, Smith recorded poet Allen Ginsberg's performances, his most important work during the decade. In 1981, he released the *New York Blues: Rags, Ballads and Harmonium Songs*. But most of Smith's attention was focused on other pursuits.

For the rest of his life, Smith filmed and recorded Native American peyote ceremonies, researched and constructed string games, and gathered a huge collection of paper planes that would be donated to the Smithsonian Air and Space museum. He moved frequently around New York City. Despite declining health, he survived to witness the reissue of *Anthology of American Folk Music* and was gratified by praise for the collection. On November, 27, 1991, he died at the Chelsea Hotel in New York City.

Harry Smith was a folk music historian, American archivist, student of anthropology, record collector, ethnomusicologist, experimental filmmaker, artist, and mystic. He was also a Bohemian, an original, an innovator, an oddball, a hermit, a critic, and a loner. In one stroke, with the release of *Anthology of Folk Music*, he assured himself a place in the annals of American folk music history.

Smith raised awareness of American musical heritage. He had a hand in preserving folk, old-time, traditional country, Cajun, folk-rock and country blues. His sense of enshrining the past also extended to Native American culture.

Smith is as responsible for the appreciation of roots music as anyone else in the modern era. His anthology fueled the folk revival and planted the seeds for the folk-rock explosion. Without his three-volume set, the folkies of the late 1950s and early 1960s would not have had an essential foundation, and many of the earlier contributors would not have enjoyed a career renaissance.

Smith was an experimental filmmaker and worked on abstract cartoons. They were strange works which would later receive some critical attention. Sometimes, he accompanied his films with jazz, blues, Cajun and old-time folk music. His topics included colors, magic, the planets and drug-influenced visions. Although he was an interesting filmmaker, his efforts in this field were strange and attracted little commercial interest.

Smith was an artist whose freeform abstractions were inspired from the collected roots material. His large paintings featured mysticism, drugs and planets. Many of his art works were destroyed by Smith himself or lost through the years during his many moves.

Although remembered for his music collecting, compilations, art work, and film, Smith also played a major role in raising awareness of offbeat American culture and anthropological subjects. He carefully documented his findings.

Many have studied the fragmented life of Harry Smith. Despite his numerous endeavors, most believe he never fully tapped his potential. He was a complex person who saw the world through a much different lens than others, including those in the folk world.

In 1991, he received the lifetime achievement Chairman's Merit Award at the Grammy celebration. The award was controversial because of his art and lifestyle. To many, Smith managed to produce one great thing — the anthology — which was his true legacy.

Harry Smith was a pivotal figure in the development and preservation of the modern folksong. His efforts served as fuel for the boom of the 1950s and 1960s. Because of this, he will always be remembered as the anthologist.

DISCOGRAPHY:

A Live Tribute to the Anthology of Folk Music, Smithsonian Folkways 88247.

Bibliography

Abernathy, Francis Edward, ed. *Texas Folklore Society, 1909–1943*. Denton: University of North Texas Press, 1992.

Armstrong, Robert Bruce. *The Irish and Highland Harp*. Edinburgh: David Douglass, 1904.

Asaf'ev, B.V. *Russian Music from the Beginning of the Nineteenth Century*. Ann Arbor, MI: J.W. Edwards, 1953.

Bealle, John. *Old-time Music and Dance: Community and Folk Revival*. Beverly, MA: Quarry Books, 2005.

Bohlman, Phillip. *Central European Folk Music: An Annotated Bibliography of Sources in German (Garland Reference Library of the Humanities)*. New York: Routledge, 1996.

Botkin, B.A. *Treasure of Southern Folklore: Deluxe Edition*. New York: Random House Value Publishing, 1988.

Breathnach, Breandán. *Irish Folk Music and Dances*. Cork & Dublin, Ireland: Mercier Press, 1977.

Bronner, Simon J. *Following Tradition: Folklore in the Discourse of American Culture*. Logan: Utah State University Press, 1998.

Brunvand, Jan Harold. *The Study of American Folklore: An Introduction*. New York: Norton, 1968.

Bunting, Edward. *Ancient Irish Music*. Dublin, Ireland: W. Power, 1796.

Canainn, Tomás Ó. *Traditional Music in Ireland*. New York: Music Sales Corporation, 1993.

Cartwright, Garth. *Princes Amongst Men: Journeys with Gypsy Musicians*. London: Serpent Tail, 2005.

Cavalier, Debbie. *Folk Dances from Around the World*. Van Nuys, CA: Alfred, 1997.

Cohn, Amy, and Molly Bang. *From Sea to Shining Sea: A Treasury of American Folklore and Folk Songs*. New York: Scholastic, 1993.

Complete Works of O'Carolan. Cork City, Ireland: Ossian, 1997.

Courlander, Harold. *Negro Folk Music U.S.A.* New York: Columbia University Press, 1964.

Czekanowska, Anna. *Polish Folk Music: Slavonic Heritage, Polish Tradition, Contemporary Trends*. Cambridge, MA: Cambridge University Press, 2006.

Denisoff, R. Serge. *Great Day Coming: Folk Music and the American Left*. Baltimore, MD: Penguin, 1973.

Dorson, Richard M. *American Folklore*. Chicago: University of Chicago Press, 1959.

Dow, Daniel. *A Collection of Ancient Scots Music*. Edinburgh: Scottish Music Centre, 1776.

Dunaway, David. *How Can I Keep from Singing: Pete Seeger*. New York: Da Capo, 1981.

Fletcher, Alan. *Drama and the Performing Arts in Pre-Cromwellian Ireland: A Repertory of Sources and Documents from the Earliest Times until c.1642*. Cambridge, England: D.S. Brewer, 2001.

Fowke, Edith. *Folklore of Canada*. Toronto: McClelland and Stewart, 1976.

_____. *Lumbering Songs from the Northern Woods*. Toronto: NC Press, 1985.

_____. *The Penguin Book of Canadian Folk Songs*. Toronto: Penguin, 1973.

_____. *Sally Go Round the Sun: 300 Songs, Rhymes and Games of Canadian Children.* Toronto: Doubleday, 1969.

_____, and Joe Glazer. *Songs of Work and Freedom.* Chicago: Roosevelt University, 2004.

_____, and Richard Johnston. *Folk Songs of Canada.* Waterloo, Ontario: Waterloo Music, 1955.

Fox, Charlotte Milligan. *Annals of the Irish Harpers.* London: John Murray, 1917.

Fox, Dan, Dick Weissman, and Sarah Wilkins. *The Great Family Songbook: A Treasury of Favourite Folk Songs, Popular Tunes, Children's Melodies, International Songs, Hymns, Holiday Jingles and More for Piano and Guitar.* New York: Black Dog & Leventhal, 1985.

Goertzen, Chris. *Fiddling for Norway: Revival and Identity.* Chicago: University of Chicago Press, 1997.

Golden Encyclopedia of Folk Music. Milwaukee: Hal Leonard, 1985.

Gunn, John. *An Historical Enquiry Respecting the Performance on the Harp in the Highlands of Scotland.* London: Constable, 1807.

Guthrie, Woody. *Bound for Glory.* New York: Plume Books, 1983.

Harper, Sally. *Music in Welsh Culture Before 1650: A Study of the Principal Sources.* Surrey, England: Ashgate, 2007.

Hast, Dorothea E., and Stan Scott. *Music in Ireland: Experiencing Music, Expressing Culture.* New York: Oxford University Press, 2004.

Hopkins, Pandora. *Aural Thinking in Norway: Performance and Communication with the Hardingfele.* New York: Human Sciences Press, 1986.

Jackson, George Pullen. *White Spirituals in the Southern Uplands: The Story of the Fasola Folk, Their Songs, Singings, and "Buckwheat Notes."* Chapel Hill: University of North Carolina Press, 1933.

Jones, Loyal and John M. Forbes. *Minstrel of the Appalachians: The Story of Bascom Lamar Lunsford.* Lexington: University Press of Kentucky, 2002.

Karpeles, Maud. *Cecil Sharp: His Life and Work.* Chicago: University of Chicago Press, 1967.

Klein, Joe. *Woody Guthrie: A Life.* New York: Knopf, 1980.

Kodaly, Zolton. *Folk Music of Hungary.* New York: Macmillan, 1960.

Lawless, Ray M. *Folksingers and Folksongs in America.* Westport, CT: Greenwood Press, 1981.

Ling, Jan, Linda Schenck and Robert Schenck. *A History of European Folk Music.* Rochester, NY: University of Rochester Press, 1998.

Lloyd, A.L. *Come All Ye Bold Miners (Ballads & Songs of the Coalfield).* London: Lawrence & Wishart, 1952.

_____. *Folk Song in England.* London: Lawrence & Wishart, 1967.

_____. *The Singing Englishman: An Introduction to Folksong.* London: Workers Music Association, 1944.

Logan, James. *The Clans of the Scottish Highlands.* London: 1985.

Lomax, Alan. *The Land Where the Blues Began.* New York: Pantheon, 2002.

_____. *Mister Jelly Roll: The Fortunes of Jelly Roll Morton, New Orleans Creole and "Inventor of Jazz."* Berkeley: University of California Press, 2001.

_____. *Selected Writings, 1934–1997.* Florence, KY: Routledge, 2005.

_____. *Songs of North America.* Jackson, TN: Main Street Books, 1975.

Lomax, John A. *Adventures of a Ballad Hunter.* New York: Macmillan, 1947.

_____. *Cowboy Songs and Other Frontier Ballads.* New York: Sturgis & Walton, 1910.

_____. *Songs of the Cattle Trail and Cow Camp.* New York: Macmillan, 1919.

_____, and Alan Lomax. *American Ballads and Folk Songs.* New York: Macmillan, 1935.

_____, _____, and Ruth Crawford Seeger. *Our Singing Country.* New York: Macmillan, 1941.

Lvov, Nikolai and Ivan Prach. *A Collection of Russian Folk Songs.* Rochester, NY: University of Rochester Press, 1987.

MacInnes, Sheldon. *Buddy MacMaster: The Judique Fiddler.* Halifax, Nova Scotia: Pottersfield Press, 2007.

_____. *A Journey in Celtic Music, Cape Breton Style.* Cape Breton, Nova Scotia: University of Cape Breton Press, 1997.

Monath, Norman, William Cole, and Edward Ardizzone. *Folk Songs of England, Ireland, Scotland, and Wales.* Van Nuys, CA: Alfred, 1999.

Moncrieffe, I., and D. Hicks. *The Highland Clans.* Manchester, England: Bramhall House, 1984.

Nathan, Hans, and Philip V. Bohlmann. *Israeli Folk Music: Songs of the Early Pioneers.* Middleton, WI: A–R Editions, 1995.

O'Hara, Aidan. *I'll Live Till I Die: The Delia Murphy Story.* Minneapolis: Irish Books & Media, 1997.

O'Neill, Francis. *Irish Folk Music: A Fascinating Hobby.* Bel Air, CA: Folcroft Library Editions, 1975.

Porterfield, Nolan. *Last Cavalier: The Life and Times of John A. Lomax, 1867–1948.* Chicago: University of Chicago Press, 2001.

Raim, Walter. *The Josh White Songbook.* New York: Quadrangle Books, 1963.

Reuss, Richard A., with JoAnne C. Reuss. *American Folk Music and Left-Wing Politics, 1927–1957.* Lanham, MD: Scarecrow Press, 2000.

Ritchie, Jean. *The Dulcimer Book.* San Francisco: Oak Publications, 1974.

_____. *Folk Songs of the Southern Appalachians as Sung by Jean Ritchie.* Lexington: University of Kentucky Press, 1997.

_____. *Garland of Mountain Songs.* New York: Broadcast Music, 1953.

_____. *Jean Ritchie Celebration of Life, Her Songs ... Her Poems.* New York: Geordie Music, 1971.

_____. *Jean Ritchie's Dulcimer People.* New York: Oak Publications, 1975.

_____. *Singing Family of the Cumberlands.* Lexington: University of Kentucky Press, 1988.

Robb, John D. *Hispanic Folk Music of New Mexico and the Southwest: A Self-Portrait of a People.* Norman: University of Oklahoma Press, 1979.

Rosenbaum, Art. *Visions and Voices: Traditional Music and Song in North Georgia.* Athens: University of Georgia Press, 1983.

Sandberg, Larry. *The Folk Music Source Book.* New York: Random House Trade Paperbacks, 1976.

Seeger, Pete. *How to Play the 5-String Banjo.* 3rd ed., revised. Milwaukee, WI: Pete Seeger, 2006.

_____. *Where Have All the Flowers Gone? A Singer's Stories, Songs, Seeds, Robberies.* Bethlehem, PA: Sing Out Publications, 1997.

Sharp, Cecil J., and Olive Dame Campbell. *English Folk Songs from the Southern Appalachians.* Whitefish, MT: Kessinger, 2008.

Shields, Hugh. *Narrative Singing in Ireland: Lays, Ballads, Come-All-Yes and Other Songs.* Dublin, Ireland: Irish Academic Press, 1993.

___. *Shamrock, Rose and Thistle: Folk Singing in North Derry.* Belfast, Ireland: Blackstaff Press, 1981.

___. *Tunes of the Munster Pipers: Irish Traditional Music from the James Goodman Manuscripts.* Dublin, Ireland: Irish Traditional Music Archive, 1998.

Siegel, Dorothy Schainman. *The Glory Road: The Story of Josh White.* San Diego, CA: Harcourt Brace Jovanovich, 1987.

Stambler, Irwin, and Lyndon Stambler. *Folk & Blues: The Encyclopedia.* New York: Thomas Dunne Books, 2001.

Stewart, Sheila. *Queen Among the Heather: The Life of Belle Stewart.* Edinburgh: Birlinn, 2006.

Taruskin, Richard. *Defining Russia Musically.* Princeton, NJ: Princeton University Press, 1997.

Wald, Elijah. *Josh White: Society Blues.* Amherst: University of Massachusetts Press, 2000.

Weissman, Dick. *Which Side Are You On? An Inside History of the Folk Music Revival in America.* London: Continuum International Publishing Group, 2006.

Wenberg, Michael. *Elizabeth's Song.* Hillsboro, OR: Beyond Words, 2002.

Willens, Doris., and Pete Seeger. *Lonesome Traveler: The Life of Lee Hays.* Winnipeg, Manitoba: Bison Books, 1993.

Williams, Ralph Vaughan., and Albert Lancaster. *The Penguin Book of English Folk Songs.* New York: Penguin, 1990.

Woods, Sylvia. *40 O'Carolan Tunes for All Harps.* Milwaukee, WI: Hal Leonard Corporation, 1987.

_____. *Music Theory and Arranging Techniques for Folk Harps.* Milwaukee, WI: Hal Leonard Corporation, 1987.

Woog, Adam. *The History of American Folk Music.* Farmington Hills, MI: Lucent Books, 2006.

Index

Numbers in **bold italics** indicate main entries.